Taboos and Controversial Issues in Foreign Language Education

This edited volume provides innovative insights into how critical language pedagogy and taboo topics can inform and transform the teaching and learning of foreign languages.

The book investigates the potential as well as the challenges involved in dealing with taboo topics in the foreign language classroom. Traditionally subsumed under the acronym PARSNIP (politics, alcohol, religion, sex, narcotics, isms, and pork). By examining how additional controversial topics such as disability, racism, conspiracy theories and taboo language can be integrated into conceptual teaching frameworks and teaching practice, this edited volume draws on examples from literary texts and pop culture such as young adult novels, music videos, or rap songs and investigates their potential for developing critical literacies. The book considers foreign language teaching outside of English teaching contexts and sets the groundwork for addressing the integration of taboo topics in foreign language education theory, research, and practice.

Filling an important gap in educational research, the book will be of great interest to researchers, academics, and students of foreign language education, critical pedagogy, and applied linguistics. It will also be useful reading for teacher trainers and educators of foreign language education.

Christian Ludwig is Visiting Professor of Teaching English as a Foreign Language at the Freie Universität, Berlin, Germany.

Theresa Summer is Associate Professor of Teaching English as a Foreign Language at the University of Bamberg, Germany.

Routledge Research in Language Education

The *Routledge Research in Language Education* series provides a platform for established and emerging scholars to present their latest research and discuss key issues in Language Education. This series welcomes books on all areas of language teaching and learning, including but not limited to language education policy and politics, multilingualism, literacy, L1, L2 or foreign language acquisition, curriculum, classroom practice, pedagogy, teaching materials, and language teacher education and development. Books in the series are not limited to the discussion of the teaching and learning of English only.

Books in the series include:

The Acquisition of English Grammar and Phonology by Cantonese ESL Learners
Challenges, Causes and Pedagogical Insights
Alice Yin Wa Chan

Using Digital Portfolios to Develop Students' Writing
A Practical Guide for Language Teachers
Ricky Lam and Benjamin Luke Moorhouse

Enhancing Beginner-Level Foreign Language Education for Adult Learners
Language Instruction, Intercultural Competence, Technology, and Assessment
Edited by Ekaterina Nemtchinova

Taboos and Controversial Issues in Foreign Language Education
Critical Language Pedagogy in Theory, Research and Practice
Edited by Christian Ludwig and Theresa Summer

For more information about the series, please visit www.routledge.com/Routledge-Research-in-Language-Education/book-series/RRLE

Taboos and Controversial Issues in Foreign Language Education

Critical Language Pedagogy in Theory, Research and Practice

Edited by
Christian Ludwig and
Theresa Summer

First published 2023
by Routledge
4 Park Square, Milton Park, Abingdon, Oxon OX14 4RN

and by Routledge
605 Third Avenue, New York, NY 10158

Routledge is an imprint of the Taylor & Francis Group, an informa business

© 2023 selection and editorial matter, Christian Ludwig and Theresa Summer; individual chapters, the contributors

The right of Christian Ludwig and Theresa Summer to be identified as the authors of the editorial material, and of the authors for their individual chapters, has been asserted in accordance with sections 77 and 78 of the Copyright, Designs and Patents Act 1988.

With the exception of Chapter 1, no part of this book may be reprinted or reproduced or utilised in any form or by any electronic, mechanical, or other means, now known or hereafter invented, including photocopying and recording, or in any information storage or retrieval system, without permission in writing from the publishers.

Chapter 1 of this book is available for free in PDF format as Open Access from the individual product page at www.taylorfrancis.com. It has been made available under a Creative Commons Attribution 4.0 International license. Funded by the University of Bamberg.

We acknowledge support by the Open Access Publication Fund of the Otto-Friedrich-Universität Bamberg.

Trademark notice: Product or corporate names may be trademarks or registered trademarks, and are used only for identification and explanation without intent to infringe.

British Library Cataloguing-in-Publication Data
Names: Ludwig, Christian, 1981- editor. | Summer, Theresa, editor.
Title: Taboos and controversial issues in foreign language education : critical language pedagogy in theory, research and practice / edited by Christian Ludwig and Theresa Summer.
Description: Abingdon, Oxon ; New York, NY : Routledge, 2023. | Series: Routledge research in language education | Includes bibliographical references and index.
Identifiers: LCCN 2022043862 (print) | LCCN 2022043863 (ebook) | ISBN 9781032116075 (Hardback) | ISBN 9781032116105 (Paperback) | ISBN 9781003220701 (eBook)
Subjects: LCSH: Language and languages—Study and teaching—Social aspects. | Critical pedagogy. | LCGFT: Essays.
Classification: LCC P53.8 .T33 2023 (print) | LCC P53.8 (ebook) | DDC 418.0071—dc23/eng/20221221
LC record available at https://lccn.loc.gov/2022043862
LC ebook record available at https://lccn.loc.gov/2022043863

ISBN: 978-1-032-11607-5 (hbk)
ISBN: 978-1-032-11610-5 (pbk)
ISBN: 978-1-003-22070-1 (ebk)

DOI: 10.4324/9781003220701

Typeset in Galliard
by codeMantra

Contents

List of Figures   ix
List of Tables   xi
List of Editors and Contributors   xiii
Acknowledgements   xix

Introduction

1 Approaching Taboos and Controversial Issues in Foreign Language Education   3
CHRISTIAN LUDWIG AND THERESA SUMMER

PART I
Theoretical Considerations and Insights

2 Between Recognition and Redistribution – The Political Economy of Taboos in Foreign Language Education   23
JOHN GRAY

3 Facing the Invisible – Taboos as Texts and Cultural Learning in English Language Education   31
DANIEL BECKER

4 Integrating Critical Approaches into Language Teacher Education   40
DAVID GERLACH AND MAREEN LÜKE

5 Taboo or Not Taboo? To Talk or Not to Talk? These Are the Questions   49
GRIT ALTER AND STEFANIE FUCHS

6 Promoting Resilience in the Foreign Language Classroom – A Basic Requirement for Working with Taboo Topics   57
ALINE WILLEMS

PART II
Empirical Inquiries

7 Learner Perceptions of Taboo Topics in English Language Teaching   71
THERESA SUMMER AND JEANINE STEINBOCK

8 Taboos in Language Teacher Education: A Survey of Pre-Service Teachers' Attitudes   81
THERESA SUMMER AND CHRISTIAN LUDWIG

9 Teaching "13 Reasons Why": A Study on the Importance of a Pedagogical Alliance in ELT   93
CHRISTINE GARDEMANN

PART III
Specific Taboos and Practical Examples

10 Swear/Taboo Words in English Rap Lyrics: Linguistic Analysis and Implications for Foreign Language Education   103
VALENTIN WERNER

11 Disability Awareness Education in ELT: Addressing Disability through Short Animation Films   113
KATRIN THOMSON

12 #mentalhealthmatters – Exploring Borderline Personality Disorder in ELT through Poetry Slams   126
CHRISTIAN LUDWIG AND VERONIKA MARTINEZ

13 Let's Talk about Sexting: Discussing Erotic and Sexually Explicit Messaging in Foreign Language Education   141
CHARLOTTE HASKINS AND CHRISTIAN LUDWIG

14 Making the Unseen Seen: Exploring Human
   Trafficking through Comics and Graphic Novels in ELT   155
   CHRISTIAN LUDWIG

15 I'm Not Racist! – Addressing Racism in
   Predominantly White Classrooms with Cooperatively
   Designed Multimodal Text Ensembles   168
   SILKE BRASELMANN

16 Critical Animal Pedagogy and Global Education in the
   EFL Classroom   181
   MARIA EISENMANN

17 Death, Extinction, and the Limits of Literacy   195
   ROMAN BARTOSCH

18 Cultural Taboos from a Sri Lankan Perspective:
   Developing Taboo Literacy with Feature Films   206
   ANCHALA AMARASINGHE AND SUSANNE BORGWALDT

19 *La pobreza, las drogas y el sida:* Using Series Like Élite
   as a Means of Making the Unspeakable Speakable   218
   JANINA REINHARDT

20 Addressing South African Perspectives on Taboos and
   Tricky Topics in European Literature Classrooms   228
   SANDRA STADLER-HEER

21 Addressing Taboo Topics in Translator and Interpreter
   Training   237
   EVA SEIDL

Conclusion

22 International Perspectives on Taboos in Foreign
   Language Education   249
   TYSON SEBURN

Appendix   261
Index   263

Figures

1.1	Parsnippy Topics	8
1.2	Contemporary Taboos and Controversial Topics	10
1.3	A Pedagogic Framework for Taboos	12
4.1	Principles for Critical Language Teacher Programmes	44
7.1	Responses to Q4: "In My View, Dealing with Taboo Topics in Class is…"	76
8.1	Taboo Topics Pre-Service Teachers Show Most Interest in	84
8.2	Formats Through which Pre-Service Teachers Encounter the Topic Racism	85
8.3	Potential Challenges when Dealing with Taboos	88
10.1	STW Categories (Synthesized from Claire, 1998; Jay, 2009; Stapleton, 2010)	104
10.2	Multiple Functions of STWs (following Claire, 1998; Dewaele, 2004, 2015; Horan, 2013; Liyanage et al., 2015; Stapleton, 2010)	105
11.1	Adding an Abstract Level of Meaning: Ian Is Being Pulled through the Fence	120
11.2	Dissolve and Disintegration Effect in *Ian* (2018)	120
12.1	Key Terms Explained (based on American Psychiatric Association, n.d.; WHO, n.d.)	128
12.2	Components of Mental Health Literacy (based on Jorm, 2000, p. 396)	129
12.3	Screenshot from Nayo Jones' Performance of "Healing" (SlamFind, 2016), Including Quotes	135
13.1	Types of Sexting	144
13.2	Example of a Sexting Situation	150
14.1	A Panel Sequence from H.E.A.T. Watch Series	160
14.2	Excerpt from H.E.A.T. Watch Series	161
14.3	An Example of a Social Media Post in which a Teenager Is Cyber Groomed	163
14.4	The Polaris Power and Control Wheel to Explore Comic and Graphic Novel Renderings of Human Trafficking	164

15.1	Practical Example of a Collaboratively Created Mind Map for the Word Field "Discrimination"	175
15.2	Practical Example of a Collaboratively Created Mind Map for the Word Field "Privilege"	176
18.1	Domains of Cultural Taboos in Sri Lanka	207
19.1	Controversial Topics in the First Season of Élite (following 1.2 in Ludwig & Summer, this volume)	220
19.2	Fake Chat in Text Messenger for Creative Writing (Fake Chat App, n.d. [Screenshot taken 10 July 2022])	226

Tables

1.1	Educational Guidelines for Dealing with Taboos	15
4.1	Workshop on Critical Language Education	46
6.1	Personal Resources/Resilience Factors	59
6.2	Social Resources/Resilience Factors	60
7.1	Survey Questionnaire: "Taboo Topics" in Focus	73
7.2	Taboo Topics Dealt with at School ("Very Often"/"Often")	75
7.3	Taboos: Average Rating of Interest in English Lessons (1 = Not at All; 5 = Very Much)	77
8.1	Top Five Neglected Taboo Topics at Schools	86
8.2	Pre-Service Teachers' Opinion on Dealing with Taboos in the English Classroom	87
10.1	Usages of *Nigga* and *Fuck* in Rap Lyrics	108
11.1	Overview: Teaching Sequence on *Ian*	119
12.1	A Sample Lesson Sequence on BPD	136
13.1	Relating Selected Components of the DigComp 2.1 to Sexting	148
15.1	Overview of the Teaching Sequence on "Racism and Discrimination"	174
15.2	Suggestions for a Text Ensemble for Racism, Discrimination, and Privilege	177
17.1	Parsnippy Topics	200
18.1	Teaching Suggestion: Dealing with the Cultural Taboo of Smoking among Females	212
18.2	Teaching Suggestion: Dealing with the Cultural Taboo of Eating with Hand	212
19.1	Overview of Selected Key Scenes and Themes of the First Season of the Series Élite	223
19.2	Sequence of Activities on Marina's HIV Outing	224
19.3	Sources for Internet Research on AIDS and HIV	225
20.1	Lesson Sequence: Debating Selected South African Tricky Topics (B2+ to C1)	233
20.2	Suggested Activities for a Task Cycle (Tasks in Part II are Adapted from Poelzleitner, 2010)	234
21.1	Practical Examples for the Translation-Oriented LX Classroom	243

Editors and Contributors

Grit Alter is Professor of Teaching English as a Foreign Language at the University College of Teacher Education in Innsbruck, Austria. She finished her Ph.D. on inter- and transcultural learning in the context of Canadian young adult fiction in 2015. Her research interests lie with literary and cultural learning, using children's literature and young adult fiction in language classrooms, textbook research, critical media literacy, and critical pedagogy. She is currently involved in projects on authenticity and curricula research as well as visual literacy and diversity.

Anchala Amarasinghe received a B.A. in German, English and Linguistics and an M.A. in Linguistics from the University of Kelaniya, Sri Lanka. She has been teaching German in Sri Lanka, at the University of Kelaniya and at the Goethe Institute in Colombo. Currently, she is working on her Ph.D. in German as a Foreign Language, researching ways to deal with cultural taboos in foreign language teaching.

Roman Bartosch is a Professor of Teaching Anglophone Literatures and Cultures and Director of the Interdisciplinary Research Centre for Teaching in the Humanities at the University of Cologne, Germany. He is the author and editor of more than 12 books and over 50 scholarly articles spanning environmental and transcultural learning, inclusive education, and the intersections of literature pedagogy and literary theory. His current work explores questions of educational philosophy, especially in terms of modelling learning objectives in times of large-scale extinction and climate catastrophe, and the phenomenon of dissent in language and literature pedagogy.

Daniel Becker studied English, History, and Educational Studies at the University of Koblenz Landau. After graduating in 2011, he completed his post-graduate teacher training at the Studienseminar Trier. He recently defended and completed his Ph.D. in literary studies. Since October 2018, Daniel Becker has been working as a TEFL lecturer at the University of Münster. His research interests include teaching literature and culture, global learning, multiliteracies, and digital media.

Susanne Borgwaldt studied Theoretical Linguistics at the Ludwig Maximilian University of Munich and received a Ph.D. in Psychology from the University of Amsterdam. After two postdoctoral appointments at the University of Alberta and Sydney University, she has been teaching and researching in Germany at the universities of Bamberg, HU Berlin, Braunschweig, Erfurt, and Siegen. Currently, she is working at the RWTH Aachen.

Silke Braselmann is Postdoctoral Researcher and Lecturer for Teaching English as a Foreign Language at Friedrich-Schiller-Universität Jena. Her current research focuses on anti-racist ELT and teacher education, Young Adult Literature, critical media literacy/multiliteracies, as well as inter- and transcultural learning in digital spaces. She has published a monograph about the role of (young adult) literature and film in the construction of the school shooting discourse and several articles about anti-racist, multiperspective, or social media-based ELT.

Maria Eisenmann is Professor of EFL Teaching at the Julius-Maximilians-University Würzburg, Germany. After finishing her Ph.D. and working as a teacher in school, she taught at the University of Education in Freiburg as well as at the University of Erlangen-Nuremberg and held the chair for EFL Teaching at the University of Duisburg-Essen. Her primary research interests lie in the fields of global education, (digital) media literacy, as well as teaching literature including individual differences. She has published widely in the fields of foreign language education, critical environmental literacies, as well as digital and literary literacy in the EFL classroom.

Stefanie Fuchs is Lecturer at the TEFL Department of the Ludwig Maximilian University of Munich, Germany. She studied German and English at the University of Erfurt, where she also worked as a research assistant for the Department of Psychology and obtained her doctorate. She has worked as a teacher for German and English and as a lecturer in the English Department of the Leibniz University of Hannover. Her research interests encompass learning and teaching grammar, gender and diversity studies, and psychological aspects of language learning. Her current research project focuses on non-native students' perception of English grammar.

Christine Gardemann is a Visiting Professor at the University of Marburg. Before that, she worked as a Postdoctoral Researcher at the University of Bielefeld, and as a teacher of English, German, and Media at a bilingual grammar school in Hamburg. She received her Ph.D. at the University of Hamburg with a mixed-methods study at the nexus of English literary didactics and professionalism research. For the project, almost 400 secondary school English teachers were surveyed on their use of literary texts in EFL in years 5–10. Subsequently, qualitative case studies were used to reconstruct teachers' implicit knowledge and beliefs on teaching and using literature.

David Gerlach is Professor at the University of Wuppertal (Germany). His research and teaching focus on professional development of language teachers, critical literacy and critical pedagogy, learning difficulties, and inclusive language teaching. Lately, together with colleagues, he has been involved in conceptualising a more critical perspective for the language teaching practice in Germany and wants to extend this to the practice of language teacher education within the German structures.

John Gray is co-director of the UCL Centre for Applied Linguistics and Professor of Applied Linguistics and Education at IOE, UCL's Faculty of Education and Society, UK. He is the author of several books, the most recent of which are *Social Interaction and English Language Teacher Identity* (2018), published by Edinburgh University Press and co-authored with Tom Morton, and *Education and the Discourse of Global Neoliberalism* (2021), published by Routledge and edited with John P. O'Regan and Catherine Wallace.

Charlotte Haskins is an adjunct who teaches English at several universities in Germany. At the University of Education Karlsruhe, she holds lectures on Gothic literature and linguistics, which are attended by future English teachers. In addition, she teaches Technical English at the levels B1 and B2 to engineering students at the Universities of Applied Sciences in Frankfurt and Karlsruhe.

Christian Ludwig is Visiting Professor at the Freie Universität, Berlin, Germany. His research mainly focuses on using digital media and literature in English language teaching but he is also interested in the use of graphic novels and comics in the foreign language classroom. He is currently involved in several research projects, including a project on the promotion of mental health in ELT. He also works as an external consultant for Cornelsen Publishing and is Head of the IATEFL Scholarship Committee.

Mareen Lüke is Ph.D. candidate at the Philipps University of Marburg working on a concept of fostering critical awareness among teachers of English as a foreign language funded by a scholarship granted by the Friedrich-Ebert-Stiftung. Besides, her research focuses on L2 reading, language teacher education, critical pedagogy, critical literacy, and the internationalisation of language teacher education.

Veronika Martinez has been working as a Physical Education and English teacher at a vocational school in Aalen, Germany, since 2011. In her final thesis, she focused on body images of adolescents in relation to the media.

Janina Reinhardt is Lecturer in Foreign Language Didactics at Bielefeld University, Germany. Being a fully qualified teacher for English, French, Spanish, and German as a Foreign Language, she has a multilingual background and is inclined to cross-linguistic language learning. She is particularly interested in the interfaces between linguistics, didactics, and media education.

Tyson Seburn is an EMI (English Medium Instructor) lecturer and curriculum director of an EAP foundation year at New College, University of Toronto, Canada. His current area of interest focuses on exploring inclusive and critical pedagogies and their applications to language teaching contexts and in particular, materials development for ELT. He is coordinator of the IATEFL Teacher Development Special Interest Group committee.

Eva Seidl has been teaching German language classes for 20 years at the University of Graz, Austria, – in the Department for Translation Studies and at the Centre for Language, Plurilingualism and Didactics (treffpunkt sprachen). She is engaged in language teacher education, at treffpunkt sprachen (Continuing Education Program "Language learning with Adults") and at UNI for LIFE (Continuing Education Program "German as a Second and Foreign Language"). Her research interests include study abroad, cross-cultural academic literacy and oracy, and language teaching in translator and interpreter education.

Sandra Stadler-Heer is Senior Lecturer of TESOL at the Department of Linguistics and Literature, Catholic University of Eichstätt-Ingolstadt, Germany. She is co-convenor of the AILA Literature in Language Learning and Teaching Research Network and co-editor of *Taking Literature and Language Learning Online* (Bloomsbury, 2022). Her recent research focuses on developing teachers' technological pedagogical content knowledge and teaching foreign languages online.

Jeanine Steinbock is Research Assistant at the JMU Würzburg, Germany, and a Ph.D. candidate working on teachers' perspectives on using Web 2.0 tools and Apps in the EFL classroom. Her research is part of a larger research project of the Professional School of Education at the JMU Würzburg. She is also currently working on the project "CoTeach – Connected Teacher Education", where she focuses on the potential of virtual reality for inter- and transcultural learning.

Theresa Summer is Associate Professor of Teaching English as a Foreign Language at the University of Bamberg, Germany. Prior to that, she taught English and Music at secondary schools for several years. Her research interests include pop culture and songs, grammar, global education, and taboos in critical foreign language education. She is co-editor of the journal *Englisch 5–10* (Friedrich, Hannover) and she currently focuses on learners' perspectives of English language teaching and learning.

Katrin Thomson is a Postdoctoral Researcher and EFL Teacher Educator at the University of Augsburg, Germany. She received her Ph.D. from the University of Jena in 2018 and was Interim Professor for TEFL at the University of Regensburg from 04/2020 to 09/2021. She has worked as a teacher for English and German and as a TEFL lecturer at the Universities of Jena, Münster and Wuppertal. Her current research focuses on language teachers' professional development with a particular interest in teachers' classroom discourse competence (CDC). She is volume editor of and contributor to Classroom Discourse Competence. Current Issues in Language Teaching and Teacher Education (2022). In her postdoctoral project, she uses a sequential mixed-methods design for her research on prospective teachers' CDC in specific classroom scenarios of ELT. Other research interests include literary and cultural learning, film and (audio-)visual literacy, gender and diversity-sensitive language education. She has published several articles on these issues and a monograph (2020) on the negotiation of gender and gender discourses in American drama.

Valentin Werner is Associate Professor in the Department of English Linguistics at the University of Bamberg, Germany. He researches and teaches in the areas of applied linguistics (especially learner English and application of linguistic findings in language education), corpus linguistics, language variation and change (especially World Englishes), media linguistics, language and culture, and stylistics. His recent activities include the edition of the volumes *Tense and Aspect in Second Language Acquisition and Learner Corpus Research* (Benjamins, 2020; with Robert Fuchs), *Pop Culture in Language Education: Theory, Research, Practice* (Routledge, 2021; with Friederike Tegge), and *Stylistic Approaches to Pop Culture* (Routledge, 2022; with Christoph Schubert).

Aline Willems is Assistant Professor for learning and teaching of modern foreign languages at the University of Cologne and thus supports programmes for students wanting to become foreign language teachers of French, Spanish, Italian, English, Dutch, Russian, and/or Japanese (all types of schools of North Rhine-Westphalia, including special needs education). Her main research focus is on multilingualism, music, and heterogeneity in the foreign language classroom. She is also interested in the biological and neuroscientific processes concerning foreign language learning and use.

Acknowledgements

This journey into the world of taboos would not have been possible without the support of like-minded colleagues. We would like to express our gratitude to all the people who made this project possible. Our first and foremost thanks go to Maria Eisenmann, who supported our idea of a symposium on taboo issues, at which the idea for this publication was born. The great interest in taboos – from researchers, teachers, teacher educators, and university students – encouraged us to initiate the taboo symposia series. We are thankful to them for their curiosity and openness to deal with the challenging undertaking of investigating the great variety of taboos and controversial issues out there each of which brings with it different obstacles for foreign language education. We would also like to thank all authors of this book: Thank you for your cooperation, sharing your thoughts and ideas, engaging in critical discussions with us, and offering interdisciplinary insights into the vast field of taboos!

The editorial team at Routledge was very supportive throughout the publication process. Thank you Emilie Coin, Swapnil Joshi, and Kanishka Jangir for your professional guidance.

Finally, we would like to thank our colleagues and friends who supported this project by engaging in numerous discussions and helping with some additional proofreading. We greatly value your critical thoughts and eye-opening spirit! A big thank you also goes to our student assistants Paul Scheffler, Claudia Schnellbögl, and Lisa Theisen, who helped with the citations and final formatting of this volume. Any remaining errors remain ours alone.

Introduction

1 Approaching Taboos and Controversial Issues in Foreign Language Education

Christian Ludwig and Theresa Summer

Introduction

When the idea of an edited volume on taboos in foreign language education evolved, it seemed very simple. Too simple. A taboo is something that is not acceptable to talk about or do. Taboos can, for example, include restrictions on certain activities and behaviours in society as a whole but also dietary restrictions among certain religious groups, or words that are inappropriate to use in certain contexts. Despite the fact that there are still boundaries that should not be crossed, today's society seems to be increasingly open and accepting towards things that used to be frowned upon. Although traditionally discussed among anthropologists, the term *taboo* now exists across almost all disciplines, including cultural studies, social sciences, and medical studies. With regard to foreign language education, the word *taboo* covers quite a wide range of phenomena, including specific topics, verbal and non-verbal communication strategies, and behaviours. There is not only taboo language that should not be used by students but also taboo subjects, customs, and lifestyles that are often avoided as they may spark some sort of controversy. As Kaye poignantly puts it, "topics such as divorce and depression and illnesses such as cancer and AIDS may not be as taboo as they used to be" (Kaye, 2015, n.p.). Consequently, such topics may no longer be taboo in society and can thus be tackled in the (foreign language) classroom. Importantly, this requires a pedagogic framework as well as, depending on the particular taboo topic, an interdisciplinary approach and support by school psychologists or psychotherapists. In this introduction, we argue that critical foreign language pedagogy constitutes a suitable lens for discussing taboos and controversial issues as these are often defined by institutions of power. Exploring taboos and controversial issues thus allows teachers and students to explore cultural, religious, and social norms while promoting different perspectives and viewpoints, and encouraging transformative discourses.

Against this background, we first take a closer look at the concept of taboo itself, arguing that in the context of foreign language education, the terms *taboo* and *controversial* are often used synonymously to refer to something that is considered unacceptable or inappropriate. Closely related to this, we then suggest a

DOI: 10.4324/9781003220701-2

systematic yet flexible categorisation of taboos. To conclude, we introduce taboo literacy as a goal of critical literacy before shedding light upon implications for educational practices.

Taboos: Past and Present

According to the founding father of psychoanalysis, Sigmund Freud, taboos are "older than the gods and [go] back to the pre-religious age" (Freud, 1913/2010, p. 26). The word *taboo* itself comes from the Polynesian languages and was first introduced to the English language in the 1770s by Captain James Cook. During his visit to Tonga, he wrote in his log:

> Everyone of my visitors received from me such presents as I had reason to believe they were highly satisfied with. When dinner came upon table, not one of them would sit down or eat a bit of any thing that was served up. On expressing my surprize at this, they were all taboo, as they said; which word has a very comprehensive meaning but in general signifies that a thing is forbidden. Why they were under such constraints at present was not explained.
> (Cook, 1842, p. 110)

As this quote illustrates, the word *taboo* was used to refer to something that was forbidden. Importantly, the meaning of the word *taboo* has changed and expanded over time, and there seems to be no more consensus on what constitutes taboos today as the term is becoming increasingly imprecise (Horlacher, 2010, p. 3). According to the *Oxford Dictionary of English* (2015), the word *taboo*, used as a noun, adjective, or verb, refers to "a social or religious custom prohibiting or restricting a particular practice or forbidding association with a particular person, place, or thing". As such, taboos no longer need to be religious but can relate to basically any object, action, location, social and cultural practice, or person. This raises various questions such as: Why do certain individuals, groups, or societies see certain things as taboo while others do not? Who decides which customs, things, or topics are given the taboo tag, as everyone seems to have their own definition of what is taboo? What happens to taboos when society decides to finally come to grips with "outdated" norms and values? Why do some taboos become weaker, while others gain strength (Fershtman et al., 2011)?

As Kaltenbrunner (1987, p. 7 as cited in Horlacher, 2010, p. 11) emphasises, we live in an era that seems to be characterised by "its aversion towards taboos and in which ever more taboos are losing their erstwhile power". However, it seems that "under the guise of an emancipatory and critically enlightened rational thinking new taboos have been created that are no less repressive than their predecessors" (Kaltenbrunner, 1987, p. 7 as cited in Horlacher, 2010, p. 9). Furthermore, taboos even seem to be needed more than ever in a world that is becoming increasingly complex, diverse, and ambiguous as they, superficially at least, help people to find order in chaos. As Hopkins pointed out back in

1994, we should "accommodate to the turbulence, indeterminacy, and fluidity of the world outside if they [schools] are to meet the increasing demands that are laid on them [students] by economic and social circumstance, and especially the demands of our democratic society" (Hopkins, 1994, p. 7). Yet, taboos are often precluded from being openly discussed in educational contexts as the sensitivity of taboos varies from individual to individual. Despite these concerns, adolescents need opportunities to learn "how to respectfully articulate and voice opinions, but also how to listen to and receive others' opinions and viewpoints on important issues" (Groenke et al., 2010, p. 29). Here, critical pedagogy provides the perfect framework as it encourages students not only to listen to each other but also to reflect and act critically.

Critical Foreign Language Pedagogy

One of the major tenets of critical pedagogy is that beliefs and practices in society, which are related to the power and domination of certain groups over others, should be questioned and challenged. In other words, teachers should guide their students towards critically examining existing ideologies and practices, and encourage them to respond critically. The pioneer of critical pedagogy, Paulo Freire (1968/2014a, 1972), emphasised the transformative power of education, which should allow all students to develop their critical consciousness and become critical thinkers. Crucially, as Steinberg poignantly argues, "Freire didn't create a critical pedagogy, he presented multiple ways of knowing" (Steinberg, 2020, p. 5), meaning that there is a complex web of ways in which critical pedagogy can be approached.

Briefly summarised, critical pedagogy, or critical pedagogies in the Freirean sense, proposes a problem-posing approach to education, which encourages learners to change their perspectives, achieve an awareness of power structures and social (in)justices, and become critical thinkers (Gerlach, 2020a, p. 17). As Steinberg emphasises, critical pedagogy is more of a spirit rather than a rigid concept:

> [Critical pedagogy] isn't a thing, a method, a way, it's not a philosophy, not a curriculum. Critical pedagogy is a spirit, an image of what can be if we are able to see what is. It is a commitment to be teachers as activists, to be unpopular, to be humble, but be shit-stirrers, and to create pedagogical uncoverings of what we can do… what our students can do.
> (Steinberg, 2020, p. 5)

According to this perspective, critical pedagogy is not a specific teaching method or approach but rather "a social and educational process" (Crookes & Lehner, 1998, p. 327). The importance of integrating this educational process into foreign language education has been addressed by various scholars (Akbari, 2008; Crookes, 2013; Gray, 2019). As Crookes notes, scholars investigating critical pedagogy within foreign or second language education are "creating the subfield of critical language pedagogy" (Crookes, 2013, p. 8). Taking this as a starting point, this volume draws on Crookes' definition of critical pedagogy as

> teaching for social justice, in ways that support the development of active, engaged citizens who will [...] critically inquire into why the lives of so many human beings, perhaps including their own, are materially, psychologically, socially, and spiritually inadequate—citizens who will be prepared to seek out solutions to the problems they define and encounter, and take action accordingly.
>
> (Crookes, 2013, p. 8)

Within this subfield of critical language pedagogy, research has been rather scarce, especially within Europe. The volume *Kritische Fremdsprachendidaktik (Critical Foreign Language Education)* by David Gerlach (2020b), however, has started to fill an important research gap, focusing particularly on critical foreign language education within the geographical boundaries of Germany. Yet, given the complexity of today's world and the great range of social injustices becoming apparent through global movements such as Animal Rebellion, Black Lives Matter, or Extinction Rebellion, critical pedagogy is by no means an easy undertaking. In fact, as Steinberg notes, "[t]eaching, critically teaching, is hard work. It requires us to rise above the petty annoyances of those who *aren't like we are*" (Steinberg, 2020, p. 4). There are numerous intersections between the field of critical foreign language pedagogy and the teaching and learning of foreign languages that become apparent not only at the methodological level but also at the level of content, some of which are discussed in the following.

In the 1980s, the development of Communicative Language Teaching (CLT) emphasised the role of authentic and social interaction in the target language. As Kumaravadivelu states, "[t]he phrase 'competence in terms of social interaction' sums up the primary emphasis of CLT" (Kumaravadivelu, 2006, p. 60). Cooperative and collaborative approaches especially support social interaction among students as they mutually engage in a coordinated effort to understand and solve a problem—an approach which also strongly favours positive interdependence and individual accountability despite its emphasis on the group. In a similar vein, approaches and concepts such as foreign language learner autonomy (Lamb & Reinders, 2008; Little et al., 2017), inquiry-based learning (Dobber et al., 2017), differentiation (Bromley, 2019; Eisenmann, 2019), and inclusive pedagogy (Bartosch & Köpfer, 2018; Bongartz & Rohde, 2018) all emphasise the critical role of the learner in living and promoting diversity. If learners are encouraged to analyse multiple perspectives, they need opportunities to deal with issues that really matter to them and to their personal lives. As Cotterall points out:

> The learning setting must offer learners the opportunity to engage in genuine inquiry and expand their understanding of topics and ideas which

matter to them. [...] [T]hey should represent authentic questions (of personal significance to the learners) which demand real answers.

(Cotterall, 2017, pp. 103–104)

Furthermore, in order to provide an "education that lasts" (Edes, 2020, p. 90), it is indispensable to follow a dialogic approach, which builds on the voices of both teachers and learners and draws on the wealth of perspectives and ideas present in every student group. In other words, a critical pedagogy approach manifests itself through the integration of taboo(ed) topics and issues, which so far, presumably remain largely absent from education. While there is a plethora of topics and themes which students may explore in collaborative settings and through the target language, taboo and controversial topics may be particularly meaningful and beneficial to students, especially with regard to developing students' communicative competence around topics and problems they encounter in real life. Closely related to this, ignoring such topics would diminish the students' roles as critical thinkers and ignore their diverse perspectives. Against this background, the following section focuses on the great variety of taboos and controversial issues as well as their potential for implementing critical pedagogy.

Taboos and Controversial Topics

Taboos and the transgression of taboos can be found in almost any societal discourse. Despite the ubiquity of taboos and taboo-breaking, the word *taboo* itself seems to remain an ambiguous and vague term in foreign language education. In one of the few existing categorisations of taboos in foreign language education, potentially controversial issues are often subsumed under the acronym PARSNIP, referring to seven main currently present taboos: politics, alcohol, religion, sex, narcotics, -isms (e.g., communism, sexism), and pork. This acronym is a rather rigid classification of taboos, which largely ignores their ephemeral nature. This construct was modified creatively by a group of English educators who added further "alternative" uses of the acronym, such as periods and porn for "P", as Figure 1.1 illustrates.

In the context of foreign language education, the concept of PARSNIP is mostly addressed in the field of materials development. Thornbury, for example, uses the term "parsnip policy" to refer to policies of publishers that exclude controversial topics, which consequently "imbues ELT books with a certain blandness" (Thornbury, 2010, n.p.). According to Meddings, publishers thereby rule out various potentially offensive territories, which "is why teachers and learners become so familiar with units on travel and the weather" (Meddings, 2006, n.p.). Nonetheless, these topics may also include representations of alternative lifestyles, pastime activities, or non-traditional family structures. In other words, foreign language teaching materials typically focus on everyday-life topics such as families, spare-time activities, and cultural content by focusing on specific countries and their traditions. Consequently, teachers working with the textbooks are

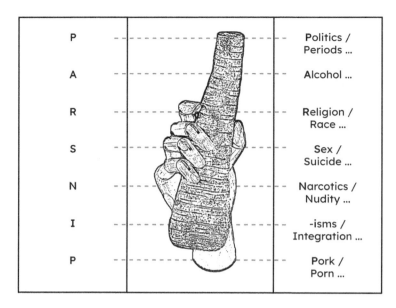

Figure 1.1 Parsnippy Topics.
Note. Authors' illustration, topics as listed in Seburn et al. (2016, p. 1).

likely to refrain from discussing taboos with their learners unless they consider themselves to be critical pedagogues. However, teachers may not only be held back by publishers, education authorities, or curricular guidelines but also by political views and agendas as the Florida "Don't Say Gay" bill illustrates.

Consequently, parsnippy topics that go beyond easy-going, communicative, and everyday-life small-talk issues are often rather scarce in published teaching materials. There are a few exceptions, however, such as the resource book *Taboos and Issues* (MacAndrew & Martínez, 2001), devoted specifically to a range of taboos, the above-mentioned ebook series called the *PARSNIPs in ELT* (Howard et al., 2016; Seburn et al., 2016; Smith et al., 2015), and *Can I Teach That?* (Linder & Majerus, 2016). The last one, for example, presents a range of stories, strategies, and advice for teachers using controversial topics and activities. Although this example does not specifically focus on foreign language education, it illustrates how spaces "for students to speak about difficult things that are happening or have happened to them" (Linder & Majerus, 2016, p. ix) can be created.

Based on this, this introduction (as well as the publication as a whole) extends the list of parsnippy topics and aspires to provide a more systematic categorisation while also offering a more flexible handling in educational contexts. First, it suggests a broader definition of taboos, understanding taboos as challenging, controversial, and tough topics that are perceived as taboo by some people or social groups in certain situations. A categorisation of taboo topics within this broad definition is crucial to enable a systematic analysis in research and a progressive conceptualisation for and an integration of taboos into teaching and learning practices. Furthermore, categories enable teachers (and students) to grasp an elusive concept such as taboo. Thus, the categorisation of taboos shown in Figure 1.2 includes a broader range of critical issues in today's society. It presents eight main flexible categories. All of the suggested taboo categories are either related to issues of social (in)justice and (un)equal power relations, which can be related to the areas of race, class, gender, and disability (Vasquez, 2017, p. 3) or to individuals' personal well-being, forms of behaviour, and ways of life. Obviously, each of the topics comes with its own challenges, especially when addressing them in the classroom. For example, before considering a discussion about suicide, one needs to be careful not to publicise suicide in order to avoid copycat suicides (Werther effect).

As concerns the presence of such taboo topics in academic literature and ELT research, a noticeable aspect is that taboos are rarely discussed among researchers and practitioners (Becker et al., 2022). This is particularly surprising for two main reasons. First, students are constantly confronted with (the changing and challenging of) taboos in their daily lives as existing social, cultural, religious, and other norms disappear and new ones are established. For example, social media platforms have potentially manifested taboos as people are promoting seemingly perfect bodies and lifestyles on Instagram and TikTok, and digital devices have contributed to the rise of new taboo issues such as sexting and cyberbullying. In fact, digital media may also expose students to potentially inappropriate or disturbing (taboo) content and language, which would not have reached them as easily a few decades ago and which raises new questions of (self-) censorship (Allan & Burridge, 2006).

A second reason why it is surprising to find only a marginal body of literature and empirical research focusing on taboos and foreign language education is the fact that English teachers across the globe are often confronted with very rigid taboos in specific countries that require a great deal of intercultural sensitivity. An example of this is the use of international and largely Western textbooks in predominantly Muslim countries that demand competence in handling taboo content among teachers. Two recent studies were conducted in this field, however, examining two different practical dimensions of working with textbooks: In a study among teachers in Saudi Arabia (in a university ELT context), Etri examined teachers' ways of handling taboo content such as dating and identified that they engage in various forms of censorship such as avoiding or skipping taboo content (Etri, 2021). A further study examined the effect of pork visuals (considered taboo among Muslim and Jewish learners) on the processing of linguistic and visual input among 40 Muslim language learners through eye-tracking, indicating that the pork content did not distract learners' attention (Dolgunsöz, 2019). These studies illustrate that taboos are existent in education and, depending on the political and cultural context of education, handling them in practice presents a challenge in legal, methodological, and ethical terms.

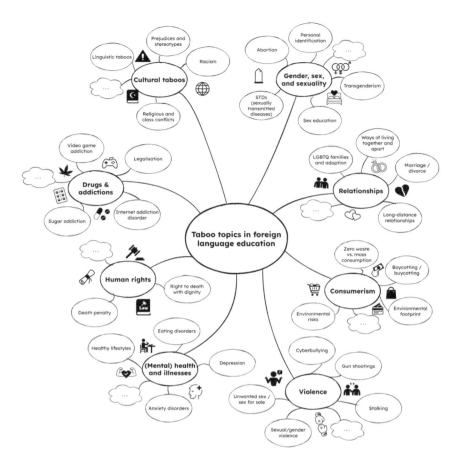

Figure 1.2 Contemporary Taboos and Controversial Topics.
Note. Authors' illustration.

Against this background, dealing with some selected taboos in the foreign language classroom cannot only help bring students in contact with views, ideas, and opinions different from their own but also motivate them to critically question and explain their own views. As Hess points out: "[t]he relative diversity of schools makes them particularly good places for controversial issue discussions. Students likely will be exposed to views different from their own and have to explain their own views during such discussions" (Hess, 2009, p. 6).

So far, we have discussed the importance of critical language pedagogy, particularly focusing on the potential of taboo topics for engaging students in critical discussions, for example, through working with various text types. Analysing and producing pop culture artefacts such as songs and TV series (Werner & Tegge, 2021) but also literary texts such as poems, multimodal novels (Delanoy et al., 2015), and graphic novels as well as born-digital texts (Ludwig & Kersten, in press) in particular can offer new and multiple perspectives on taboos, which can be explored in foreign language education among intermediate and advanced as well as young learners (the wide range of picturebooks on controversial and challenging issues may serve as an example here). Yet, adolescents, as Enriquez highlights, "are the ones most affected by exposure to these texts" and, therefore, "it is helpful to understand their definitions of controversy, the topics they consider inappropriate for the school setting, how much exposure they feel is too much" (Enriquez, 2006, p. 17).

Obviously, the aim of integrating taboos in foreign language teaching and learning is not to evoke unreflective negative responses, enhance personal stress or fear, create conflicts, or bring back negative memories. Thus, dealing with taboo topics requires careful anticipation on the part of the teacher, as well as support, feedback, and guidance in exploring certain topics and issues for (pre-service) teachers and learners alike. The next section focuses on the development of taboo literacy as a central pedagogic aim to enable learners to analyse, respond to, and create taboo(ed) artefacts and thereby reflect upon them critically.

From Critical Literacy to Taboo Literacy

In the context of foreign language education, an important concept deriving from critical language pedagogy is the goal of developing learners' critical literacy. According to Crookes, critical pedagogy commonly invites "an action response", whereas critical literacy encourages the "learner to develop tools for seeing the ways in which language has position, interests, power, and can act to disadvantage those on the lower rugs of a hierarchical society" (Crookes, 2013, p. 28). In other words, and with particular regard to foreign language learning, such explorations can uncover how "language is fundamentally tied to questions of power" (Janks, 2010, p. 11), i.e., how language and power are closely intertwined as language establishes and maintains power (cf. Fairclough, 2014). In a similar vein, Gerlach also emphasises the fact that critical theories and critical pedagogy deal with the relationship between the world, understanding the world and language (Gerlach, 2020a, p. 24). This is closely related to the definition of critical literacies from the perspective of a multiliteracies approach, which lists three dimensions of critical literacies: (1) connecting with lived experience, (2) thinking critically, and (3) taking action. At a more practical level, this includes dealing with texts from students' lives and identifying multiple perspectives (1), identifying problems and voicing concerns (2), and offering solutions or participating (3). Notably, "meaningful participation" is described as "a touchstone of critical literacy", which is, for example, facilitated through digital media and technological conditions that provide powerful opportunities for participation (Kalantzis & Cope, 2012, pp. 160–161). Consequently, dealing with taboos and controversial topics can foster the development of critical literacy or, more specifically and in the context of handling taboos, taboo literacy, in foreign language education. Learners should be offered opportunities to deal with some tough, controversial, and taboo topics and texts relevant to their lives, analyse these, and participate on the grounds of their new insights. The following section therefore addresses a range of pedagogic implications for integrating taboos and controversial topics into critical foreign language education.

A Pedagogic Framework for Taboos

This section presents a pedagogic framework that aims to relate theory and research to practice by exploring three interrelated questions. These questions, illustrated in Figure 1.3, require a new consideration of how to foster taboo literacy in practice by examining implications for curricular, pedagogic as well as methodological guidelines, and materials development. While examining these three areas, this section offers some practical suggestions for teaching practice.

First, the curriculum, which embodies decisions about the teaching objectives, content, the methods of instruction, and the evaluation of a programme (Thornbury, 2017, p. 74), can be examined for their taboo qualities, i.e., opportunities for discussing "regular" topics from a more critical perspective. Second, curricula can be analysed by detecting opportunities for dealing with taboo issues and developing guidelines for promoting taboo literacy. This primarily applies to the areas of teaching objectives (i.e., developing taboo literacy as well as other competences and skills developed through engaging with taboo issues) and the content (i.e., dealing with topics that are considered taboo).

Nonetheless, curricula for English in Europe already offer a considerable amount of freedom to teachers and learners when it comes to the choice of

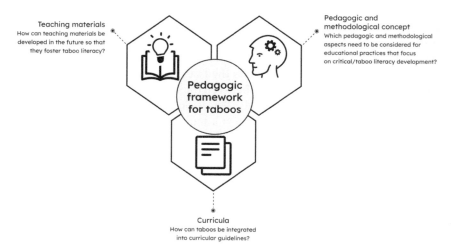

Figure 1.3 A Pedagogic Framework for Taboos.
Note. Authors' illustration.

content. In European documents such as the *Common European Framework of References* (*CEFR*), the development of communicative competence is still high on the agenda. In the new descriptors of the *Compendium Volume* to the *CEFR*, four modes of communication are listed—namely, reception, production, interaction, and mediation (Council of Europe [CoE], 2018). Evidently, an exploration of taboos in practice can facilitate the development of all of these modes. To give an example, cultural taboos such as swear words and taboo language (see Chapter 10) can be dealt with in practice by identifying the use of swear words (reception) and comparing the use of such words to other languages in a plurilingual approach (mediation). Moreover, in an example of online interaction activities listed in the *CEFR*, it is suggested that learners can personally engage "in a critical discussion of arts or music with friends online" (CoE, 2018, p. 186). This could, for instance, include a critical analysis of eco-songs (Summer, 2021), music videos, and digital art by reflecting upon the portrayal of people's relationship with the natural world, consumerism, and environmental risks.

In addition to new curricular objectives, taboos can serve to fulfil already existing ones, such as the development of intercultural competence (Byram, 1997). As taboos are a key element of every culture, they can be explored to identify cultural similarities and differences, as illustrated in the chapter in this volume by Amarasinghe and Borgwaldt (Chapter 18). It discusses taboos in Germany and Sri Lanka, not only emphasising the fact that topics which may be considered taboo in one culture are acceptable in another culture but also that one may have a blind spot for taboos in one's own culture. Closely related to this, taboos can also provide an impulse for exploring learners' potentially (trans)cultural identities. Learners can rehearse their roles as global citizens by engaging with different (trans)cultural perspectives and identifying differences and similarities across individuals, which are implicit in different texts and artefacts. Byram's (2008) concept of education for intercultural citizenship also promotes a greater focus on political, social, and cultural issues in foreign language education and thus provides a theoretical rationale for discussing taboos.

The second domain of the framework addresses pedagogic and methodological aspects—hence, questions related to the development of teaching goals (i.e., in combination with competences, skills, and content), lesson plans, as well as activity or task design. While combining the above-mentioned modes of communication (CoE, 2018) with the development of taboo literacy, the first direct implication is that current teaching materials need to be substituted with additional, authentic materials.

In addition, pedagogic implications on the methodological level require a (re)consideration of learner-centredness. As an essential principle of foreign language education, learner-centredness accounts for the subjective needs of learners involving collaborative approaches in which educators and learners share insights into their experiences and knowledge (Nunan, 2013; Tudor, 1996). For the development of taboo literacy in foreign language education, the notion of learner-centredness is absolutely crucial and, in terms of task design, it needs to be reconsidered. This is due to the potential challenges and dangers involved in handling the wide variety of taboos in educational settings. Primarily because of the power imbalances between teachers and learners, reasons against the integration of taboos into (foreign language) education are manifold. Potential risks include offending learners by violating their religious and political beliefs, their moral codex and sexuality, creating personal conflicts among learners (and teachers), and provoking extreme and negative emotional responses due to traumatic experiences of individuals, who may have been personally affected by violence, experienced personal loss, or political persecution. Rather than relating topics to learners' personal experiences, as would be the norm in communicative approaches that encourage learners to relate to personal situations and concerns, for instance, dealing with taboos requires a different approach in which the topic rather than the learners' personal views or experiences is in the foreground and in which different texts and perspectives are investigated critically. What is more, when selecting particularly controversial topics and texts for the classroom, teachers should consult school psychologists and ask for advice.

Due to the importance of creating a positive and trustworthy atmosphere in educational settings, it is important to try to cut out the negative experiences of learners—especially when it comes to controversial topics such as violence. Rather than asking learners about their experiences with regard to cyberbullying, for instance, it would be more appropriate to explore the experiences of others. As mentioned above, this could be approached through different texts and (pop culture) artefacts and by focusing on explorations that allow for multiperspective discussions, which are based on arguments and which, ideally, reach beyond the microcosm of the classroom and help students to practise for the macrocosm of the world.

Related to the aforementioned challenge, another critical aspect related to the integration of taboos and controversial issues into practice is the occurrence of eruptions. Introduced by Janks (2010), the term *eruption* refers to the occurrence of difficult situations and unexpected conflicts in the classroom. An example of such an eruption is reflected upon by West (2021), who reports on a homophobic incident in an in-service English language teaching course in South Korea, in which a video sparked a homophobic eruption. As such eruptions can theoretically happen at any time in the classroom, the integration of critical pedagogy into TEFL programmes at university and an interdisciplinary approach with psychology with a focus on handling taboos and the conflicts that come with them could potentially help teachers develop strategies for dealing with such unexpected conflicts. By engaging in an open discourse with learners and encouraging self-reflexivity, also among teachers (Buyserie & Ramírez, 2021), normativity can be challenged.

The following teaching guidelines, subsumed under the acronym TABOOS in reference to the more narrow PARSNIP model, serve as general suggestions for activity design and materials development by taking into account potential dangers and risks involved, as described above, and trying to carve out and illustrate the potential of critical language pedagogy and taboos for foreign language education (see Table 1.1). Given the great variety of taboo topics (see

Table 1.1 Educational Guidelines for Dealing with Taboos

Educational guidelines	Suggestion
T Texts and artefacts	Bringing in a variety of texts and artefacts that offer different perspectives on taboos.
A Advice and help	Creating an atmosphere of trust and specifying where learners can get help. Depending on the taboo topic in focus, a trigger warning might be important or a choice of topics/texts to avoid negative experiences among learners.
B Be fair!	Encouraging learners to be fair by listening to their classmates. This also holds true for teachers, who need to handle biased perspectives and listen to their students' points of view.
O Open: knowledge	Widening learners' horizons by providing relevant, reliable, and important information and facts on historical, social, and cultural developments.
O Open: views	Opening one's classroom for new topics, forms of discussions and interdisciplinary approaches while pushing for common ground (for example, by adhering to basic human rights), and inviting multiple perspectives.
S Student-centeredness	Considering learners' subjective needs/interests and inviting them to bring in their own materials and raise questions relevant to their lives in the on- and offline world outside the classroom, if appropriate (depending on the learners and the topic in focus).

Figure 1.2), on the one hand, and teachers' need for practical models for their everyday teaching, on the other hand, a one-approach-fits-all is inappropriate, which is why we present some basic educational guidelines and suggestions.

Overall, the educational guidelines of TABOOS highlight the importance of developing lesson plans and activities that are student-centred by addressing topics relevant to their lives but without directly involving their personal (possibly traumatic) experiences. Foreign language education should guide learners towards tracing the roots of taboos by widening their horizons and learning more about the origins of social injustices, discovering power relations and cultural conventions, exploring consequences of tabooing certain topics, and finding possible solutions.

Closely related to this, we clearly declare ourselves in favour of a negotiated syllabus, which does not avoid but embrace some controversial issues if discussed properly and which, as Clarke points out, "takes the basic principles of communicative language teaching to their logical conclusion" (Clarke, 1991, p. 13). It actively involves students in choosing topics and activities but also other key classroom processes such as evaluation, feedback, and assessment. It seems that through such radical and full student participation, contemporary taboo issues could move to the forefront, provided that students are willing to be challenged and can be encouraged to move beyond their comfort zones.

An additional, more general pedagogical aspect that deserves attention is the role of parents in dealing with taboos in education. Situations in which parents complain about religious festivities such as Christmas at school, which they feel may exclude their children, or dealing with controversial issues that are brought up in novels read at school and irritate some parents, are situations which are presumably well-known to practising teachers. If teachers begin a lesson sequence on sexting, for instance (due to conflicts that have arisen among learners), a valuable piece of advice might be to inform parents about such plans by explaining the purpose behind such a project. In this way, teaching content is not only negotiated with the students but also with parents. Furthermore, finding out more about students' backgrounds and encouraging parents to help can also guide students through taboo experiences. Ultimately, and ideally, not only students but also parents may become what Freire refers to as "critical co-investigators" (Freire, 1968/2014a, p. 81).

The third aspect of the pedagogic framework (see Figure 1.3), teaching materials, relates more specifically to how textbooks or (digital) materials can be designed to promote taboo literacy as an outcome in students. As already mentioned, "normwashed" classroom materials, which avoid discussing or even mentioning controversial issues, are common rather than unusual. Yet, they play a key role in facilitating discussions around controversial issues. Although real-world materials offer a viable and feasible solution, they also require time—mostly in terms of finding suitable materials and designing goal-oriented tasks around them. Once again, learner-centredness plays an important role here as students can bring their own materials to the classroom and produce materials which may be used for further learning. Materials can, for instance, include literary texts such as poems and young adult literature, songs and music videos, and born-digital texts. Evidently, no matter whether materials are brought to the classroom or even produced by students, they need to be carefully evaluated by teachers.

Here, guiding questions on integrating taboos in general and choosing appropriate materials such as the following may help as they shed light upon the complexities involved in dealing with taboos in education:

- How can a taboo topic be connected with existing classroom materials, such as the textbook (e.g., by supplementing it with texts from learners' lives)?
- How can students be supported in better understanding the complexity inherent to any taboo issue?
- Which approaches can be applied to reflect both on the topic as well as the classroom work that revolved around the topic?
- How can students' skills for critical dialogue and discussion be enhanced?
- How can the discussion of taboo topics be more explicitly linked to their role as (future) global citizens?

These questions hint at the fact that teacher education as well as in-service teacher training play a crucial role in promoting both critical and taboo literacy. Therefore, teacher education programmes, in which critical literacy plays a marginal role, as has been observed by Gray (2019), are bound to fail. They insufficiently raise future teachers' awareness of the importance of integrating challenging issues into their lessons, do not prepare them for addressing issues that are still (too) often avoided in education, and still omit approaches to learning foreign languages which emphasise the active and participatory role of students in all decisions and steps of learning.

According to Kelly (1986), teachers adopt four different attitudes towards discussing controversial issues: (1) exclusive neutrality, (2) exclusive partiality, (3) neutral impartiality, and (4) committed impartiality. Teachers who support exclusive neutrality (attitude 1) argue that taboos should not have a place in the classroom, which is believed to represent a neutral space. Supporters of exclusive partiality (attitude 2) avoid (creating) situations in which students get a chance to voice their opinion, which may go against the teacher's or other students' opinions. Especially teachers who belong to the first two categories seem to be likely or at least reluctant to avoid controversial issues. This attitude, detrimental to the Freirean model of education, represents an example of his banking model in which the students are the depositories, and the teacher is the depositor (Freire, 1968/2014). As Dahlgren puts it: "[a]t its most extreme and authoritarian level, teachers utilizing this approach actively shut down students who have the temerity to question the authority of their opinions and even grade students with opposing views in a punitive manner" (Dahlgren, 2008, p. 27).

A further challenge is that educators may feel incapable of dealing with specific taboos due to their own lack of crucial knowledge and skills. At the same time, however, teachers may not always be aware of their dismissive attitude towards critical issues, or they may simply be afraid of overt multiperspectivity and vocality and thus rather implicitly enforce traditional topics, roles, and materials. In contrast to these two groups, teachers with an attitude of neutral impartiality (attitude 3) promote the discussion of critical issues, while avoiding expressing their personal attitudes and opinions. Committed impartiality (attitude 4), according to Kelly (1986), represents the most satisfying attitude. Teachers who support this approach cater to the needs of today's diverse classrooms by revealing their own attitudes and views without indoctrinating or brainwashing students while, at the same time, allowing students to voice their own thoughts and ideas.

Final Remarks

Teachers play an essential role in helping students navigate this increasingly complex and diverse world. While students rely on their teachers to address issues to be more prepared for what they may encounter in real life, teachers need tools, material, and methods to address these topics appropriately. Taking this as a starting point, this volume not only offers a rationale for addressing controversial topics in the classroom by explaining why controversial issues are important but also provides concrete topics, tools, materials, and methods to help teachers make their foreign language classrooms more controversial. This edited volume emphasises the fact that today's students not only need to become more informed but also more critical, self-reflective, and open towards the perspectives of others. Without doubt, teacher education plays a key role in promoting critical and taboo literacy so that learners become critical, democratic, and active citizens.

References

Akbari, R. (2008). Transforming lives: Introducing critical pedagogy into ELT classrooms. *ELT Journal, 62*(3), 276–283.
Allan, K., & Burridge, K. (2006). *Forbidden words: Taboo and the censoring of language.* Cambridge University Press.
Bartosch, R., & Köpfer, A. (2018). *Inklusion und Nachhaltigkeit: Entwicklungslinien moderner Englischdidaktik.* Wissenschaftlicher Verlag Trier.
Becker, D., Ludwig, C., & Summer, T. (2022). Taboos in ELT through the lens of critical pedagogy. *Teacher Development Academic Journal (TDAJ), 2*(2), 9–16.
Bongartz, C., & Rohde, A. (Eds.). (2015). *Inklusion im Englischunterricht.* Peter Lang.
Bromley, M. (2019). Differentiation in the classroom. *SecEd, 10*(1), 21–27.
Buyserie, B., & Ramírez, R. (2021). Enacting a queer pedagogy in the composition classroom. *ELT Journal, 75*(2), 193–202. https://doi.org/10.1093/elt/ccaa072
Byram, M. (1997). *Teaching and assessing intercultural communicative competence.* Multilingual Matters.
Byram, M. (2008). *From foreign language education to education for intercultural citizenship: Essays and reflections.* Multilingual Matters.
Clarke, D. F. (1991). The negotiated syllabus: What is it and how is it likely to work? *Applied Linguistics, 12*(1), 13–28.
Cook, J. (1842). *The voyages of Captain James Cook* (Vol. 2). W. Smith.
Cotterall, S. (2017). The pedagogy of learner autonomy: Lessons from the classroom. *Studies in Self-Access Learning Journal, 8*(2), 102–115.
Council of Europe. (2018). *Common European framework of reference for languages: Learning, teaching, assessment. Companion volume with new descriptors.* Council of Europe.
Crookes, G. (2013). *Critical ELT in action: Foundations, promises, praxis.* Routledge.
Crookes, G., & Lehner, A. (1998). Aspects of process in an ESL critical pedagogy teacher education course. *TESOL Quarterly, 32*(2), 319–328.
Dahlgren, R. L. (2008). *Experiences of social studies teachers with teaching controversial public issues in the classroom* [Doctoral dissertation, University of Florida]. UF Digital Collections. https://ufdc.ufl.edu/UFE0022576/00001/pdf
Delanoy, W., Eisenmann, M., & Matz, F. (Eds.). (2015). *Learning with literature in the EFL classroom.* Peter Lang.
Dobber, M., Zwart, R. C., Tanis, M., & van Oers, B. (2017). Literature review: The role of the teacher in inquiry-based education. *Educational Research Review, 22*, 194–214.
Dolgunsöz, E. (2019). The effect of taboo content on incidental vocabulary acquisition in a foreign language: A facial expression analysis study. *Studia Psychologica, 61*(1), 3–16. https://doi.org/10.21909/sp.2019.01.768
Edes, I. (2020). Listening to student voice. *Taboo: The Journal of Culture and Education, 19*(2): 81–91.
Eisenmann, M. (2019). *Teaching English: Differentiation and individualisation.* UTB.
Enriquez, G. (2006). The reader speaks out: Adolescent reflections about controversial young adult literature. *The ALAN Review, 33*(2), 16–26.

Etri, W. (2021). Strategies for withstanding the inevitable at ground zero: an analysis of intercultural sensitivity in the ELT classroom. *Open Journal of Modern Linguistics, 11*, 34–48. https://doi.org/10.4236/ojml.2021.111003

Fairclough, N. (2014). *Language and power*. Routledge.

Fershtman, C., Gneezy, U., & Hoffman, M. (2011). Taboos and identity: Considering the unthinkable. *American Economic Journal: Microeconomics, 3*(2), 139–164.

Freire, P. (1972). *Cultural action for freedom*. Penguin.

Freire, P. (2014). *Pedagogy of the oppressed*. Bloomsbury. (Original work published 1968).

Freud, S. (2010). *Totem and taboo: Resemblances between the psychic lives of savages and neurotics* (A. A. Brill. Trans.). Lits. (Original work published 1913).

Gerlach, D. (2020a). Einführung in eine Kritische Fremdsprachendidaktik. In D. Gerlach (Ed.), *Kritische Fremdsprachendidaktik: Grundlagen, Ziele, Beispiele* (pp. 7–32). Narr.

Gerlach, D. (Ed.). (2020b). *Kritische Fremdsprachendidaktik: Grundlagen, Ziele, Beispiele*. Narr.

Gray, J. (2019). Critical language teacher education? In S. Walsh, & S. Mann (Eds.), *The Routledge Handbook of English Language Teacher Education* (pp. 68–81). Routledge.

Groenke, L. S., Maples, J., & Henderson, J. (2010): Raising "Hot Topics" through Young Adult Literature. *Voices from the Middle, 17*(4), 29–36.

Hess, D. E. (2009). *Controversy in the classroom: The democratic power of discussion*. Routledge.

Hopkins, R. L. (1994). *Narrative schooling: Experiential learning and the transformation of American education*. Teachers College Press.

Horlacher, S. (2010). Taboo, transgression, and literature: An introduction. In S. Horlacher, S. Glomb, & L. Heiler (Eds.), *Taboo and transgression in British literature from the renaissance to the present* (pp. 3–21). Palgrave Macmillan.

Howard, R., Lam, N., Petrie, D., Simpson, A., Smith, M., Veigga, T., & Wade, P. (2016). *Parsnips in ELT: Stepping out of the comfort zone* (Vol. 2). http://research.sabanciuniv.edu/29356/1/parsnips-in-elt-stepping-out-of-the-comfort-zone-vol-2.pdf

Janks, H. (2010). *Literacy and power*. Routledge.

Kalantzis, M., & Cope, B. (2012). *Literacies*. Cambridge University Press.

Kaltenbrunner, G. K. (1987). Vorwort des Herausgebers. In G. -K. Kaltenbrunner (Ed.), *Der innere Zensor. Neue und alte Tabus in unserer Gesellschaft* (pp. 7–18). Herder.

Kaye, P. (2015). *Taboo in the classroom*. British Council. https://www.teachingenglish.org.uk/article/taboo-classroom

Kelly, T. E. (1986). Discussing controversial issues: Four perspectives on the teacher's role. *Theory and Research in Social Education, 14*(2), 113–138.

Kumaravadivelu, B. (2006). TESOL methods: Changing tracks, challenging trends. *TESOL Quarterly, 40*(1), 59–81.

Lamb, T., & Reinders, H. (Eds.). (2008). *Learner and teacher autonomy: Concepts, realities, and responses*. John Benjamins Publishing.

Linder, S., & Majerus, E. (2016). *Can I teach that? Negotiating taboo language and controversial topics in the language arts classroom*. Rowman & Littlefield Publishers.

Little, D., Dam, L., & Legenhausen, L. (2017). *Language learner autonomy: Theory, practice and research*. Multilingual Matters.

Ludwig, C., & Kersten, S. (Eds.). (in press). *Born-digital texts in language learning and teaching*. John Benjamins Publishing.

MacAndrew, R., & Martínez, R. (2001). *Taboos and issues: Photocopiable lessons on controversial topics*. Thomson Learning.

Meddings, L. (2006, January 20). *Embrace the parsnip*. The Guardian. https://www.theguardian.com/education/2006/jan/20/tefl4

Nunan, D. (2013). *Learner-centered English language education: The selected works of David Nunan*. Routledge.

Oxford University Press. (2010). Taboo. In *Oxford Dictionary of English*. https://www.oxfordreference.com/view/10.1093/acref/9780199571123.001.0001/m_en_gb0840030

Seburn, T., Finegan, K., Greene, S., Howard, R., Lam, N., Petrie, D., & Veigga, T. (2016). *Parsnips in ELT: Stepping out of the comfort zone* (Vol. 3). Smashwords. https://www.smashwords.com/books/view/669186

Smith, M. JC, Lemos, C., Petrie, D., Simpson, A., Bilsborough, K., Lam, N., & Wade, P. (2015). *Parsnips in ELT: Stepping out of the comfort zone* (Vol. 1). Smashwords. http://research.sabanciuniv.edu/27130/1/parsnips-in-elt-stepping-out-of-the-comfort-zone-vol-1.pdf

Steinberg, S. R. (2020). Special issue introduction: 50 years of critical pedagogy and we still aren't critical. *Taboo: The Journal of Culture and Education, 19*(2), 3–5.

Summer, T. (2021). Eco-songs in foreign language education. In V. Werner, & F. Tegge (Eds.), *Pop culture in language education: Theory, research, practice*. Routledge.

Thornbury, S. (2010, June 27). T is for taboo. *An A-Z of ELT: Scott Thornbury's Blog*. https://scottthornbury.wordpress.com/2010/06/27/t-is-for-taboo/

Thornbury, S. (2017). *The new A-Z of ELT: A dictionary of terms and concepts*. Macmillan.

Tudor, I. (1996). *Learner-centredness as language education*. Cambridge University Press.

Vasquez, V. M. (2017). Critical literacy. In *Oxford research encyclopedia of education*. 10.1093/acrefore/9780190264093.013.20

Werner, V., & Tegge, F. (Eds.) (2021). *Pop culture in language education: Theory, research, practice*. Routledge.

West, G. B. (2021). 'Is this a safe space?': Examining an emotionally charged eruption in critical language pedagogy. *Education Sciences, 11*(186), 1–14. https://doi.org/10.3390/educsci11040186

Part I
Theoretical Considerations and Insights

2 Between Recognition and Redistribution – The Political Economy of Taboos in Foreign Language Education

John Gray

Introduction

As the Introduction to this volume points out, taboos have a long, complicated and evolving cultural history. In the modern world, they continue to exist for a complex variety of reasons and can take very different forms in which linguistic prohibitions and the power to limit what can be encoded in language are often central. This is particularly true of foreign language teaching. Perhaps one of the most deep-seated prohibitions teachers of my generation (trained in the communicative approach in the 1980s) were exposed to was the taboo against the use of the mother tongue or the home language(s) in the classroom. As novice teachers, we were expected to teach English through English and our students were expected to learn it with no (or minimal) recourse to their existing linguistic repertoires. Use of a language other than English on the part of a teacher was taken as evidence of deficient pedagogical skill, or an indication of a student's wilful attachment to what was ultimately seen as a source of interference. This taboo had clear educational consequences in terms of classroom practice, but it also had economic consequences for the Anglophone English language teaching (ELT) Edu-business promoting it – monolingual textbooks for global consumption were cheaper to produce than country-specific bilingual materials, monolingual learner dictionaries were marketed as state-of-the-art learning resources by leading ELT publishers and of course (frequently monolingual) Anglophone English language teachers trained in monolingual methodology became key promotional features of the burgeoning global commercial sector from the last quarter of the 20th century onwards. Increasingly, however, under the aegis of the "multilingual turn" (Cenoz & Gorter, 2015) and calls to decolonise the curriculum (Macedo, 2019), this insistence on monolingualism is understood as being politically, ethically, educationally and cognitively questionable. Commenting on this linguistic taboo, Alistair Pennycook (2019, p. 175) argues that "one of the great crimes of the global hegemony of communicative language teaching" is the way in which it served to "promote a monolingual, native-speaker norm-based, and educationally shallow version of English". While this may be a little harsh on communicative language teaching (CLT) as originally conceived, it is undeniable that CLT quickly became associated with a

DOI: 10.4324/9781003220701-4

rigid monolingualism and narrow view of language using. Grammar translation, contrastive analysis and literature were edged out of many teaching settings, particularly in the powerful commercial sector, where an instrumental, skill-based view of language came to predominate. This impacted hugely on the production of materials, many of which originated in the commercial sector before eventually finding their way into schools and universities. My point, in raising this at the outset of this chapter, is that taboos exist for a reason and that, in exploring them, it behoves us to consider their underpinnings from a political economy perspective.

This chapter argues that many of the taboos found in the foreign language classroom can be considered as forms of erasure and raise issues related to social justice which are in need of redress. The chapter focuses on two salient taboos in ELT materials, namely those which avoid referring to the working class and those which proscribe mention of LGBTQ+ identities, as well as any treatment of issues related to them. The following section outlines the theoretical perspective adopted in this chapter in greater detail, before moving on to a consideration of the pedagogical implications of these erasures and the case for their removal.

Theoretical Background

As stated, key to my understanding of taboos in foreign language education is the concept of erasure, by which I mean the systematic editing out of the curriculum of certain categories of person, identities, events, injustices and histories for ideological, cultural or commercial reasons. As Judith Irvine and Susan Gal point out, specifically with regard to language:

> Erasure is the process in which ideology, in simplifying the sociolinguistic field, renders some persons or activities (or sociolinguistic phenomena) invisible. Facts that are inconsistent with the ideological scheme either go unnoticed or get explained away. So, for example, a social group or a language may be imagined as homogenous, its internal variation disregarded.
> (2000, p. 38)

This is particularly noticeable in the way in which language is represented for teaching purposes in pedagogical materials. The fact that students, if they go on to use the language they are learning beyond the classroom, will encounter a range of accents and grammars is not taken into consideration. But erasure is not simply a matter of ignoring certain accents (both L1 and L2) or linguistic variation, although they are important, it is also in many cases a matter of withholding lexis so as to make certain topics literally unspeakable, a point I will return to below. From this perspective, erasure is fundamentally a matter of injustice, and for those teachers who take the view that a commitment to education is perforce a commitment to social justice, this raises a number of issues. It is here that the work of Nancy Fraser (1995) is particularly useful (see also Fraser & Honneth, 2003). Fraser argues that social justice in the world today requires redress on two fronts. On the one hand, there is the *socioeconomic injustice* exacerbated by neoliberalism (discussed below) dating from the late 1970s. This has seen the extraordinary growth of material inequality across much of the world, the immiseration of those working in the gig economy and on zero-hour contracts, the proliferation of food banks in the rich countries of the Global North, as well as the impact of the Coronavirus pandemic on poorly paid key workers. Collectively these injustices may be said to require a politics of redistribution which would entail a political-economic restructuring of the economy.

At the same time, there is the *cultural injustice* suffered by minority groups, such as racial and ethnic minorities, religious minorities and sexual and gender minorities whose marginalisation also calls out for a politics of recognition. With regard to the latter group, although there has been a great deal of legislation granting rights to LGBTQ+ people in many countries around the world in recent years, recognition remains noticeably absent from pedagogical materials. Socioeconomic injustice raises the issue of social class and redistribution, while cultural injustice raises issues of identity and recognition. Of course, there is overlap between these and as Fraser points out, "this distinction between economic injustice and cultural injustice is analytical. In practice the two are intertwined" (Fraser, 1995, p. 72). At the same time, it is important to clarify that the economically disadvantaged do not seek recognition *as disadvantaged* but rather the removal of their disadvantage – while LGBTQ+ people seek recognition as socially legitimate and equal members of society. From this perspective, a cultural politics of difference (including a critical foreign language pedagogy) that does not include an intersectional awareness of the role of class will not succeed in alerting students to the ways in which issues of recognition articulate with those of redistribution. With this in mind, I will argue that representation, by which I mean the semiotic processes whereby meanings are made and received, is important with regard to *both* types of injustice, particularly when it comes to education. In the following section, I consider research on the relevance of these issues for classroom practice, specifically with regard to the representation of the working class and that of LGBTQ+ identities and related issues.

Relevance for the Classroom

A number of recent studies show that language teaching materials for several decades have been characterised in many settings by an unproblematised and celebratory take on neoliberalism (Bori, 2018; Copley, 2018; Gray & Block, 2014). By neoliberalism, I refer to the forms of market fundamentalism which have characterised the current phase of capitalism since the late 1970s. These studies show that language teaching materials are key sites for situating language learners not only as would-be users of the languages being taught but also as particular kinds of people who embody the resilience, entrepreneurialism and individualism so characteristic of the ideal neoliberal citizen. In this way, the dominant ideology of contemporary global capitalism is repeatedly reproduced in the second language classroom. One good example of this is the way in which mobility (whether for work or leisure) is dealt with in textbooks. Willingness to relocate geographically for work is a key neoliberal value, and textbooks repeatedly associate English with unproblematic work-related migration. In *Navigate* (Roberts et al., 2015), a unit on ambitions focuses entirely on work. In one listening exercise, three typical textbook characters describe their positive experiences of relocation. Maria, an unemployed Greek architect from Athens, describes her experience as follows:

> I'd been unemployed for over a year when I decided to try Australia. I still haven't been able to find work as an architect in Melbourne, but I have been able to retrain as a landscape designer, designing gardens instead of houses. It's great being outside so much, because the weather's nearly always good. I also have a lot of job satisfaction now.
>
> (Roberts et al., 2015, p. 167)

When asked by the interviewer if she plans to stay, Maria answers in the affirmative. In this extract, the unemployed speaker is shown to agentively decide to relocate as a consequence of redundancy. There is no mention of the difficulties this may have entailed, the financial implications or any of the other problems less fortunate migrants face – such as exploitation, physical danger and racism. Even when she is unable to obtain work as an architect in Australia, Maria unproblematically describes her self-reinvention as a landscape designer and finds that it offers her job satisfaction and the chance to work outdoors. Resilient, individualistic and unquestioning with regard to the structural forces underpinning such migration, Maria is in every way an ideal neoliberal citizen. That she speaks English need not even be mentioned – it is part of what makes her such an ideal.

Although neoliberalism is far from being a seamless phenomenon globally and has evolved over time, integral to its rhetoric is a repudiation of the concept of social class and the primacy of the individual. While the financial crisis of 2007–2008 and its aftermath saw a tentative return to the concept of class in the British media and political discourse, most politicians on the right avoid the term completely and those on the centre left still prefer to talk of hard-working or working families for fear of being seen to subscribe to a view of society deemed outdated. That said, many scholars still consider the concept of class to be important, and its attempted erasure from public discourse as part of an ideological denial of class as a social fact and an attack on organised labour and human collectives more generally.

In our study of the representation of the working class and the treatment of class in general, David Block and I carried out an analysis of a set of six best-selling ELT textbooks published between 1970 and 2010 (Gray & Block, 2014). In setting about categorising representations of the working class, we drew on a classical Marxist definition:

> Classes are large groups of people which differ from each other by the place they occupy in a historically determined system of social production, by

their relation (in most cases fixed and formulated in law) to the means of production, by their role in the social organization of labour and, consequently, by the dimensions and method of acquiring the share of the social wealth of which they dispose. Classes are groups of people one of which can appropriate the labour of another owing to the different places they occupy in a definitive system of social economy.

(Lenin, 1982, p. 57)

This was complemented by a Bourdieusian perspective in which property ownership, disposable income, occupation, place of residence, education, social networking, consumption patterns and types of symbolic behaviour such as the way one speaks, the clothes one wears and leisure activities are added to the mix. Our point of entry was employment as this was often clear (although on its own not a sufficient determiner of class location) and then we looked at other dimensions to make our decision as to whether or not the representation could be included in our analysis.

The analysis revealed a progressive decline in the representation of working-class characters, mentions of working-class employment and themes relating to working-class experience over the four decades covered by our sample – a period which is coterminous with the entrenchment of neoliberal government (regardless of party) in the UK, and elsewhere in the world. The study also showed that where limited representation of working-class characters did occur (in textbooks from the 1970s), students were not invited to identify with them and there was generally no serious engagement with issues relating to working conditions, union activity and disputes – although these were mentioned in passing. In subsequent textbooks, however, working-class characters are shown to have been erased and replaced by a collection of property-owning, professionally successful, globe-trotting characters with whom students *are* repeatedly invited to identify.

Such erasure is not only a refusal to recognise the existence of the working class by focusing only on middle-class representations, nor is it simply a denial of the existence of working-class students who may be learning English; it is also an active withholding of lexis related to working-class life and struggles. This serves to make certain topics literally unspeakable in the classroom. Without the language to discuss their lives and their perspectives on the world, working-class students are being asked to learn a foreign language in which the content they engage with erases them and their concerns.

When it comes to LGBTQ+ language learners the situation is similar – although there are important differences. Here again, studies show that erasure is pervasive (Gray, 2013; Thornbury, 1999), but unlike decreasing working-class representation, there was never a time when LGBTQ+ had featured. A major global report carried out by UNESCO (2016) concluded that, despite legislation recognising and protecting sexual and gender minorities across much of the world from the late 20th century onwards, the education sector as a whole appeared to be reluctant to accord recognition to LGBTQ+ students. The report pointed out that materials remained firmly heteronormative in character, stereotypical in terms of gender roles and blind to varieties of gender and sexual diversity. The report, which focused on violence against LGBTQ+ students in educational settings, argued that pedagogical materials needed to reflect the changing legal panorama if actual social change was to occur and the lives and educational opportunities of LGBTQ+ students were to be improved. Physical violence aside, there is increasing evidence to suggest that being erased from the curriculum is experienced as a form of symbolic violence by LGBTQ+ students. As the young, queer Black novelist Paul Mendez explained, reflecting on his own experience of schooling:

> One of the reasons it took me so long to write [my first novel] is that there were so few Black male (and queer Black male) names on my shelves to give me confidence and permission. My secondary-level English literature curriculum was centred entirely around canonical, dead white men, and I wonder what might have been different for me had I been introduced to James Baldwin and Caryl Phillips – let alone Toni Morrison and Buchi Emecheta – at that age.
>
> (2020, n.p.)

Here, we see the coming together of the erasures of sexual orientation and race in ways which Mendez suggests delayed his potential to flourish as a writer. Specific erasure related to gender and sexual orientation in ELT can be traced to the political economy of the British publishing industry. British materials are sold globally in counties which have legalised same-sex marriage but also in countries whose governments are hostile to sexual and gender diversity in which state-sponsored homophobia may be actively promoted. The lucrative sales of ELT materials produced by leading publishers are used to subsidise their more prestigious academic lists. Given the political and economic risks posed by LGBTQ+ recognition, and the profit-reducing consequences of producing country-specific materials, this particular taboo is unlikely to be removed any time soon. What then, it might be asked, are teachers concerned with such erasure to do? In the following section, I suggest one possible way forward.

Practical Examples

Despite decades of critique, demands that ELT textbooks address these erasures have fallen largely on deaf ears. For that reason, it falls to educators themselves to attempt to fill the gap, and it is here that literature and other forms of so-called authentic materials can be of use (see Eisenmann & Ludwig, 2018; Gray, 2021). Well-chosen literary texts provide an opportunity to address a cultural politics of difference while also providing an intersectional awareness of the role of class. A good example is found in the collection *Everything I have is Blue: Short Fiction by Working Class Men about More-or-less Gay Life* edited by Wendell Ricketts (2005). Also, useful and easily exploitable short engaging texts can be found online in sites such as Gay Flash Fiction (https://

gayflashfiction.com/). As several of the contributions to the theoretically informed and eminently practical *Queer Beats* (Eisenman & Ludwig, 2018) volume show, literary texts can also be used alongside other types of material such as films, blogposts and journalism. Films such as *Pride* (Warchus, 2014) and *Beautiful Thing* (Macdonald, 1996) address different aspects of queer working-class life. In the case of the former, there is the true story of the involvement of a group of lesbian and gay activists in the British miners' strike of 1984–1985, and in the case of the latter, the story of an emerging love affair between two teenagers who live on a housing estate in south London. Such films are important not only for providing an alternative to a sanitised version of middle-class gay life found in much of the media but also for another reason – namely, the inclusion of regional accents which are often (but not necessarily) markers of working-class speech and which learners of English are often deprived of exposure to in mainstream materials.

Conclusion

In this short chapter, I have argued that two very different erasures characterise UK-produced materials and that this is linked to the political economy of ELT publishing. Following Fraser, I have taken the view that while the politics of redistribution and recognition are different, they are not unrelated. As educators, we are necessarily constrained by what we can achieve in terms of social transformation. We can, however, seek to recognise our students in all their difference, and that may make a modest, but not insignificant impact on them. In concluding with the suggestion that the use of literary (and other kinds of so-called authentic) texts can be of use, it seems appropriate to finish with a quotation from a lesbian feminist poet who had much to say about education. Adrienne Rich writes

> When those who have power to name and to socially construct reality choose not to see you or hear you [...] when someone with the authority of a teacher, say, describes the world and you are not in it, there is a moment of psychic disequilibrium, as if you looked in the mirror and saw nothing.
>
> (1987)

In the case of the textbooks I have described, it is not just those who are LGBTQ+ and those who are working class who see nothing – those who are neither LGBTQ+ nor working class are also denied access to a fuller picture. The consequences for both are different though. In the case of the former, there is the denial of recognition and the attendant psychic disequilibrium, while in the case of the latter, there is the denial of the opportunity to see the world in its more of its human complexity. For all students though regardless of class, sexual orientation and gender identification, the potential for the development of critical consciousness is seriously curtailed.

References

Bori, P. (2018). *Language textbooks in the era of neoliberalism*. Routledge.
Cenoz, J., & Gorter, D. (Eds.). (2015). *Multilingual education: Between language learning and translanguaging*. Cambridge University Press.
Copley, K. (2018). Neoliberalism and ELT coursebook content. *Critical Inquiry in Language Studies, 15*(1), 43–62.
Eisenmann, M., & Ludwig, C. (Eds.). (2018). *Queer beats: Gender and literature in the EFL classroom*. Peter Lang.
Fraser, N. (1995). From redistribution to recognition? Dilemmas of justice in a 'postsocialist' age. *New Left Review, 212*, 68–149.
Fraser, N., & Honneth, A. (2003). *Redistribution or recognition? A political-philosophical exchange*. Verso.
Gray, J. (2013). LGBT invisibility and heteronormativity in ELT materials. In J. Gray (Ed.), *Critical perspectives on language teaching materials* (pp. 40–63). Palgrave Macmillan.
Gray, J. (2021). Addressing LGBTQ erasure through literature in the ELT classroom. *ELT Journal, 75*(2), 142–151.
Gray, J., & Block, D. (2014). All middle class now? Representations of the working class in the neoliberal era: The case of ELT textbooks. In N. Harwood (Ed.), *English language teaching textbooks: Content, consumption, production* (pp. 45–71). Palgrave Macmillan.
Irvine, J. T., & Gal, S. (2000). Language Ideology and Linguistic differentiation. In P. V. Kroskrity (Ed.), *Regimes of language: Ideologies, politics, and identities* (pp. 35–84). School of American Research Press.
Lenin, V. I. (1982). The abolition of classes. In A. Giddens, & D. Held (Eds.), *Classes, power and conflict: Classical and contemporary debates* (pp. 57–59). University of California Press. (Reprinted from *A great beginning. The heroism of the workers in the rear. On "Communist Subbotniks"*, by V. I. Lenin, 1919).
Macdonald, H. (Director). (1996). *Beautiful thing* [Film]. FourFilm Distributors.
Macedo, D. (Ed.). (2019). *Decolonizing foreign language education: The misteaching of English and other colonial languages*. Routledge.
Mendez, P. (2020, July 31). Where are the hotshot British male novelists? BAME authors may know. The Guardian. https://www.theguardian.com/books/2020/jul/31/where-are-the-hotshot-british-male-novelists-bame-authors-may-know
Pennycook, A. (2019). From translanguaging to translingual activism. In D. Macedo (Ed.), *Decolonizing foreign language education: The misteaching of English and other colonial languages* (pp. 169–185). Routledge.
Rich, A. (1987). *Blood, bread, and poetry: Selected prose, 1979–1985*. Virago.
Ricketts, W. (2005). *Everything I have is blue: Short fiction by working class men about more-or-less gay life*. Suspect Thoughts Press.
Roberts, R., Buchanan, H., & Pathare, E. (2015). *Navigate: B1+ intermediate*. Oxford University Press.
Thornbury, S. (1999). Window-dressing vs cross-dressing in the EFL sub-culture. *Folio, 5*(2), 15–17.
UNESCO. (2016). *Out in the open: Education sector responses to violence based on sexual orientation and gender identity/expression*. UNESCO. https://unesdoc.unesco.org/ark:/48223/pf0000244756
Warchus, M. (Director). (2014). *Pride* [Film]. Twentieth Century Fox.

3 Facing the Invisible—Taboos as Texts and Cultural Learning in English Language Education

Daniel Becker

Introduction

Taboos, which can be understood as "proscriptions of behavior arising out of social constraints" (Allan, 2016, n.p.), are an integral part of social and cultural life. In fact, they fulfil a most important regulatory function, since declaring something as "taboo" becomes an act of contouring a society's cultural and moral fabric. Taboos are protected spaces that separate the acceptable from the unacceptable and influence "[t]he way we behave, dress, eat, and drive, as well as our sex life" (Fershtman et al., 2011, p. 139). As such, they establish an important prerequisite for dynamically constituting one's own identity and a meaningful relationship to the world.

With this essential importance in mind, taboos are also inextricably linked to the notion of cultural participation. More precisely, if taboos permeate the very foundation of cultural meaning-making, then becoming an active participant, who is involved in a culture's "shared sets of meanings" (Freitag-Hild, 2018, p. 161), necessarily rests upon one's ability to understand taboos and the way they function. This, in turn, makes taboos relevant also for school education and its goal of preparing future citizens and social agents (Council of Europe, 2018). Yet, taboo education is a challenging endeavour. Not only are taboos associated with feelings of shame and discomfort that learners need to deal with, but they are also, by design, "invisible" and hard to grasp as learning objects (Eggert, 2002). However, in order for learners to understand taboos, they need to be taken out of their invisible realm and made accessible, at least to a certain extent.

The present contribution focuses on English language education, arguing that the subject of English can achieve exactly that: Based on Hallet's textual approach to cultural learning (2002, 2007), it will be shown that the English as a foreign language (EFL) classroom has the potential to make taboos visible in their discursive and textual constitution and, therefore, enables learners to access and analyse the culturally constructed nature of the prohibited. The paper proceeds in three parts: The first part discusses Hallet's textual understanding of culture as a theoretical foundation. The second part highlights the specific relevance of Hallet's approach for capturing taboos by discussing the inherent discursivity and textuality of taboos as cultural phenomena. Finally, the last part brings the two previous steps together by illustrating how taboos can be implemented in the classroom through Hallet's textual lens.

Cultural Learning in the EFL Classroom: Hallet's Intertextual Approach

English language education aims at preparing learners for "reading the world" by letting them explore the complex relationship between language and culture (Küchler, 2011). This makes the notion of "cultural learning" an essential pillar of the contemporary EFL classroom. More precisely, learners are meant to develop intercultural communicative competence (ICC; Byram, 1997), which enables them to negotiate and reflect on differences and similarities between their own and other cultures. One approach to foster this intercultural negotiation process, which has become specifically influential in the German EFL context, is Hallet's intertextual understanding of culture (2002, 2007).

On its most fundamental level, Hallet's (2002) understanding of culture is based on the anthropological metaphor of "culture as text". According to this metaphor, culture is as a constellation of texts which—beyond the written or spoken word—also manifests in rituals, theatre, gestures, festivities etc. (Bachmann-Medick, 2004). Culture, in other words, is a "giant text and discourse space" and a continuous semiotic practice, as shared beliefs do not exist outside a culture's numerous text productions but are only constituted in this ever-changing textual web of signification (Hallet, 2007). Thus, for instance, how a culture interprets taboo topics such as mental disorders is not a predetermined notion but is actively negotiated in the texts (in the broadest sense) that address this topic in one way or another; which makes taboo a textual phenomenon (see below). This means that a culture's representation, stigmatisation and belief about mental health are the result of every single text—ranging from news reports (e.g., negative reports on mental illness in the context of school shootings), to young adult literature (e.g., romantic depiction of mental disorders in John Green's (2008) *Paper Towns*) and YouTube videos [e.g., more scientific portrayals in explanation videos like "7 Signs of Depression" by Psych2Go (2019)]—and their individual perspective they contribute to the overall cultural discussion.

In order to outline this web of signification in more detail, Hallet furthermore uses the poststructuralist notion of intertextuality. Following Bachtin's idea of polyphony, as well as Kristeva's and Barthes' text theories, he argues that meaning in culture is not created in *isolated* texts but in the "interplay" between different texts in the broadest sense (Hallet, 2002, p. 58). Referring to the mental health example above, this means that individual perspectives expressed in single picturebooks (e.g., Matthew Johnstone's (2007) *I had a Black Dog*), movies (e.g., Lars van Trier's (2011) *Melancholia*) or video games (e.g., *Celeste* (Thorson, 2018)) often influence each other in their portrayal of mental health concerns. As such, they might indirectly complement or contradict each other—for example, many social media posts made by teenagers implicitly share a romantic portrayal of mental disorders (Singh, 2018)—or they more explicitly integrate another text's voice in their own textual landscape. Hallet thus perceives cultural meaning-making (e.g., the negotiation of taboos) as a multimodal, multimedial and, overall, intertextual practice, in which the individual text becomes a genuinely interactive entity. Like the poststructuralists, he conceptualises text as an open cultural space where different (and often conflicting) discourses intersect and where under its linear and monologic surface different voices and speeches can be recognised (Hallet, 2002). Each culture, therefore, inherently consists of a plurality of overlapping textual voices at all times.

This intertextual view harbours important implications for cultural learning. More precisely, since the cultural negotiation of meaning is firmly located on a concrete textual level, learning to understand other (English language) cultures necessarily needs to focus on the "material productions" of these cultures (Hallet, 2007, p. 39). Thus, based on the intertextual approach, learners can only negotiate cultural similarities and differences (e.g., differences in how openly a culture's textual network represents the topic of depression) if they gain access to the different textual landscapes from which these differences and similarities originate (Hallet, 2002). Cultural learning becomes textual learning, and learners turn into intertextual readers and text analysts who explore the communicative, rhetorical or narrative strategies at the very centre of a culture, as a way of comparing their different semiotic roots.

Considering its textual point of view on learning, Hallet's approach provides a valuable foundation for addressing taboos in the EFL classroom. By focusing on texts, the "culture as text" approach can also include taboos in the learning process, since, despite their invisibility in public communication, they do in fact have a discursive and textual presence of their own, as the following section will show.

The Discursivity and Textuality of Taboos

Taboos are not natural. Rather, they are culturally constructed and conventionally agreed upon spaces of the forbidden, which can change in different cultural contexts and which are protected by collective feelings of danger, disgust or the fear of contamination (Freitas, 2008). As such, tabooed topics obtain an aura of the untouchable and invisible, which need to be avoided to protect oneself from harm and/or social sanctions (Eggert, 2002).

Yet, they are not entirely invisible. Since they are actively constructed in cultural debates, taboos are always an integral part of discourse formation—and, as such, they become partly visible. Discourses represent "the production of knowledge through language" (Hall, 2001, p. 72) and are a most dominant social practice of meaning-making. They represent one particular perspective on a given topic, which shapes how people think and act in their private and public environments (Taylor, 2013)—for example how people think about the topic of mental health. These discursive perspectives are actively constructed in a continuous process of "monosemination" (Höhne, 2010, p. 427): Any topic or event discussed in society is genuinely "polysemous" (Höhne, 2010, p. 428), which means that it can potentially be interpreted from a multitude of perspectives.

The topic of depression, for instance, can be seen as an illness that requires treatment or it can be treated as an uncomfortable and even unwanted phenomenon, among many other interpretations. Discourses, however, are defined by the fact that they actively promote *one* single perspective over all the others—hence *mon-osemination*. They "condense" meaning by repeatedly shifting certain elements of a topic to the centre of attention, while marginalising or leaving out others that do not fit their discursive agenda. As such, discourses mould a particular image of a topic through a constant communicative interplay between thematic inclusion and exclusion (Höhne, 2010).

It is at this point that taboos take part in discourse formation. In the constant interplay between thematic inclusion and exclusion, taboos represent the excluded and all the elements that do not fit a discursive perspective. As Trumm (2014) points out, in the selective process of discursive meaning-making, taboos play the vital role of the semantic "other". They are contouring devices to shape a discursive view *ex negativo*, as they contrast the desirable and reasonable with the dangerous. Hence, they take part in the dialectics of difference (Höhne, 2010), which lies at the very foundation of discourse formation, so that in order to understand discourses, learners must not neglect taboos in the process.

This interaction between discourse and taboo does not happen in a cultural vacuum but rather, based on the "culture as text" approach, manifests in a cultural constellation of texts. This means that the discursive interplay between thematic inclusion and exclusion takes place on a concrete textual level on which taboos, as a vital part of discourse formation, gain an observable textual presence of their own. This textual visibility can be described more precisely with Bachtin's notion of polyphony. Bachtin perceives texts as open spaces of negotiation which are defined by the dialogue and often friction of many voices (Lachmann, 1984). It can be argued that this understanding also applies to the textual formation of discourses and taboos. If discourses rely on taboos as the semantic other, then texts do not only advocate one dominant perspective on a topic, but they still also include the "other" voices that are in "semantic friction" with this perspective (Ternès, 2016, p. 116). This means that although these other (tabooed) voices might not be overtly visible in every text, they nonetheless leave latent traces in a text's fabric and, thus, can be made visible.

One prominent way of making tabooed voices visible is through analysing a text's circumvention strategies. Circumvention strategies can be described as a linguistic etiquette used in a variety of oral and written texts (Trumm, 2014). In more detail, while taboos are not meant to be addressed, they cannot always be completely avoided in the course of communication. In this context, circumvention refers to any rhetorical technique in texts by which tabooed areas can be bypassed or kept as implicit as possible (Braun, 2015). These techniques might include shifting one's communicative style to a scientific register (e.g., using the term "sex organs" to more neutrally talk about potentially uncomfortable topics surrounding sexuality) using textual gaps (i.e., leaving empty spaces or pauses in a text where a taboo word would occur) or relying on jokes and euphemisms to tackle uncomfortable topics from a safe distance (e.g., to describe death as "kicking the bucket"; Braun, 2015). Paradoxically, though, this shift in style also makes a taboo visible. In Graham Swift's (1985) classic novel *Waterland*, for example, the incest taboo has the power to disrupt the narrator's text in some passages, since, in trying to avoid addressing the topic, he suddenly produces elliptic sentences. In these gaps, the taboo is re-inscribed in the text, as it becomes the unspoken voice that indirectly fills the rest of the page and, thus, still indirectly echoes in how it bends the rules and disrupts the style of communication at particular points in a text. In these instances, they obtain their own textuality and an otherwise elusive phenomenon suddenly becomes visible on the surface.

Taboos in the EFL Classroom: Applying Hallet's Intertextual Approach

It is this latent (inter-)textual embodiment of taboos that makes them relevant learning materials for English language education. More precisely, since taboos leave traces on a textual level and establish the "other" voices in a textual network, a "culture as text"-based EFL classroom has the potential to illuminate these otherwise hidden phenomena—and use them for intercultural learning. As pointed out in the Section on 'Cultural Learning in the EFL Classroom' understanding different cultures and their discourses means understanding the textual landscape of different cultures. Since taboos are an integral part of discourse, they must not be left aside when comparing multiple cultural spheres in order to successfully develop intercultural communicative competence. Hallet's concept proves helpful for this purpose, as it offers the conceptual capacity to not only dissect prominent discourses but also take into account the textualised zones of prohibition that accompany them. The approach establishes a differentiated analytical scope that does not exclude voices in the margins or the latent deep structures of a textual network. Rather, in focusing learners' attention on all kinds of (inter-)textual strategies by which discourses are shaped, it can highlight these voices as equal parts of a culture's textual and discursive fabric and can thus help the intercultural learner to understand and negotiate differences on a more profound and structural level (Hallet, 2007). Hallet's take on cultural learning, therefore, offers a framework for capturing taboos as an important part of cultural meaning-making and broadens the spectrum of intercultural analysis towards additionally understanding what is *not* being said in cultural self-presentations. This, in turn, allows learners to critically reflect their own position in shaping a society's line between the acceptable and the unacceptable, as they can recognise their own agency as readers and writers of textualised taboos.

On the level of concrete teaching practices, this potential of Hallet's approach can be implemented with the help of four guiding principles (adapted from Hallet, 2007):

Textual Networks

First, taboos, which must be immediately relevant for learners' everyday experiences (Hallet, 2007), should be approached through individual texts. If, for instance, learners are meant to explore the topic of mental health as part of their intercultural learning process, they need to work with specific text examples, such as the discussion of the topic in a literary text (e.g., Faith Gardner's (2021) *Girl on the Line*). More precisely, since taboos are generated in an entire network of interrelated texts (see Section 'The Discursivity and Textuality of Taboos'), learners can only understand the complex construction of taboos if the EFL classroom provides a *multitude* of related texts accordingly—so next to *Girl on the Line*, one could also include (samples from) other literary texts, such as Jennifer Niven's (2015) *All the Bright Places* or *Release* by Patrick Ness (2017). For pragmatic and pedagogic reasons, this multitude of texts is only a selection of an almost infinite number of text productions in any culture. It is therefore all the more important that the selection inside the classroom, as Hallet (2007) insinuates, is somehow representative of the more extensive network outside. In practice, this means that teachers need to use different text types in the classroom and also select these according to the different perspectives they offer on a topic (e.g., texts portraying depression as an illness vs. texts portraying depression as dangerous and unwanted).

Multimediality

In order to let learners explore the complexity of textual taboo constructions, the selection of texts furthermore needs to consist of different text and media genres, as each different kind of text employs different communicative or narrative strategies to shape the unwanted (see Specific Taboos and Practical Examples). Thus, engaging with mental health, for example, becomes a process of working with movies, tweets, blogs, podcasts, newspaper articles, video games, YouTube videos, literary texts or spoken presentations, as each text grants an individual entry point to more holistically understand the phenomenon. Learners develop competencies to decipher and analyse the numerous semiotic modes, languages and textualisations by which taboos, much like discourses, are constituted and become visible overall. The EFL classroom, in other words, needs generic diversity.

Different Perspectives on Taboos

Aside from displaying different textual strategies and types, the selection of texts should also include different social perspectives on taboos. Seen as a part of discourse formation, understanding taboos is not only a matter of uncovering the different methods and techniques by which they are (textually) created but is also related to becoming aware of the social power dynamics by which these constructed taboos are maintained and reinforced (Stenzel, 2015). Consequently, in the EFL classroom texts might be chosen which all deal with one specific taboo (e.g., depression) but they need to do so from both the angles of those who create taboos and those who challenge or even transgress them (Kraft, 2004). As such, the EFL classroom should become a space where different (textual) voices come together and where learners can become aware of the fact that taboos are inherently formed out of the friction between different perspectives. Guided by the paradigm of multiperspectivity, they can understand that taboos are not constructed as homogeneous and universal entities but obtain their meaning depending on the social group in which they are negotiated (Eggert, 2002). In that way, teaching taboos is meant to show learners that the textual construction of taboos is inextricably linked to the question of social power and that learners themselves play a part in the negotiation and, in the spirit of critical pedagogy, can locate their position in juxtaposition to other points of view.

Integrating Literary Texts and Films

Finally, in the process of making taboos visible to learners, literary texts and films play a most important role in the textual network selected for the EFL classroom. More precisely, they are important because they offer the potential of dramatisation. As Bredella (2008, p. 14) points out, in literary texts "something is taken out of its ordinary context so that we as spectators can watch it, respond to it and comment on it". Literature (and film), in other words, can examine discourses in isolation, as it lifts them onto a literary stage, where it accentuates its forms and functions to readers. This potential becomes all the more important for taboos. Literature and film are not necessarily obligated to adhere to a culture's moral conventions but can be seen as a meta-space within a social system, where, in the safe realm of fictionality, current values and norms can be openly reflected, experimented with and transformed (Horlacher, 2010). They make stigmatised phenomena directly visible and, hence, become an ideal foundation for learners to dissect taboos in all their features and functions. Ned Vizzini's (2007) *It's Kind of a Funny Story*, for example, provides readers with first-hand insights into anxiety and panic attacks and can make learners aware of the causes and effects accompanying these conditions.

Conclusion

Taboo education remains a challenge since it faces the paradox of attempting to illuminate what usually exists in the dark. This chapter examines in how far English language education can facilitate this effort by showing that the EFL classroom can capture taboos as texts. In that way, it contributes to making taboos accessible to learners in the first place and offers a foundation to analyse their cultural constructedness. More specifically, in a text-based EFL classroom, learners analyse the different textual strategies and mechanisms underlying taboos (e.g., circumvention in different genres) and can thus engage in reinforcing or transforming taboos themselves.

However, this is not the only potential the EFL classroom has to offer for taboo education. As the present contribution solely zoomed in on the area of cultural/textual learning, other components of contemporary language teaching were neglected. Thus, future contributions still need to clarify in what ways, for instance, communicative competences and more recent developments in digital and multi-literacies might provide alternative frameworks for learning with and through taboos in an EFL context.

References

Allan, K. (2016). Taboo. In *The Wiley Blackwell encyclopedia of gender and sexuality studies*. https://onlinelibrary.wiley.com/doi/full/10.1002/9781118663219.wbegss539

Bachmann-Medick, D. (2004). Einleitung. In D. Bachmann-Medick (Ed.), *Kultur als Text* (2nd ed.) (pp. 7–64). Francke.

Braun, M. (2015). Grüezen statt biligen: Verbale Tabus im Minnesang. In A. Dingeldein, & M. Emrich (Eds.), *Texte und Tabu: Zur Kultur von Verbot und Übertretung von Spätantike bis zur Gegenwart* (pp. 19–40). Transcript.

Bredella, L. (2008). What makes reading literary texts pleasurable and educationally significant? *Fremdsprachen Lehren und Lernen*, 37, 12–26.

Byram, M. (1997). *Teaching and assessing intercultural communicative competence*. Multilingual Matters.

Council of Europe. (2018). *Common European framework of reference for languages: Learning, teaching, assessment. Companion volume with new descriptors*. Council of Europe.

Eggert, H. (2002). Säkulare Tabus und die Probleme ihrer Darstellung – Thesen zur Eröffnung der Diskussion. In H. Eggert, & J. Golec (Eds.), *Tabu und Tabubruch: Literarische und Sprachliche Strategien im 20. Jahrhundert* (pp. 15–24). Metzler.

Fershtman, C., Gneezy, U., & Hoffman, M. (2011). Taboos and identity: Considering the unthinkable. *American Economic Journal: Microeconomics*, 3(2), 139–164.

Freitag-Hild, B. (2018). Teaching culture – Intercultural competence, transcultural learning, global education. In C. Surkamp, & B. Viebrock (Eds.), *Teaching English as a foreign language* (pp. 159–175). Metzler.

Freitas, E. S. L. (2008). *Taboos in advertising*. John Benjamins.

Gardner, F. (2021). *Girl on the line*. HarperTeen.

Green, J. (2008). *Paper towns*. Dutton.

Hall, S. (2001). Foucault: Power, knowledge and discourse. In S. Yates, S. Taylor, & M. Wetherell (Eds.), *Discourse theory and practice: a reader* (pp. 72–81). Sage.

Hallet, W. (2002). *Fremdsprachenunterricht als Spiel der Texte und Kulturen: Intertextualität als Paradigma einer kulturwissenschaftlichen Didaktik*. WVT.

Hallet, W. (2007). Literatur und Kultur im Unterricht: Ein kulturwissenschaftlicher didaktischer Ansatz. In W. Hallet, & A. Nünning (Eds.), *Neue Ansätze und Konzepte der Literatur- und Kulturdidaktik* (pp. 31–48). WVT.

Höhne, T. (2010). Die thematische Diskursanalyse – dargestellt am Beispiel von Schulbüchern. In R. Keller, A. Hirseland, W. Schneider, & W. Viehöver (Eds.), *Handbuch sozialwissenschaftliche Diskursanalyse* (pp. 423–455). VS Verlag.

Horlacher, S. (2010). Taboo, transgression, and literature: An introduction. In S. Horlacher, S. Glomb, & L. Heiler (Eds.), *Taboo and transgression in British literature from the Renaissance to the present* (pp. 3–21). Palgrave.

Johnstone, M. (2007). *I had a black dog*. Robinson.

Kraft, H. (2004). *Tabu: Magie und soziale Wirklichkeit*. Patmos.

Küchler, U. (2011). Linking foreign language education and the environment. In S. Oppermann, & U. Özdag (Eds.), *The future of ecocriticism: New horizons* (pp. 436–452). Cambridge Scholars Publishing.

Lachmann, R. (1984). Bachtins Dialogizität und die akmeistische Mythopoetik als Paradigma dialogisierter Lyrik. In K. Stierle, & R. Warning (Eds.), *Das Gespräch: Poetik und Hermeneutik* (pp. 489–515). Wilhelm Fink.

Ness, P. (2017). *Release*. HarperTeen.

Niven, J. (2015). *All the bright places*. Ember.

Psych2Go. (2019, March 30). *7 signs of depression* [Video]. YouTube. https://www.youtube.com/watch?v=o3rGwIOvUZQ

Singh, P. (2018, June 27). *Why are we romanticizing mental illness on social media?* Feminism in India. https://feminisminindia.com/2018/06/27/romanticising-mental-illness-social-media/

Stenzel, J. (2015). Der umgekehrte kategorische Imperativ: Versuch zu einer Typologie von Tabu. In A. Dingeldein, & M. Emrich (Eds.), *Texte und Tabu: Zur Kultur von Verbot und Übertretung von Spätantike bis zur Gegenwart* (pp. 41–57). Transcript.

Swift, G. (1985). *Waterland*. Picador.

Taylor, S. (2013). *What is discourse analysis?* Bloomsbury.

Ternès, A. (2016). *Intertextualität: Der Text als Collage*. Springer.

Thorson, M. (2018). *Celeste* [Video game]. Matt Makes Games.

Trumm, T. (2014). *Dem Schweigen Worte geben: Wege der Annäherung an Tabu und Tabuisierung im Deutschunterricht*. Schneider.

van Trier, L. (Director). (2011). *Melancholia* [Film]. Zentropa.

Vizzini, N. (2007). *It's kind of a funny story*. Miramax Books.

4 Integrating Critical Approaches into Language Teacher Education

David Gerlach and Mareen Lüke

Critical Approaches and Language Teacher Education

Climate change, right-wing politics, poverty – students deal with such topics every day. Although one might argue that teachers must be neutral and should not convey political views, no classroom setting can ever be neutral. This is because "educational systems are reflections of the societal systems within which they operate, and since in all societal systems we have discrimination and marginalisation […] the same biases are reproduced in educational systems" (Akbari, 2008, p. 276). In order to unearth existing inequalities, teachers need to address existing discriminations and power relations in teaching and in the classroom itself. Regarding the need to address discriminatory practices in education, Hawkins and Norton argue that

> [b]ecause language, culture, and identity are integrally related, language teachers are in a key position to address educational inequality, both because of the particular learners they serve, many of whom are marginalized members of the wider community, and because of the subject matter they teach – language – which can itself serve to both empower and marginalize.
> (Hawkins & Norton, 2009, p. 32)

Following the critical agenda in teacher education introduced by Hawkins and Norton, other scholars (e.g., Abednia, 2012; Gray, 2019) began to focus on critical language teacher education at an international level. Yet, many of the challenges of integrating critical approaches into both language education and teacher education stem from growing educational standardization and transmission orientation, that is, teaching that focuses on knowledge instruction without considering students' needs, which, in turn, leads to fewer opportunities for teachers' active participation and agency in their development process (Gerlach & Fasching-Varner, 2020; Gray, 2019). The following contribution, therefore, aims at providing principles for critical language teacher programmes and a concrete example of a professional development opportunity for critical language teacher education. In order to prepare the conceptual foundation for that, we will first provide an overview of critical approaches and their role in language teacher

DOI: 10.4324/9781003220701-6

education before discussing a model of general principles for critical language teacher education.

Criticality in Language Teaching and Language Teacher Education

According to Banegas and Villacañas de Castro (2016, p. 455), "criticality refers to the practice of socially situated reflection and evaluation. It means considering an issue from multiple perspectives, even when these involve self-critiquing." Thus, if English language teachers take a critical perspective in their teaching, they will initiate socially situated reflection and critique on the content and practices of their teaching from multiple perspectives. With this aim, critical approaches take a sociocultural approach to language teaching based on principles of critical theory related to the Frankfurt School (Gerlach, 2020) by focusing on

> challenging deficit representations of language learners and related subtractive paradigms of language, literacy, and culture with keen attention to a nexus of sociocultural factors such as majority-minority relations, social class difference, linguicism, patriarchy, language attitudes and prestige, and others.
>
> (Chang & Salas, 2020, p. 15)

Related to the work of Paulo Freire (1968/2014), critical approaches aim to make students as well as teachers aware of discriminatory practices in education in order to help change and transform such practices (e.g., gender stereotypes in teaching materials) into socially relevant actions (Gerlach, 2022). Although there are various intersectional domains of critical approaches (e.g., feminist or environmental education), most of these approaches have critical pedagogy as their theoretical basis (Crookes, 2013; Gerlach, 2020). According to Akbari,

> CP [critical pedagogy] deals with questions of social justice and social change through education. Critical pedagogues argue that educational systems are reflections of the societal systems within which they operate, and since in all social systems we have discrimination and marginalization in terms of race, social class, or gender […], the same biases are reproduced in educational systems.
>
> (Akbari, 2008, p. 276)

Taking a more language-specific stance, critical literacy is another prominent approach focusing on critically reflecting and transforming power relations in texts (Abednia & Crookes, 2019). According to Janks, critical literacy

> focuses specifically on the role of language as a social practice and examines the role played by text and discourse in maintaining or transforming these

orders. The understanding and awareness that practices can be transformed opens up possibilities, however small, for social action.

(Janks, 2014, p. 349)

When speaking of text, critical literacy uses a rather broad definition including various forms of texts and genres, such as pictures, videos, advertisements, or picturebooks (Abednia & Crookes, 2019). According to Breidbach et al. (2014), critical literacy can thus also be considered part of the pedagogy of multiliteracies focusing on the constantly changing modes of communication as well as considering the growing cultural and linguistic diversity (The New London Group, 1996).

Although such approaches could lead to a more socially just way of language teaching, our argument here is that teachers need to be prepared for critical language teaching. This preparation must include the development of a critical consciousness about (language) teaching in order to become aware of power relationships or discriminatory teaching practices that already exist in classrooms and classroom materials (e.g., Chun, 2013; Gray, 2019). Such practices might occur due to rather traditional views of language and education within society or the neoliberal turn in English language teaching focusing on "the production of citizens with the knowledge and dispositions appropriate for servicing the economy" (Gray, 2019, p. 70). As a way to challenge such traditional or even neoliberal tendencies, critical language teacher education conceptualizes language teachers as transformative intellectuals "who combine scholarly reflection and practice in the service of educating students to be thoughtful, active citizens" (Giroux, 1988, p. 122). To "exercise agency in their roles as teachers" (Fairley, 2020, p. 2) and to critically reflect on their knowledge and practice, the language teachers' constantly developing identities must be put at the centre of teacher education.

In international research on language teacher education, language teacher identities have gained traction in the last 20 years (Banegas & Gerlach, 2021; Kayi-Adar, 2019). According to Norton (2013, p. 45), identity is "how a person understands his or her relationship to the world, how that relationship is constructed across time and space, and how a person understands possibilities for the future." Teachers' identities are, therefore, changing and varying all the time because they are socially constructed and often challenged (Fairley, 2020). Thus, they can and should intentionally develop through a process of identification, positioning, and negotiation of meaning (Tsui, 2007; Varghese et al., 2005). On the one hand, there may be normative assumptions and biographical self-reflections that shape language teacher identities. On the other hand, language teacher identities are influenced by sociocultural contexts (Banegas & Gerlach, 2021; Golombek, 2017) or ethical backgrounds (e.g., Fairley, 2020; Miller et al., 2017; Vásquez, 2011). Despite the need for critical reflection on language teacher identities, Fairley notes that language teacher education programmes do not consider (nor respect) language teacher identities well enough, which the author tries to address with a competence-oriented approach. She regards "critical reflexivity, emotional literacy, collaboration, and responsiveness" (Fairley, 2020, p. 9) as core competencies for the development of transformative language teacher identities, which could be acquired through narrative writing or artistic expression activities, among other things.

Principles of Critical Language Teacher Education

Based on the sociocultural embeddedness of language teaching and language teacher education as well as the need to consider the development, contexts, and backgrounds of language teacher identities, we now outline two major (context-sensitivity and criticality) and two subordinate principles (cooperation and dialogic practice) for critical language teacher education. We understand the two superior principles as the foundation on which critical language teaching takes place, whereas the two subordinate principles should be put at the centre when (e.g., future) teachers interact with each other in learning and teaching activities, such as materials development. Besides, we will present four activities, with which these principles can be addressed. Before that, we will shortly sum up the goals of critical language teacher education primarily based on Gerlach and Fasching-Varner (2020): the development of (1) a critical consciousness, (2) a broad knowledge base, and (3) agency.

First and as a precondition for critical language teaching, teachers should question their mission for teaching English to develop a critical consciousness about discriminatory practices and to initiate identity development (see above; Gerlach & Fasching-Varner, 2020; Hawkins & Norton, 2009). Secondly, critical language teachers need a broad theoretical knowledge base about language, language teaching, and the school system, to be able to position themselves and pose critical questions about the structures and institutions they are working in and about the materials they are working with. Thirdly, the ultimate goal is to increase individual agency within these structures (Banegas & Gerlach, 2021). Based on a solid knowledge base, critical language teachers can develop a critical consciousness of their language teaching practice. In addition to that, critical language teachers become more aware of their own private and professional identities to understand how biography, culture, politics, and social background are influencing one's own language teaching. The development of a critical consciousness might (and probably should) lead to questioning one's knowledge base and one's identities.

In order to achieve such goals and initiate identity development as described above, researchers have proposed a variety of principles (e.g., Fairley, 2020; Hawkins & Norton, 2009), activities (e.g., Ahmadian & Maftoon, 2016; Fairley, 2020; Sharma & Phyak, 2017) and methods that can be implemented in critical teacher education and development (Figure 4.1). Based on this research (see above), we developed a model (Figure 4.1) for educating language teachers on a more critical perspective. It shows the two major (context-sensitivity and criticality) and the two subordinate principles (cooperation and dialogic practice) for critical language teacher education, which will be supported by four possible methods (exploration of teaching practice, lesson planning, reflective tasks, and materials development). We are fully aware that these suggestions sound very normative at first and, therefore, might be against Freire's understanding of teacher autonomy. However, we would like to stress that these principles and approaches attempt to empower language teachers within rather structured, standards-oriented, and – in Freire's words – oppressive institutions. We implement these principles in order to help support teachers form a critical perspective and develop agency through a bottom-up approach.

To explain Figure 4.1, critical language teacher education in practice needs to promote context-sensitivity and, most significantly, criticality. Being context-sensitive should be a precondition for criticality and aims at raising consciousness and sensitivity for various contexts English language teaching is affected by. Taking critical pedagogy and critical literacy seriously, foreign language teachers should proceed to integrate local needs, ideas, and experiences of students and, therefore, promote situated practice and context-sensitivity (Bax, 2003). Related to situated practice, one core principle of critical language teacher education should be enhancing criticality and critical discourse. Only if English language teachers consider and let learners consider multiple perspectives and question dominant ideologies during lessons both groups will be able to initiate critical reflection and transformation of texts and materials collaboratively (Banegas & Villacañas de Castro, 2016). English language teacher education can use different methods to enhance criticality and context-sensitivity. First, teachers can engage in materials development activities. Through developing materials, teachers learn to reflect on existing materials they use and they can modify or extend them critically. Teachers are likely to reflect on power relations incorporated in materials and texts and consider the local specifics or contexts of language classrooms when developing teaching materials (Gerlach & Fasching-Varner, 2020; Hawkins & Norton, 2009; Sharma & Phyak, 2017).

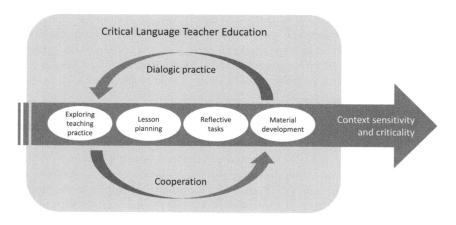

Figure 4.1 Principles for Critical Language Teacher Programmes.

In order to reflect on potentials and difficulties when using the newly developed materials, language teachers can engage in lesson planning activities leading to the exploration of one another's teaching practices. If teachers collaboratively plan, research, and theorize (critical) teaching, they might be more empowered to emancipate themselves from the dominant methods, such as the ones presented in textbooks (e.g., reading canonical literature without taking a socially just stance). By observing and reflecting as well as advising on one another's critical teaching and situated practice, equity-based cooperation and critical awareness are enhanced (Ahmadian & Maftoon, 2016; Burns, 2019; Gerlach & Fasching-Varner, 2020). Before, while and after practicing critical teaching, critical language teacher education needs to initiate reflective phases for language teachers to explore their own identities in order to develop a more socially just and autonomous mission for language teaching. Such reflective activities help to make critical language teaching more relevant to language teachers because they might have been the subject of discriminatory practices themselves or they might have greater awareness of discriminatory practices occurring in their immediate environment (Ahmadian & Maftoon, 2016; Hawkins & Norton, 2009; Zeichner, 2011).

As illustrated in Figure 4.1, these activities for critical language teacher education are framed by cooperation and dialogic practice. Through this practice and cooperation, teachers can extend and co-construct their knowledge base about language and language teaching and pose critical questions from multiple points of view provided by their teacher colleagues. This dialogue can lead to a critical consciousness and enhance communication on equitable terms so that each participant can equally contribute. Moreover, cooperation and dialogic practices help language teachers when they face difficulties arising from critical teaching (e.g., the question of how to discuss sensitive and intimate topics with students) (Ahmadian & Maftoon, 2016; Fairley, 2020; Gerlach, 2022; Hawkins & Norton, 2009).

In order to illustrate these principles, we will outline a practical example from a workshop on critical language education for English language teachers in Germany. The workshop activity aims to raise critical awareness about discriminatory practices in teaching materials in order to, then, modify them (Table 4.1).

The practical example illustrated in Table 4.1 can help language teachers critically reflect on criteria for developing language teaching materials from a more socially just perspective. It can be extended to different contexts and it can trigger collaborative lesson development.

Conclusion

Based on research into critical approaches to language teaching (e.g., Norton & Toohey, 2004) and language teacher education (e.g., Hawkins & Norton, 2009), this contribution outlined general principles for critical language teacher development. Central to these ideas are the principles of context-sensitivity and criticality, both of which can be enhanced through cooperative and dialogic

Table 4.1 Workshop on Critical Language Education

1.	*Teachers discuss possible criteria for more socially just TEFL materials.*
	To do so, they can use the following principles of critical pedagogy formulated by Crookes (2009, p. 184; slightly shortened):
	• The purpose of education is to develop critical thinking by presenting [a student's] situation to them as a problem so that they perceive, reflect and act on it;
	• The content of curriculum derives from the life situation of the learners as expressed in the themes of their reality;
	• The learners produce their own learning materials;
	• The task of planning is first to organize generative themes and second to organize subject matter as it relates to those themes;
	• The teacher participates […] as a learner among learners;
	• The teacher […] contributes his/her ideas, experiences, opinions, and perceptions to the dialogical process;
	• The teacher's function is one of posing problems;
	• The students possess the right to and power of decision-making.
2.	*Teachers present (discriminatory) TEFL materials they bring to the workshop.*
	The following guiding questions can be used for the presentation:
	• How do these materials show discriminatory practices?
	• Would you use such materials in your TEFL lessons? If yes:
	• In which grades would you use the materials?
	• What is the curricular context in which you would embed the materials?
3.	*Teachers gather ideas for critically modifying and transforming materials in teams.*
	The following guiding questions can assist them in the discussion:
	• How can you use the material to address topics that are relevant for more socially just teaching?
	• What might be of interest to your learners in the material or topic?
	• How can you enhance cultural and language learning with these materials?
	• What contexts (e.g., experiences of learners, family background) do I need to consider when modifying the material?
4.	*Teachers present and discuss the modified materials.*
5.	*Teachers reflect on the learning process.*
	The language teachers use this reflective task to think about their experiences during their collaborative work using and transforming materials. Through this reflection opportunity, they may gain insight into their own positioning as well as language teacher identities, which may help them to develop/select certain materials within the process (and future planning stages).

methods such as materials development or reflective tasks. To illustrate these key concepts, we provided a set of tasks that focuses on developing teachers' critical consciousness and initiating materials development. Since intervention research into critical language teacher education seems to indicate a promising effect on language teachers' identities (e.g., Abednia, 2012), the practicability and usefulness of the principles presented above should be empirically studied further in all contexts, e.g., in school (i.e., teacher development) and higher education (i.e., language teacher education). Especially, the processes of teachers' identity development need to be considered and reconstructed in order to become aware of possible tensions or conflicts when implementing critical approaches in standardized and transmission-oriented language teaching settings. As a starting point, the principles outlined in this contribution offer the opportunity to initiate critical language teacher education which

> recognizes the specific social, cultural and economic situatedness of the classroom, the unpredictability of teaching and the necessarily dialogic nature of a type of pedagogy that seeks to do more than provide students with the skills deemed necessary to service the needs of the economy
>
> (Gray, 2019, p. 78)

References

Abednia, A. (2012). Teachers' professional identity: Contributions of a critical EFL teacher education course in Iran. *Teaching and Teacher Education, 28*(5), 706–717.

Abednia, A., & Crookes, G. (2019). Critical literacy as a pedagogical goal in English language teaching. In G. Xuesong (Ed.), *Second handbook of English language teaching* (pp. 255–275). Springer.

Ahmadian, M., & Maftoon, P. (2016). Enhancing critical language teacher development through creating reflective opportunities. *The Journal of Asia TEFL, 13*(2), 90–101.

Akbari, R. (2008). Transforming lives: Introducing critical pedagogy into ELT classrooms. *ELT Journal, 62*(3), 276–283.

Banegas, D. L., & Gerlach, D. (2021). Critical language teacher education: A duoethnography of teacher educators' identities and agency. *System, 98*(1), 102474.

Banegas, D. L., & Villacañas de Castro, L. S. (2016). Criticality. *ELT Journal, 70*(4), 455–457.

Bax, S. (2003). The end of CLT: A context approach to language teaching. *ELT Journal, 57*(3), 278–287.

Breidbach, S., Medina, J., & Mihan, A. (2014). Critical literacies, multiliteracies and foreign language education. *Fremdsprachen Lehren und Lernen, 42*(2), 91–106.

Burns, A. (2019). Action research in English language teaching: Contributions and recent developments. In G. Xuesong (Ed.), *Second handbook of English language teaching* (pp. 991–1005). Springer.

Chang, B., & Salas, S. (2020). Disrupting method: Critical pedagogies and TESOL. In P. Vinogradova, & J. Kang Shin (Eds.), *Contemporary foundations for teaching English as an additional language: Pedagogical approaches and classroom applications* (pp. 15–44). Routledge.

Chun, C. W. (2013). The 'neoliberal citizen': Resemiotising globalised identities in EAP materials. In J. Gray (Ed.), *Critical perspectives on language teaching materials* (pp. 64–87). Palgrave Macmillan.

Crookes, G. (2009). *Values, philosophies, and beliefs in TESOL: Making a statement*. Cambridge University Press.

Crookes, G. (2013). *Critical ELT in action: Foundations, promises, praxis*. Routledge.

Fairley, M. J. (2020). Conceptualizing language teacher education centered on language teacher identity development: A competencies-based approach and practical applications. *TESOL Journal, 78*(3), 1–28.

Freire, P. (2014). *Pedagogy of the oppressed*. Bloomsbury. (Original work published 1968).

Gerlach, D. (2020). Einführung in eine Kritische Fremdsprachendidaktik. In D. Gerlach (Ed.), *Kritische Fremdsprachendidaktik: Grundlagen, Ziele, Beispiele* (pp. 7–31). Narr.

Gerlach, D. (2022). Addressing critical perspectives in language teacher education: Challenging norms and structures. In D. L. Banegas, & N. Govender (Eds.), *Gender and sexuality in English language education: New transnational voices* (pp. 175–191). Bloomsbury.

Gerlach, D., & Fasching-Varner, K. (2020). Grundüberlegungen zu einer kritischen Fremdsprachenlehrer*innenbildung. In D. Gerlach (Ed.), *Kritische Fremdsprachendidaktik: Grundlagen, Ziele, Beispiele* (pp. 217–234). Narr.

Giroux, H. (1988). *Teachers as intellectuals: Toward a critical pedagogy of learning*. Bergin & Garvey.

Golombek, P. (2017). Innovating my thinking and practices as a language teacher educator through my work as a researcher. In T. S. Gregersen, & P. MacIntyre (Eds.), *Innovative practices in language teacher education* (pp. 15–31). Springer.

Gray, J. (2019). Critical language teacher education. In S. Walsh, & S. Mann (Eds.), *The Routledge handbook of English language teacher education* (pp. 68–81). Routledge.

Hawkins, M., & Norton, B. (2009). Critical language teacher education. In A. Burns, & J. C. Richards (Eds.), *Cambridge guide to second language teacher education* (pp. 30–39). Cambridge University Press.

Janks, H. (2014). Critical literacy's ongoing importance for education. *Journal of Adolescent & Adult Literacy*, 57(5), 349–356.

Kayi-Aydar, H. (2019). Language teacher identity. *Language Teaching*, 52, 281–295.

Miller, E. R., Morgan, B., & Medina, A. L. (2017). Exploring language teacher identity work as ethical self-formation. *The Modern Language Journal*, 101, 91–105.

Norton, B. (2013). *Identity and language learning. Extending the conversation* (2nd ed.). Multilingual Matters.

Norton, B., & Toohey, K. (Eds.). (2004). *Critical pedagogies and language learning*. Cambridge University Press.

Sharma, B. K., & Phyak, P. (2017). Criticality as ideological becoming: Developing English teachers for critical pedagogy in Nepal. *Critical Inquiry in Language Studies*, 14(2–3), 210–238.

The New London Group. (1996). A pedagogy of multiliteracies: Designing social futures. *Harvard Educational Review*, 66(1), 60–92.

Tsui, A. B. (2007). Complexities of identity formation: A narrative inquiry of an EFL teacher. *TESOL Quarterly*, 41, 657–680.

Varghese, M., Morgan, B., Johnston, B., & Johnson, K. A. (2005). Theorizing language teacher identity: Three perspectives and beyond. *Journal of Language, Identity, and Education*, 4(1), 21–44.

Vásquez, C. (2011). TESOL, teacher identity, and the need for 'small story' research. *TESOL Quarterly*, 45, 535–545.

Zeichner, K. (2011). Teacher education for social justice. In M. Hawkins (Ed.), *Social justice language teacher education* (pp. 7–22). Multilingual Matters.

5 Taboo or Not Taboo? To Talk or Not to Talk? These Are the Questions

Grit Alter and Stefanie Fuchs

Introduction

Secrecy often makes things more exciting. If one is forbidden to open a door, curiosity to do so increases and one is tempted to sneak a peek anyway. A similar process is said to be activated when the discourse on tabooed topics suggests that these are beneficial and more motivating for teenage learners than talking about the weather or creating another dialogue on making a reservation in a hotel. Even so, our discussion of the topic led to rather critical reflections. Hence, this contribution addresses more fundamental questions about the potential of tabooed topics in foreign language teaching (FLT).

Our line of argument is based on two main issues. One, we observe a rather vague use of terminology for labelling the very concept within the discourse on tabooed topics, and we would like to critically reflect upon it. Two, we address ethical and pragmatic questions concerning aspects such as classroom practice, students' willingness to discuss tabooed topics with their teachers, aspects of teacher education and the teacher's personality.

We would like to acknowledge Prof. Dr. Lotta König's valuable contributions to this contribution.

Dimensions

Terminology and Concept

Two challenges of reflecting on tabooed issues are the terminology with which these are labelled and which topics are included in such a label. As this volume and further publications (e.g., MacAndrew & Martínez, 2001) show, respective terms include "taboo," "controversial issues," or "regular topics from a critical perspective." In a strict sense, taboo can relate to something that is prohibited or restricted, something that one is forbidden to interact and engage with for moral or ethical reasons; to do so could be considered dangerous or harmful. Thus, and we agree to this narrow understanding as well, tabooed topics concern topics one should not talk about, objects one should not touch and places one should not go (Alter & Merse, 2014). This "should" indicates a strong normative, moral

DOI: 10.4324/9781003220701-7

and ethical notion. That one is not to engage with tabooed issues is usually not based on legal matters and one does not have to fear legal repercussions. Rather, the restrictions are based on socio-cultural norms a society has, maybe even coconsciously, agreed upon.

Compared to that, controversial issues refer to topics or circumstances that could be openly discussed, but which are approached from different points of view, and to which people offer differing perspectives which then result in a controversy. While taboos are to remain silenced for socio-cultural and normative restrictions, controversial issues demand negotiations which at times could be heated. In case the participants in such negotiations risk serious conflict, a controversial issue may be pronounced a taboo to avoid a breakdown of communication.

Depending on students' and teachers' background and experiences, certain topics and themes suggested in curricula could indeed touch upon issues that some may regard as a taboo or that make them feel uncomfortable. On the one hand, this could lead to incidents in which reflecting upon assumably regular topics results in silence. On the other hand, it could and needs to be seen as an opportunity to encourage participation, as any discussion about regular topics from a critical perspective contributes to fostering critical thinking and developing critical literacy (e.g., Shor, 1999). Even so, we would like to be careful with labelling the resulting competence as taboo literacy but rather remain within the concept of critical literacy as this entails asking critical questions and challenging taken-for-granted assumptions. The regular topics as such are not forbidden and not silenced from public discourse, and approaching these from critical perspectives does not transcend normative regulations. Rather, critically thinking about regular topics is necessary to challenge information offered through media, politics and further public areas.

The issue of genital mutilation shall illustrate these conceptual differences. When a society does not speak about genital mutilation and restricts and morally forbids all discourse about it, the topic is a taboo. Due to shame, embarrassment, insecurity or ignorance, people may not be able to talk about this practice. When a group of people starts to discuss it anyway, collects information on it and enters a discourse while being aware of its disputed standing, possibly to change the patriarchal expression of power, they engage with genital mutilation as a controversial issue by negotiation differing opinions. Given circumstances in which this group is fairly successful with de-silencing genital mutilation and in which a broader public joins the debate, the topic that has formerly been considered a taboo, shifts to a more regular topic that can be reflected from various perspectives such as health, human and women's rights, but also considers people's cultural identities and local norms, values and customs. These shifts a topic can undergo, depending on how people are willing and able to relate to it, indicate that a tabooed topic is not determined as such, but that the degree to which it is silenced can change. These shifts also indicate that there is a normative process involved that declares topics as tabooed, but that can also challenge this status.

The attentive reader has recognized that we use the term "tabooed topics" rather than "taboo topics." We prefer this participle phrase as it emphasizes that there are no taboos as such, but topics that have been silenced and actively, whilst maybe coconsciously, banned from public discourse. Reasons why may vary. However, it is safe to say that there is always some kind of discomfort, unease and shame attached to not being able or willing to address certain topics. Using "tabooed" as a participle to qualify these topics indicates that tabooed topics are not ontological truths but that these develop due to socio-cultural limitations. The participle also draws attention to processes of "tabooing;" it is precisely these processes that need to be critically reflected as this helps to understand why and how a society silences certain issues from public discourse.

These differentiations emphasize why it makes a difference whether teachers include tabooed topics in their classrooms or reflect regular topics from critical perspectives to foster critical literacy. They need to be aware of who their students are, how students from various backgrounds may be differently affected by an issue, how the students' language level advances or hinders (deep) discussions, and that, therefore, they may have to apply a different methodology (see below).

We are here careful with naming tabooed topics because it is hardly possible to do so without the necessary research. In order to identify tabooed topics, one would have to conduct surveys in particular age and cultural groups to find out in how far an issue is actually tabooed (focusing on a pre-selected list of taboo topics see Summer & Steinbock in this volume). For teachers, doing such surveys in their own classes could be helpful in determining what kind of topics their students consider to be tabooed and also what kind of topics they would like to de-silence. A topic may also be tabooed depending on how one is personally affected.

With these two dimensions in mind, the openness of tabooed topics to change and their context-sensitivity, it is surprising that publications on tabooed topics in education published between 2001 and 2016 (e.g., Alter & Merse, 2014; Linder & Majerus, 2016; MacAndrew & Matrínez, 2001) mention (homo-)sexuality, death and abortion, but also lying, organ trafficking and sport and money as issues that fit into this category. While these publications span 15 years, they include rather similar (if not the same) topics, despite socio-cultural developments and various rights movements such as LBGTQI* or crip studies.

Ethical and Practical Questions

The ethical and practical questions we take into consideration refer to teacher education, identity formation and students' privacy, as well as foreign language classroom practice. Each of these will be critically reflected in the following section.

If teachers like to engage with tabooed topics, they need background knowledge to do so. However, a teacher's ability to address tabooed topics in classrooms not only depends on this, but more importantly, on personality and character traits like openness, honesty, their ability to develop trust among learners and a respectful and trustworthy relationship to their students as well as among students. Whereas knowledge about various topics can be gained, personality-related aspects are more difficult and lengthier to foster. Teachers also need to be aware that reflections on tabooed topics can trigger unexpected reactions in themselves. After all, they do not know in which direction students may lead discussions. When touching upon tabooed topics, they need to be willing and able to endure this and consider how far they themselves like to open up in front of their students.

The construction and negotiation of identity is a prime issue during puberty (Fuchs, 2013). This process is closely connected to discovering, creating and trying out new aspects of self and to see how these contribute to identity formation. Becoming aware of and talking about tabooed topics is one example of transcending given socio-cultural limitations and the familiar sphere. Learners may feel a certain excitement when encountering the secrecy surrounding tabooed topics. For some learners, it may also be inevitable to face tabooed topics because they are affected by processes of silencing, for example, when becoming aware of their fluid sexual identities. De-silencing issues regarded as tabooed topics raises awareness of these processes and, in the individual, enables skills of decision-making, reasoned argument and bringing critical approaches to evidence. Results from Hahn's study for which she interviewed, surveyed and observed 15- to 19-year-old students in 50 schools in five countries (the USA, GB, Germany, Netherlands, Denmark) show that students who were encouraged to explore controversial issues developed a higher level of political efficacy, interest, trust and confidence as well as positive attitudes to civic participation (Hahn, 1998, as cited in Cowan & Maitles, 2012). Similar processes could be valid for tabooed topics. Exposing learners to tabooed topics, teachers can engage them with topics they might otherwise not even have thought of (König & Rohrbach, 2015). Thus, they are exposed to a diversity of voices and opinions, even when their own contributions seem inhibited by a lack of linguistic means or other invisible factors, such as the fact that tabooed topics are likely to touch upon very personal issues and learners may simply not want to talk about these with their teachers and classmates. Also, instead of really considering a tabooed topic, students may offer responses that appear socially desirable, simply doing their "student job." Reflecting on tabooed topics may also put individual students into an uncomfortable spotlight or assume students' expertise in a specific area.

One assumption in the context of FLT is that including topics that are relevant to students increases their participation and engagement (Gudjons, 2007). Given that tabooed topics are said to be relevant, mainly due to their public secrecy or students' interest in these may be beneficial for eliciting speech production and lead to meaningful discussions in the foreign language. Foreign language classrooms could be predestined for such reflections as they are said to offer a "safe space" for the students to discuss sensitive issues (Boostrom, 1998). Furthermore, since language and culture are so deeply intertwined, it would sometimes be easier to speak about a tabooed topic in another language than one's first. Simultaneously, Wilson's (2013) study revealed that students gained freedom when speaking a foreign language. Despite this, Dewaele and Nakano's (2013) research with adult learners revealed that multilinguals feel different when switching a language; they feel less logical, less serious, less emotional and increasingly fake. These results show that while teenage learners may be able and willing to speak more openly in a foreign language, their utterances may also be less truthful and their reflections less personal. Thus, students could use the foreign language for protecting their privacy. One of König's students confirmed this when after a unit on gender and different sexualities commented that it was a relief to speak about these issues in a tentative way, using a language in which no one expected you to already perfectly phrase what you mean when you only start framing your thoughts on it (König, 2018).

Another aspect of classroom practice is that teachers have the choice to use different materials. They have the privilege to bring in various texts which offer different perspectives. Especially fictional characters, but also autobiographical narratives such as narrative texts, TV shows or online forums, allow us to get insights and speak about the effect of tabooed topics at the example of someone else, removed from students' own perspectives (Fuchs, 2021). The students could relate to them but do not have to speak about themselves.

In terms of participating in classroom discourses, it is questionable in how far all students possess the language to talk about rather complex issues such as death, abortion, organ trafficking or sexually transmitted diseases, linguistic barriers and a lack of linguistic means could actually prevent communication: When too much language work is necessary for an in-depth reflection, this could not only reduce the students' motivation to talk about tabooed topics but also lead to frustration which could result in students feeling even more insecure or inhibited to talk. Furthermore, a reflected discussion of tabooed topics requires a large amount of language material on different perspectives as well as cognitive resources. Handling this could be a challenge for teachers and learners alike.

Both, the complexity of language and the material could be particularly demanding for students who have difficulties learning and speaking the foreign language. The classroom community needs to ensure that everyone can participate in the discourse and that no one is excluded from reflections on tabooed topics. Certainly, one should not make the mistake and believe that due to their complexity and assumed demand of maturity, tabooed topics are reserved for grammar school students. On the contrary, reflections on such issues are important to all students at all schools.

One suggestion to solve the controversy of whether to discuss tabooed topics in FLT lies with the question of "how?". Teachers should establish a communicative atmosphere in the classroom characterized by openness and respect, so that all learners can participate in the discourse. However, it is sometimes difficult to keep a respectful atmosphere intact in which every student is willing and allowed to openly contribute to discussions without fear of derogative comments and devaluation – either in school or afterwards.

Beyond the classroom atmosphere, dealing with tabooed topics also regards appropriate language scaffolding without giving away too much content and opinion. By offering sentence starters or sentence structures, for example, to express surprise or disbelief, teachers can foster respectful communication. Additionally, some simple ways of expressing an opinion, for example, yes or no options as responses to general statements (see below), can serve as a starting point for further discussions or group debates.

Methods and approaches which allow students to address tabooed topics without putting themselves on the spot too much are, for instance:

- *Fold your answer*: Before responding to a tabooed topic, students fold a piece of paper in half. On the inside, they take notes they like to remain private and do not want to share; on the outside, they note down aspects they do want to contribute to a discussion. Thus, their privacy is respected; they can keep a distance between their student role and private person. During the discussion, they may also reflect on the reasons why they have used both sides of their folded paper. Thus, they simultaneously reflect on the socio-cultural context of the tabooed topic (Alter, 2015).
- *Privacy*: The teacher offers statements to a tabooed topic, e.g., "I dislike certain parts of my body," "I would do minor plastic surgery," "Someone else/I've made comments on someone else's body which made them feel ugly" for the topics body norms, body shaming and beauty surgery (König, 2020). Students write "yes" or "no" on a piece of paper and enter it into a bag hidden from view. Before the answers to each statement are counted, the students guess how many yes or no answers are in the bag. Here, they can talk about tabooed topics without having to "out" themselves and still get an impression of what their classmates think. The class could then enter a discussion about the respective topic on a meta-level.
- *Using pictures (on social media)*: Teachers can work with images of famous people from social media. These images or portraits mostly tell a story and enable the recognition, discovery and discussion of different perspectives. While analysing the images students reflect on tabooed topics such as (fluid) sexual identities. Social media are suitable here because, on the one hand, they tie in with the students' lifeworlds and are authentic material, but on the other hand, they can also be critically scrutinized without a student taking centre stage with their own reports. Methods need to be chosen according to learning goals and learners' needs (Fuchs, 2021).

Additionally, one can make productive use of students' first language for a meta-reflection. However, this practice is often considered a taboo of FLT itself.

Conclusion

What is the objective of FLT? Referring to this contribution, this question seems to be rather broad, but its critical consideration contributes to solving the issue of whether or not tabooed topics should be made part of FLT. Certainly, one can offer good reasons to do so (see Introduction). Yet, first and foremost, one objective of FLT is to develop the skills and competences paramount in the 21st century. These include, e.g., critical thinking, (international) cooperation and digital literacy (Battelle for Kids, 2019). In connection with tabooed topics, the complex reflections demand and develop discourse competences (Hallet, 2008; Plikat, 2017) and symbolic competence (Kramsch, 2006) as well as critical literacy (Shor, 1999) as central competences students need. Depending on the classroom situation, students' interests and teachers' preparedness, tabooed topics can contribute to developing these. Even so, thoroughly investigating pitfalls and benefits of addressing tabooed topics, controversial issues or regular topics from critical perspectives is inevitable. After all, tabooed topics may also uncover individual traumata, and teachers are teachers, not psychologists.

This contribution adds a critical perspective to tabooed topics in (foreign language) education. The German term "hinterfragen," to look, go and step behind an issue, to try and see what else is there, upon which assumptions certain questions and answers are grounded, carries a lot of meaning. We do not only attempt to question the existence and establishment of tabooed topics in society but also to interrogate ideas that too quickly jump on the bandwagon of new and exciting moves within our discipline. One part of this would be to pay more attention to what is actually happening in classrooms compared to lofty academic ideas.

References

Alter, G. (2015). *Inter- and transcultural learning in the context of Canadian young adult fiction*. LIT.
Alter, G., & Merse, T. (2014). Das Potenzial tabuisierter und kontroverser Texte für das literarisch-ästhetische Lernen innerhalb der pluralen Bildung. In C. Fäcke, M. Rost-Rot, & E. Thaler (Eds.), *Sprachenausbildung, Sprachen bilden aus, Bildung aus Sprachen. Dokumentation zum 24. Kongress für Fremdsprachendidaktik der Deutschen Gesellschaft für Fremdsprachenforschung (DGFF) Augsburg, 25–28 September 2013* (pp. 161–171). Schneider.
Battelle for Kids. (2019). *Framework for 21st century skills*. Columbus.
Boostrom, R. (1998). "Safe spaces": Reflections on an educational metaphor. *Journal of Curriculum Studies, 30*(4), 397–408.
Cowan, P., & Maitles, H. (Eds.). (2012). *Teaching controversial issues in the classroom. Key issues and debates*. Continuum.
Dewaele, J.-M., & Nakano, S. (2013). Multilinguals' perceptions of feeling different when switching languages. *Journal of Multilingual and Multicultural Development, 34*(2), 107–120. https://doi.org/10.1080/01434632.2012.712133
Fuchs, S. (2013). *Geschlechtsunterschiede bei motivationalen Faktoren im Kontext des Englischunterrichts. Eine empirische Studie zu Motivation, Selbstkonzept und Interesse im Fach Englisch in der Sekundarstufe I*. Peter Lang.
Fuchs, S. (2021). Focus on identity in English language education: Doing gender in digital spaces. In T. Merse, & C. Lütge (Eds.), *Digital teaching and learning: Perspectives for English language education* (pp. 167–183). Narr.
Gudjons, H. (2007). *Neue Unterrichtskultur – veränderte Lehrerrolle*. Klinkhardt.

Hahn, C. (1998). *Becoming political. Comparative perspectives on citizenship education.* SUNY Press.
Hallet, W. (2008). Diskursfähigkeit heute. Der Diskursbegriff in Piephos Theorie der kommunikativen Kompetenz und seine zeitgemäße Weiterentwicklung für die Fremdsprachendidaktik. In M. K. Legutke (Ed.), *Kommunikative Kompetenz als fremdsprachendidaktische Vision* (pp. 76–96). Narr.
König, L. (2018). *Gender-Reflexion mit Literatur im Englischunterricht. Fremdsprachendidaktische Theorie und unterrichtspraktische Beispiele.* Metzler.
König, L. (2020). On beauty ideals and body norms. Schönheits- und Körpernormen als Thema in einer Kritischen Fremdsprachendidaktik. In D. Gerlach (Ed.), *Kritische Fremdsprachendidaktik. Grundlagen, Ziele, Beispiele* (pp. 125–144). Narr.
König, L., & Rohrbach, J. (2015). Grenzen im Denken auflösen. *Der Fremdsprachliche Unterricht. Englisch, 49*(135), 44–45.
Kramsch, C. (2006). From communicative competence to symbolic competence. *The Modern Language Journal, 90*(2), 249–252.
Linder, S., & Majerus, E. (2016). *Can I teach that? Negotiating taboo language and controversial topics in the language arts classroom.* Rowman & Littlefield Publishers.
MacAndrew, R., & Matrínez, R. (2001). *Taboos and issues: Photocopiable lessons on controversial topics.* Helbling Languages.
Plikat, J. (2017). *Fremdsprachliche Diskursbewusstheit als Zielkonstrukt des Fremdsprachenunterrichts.* Peter Lang.
Shor, I. (1999). What is critical literacy? *Journal of Pedagogy, Pluralism, and Practice, 1*(4), 2–32.
Wilson, R. (2013). Another language is another soul. *Language and Intercultural Communication, 13*(3), 298–309. https://doi.org/10.1080/14708477.2013.804534

6 Promoting Resilience in the Foreign Language Classroom – A Basic Requirement for Working with Taboo Topics

Aline Willems

Introduction

As Summer and Ludwig explain in the introduction to this volume, teaching according to the ideas of critical language pedagogy is "hard work" (Steinberg, 2020, p. 4). Unfortunately, sometimes teachers shy away from taking a critical pedagogy turn because they are unfamiliar with it or feel they do not have the necessary knowledge and skills to implement critical pedagogy in their classrooms. Yet, apart from the prerequisites that teachers must have, it is equally important to question when and whether students are capable of being confronted with taboo topics in the sense of critical foreign language pedagogy. In this context, the construct of resilience – defined as "the coping behaviour demonstrated by an individual or a system in the face of substantial risk or adversity" (Mukherjee & Kumar, 2017, p. 3) – plays an important role. At first glance, it may seem surprising to call for resilience as a prerequisite for foreign language teaching, but any engagement with taboos challenges students to deal with issues on an emotional, affective, and personal level – especially those students who may be particularly triggered by individual biographical experiences.

Against this background, the first hypothesis of this contribution is that it is easier to treat taboo topics with resilient students than with those lacking resilience. This assumption will be supported in the subsequent section by means of a theoretical discussion of and empirical evidence for the importance of resilience and resilience strategies. Since the majority of studies on resilience do not take place in the immediate school context and certainly not with reference to foreign language teaching, the third section will illustrate how to promote resilience in foreign language teaching without much additional effort. It will be made clear that the measures to promote resilience largely intersect with common principles of today's foreign language teaching. Based on examples of vocabulary learning, it will be shown that many of the things teachers already do – often unconsciously – promote the resilience of their students. If they use these techniques consciously and adapt the ones presented here for other teaching-learning situations, the protective factors of the students can be positively influenced more extensively.

DOI: 10.4324/9781003220701-8

Resilience – A Theoretical Approach

On a very fundamental level, resilience can be defined as "the capacity of a dynamic system to adapt successfully to disturbances that threaten system function, viability, or development" (Masten, 2014a, p. 6). Grounded on general systems theory, the construct has been researched and used as an explanatory approach in psychology and ecology since the 1970s (cf. Masten, 2014a). However, the underlying ideas go back further. In the field of child development research, which is of particular importance for school teaching and thus for this contribution, corresponding investigations began as early as around World War II and continued in relation to other disasters – also referred to as mass-trauma events (cf. Masten, 2014a; Wustmann Seiler, 2020). The COVID-19 pandemic (cf. Masten, 2021a; Masten & Motti-Stefanidi, 2020), as well as recent armed conflicts, such as the war in Ukraine can certainly be considered some of the latest mass-trauma events.

Based on extensive research, children's resilience is defined as their psychological resistance to biological, psychological and psychosocial development risks (cf. Wustmann Seiler, 2020). Until today, however, members of the scientific community do not agree on the nature of those developmental risks and possible coping strategies on which an all-encompassing definition of resilience could be based on. Instead, different researchers propose different sets of risk factors, reaching from a "significant threat to child development" (Wustmann Seiler, 2020, p. 18) to "daily challenges" at school (Smith, 2020, p. 1). In other words,

> [t]he resilience of an individual over the course of development depends on the function of complex adaptive systems that are continually interacting and transforming. As a result, the resilience of a person is always changing and the capacity for adaptation of an individual will be distributed across interacting systems.
> (Masten, 2014a, p. 9; cf. Masten, 2021b; Wustmann Seiler, 2020)

What scientists agree upon, however, is the fact that resilience is based on a set of protective factors/resources that, in turn, compete with potential risk factors. In a very simplified way, one could imagine the protective factors and the risk factors on a balance scale. If the effect of the protective factors equals or exceeds that of the risk factors, i.e., the scale is in balance or the protective factors are "heavier" than the risk factors, one speaks of resilience. The proposed protective and risk factors are nearly as diverse as the number of prominent studies on resilience in childhood and adolescence (cf. Feder et al., 2011; Fröhlich-Gildhoff & Rönnau-Böse, 2019; Masten, 2021a; Provitolo & Reghezza-Zitt, 2015; Smith, 2020; Wustmann Seiler, 2020).

Potential risk factors that can negatively affect a child's development can be subdivided into *vulnerability factors*, based on intrapersonal psychological and biological characteristics of the child, and *risk factors/stressors*. The latter act on the child from its environment. Examples of vulnerability factors are neuropsychological deficits, chronic diseases, insecure attachment patterns, and poor self-regulation of tension and relaxation (cf. Wustmann Seiler, 2020). While it is possible to reduce some of those vulnerability factors through appropriate treatment and assistance, decreasing or even eliminating the number of risk factors would only be imaginable in an ideal world or through extensive training and support from parents. This becomes particularly clear when looking at selected examples of risk factors: low socio-economic status, aversive living environment (e.g., residential area with a high crime rate), chronic family disharmony, parental alcohol and drug abuse, mental disorders or illnesses of one or both parents, frequent moves, frequent changes of school, migration background, and traumatic experiences (cf. Wustmann Seiler, 2020).

Although a certain number of students might be affected by one or more of the reported vulnerability and/or risk factors, some of them are better able to cope with challenges than others. Scientists suggest that those children dispose of different levels of *protective factors* that confront and counteract the negative factors. Based on numerous studies, Wustmann Seiler (2020, pp. 115–116) categorises central protective factors into personal (see Table 6.1) and social resources/resilience factors (see Table 6.2).

Table 6.1 Personal Resources/Resilience Factors

- Positive temperament characteristics that evoke social support and attention from caregivers
- Intellectual ability
- Problem-solving skills
- Self-efficacy beliefs
- Positive self-concept/self-confidence/high self-esteem
- Internal belief in control
- Realistic attribution style [note: Attribution theories are based on a particular branch of motivation studies which examine how people explain their success or failure in a certain situation. According to Weiner (2010), some of the most frequent attributions are ability, effort, task difficulty, and luck.]
- High social skills: empathy, ability to cooperate and make contacts (combined with good language skills), taking on social perspectives, assuming responsibility, humour
- Active and flexible coping behaviour
- Secure attachment behaviour [note: Based on Bowlby (1969), attachment is understood as a developmental process. Babies develop internal working models of relationships which evolve over time due to experiences. Those internal working models influence the way we experience and construct relationships throughout life. The more stable or secure the individual attachment behaviour the better for our resilience.]
- Enthusiasm for learning, commitment to school
- Optimistic outlook on life
- Religious belief, spirituality
- Talents, interests, hobbies
- Goal orientation, planning competence
- Creativity
- Physical health resources

Source: Taken from Wustmann Seiler (2020, p. 115). See also Masten (2014b).

Table 6.2 Social Resources/Resilience Factors

Resilience Factors within the family	Resilience Factors in educational institutions	Resilience Factors in the wider social environment
• At least one stable caregiver who promotes trust and autonomy • Authoritative/democratic parenting style (emotionally positive, supportive and structured parenting behaviour, sensitivity, and responsiveness) • Cohesion, stability, and constructive communication in the family • Age-appropriate household responsibilities assigned to the child • High level of education of parents • Supportive family network (relatives, friends, neighbours) • High socio-economic status	• Clear, transparent, and consistent rules and structures • Appreciative climate (warmth, respect, acceptance of the child) • High but adequate standard of performance • Positive reinforcement of the child's performance and willingness to exert themselves • Positive peer contacts/ positive friendship relationships • Cooperation with the parental home and other social institutions	• Competent and caring adults outside the family who promote trust, convey security, and serve as positive role models • Resources at the municipal level • Good job and employment opportunities • Presence of prosocial role models, norms, and values in society

Source: Taken from Wustmann Seiler (2020, p. 116). See also Masten (2014b).

While the personal resilience factors (Table 6.1) – as the name already suggests – are inherent to individual students, the social resilience factors (Table 6.2) are external factors that can have an impact on a person's resilience.

As shown in Table 6.2, social resilience factors can be grouped into three different categories: within the family, in educational institutions, and in the wider social environment. These categories are based on the contexts of the specific resilience studies in which the factors manifested themselves. For example, if clear, transparent and consistent rules and structures are identified as a resilience factor in educational institutions, this does not mean that they cannot also be beneficial within the family or in the wider social environment. It simply says that there are no specific resilience studies that have examined the effects of clear, transparent, and consistent rules and structures in the family or social environment on promoting resilience.

Table 6.1 illustrates that resilience factors are very congruent with the current principles of today's foreign language teaching. Since it is not possible here to go into detail about those numerous concepts and principles, I will only mention selected examples, including critical foreign language pedagogy (cf. Crookes, 2013; Gerlach, 2020; Ludwig & Summer, this volume), learner autonomy or learner agency (cf. Deters et al., 2015; Teng, 2019), critical digital literacy/competence (c.f. Becker, 2019; CoE, 2019), political education/education for democratic culture (cf. CoE, 2018), inter-/transcultural learning (cf. Byram, 2008; Candelier et al., 2012; Plikat, 2017), and global education/education for sustainable development (cf. Bourn, 2020; Lütge, 2015; UNESCO, 2021).

Many of the mentioned vulnerability and risk factors overlap with topics/aspects that are classified as taboo topics in this edited volume. Following the construct of resilience and remembering the scale metaphor, it can be concluded that it is easier to discuss these tabooed issues with affected students who are more resilient because they have enough protective factors on the scale that level out the risk factors on the opposite side of the scale. Even if students are not faced with any of the risk factors, dealing with taboo topics in the classroom can be emotionally challenging for them, which could cause their balance to drop on the side with the negative. Thus, improving their protective factors might also be helpful for the students before addressing taboo topics. However, two questions remain unanswered: How can resilience be promoted in school without considering any subject-specific aspects? What are the specific possibilities in foreign language teaching? This will be explored in the following section.

Promoting Resilience in the Classroom

Recommendations for All School Subjects

The range of general programmes fostering resilience for schools and the extracurricular sector is very large (cf. Goldstein & Brooks, 2013; Goncalves Viana, 2019; Lundgaard, 2018; Smith, 2020). Moreover, the number of programmes has been increasing massively since the COVID-19 pandemic as related lockdown measures are considered to be very stressful for many children and young people (cf. Shaver, 2021). However, many of these programmes have not been specifically developed for foreign language teaching but education in general. Thus, the following ten recommendations suggested by the American Psychological Association (APA) can support teachers of all subjects in designing lessons that strengthen students' resilience:

- Make connections
- Avoid seeing crises as insurmountable problems
- Accept that change is a part of living
- Move towards your goal
- Take decisive actions
- Look for opportunities for self-discovery
- Nurture a positive view of yourself
- Keep things in perspective
- Maintain a hopeful outlook
- Take care of yourself (Lundgaard & de Lima, 2018, p. 5).

There are different ways in which these recommendations can be implemented in the classroom. For example, teachers can include them into individual feedback for their students. Some counsels could also be taken as a starting point for specific tasks – if possible in the foreign language if not in the language used for other subjects in the school: Considering the advice "Move towards your goal" (Lundgaard & de Lima, 2018, p. 5) a first task could be to specify the goals like "In three weeks from now, what would you like to have reached?". In the foreign language classroom answers might be "I would like to have read a Harry Potter novel by then" or "I would like to have finished my YouTube video about my favourite hobby by then". The next task could be to write down the steps one has to take in order to reach these goals. The results could be compared, checked, and corrected or complemented if needed in a short session with a partner and further on with the whole class. The results from the plenary session could then be visualised on a poster or in a checklist with boxes to tick, when steps are fulfilled. At the end of the three weeks, the students would reflect if they reached their goals and why or why not. Thereby they might gain a "realistic attribution style", extend their "problem-solving skills" by learning strategies for reaching one's goals, and increase their "planning competence" (see Table 6.1; Wustmann Seiler, 2020, p. 115).

Looking back at one of the other recommendations by the APA, the counsel "Take care of yourself" could also be a starting point for a self-reflection initiated by the teacher: First, the students could collect ideas about what it means to take care of oneself. Those ideas could be discussed subsequently and each of the students might choose up to five suggested ideas that suit him/herself best. Then little cards with those ideas could be creatively designed and further on be used as little reminders during the (school) day to do things that help taking care of oneself. Alternatively, the task can be extended to "take care of yourself and your best friend". Some days or weeks later, the students should reflect if the ideas they chose for themselves suited them the way they had thought or if they would like to exchange some of the formerly chosen ideas. Through this the students could learn to focus on their "physical (and mental) health resources" and at best they can increase them (see Table 6.1; Wustmann Seiler, 2020, p. 115). Furthermore, they might as well enhance their "self-efficacy beliefs", their "self-confidence" and, if the task was extended to "…and your friend", their "social skills" (see Table 6.1; Wustmann Seiler, 2020, p. 115).

But in order to promote resilience in school, teachers do not necessarily have to invest a lot of time in tasks like those suggested above. Smaller things can also be helpful, which are often already known and used anyway, but whose connection to resilience promotion may not yet have been disclosed. By constructing and using helper systems or scaffolding that reduce the complexity of a task, for example, aspects like "problem-solving skills, self-efficacy beliefs, positive self-concept, internal belief in control, realistic attribution style, active and flexible coping behaviour, enthusiasm for learning and commitment to school", as well as "goal orientation", and "planning competence" (see Table 6.1; Wustmann Seiler, 2020, p. 115) could be fostered. Those aspects could also be promoted by creating opportunities to act independently and control one's own behaviour, by creating social learning situations, for instance via cooperative and collaborative learning, and by using advance organisers for planning. By introducing and performing rituals, the students can experience stability and structure – two further resilience factors (see Table 6.2; Wustmann Seiler, 2020). Finally, it can also be helpful not to overstrain the room design as this could lead to distraction and visual overload.

These recommendations are by no means new, but already being widely implemented in the classroom, though so far often without reflecting on their resilience-promoting properties. In other words, promoting resilience in the classroom can be achieved without much additional effort if teaching and learning are based on current principles. If so far teachers have shied away from the extra workload often associated with the introduction of helper systems, scaffolding, etc., then the fact that they can increase not only their students' learning outcome but also their resilience may be a further motivation.

Promoting Resilience in the Foreign Language Classroom

Foreign language teaching offers specific teaching and learning situations: Teachers are supposed to foster their students' speaking, writing, listening, and reading skills, promote intercultural competences, and expand their students' language awareness and language learning competences and much more. As examining all of those teaching and learning skills and competence domains with regard to their possibilities to promote resilience would represent a project that would be too comprehensive for this article, one example is chosen here to illustrate the intended argument: promoting resilience when teaching and learning vocabulary. This example was chosen as vocabulary work is considered one of the basic components of successful language competence development.

Before starting to confront students with new words, three general aspects should be taken into account which foster resilience but are not necessarily of a task-specific nature:

1. create an environment that is as free of disturbances (especially noise) as possible,
2. create a situation that is as stress-free/-reduced as possible, and
3. implement and/or use learning strategies – with the option for the students to decide consciously against the use of a strategy (cf. Deters et al., 2015; Nation, 2013, 326).

The third recommendation refers to general language learning strategies and techniques (cf. Oxford, 1990) as well as those that specifically support vocabulary learning (cf. LaBontee, 2021; Nation, 2013). In addition to the frequently cited suggestions by Nation (2013), the following strategies can be particularly helpful when learning new words: If the information concerning a new word might overstrain the students, reduce the amount of input, for example, by presenting the written and phonetic presentation separately. Especially if the oral code differs a lot from the written code or the phonem-graphem relation is rather different in the target language than in the languages the students already know – e.g., for English L1 speakers: fr. *équation* [ekwasjɔ̃], fr. *heureux* [ørø], fr. *lundi* [lœ̃di] – or if the students might think that the phonem–graphem correspondence is very arbitrary – e.g., for German L1 speakers: engl. *infinite* [ɪnfɪnɪt] vs. *finite* [faɪnaɪt] or *butcher* [bʊtʃə] vs. *but* [bʌt] – or if the writing system is new to the learners as well, like when being exposed to the Cyrillic alphabet or the Japanese character code, concentrating on one medium can help, especially in the beginning. To support learners even more, creating meaningful pictures for words and pairing them with pronunciation and/or spelling may help. If the target language has a grammatical gender, it may help to mark the different articles or words in colours according to their gender. A further method that can help learners acquire new vocabulary is to connect single words or chunks – mainly in spoken language – with a gesture that is used during pronunciation. This movement can be connected to the meaning of the word. For example, one could sit down while saying "to sit", "s'assoir", "zitten", "座る" – whichever language should be learned (cf. Janzen Ulbricht, 2020; Janzen Ulbricht & Spindler, 2022). Yet scientific findings from the field of embodiment also show that the gesture which accompanies the pronunciation of a word does not necessarily have to represent the word's meaning to support learning (cf. Borghi, 2014). In addition, of course, all the other measures commonly used in foreign language teaching are helpful in learning vocabulary, such as learning in chunks, contextualising words, and recognising the communicative value of newly learned words.

Helping students to cope successfully with learning situations – such as vocabulary learning – can, among other things, increase their enthusiasm for learning, their commitment for school, their self-esteem, and their intellectual ability (see Tables 6.1 and 6.2). If they are enabled to recognise which potential learning techniques can be helpful for them personally and if they are empowered to decide whether and which strategy to use, then this can particularly promote their problem-solving ability, their self-efficacy beliefs, their internal belief in control, their self-confidence, as well as their goal orientation and planning competence (see Table 6.1). In other words, successfully coping with learning situations while at the same time feeling self-efficacious, for example, through selecting and applying appropriate learning strategies, can support many of the factors that were named as protective factors at the beginning (cf. Wustmann Seiler, 2020). Experienced teachers will now rightly object that the proposed measures are not new in foreign language teaching. That is precisely the advantage. Teachers do not have to change or additionally integrate anything in a foreign language classroom designed according to current principles in order to promote resilience. However, one small restriction should be mentioned: Learners should be made aware of these protective factors and come to appreciate them. This can be supported, for example, by promoting group and individual reflection, for example, after a task or at the end of a unit.

Although vocabulary work is only one component of foreign language teaching, it should have become clear that promoting protective factors can easily be integrated into regular lessons without much additional effort. Other areas of foreign language teaching can promote students' resilience in addition to their foreign language competences with equivalent teaching methods that reduce the complexity of tasks, suggest concrete techniques and problem-solving strategies, and thus increase the chance of learning success. Similarly, successfully mastered situations related to intercultural competence can promote protective factors, if self-efficacy is achieved, active and flexible coping behaviour could be used and/or control of the situation could be made perceptible.

Conclusion

This contribution has shown that resilience – not being innate, but something that needs to be developed in the course of life – can be fostered without having to rely on resilience programmes but more or less *en passant* during regular lessons. Thereby, it is important to bear in mind that the levels of resilience depend, among other things, on the situation in which resilient behaviour is required as well as on vulnerability factors/risk factors and on protective factors/resources. Looking at the list of vulnerability factors and risk factors, it becomes clear that there is a high overlap with taboo topics. This implies that dealing with taboo topics in class is also a challenge that can have an impact on resilience. Let us return to the image of the balance scale in which risk factors and protective factors face each other: If dealing with taboo topics could pull down the balance scale on the side of the risk factors, it could be advantageous to strengthen the protective factors on the other side of the scale beforehand in order to achieve at least a balance, or even better, an overweight on the side of the protective factors and thereby resilience.

It is therefore important to build up learners' protective factors as early as possible in foreign language teaching and to make students aware of them. In this way, the learners can be strengthened in dealing with taboo topics in the classroom as well as in their daily lives. Of course, the promotion of protective factors can also take place parallel to the treatment of taboo topics, for example, by consciously using learning strategies and techniques and finally reflecting on their use. Furthermore, the teaching methods used to foster resilience are already widely spread as they are helpful to reduce the complexity of a task and to increase the learning success, like for example, helper systems, scaffolding, using advance organisers. This means the methods are not new to teachers and therefore do not consume extra time and effort to implement and use them, "only" to promote resilience. But teachers can rely on well-known teaching and learning strategies. They should only make themselves and the students aware of the way in which this promotes resilience in addition to the other learning goals in the classroom. Furthermore it is important to let the students reflect on the strategies and techniques used in order to find the ones that suit them best.

References

Becker, D. (2019). The digital citizen 2.0 – Re-negotiating issues of digital citizenship education. *Arbeiten aus Anglistik und Amerikanistik, 44*(2), 167–193.

Borghi, A. M. (2014). Embodied cognition and word acquisition: The challenge of abstract words. In C. Müller, A. Cienki, E. Fricke, S. H. Ladewig, D. McNeill, & J. Bressem (Eds.), *Body – language – communication. An international handbook on multimodality in human interaction*. De Gruyter Mouton.

Bourn, D. (Ed.). (2020). *The Bloomsbury handbook of global education and learning*. Bloomsbury Academic.

Bowlby, J. (1969). *Attachment and loss* (Vol. 1), *Attachment*. Hogarth Press.

Byram, M. (2008). *From foreign language education to education for intercultural citizenship*. Multilingual Matters.

Candelier, M., Camilleri-Grima, A., Castellotti, V., de Pietro, J.-F., Lőrincz, I., Meißner, F.-J., Noguerol, A., & Schröder-Sura, A. (2012). *FREPA – A framework of reference for pluralistic approaches to languages and cultures: Competences and resources*. Council of Europe Publishing. https://www.ecml.at/Portals/1/documents/ECML-resources/CARAP-EN.pdf?ver=2018-03-20-120658-443

Council of Europe. (2018). *Reference framework of competences for democratic culture: Context, concepts and model* (Vol. 1) [online]. https://rm.coe.int/prems-008318-gbr-2508-referenceframework-of-competences-vol-1-8573-co/16807bc66c

Council of Europe. (Ed.). (2019). *Digital citizenship education handbook: Being online, well-being online, rights online*. https://rm.coe.int/168093586f

Crookes, G. V. (2013). *Critical ELT in action: Foundations, promises, praxis*. Routledge.

Deters, P., Gao, X. A., Miller, E. R., & Vitanova, G. (Eds.). (2015). *Theorizing and analyzing agency in second language learning – Interdisciplinary approaches*. Multilingual Matters.

Feder, A., Charney, D., & Collins, K. (2011). Neurobiology of resilience. In S. Southwick, B. Litz, D. Charney, & M. Friedman (Eds.), *Resilience and mental health: Challenges across the lifespan*. Cambridge University Press.

Fröhlich-Gildhoff, K., & Rönnau-Böse, M. (2019). *Resilienz*. Ernst Reinhardt.

Gerlach, D. (Ed.). (2020). *Kritische Fremdsprachendidaktik: Grundlagen, Ziele, Beispiele*. Narr Francke Attempto.

Goldstein, S., & Brooks, R. B. (Eds.). (2013). *Handbook of resilience in children*. Springer.

Goncalves Viana, S. (2019). *Developing children's resilience and mental health*. Routledge.

Janzen Ulbricht, N. (2020). The embodied teaching of spatial terms: Gestures mapped to morphemes improve learning. *Frontiers in Education, 2020*(5). https://www.frontiersin.org/articles/10.3389/feduc.2020.00109/full

Janzen Ulbricht, N., & Spindler, B. (2022). Learning a play through gestures: A dentist to the rescue. In C. Ludwig, & M. Sambanis (Eds.), *English and beyond: Impulse zur Förderung von Mehrsprachigkeit im Englischunterricht*. Brigg-Verlag.

LaBontee, R. (2021). Vocabulary learning strategy surveys in second language acquisition: Design, context and content. In Z. Gavriilidou, & L. Mitits (Eds.), *Situating language learning strategy use: Present issues and future trends*. Multilingual Matters.

Lundgaard, P. (Ed.). (2018). *Developing resilience in children and young people – A practical guide*. Routledge.

Lundgaard, P., & de Lima, S. (2018). What is resilience? The background of The Resilience Programme. In P. Lundgaard (Ed.), *Developing resilience in children and young people – A practical guide*. Routledge.

Lütge, C. (Ed.). (2015). *Global education: Perspectives for English language teaching.* Lit-Verlag.

Masten, A. (2014a). Global perspectives on resilience in children and youth. *Child Development, 22*(1), 6–20.

Masten, A. (2014b) *Ordinary magic – Resilience in development.* Guilford Press.

Masten, A. (2021a). Resilience in developmental systems: Principles, pathways, and protective processes in research and practice. In M. Ungar (Ed.), *Multisystemic resilience: Adaptation and transformation in contexts of change.* Oxford University Press.

Masten, A. (2021b). Resilience of children in disasters: A multisystem perspective. *International Journal of Psychology, 56*(1), 1–11.

Masten, A., & Motti-Stefanidi, F. (2020). Multisystem resilience for children and youth in disaster: Reflections in the context of COVID-19. *Adversity and Resilience Science, 1,* 95–106.

Mukherjee, S., & Kumar, U. (2017). Psychological resilience: A conceptual review of theory and research. In U. Kumar (Ed.), *The Routledge international handbook of psychosocial resilience.* Routledge.

Nation, I. S. P. (2013). *Learning vocabulary in another language.* Cambridge University Press.

Oxford, R. L. (1990). *Language learning strategies: What every teacher should know.* Heinle & Heinle.

Plikat, J. (2017). *Fremdsprachliche Diskursbewusstheit als Zielkonstrukt des Fremdsprachenunterrichts: eine kritische Auseinandersetzung mit der Interkulturellen Kompetenz.* Peter Lang.

Provitolo, D., & Reghezza-Zitt, M. (2015). Resilience and vulnerability: From opposition towards a continuum. In M. Reghezza-Zitt, & S. Rufat (Eds.), *Resilience imperative: Uncertainty, risks and disasters.* Iste.

Shaver, A. (2021). Resilience and teaching: New resources coming soon for teachers – Four lessons for high school students will promote resilience. *American Psychological Association.* https://www.apa.org/ed/precollege/psychology-teacher-network/introductory-psychology/resilience-teaching-resources

Smith, M. (2020). *Becoming buoyant: Helping teachers and students cope with the day to day.* Routledge.

Steinberg, S. W. (2020). Special issue introduction: 50 years of critical pedagogy and we still aren't critical. *Taboo: The Journal of Culture and Education, 19*(2), 3–5.

Teng, F. M. (2019). *Autonomy, agency, and identity in teaching and learning English as a foreign language.* Springer.

UNESCO. (Ed.). (2021). *Education for sustainable development.* https://en.unesco.org/themes/education-sustainable-development

Weiner, B. (2010). The development of an attribution-based theory of motivation: A history of ideas. *Educational Psychologist, 45*(1), 28–36.

Wustmann Seiler, C. (2020). *Resilienz: Widerstandsfähigkeit von Kindern in Tageseinrichtungen fördern.* Cornelsen.

Part II
Empirical Inquiries

7 Learner Perceptions of Taboo Topics in English Language Teaching

Theresa Summer and Jeanine Steinbock

Introduction

At schools, curricular guidelines commonly provide the basis for English language teaching (ELT). Amidst the number of competences learners should develop, however, English language teachers have a certain scope for decision-making with regard to the content they choose for developing various competences. Due to the certain degree of freedom teachers have when selecting content and topics, controversial and taboo topics that are relevant to learners' lives could potentially play a key role in increasing learners' interest and motivation. Furthermore, they could pave the way for critical foreign language education, which is considered essential to "aggressively name and interrogate potentially harmful ideologies and practices" in classrooms (Bartolomé, 2004, p. 98). Finding out which topics learners are interested in and which topics they would like to encounter in English lessons is thus a prerequisite for the development of teaching practices and resources.

Listening to students' voices is a central paradigm within critical language pedagogy. As Edes (2020) highlights, "[s]tudent voice is not just a privilege for students, but a must for proper and sustainable education" (p. 81). Edes further emphasises that students should be encouraged to make their own choices in educational settings. This applies to learners' choices of subject matter and content in English language education, which should derive from their immediate social, cultural, and political surroundings (Abendroth-Timmer, 2020). In this context, a frequently discussed problem is that textbooks do and cannot always meet those demands due to strict political regulations, the long publication process and copyright restrictions involved in their development. As Gray criticises, textbooks are often "sanitized for commercial purposes", which thus "neutralizes the material and often prevents linguistic engagement with certain topics" (Gray, 2002, pp. 159–160). What is more, as publishers often avoid parsnippy themes in textbooks (see Ludwig & Summer, this volume), these materials can, to a certain degree, be described as "meaningless" (Leonhardt & Viebrock, 2020, p. 42). In a study investigating topic preferences among Turkish ELT students and teachers in textbooks, Kazazoğlu and Sarıçoban (2012) found that the large majority of ELT students had an unfavourable attitude towards current

DOI: 10.4324/9781003220701-10

textbook topics – thus suggesting that taboos should be included in textbooks to increase student motivation and participation.

Against this background, our aim was to identify which topics play a central role in learners' lives. Previous studies examined children and adolescents' interests in general, such as the Shell youth study that investigated adolescents' perception of the future from personal and social viewpoints indicating an increase in the awareness of holistic social problems such as environmental protection (Albert et al., 2019). Other studies, such as the study "Jugendsexualität" (youth sexuality), for instance, are issue specific, focusing on adolescents' attitudes towards sexuality (BZgA, 2019). To date, no studies have focused specifically on various taboos that may increasingly influence learners through digital media. To fill this gap, this study examined learners' perspectives concerning taboo topics in Germany, focusing on the following three research questions:

1 Which taboos are learners interested in and confronted with in their spare time?
2 Which taboos have learners encountered in classroom settings and which topics would they like to deal with in classroom settings?
3 What is the potential of taboos for ELT?

After a presentation of our research interests and an outline of the questionnaire, we present and discuss the main findings of the survey.

Research Methodology

Survey Design

We developed the online survey "Topics in school education" (issued in German: "Themen im Unterricht") out of the hypothesis that learners are frequently confronted with taboos in their daily lives but are only rarely given the opportunity to deal with such topics in school and in English lessons. To examine the questions listed above, we developed an online questionnaire using the platform Soscisurvey with a total of eight closed-ended questions and one open-ended question (see Appendix). The sampling method involved distributing the online survey through an advertising campaign on Facebook and Instagram using a self-designed meme and offering vouchers as incentives during a two months period from July 2020. This sampling method allowed us to reach out to participants across Germany. This evidently meant that only adolescents using Facebook or Instagram were actively invited to participate.

Both in the title and in the introduction of the survey, we refrained from using the term *taboo topics* to avoid a priming effect indicating a negative connotation (Hermans et al., 1994). Instead, we introduced participants to a questionnaire on topics they might encounter in their everyday lives. Later in the questionnaire, we introduced the term *taboo topics*. To avoid possible negative effects on participants finding themselves in a currently difficult personal situation, we discussed our questionnaire with a psychotherapist and added a note on where to find help. The preselected topics allowed us to compare learners' interests and examine their perceptions of taboos with regard to ELT, as outlined in the following.

Selecting Taboos and Challenging Topics

The survey focused on 18 different topics (see Table 7.1) that set the basis for the research project "Taboos in ELT" (see also Summer & Ludwig, this volume). The chosen topics derive from research within two areas: (1) the field of critical language pedagogy in which social justice issues related to the categories of race/ethnicity, class, gender/sexuality, and disabilities play a key role (Crookes, 2013; Freire, 2014; Giroux, 1983; Pennycook, 2001) and (2) an analysis of previously published resource materials focusing on taboo, controversial, and tough topics. Concerning the latter, we analysed teaching resources that address taboo topics. Given that materials on taboos are "rather under-developed" (Crookes, 2013, p. 13), we focused on two main resources: *Taboos and Issues* (MacAndrew & Martínez, 2001) and the journal *PARSNIP in ELT: Stepping out of the comfort zone* (Volumes 1–3; Seburn et al., 2016).

The topics that emerged from this research resulted in a very extensive and detailed list of topics, including various subtopics (see mindmap in Ludwig & Summer, this volume). For the "Taboos in ELT" research project, we decided to focus on 18 topics that we considered politically and socially relevant and partly also potentially suitable for the development of various competencies within ELT. Criteria for selecting the topics were that they covered a great variety of issues within the different domains of social (in)justice(s) as well as topics that can be assumed to play an influential role in the lives of adolescents. Given the fluidity of the 18 taboos selected for this study, this list is evidently not complete and can be updated and replaced with other topics. Therefore, the study does not claim to investigate all taboos that might potentially be of interest to learners. What is more, we are using the term *taboos* in reference to topics that we consider partly taboo (not talked about in educational settings),

Table 7.1 Survey Questionnaire: "Taboo Topics" in Focus

1. Drugs	10. Homosexuality
2. Other addictive behaviour	11. Racism
3. Gender reassignment	12. Religious conflicts
4. Illnesses	13. Migration and refuge
5. Death	14. Radicalism
6. Disabilities	15. Conspiracy theories and fake news
7. Poverty and unemployment	16. Violence
8. Sex and dangers	17. Self-mutilation
9. Sex and love	18. Environmentally destructive lifestyles

challenging, and tough in a broader sense (see Ludwig & Summer, this volume); we were *not* asking learners which topics they consider taboo or topics they do *not* wish to discuss in education. The aim was to provide a broad range of topics that relate not only to social (in)justice themes but also to social, health, and specific teenage issues such as drugs, sex, conspiracy theories and fake news, and self-mutilation. In the survey, we included short explanations for more complex topic categories and offered some examples to avoid confusion or misunderstanding.

Descriptive Survey Results

The data revealed 841 valid cases. We gathered data from adolescents across all 16 federal states in Germany, with the majority of participants coming from Bavaria (19.7%), followed by North Rhine-Westphalia (15.6%). There was a predominance of female participants (69.6%) over male participants (26.9%) and participants of diverse sex (2.3%). Fifteen-year-olds were the largest represented age group, followed by 17-year-olds. The following sections present the three main categories of the survey: learners' engagement with taboo topics (1) in their spare time, (2) in class, and (3) in English lessons.

Spare Time

The first question (Q1) asked participants which topics they were interested in their spare time and to what extent. They showed the most interest in the topics of illnesses, racism, and love and sexuality. Topics that participants showed less or no interest in were gender reassignment ("not really"/"not at all" 61.4%), drugs ("not really"/"not at all" 60.4%), and conspiracy theories/fake news ("not really"/"not at all" 50.6%). The next item (Q2) listed possible passive encounters, i.e., media formats with preselected taboo topics (drugs, sex/love, sex/danger, homosexuality, racism, radicalism, conspiracy theories/fake news, violence, and bullying), which we expected to be the most prominent taboos in adolescents' spare time. The passive encounters include pictures/photos, videos, personal conversations, online chat, forwarded links, and others. With regard to the preselected topics, more than half of the participants (n = 458) reported that they encountered the topic of sexuality and love through personal conversations, revealing parallels with the findings by the previously mentioned study on youth sexuality (BZgA, 2019). As for racism, to give another example, 455 participants reported they encountered this topic through pictures and/or photos. Overall, these outcomes indicate both the relevance of peer contacts as well as that of digital content. In other words, personal conversations and digital access to visual

Learner Perceptions of Taboo Topics in English Language Teaching 75

media in particular seem to have an impact on adolescents' interest in certain taboos such as sexuality and racism.

In Class

In Q3, we aimed to identify which topics adolescents have dealt with at school and how frequently. In the overview presented in Table 7.2, items are ranked according to frequency, adding the attributes "very often"/"often".

Among the three apparently most neglected topics in school, 57.4% of participants stated that they had never talked about homosexuality in class. 59.5% of participants had never spoken about self-mutilation and 77.6% never addressed gender reassignment in class.

In Q4, the term *taboo topics* was introduced to participants stating: "The topics you read about can also be called taboos or taboo topics. They could also be dealt with at school. Please rate the following statements". Participants were asked to attribute their degree of (dis-)agreement on whether taboo topics are "interesting", "embarrassing", "exciting", "motivating", "frightening" and "important". In total, 81.1% of participants ($n = 837$) "strongly agreed"/"agreed" with taboo topics being important to deal with in class.

Table 7.2 Taboo Topics Dealt with at School ("Very Often"/"Often")

First category (*most frequently dealt with at schools*)	*Second category*	*Third category*
• Environmentally destructive lifestyles (28.1%; $n = 836$) • Illnesses (24.1%; $n = 837$) • Racism (23.8%; $n = 834$)	• Migration and refuge (22.9%; $n = 832$) • Poverty and unemployment (21.5%; $n = 836$) • Violence (20.5%; $n = 835$) • Religious conflicts (19.0%; $n = 836$) • Drugs (16.7%; $n = 836$) • Sex and danger (16.6%; $n = 836$) • Sex and love (16.4%; $n = 836$)	• Other addictive behaviour (13.5%; $n = 836$) • Death (12.5%; $n = 835$) • Radicalism (10.2%; $n = 836$) • Disabilities (8.6%; $n = 835$) • Conspiracy theories/fake news (8.5%; $n = 836$) • Homosexuality (4.5%; $n = 836$) • Self-mutilation (4.1%; $n = 835$) • Gender reassignment (1.7%; $n = 836$)

70.0% "strongly disagreed"/"disagreed" that talking about taboo topics would be embarrassing. 76.4% noted that taboo topics would be exciting and 54.9% disagreed with taboo topics being frightening. The vast majority of participants (89.3%) stated that talking about taboos in class would be important (see Figure 7.1). As such, we can conclude that the great majority of adolescents see taboos as highly significant topics that they would like to address in school education.

English Lessons

The subsequent part of the survey focused on English lessons. Q5 asked participants, "Regardless of your current or past teacher, would you like to deal with the following topics in English lessons?", rating their answers from 5 (*very much*) to 1 (*not at all*). The topics ranking highest were racism, environmentally destructive lifestyles, and illnesses. The topics ranking lowest were sex and danger, radicalism, and gender reassignment (see Table 7.3).

Another aspect of interest in the survey was the practical dimension of working with taboos in ELT (Q6). We asked learners to rate an imaginary teaching scenario that deals with a taboo topic (e.g., drugs or racism) in an English lesson through watching a short film, analysing a song, and discussing the topic. Overall, participants expressed a significant interest in this approach: 72.3% stated they would "very much like to"/"like to" participate in such a lesson.

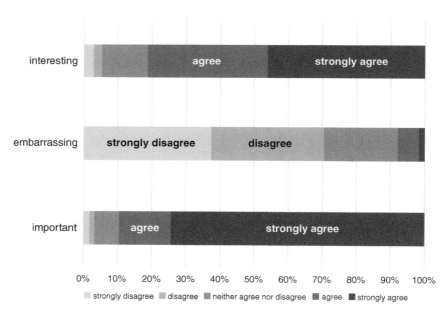

Figure 7.1 Responses to Q4: "In my View, Dealing with Taboo Topics in Class is…".

Table 7.3 Taboos: Average Rating of Interest in English Lessons (1 = Not at All; 5 = Very Much)

Taboo topic	Average rating of interest
Racism	3.28
Environmentally destructive lifestyles	3.13
Illnesses	3.10
Sex and dangers	2.72
Radicalism	2.66
Gender reassignment	2.65

The penultimate item of the closed-ended questions (Q7) asked adolescents to express their choice of media for dealing with taboos in ELT. Over 80% (81.3%, n = 839) of the participants responded that they would like to use short films when exploring taboos. Inviting affected people (68.0%) seemed about just as appealing as using the internet or social media (64.4%). 50.5% of participants would like to work with feature films, whereas the least popular text formats were the textbook (18.5%), literary texts (16.3%), graphic novels/comics (14.4%), and picturebooks (9.2%).

Personal involvement, however, seems to be an issue for some participants. When asked if they wanted to deal with taboos even though they personally affected them, 27.8% stated it to be unlikely and 18.7% stated "no".

Discussion

Based on the summary of the study's key findings presented above, this section discusses three central outcomes:

1 Participants consider taboo topics important in school education.
2 Participants seem to be interested in currently and politically relevant topics such as racism and consider these crucial for ELT.
3 Participants prefer to use audio-visual and digital texts compared to printed (literary) texts when dealing with taboos.

Considering the first major finding, participants generally showed a positive attitude towards taboo topics in class. As a generation that seems to be aware of social injustice issues such as racism (see Braselmann, this volume), they consented to the importance of addressing such topics in ELT. Yet, as mentioned above, the preselected list of topics for the survey means that only a selection of a (in reality) much greater variety of topics was in focus. Due to current political and socio-cultural events, taboo topics are always in flux, resulting in an urge to address new topics in the future that we may not have heard of today. As such, we argue for a student-centred approach to dealing with taboo topics in which teachers address the variety of topics learners encounter through peers (e.g., through text messaging) and the media in their everyday lives. If we see this as a premise for motivation and engagement in learning, ELT should take this pluralism of topics into account. A careful engagement with these issues in the protected setting of a pedagogic context could potentially prevent anxiety and equip learners with the skills needed to react appropriately in certain challenging situations. This seems to be of particular importance, as we identified a certain degree of hesitation among adolescents in dealing with topics that personally affected them. At the same time, however, it is absolutely crucial for teachers to seek professional advice, i.e., from school psychologists, especially when dealing with taboos that could lead to harm or poor (mental) health among adolescents.

For English lessons in particular, we can draw several conclusions from this study. There still seems to be a certain discrepancy between the taboos that adolescents encounter in their free time and the topics addressed in school. For instance, looking more closely at gender reassignment, 600 (71.8%) participants answered that they "never" dealt with this issue at school. Since participants see English lessons as a suitable environment for dealing with taboos, integrating them into English classrooms would therefore be worth considering.

In the context of choosing texts for English lessons, a pop-cultural approach (Summer, forthcoming) seems promising. The data of this study suggest that pop culture artefacts such as short films and songs are considered suitable and motivating by learners (72.3% would like to/very much like to participate in such lessons). At the same time, however, findings illustrating that picturebooks, for example, are less popular formats indicate that adolescents may not yet have discovered the potential of such texts because they may not have used them in secondary ELT. Working with a combination of pop-cultural and literary texts through text ensembles (see Braselmann, this volume) could thus open up avenues for developing learners' taboo literacy in foreign language education. Further research could follow up on this and evaluate the perception of this multimedia approach in the context of taboo topics and derive media-supported teaching designs for integrating taboo topics into ELT practices.

Conclusion

This survey investigated adolescents' perspectives on taboos and challenging topics in their spare time, education, and ELT in Germany. Given that, according to López-Gopar (2018), "[children's] lives must be taken seriously should we not want critical pedagogy to be yet another grand narrative and imposition in their lives" (p. 243), we consider an investigation of learners' interests as crucial for the application of critical pedagogy to educational practice. Due to the lack of surveys investigating topics that go beyond everyday life communicative issues, the aim of this questionnaire was to fill this gap in research. Despite its discussed limitations, this study provides a first insight into adolescents' voices on taboos in education. As Edes (2020) criticises, "[t]he voices of youth are not only not heard but also often ignored" (p. 84). Therefore, listening to our youth's voices is crucial so that we can take learners' lives, interests, hopes, and problems seriously. In practice, this, among other issues of course, implies that teachers, preferably called "coaches" by Edes (2020, p. 84), need to listen to their students' voices by asking them about taboos relevant to their lives. Our findings strongly suggest that adolescents agree with this while acknowledging the importance of these topics in school education and expressing an open-mindedness as well as a sense of embracing this approach, with some care and reservation, especially if they are themselves affected.

The list of topics chosen for this study presents examples of important controversial and taboo topics that will, in different places in the world and in the future, most probably look very different. Consequently, examining learners' perspectives on topics for education is important with regard to: (1) research (such as this study) that examines learners' interests in a particular country, Germany in this case, and (2) the classroom – the local level. Whereas research outcomes from studies such as this one can provide a first guideline for curriculum development and materials design, it is equally important at a local and practical level for educators to find out more about their learners' interests. They can do this by conducting short questionnaires to explore which topics learners wish to deal with in the classroom. As Freire (2014) notes, "there is no educational practice without content" (p. 103), and thus, it is crucial to explore which topics are prevalent in learners' lives and which topics are suitable for ELT, which are not, and which topics require additional support – for instance, by psychotherapists. Furthermore, the findings discussed above could be supplemented with interviews and classroom observations to delve deeper into the practical side of how to best handle taboos (and which taboos) in practical teaching.

Finally, in future research, practitioners and researchers could address two key questions: (1) How can future foreign language education consider learners' interests and integrate them in practice? and (2) How can different texts be integrated into teaching practice when addressing taboos? Finding answers to these questions could help promote the integration of critical foreign language pedagogy into ELT.

References

Abendroth-Timmer, D. (2020). Kritisch–reflexive Professionalisierung von Fremdsprachenlehrenden: Ein dramapädagogisch–hochschuldidaktischer Ansatz. In D. Gerlach (Ed.), *Kritische Fremdsprachendidaktik: Grundlagen, Ziele, Beispiele* (pp. 199–215). Narr.

Albert, M., Hurrelmann, K., & Quenzel, G. (2019). *Jugend 2019. Eine Generation meldet sich zu Wort*. Weinheim.

Bartolomé, L. I. (2004). Critical pedagogy and teacher education: Radicalizing prospective teachers. *Teacher Education Quarterly, 31*(1), 97–122.

Bundeszentrale für gesundheitliche Aufklärung (BZgA). (2019). Jugendsexualität. https://www.forschung.sexualaufklaerung.de/jugendsexualitaet/jugendsexualitaet-neunte–welle/

Crookes, G. (2013). *Critical ELT in action. Foundations, promises, praxis*. Routledge.

Dornyei, Z., & Taguchi, T. (2009). *Questionnaires in second language research: Construction, administration, and processing*. Taylor & Francis Group.

Edes, I. (2020). Listening to student voice. *Taboo: The Journal of Culture and Education*, *19*(2), 81–91. https://digitalscholarship.unlv.edu/taboo/vol19/iss2/7

Freire, P. (2014). *Pedagogy of hope. Reliving pedagogy of the oppressed*. Bloomsbury Academic.

Giroux, H. G. (1983). *Theory and resistance in education: A pedagogy for the opposition*. Bergin & Garvey.

Gray, J. (2002). The global coursebook in English language teaching. In D. Block, & D. Cameron (Eds.), *Globalization and language teaching* (pp. 151–166). Routledge.

Hermans, D., De Houwer, J., & Eelen, P. (1994). The affective priming effect: Automatic activation of evaluative information in memory. *Cognition and Emotion*, *8*(6), 515–533.

Kazazoğlu, S., & Sarıçoban, A. (2012). Topic preferences of Turkish ELT students and teachers in text books. *Sino-US English Teaching*, *9*(2), 887–892.

Leonhardt, J.-E., & Viebrock, B. (2020). Ausgewählte Materialien für einen kritisch orientierten Fremdsprachenunterricht: Jugendliteratur mit Transgender-Thematik. In D. Gerlach (Ed.). *Kritische Fremdsprachendidaktik: Grundlagen, Ziele, Beispiele* (pp. 37–52). Narr.

López-Gopar, M. E. (2018). Critical pedagogy and teaching English to children. In S. Garton, & F. Copland (Eds.), *The Routledge handbook of teaching English to young learners* (pp. 234–246). Routledge.

MacAndrew, R., & Martínez, R. (2001). *Taboos and issues: Photocopiable lessons on controversial topics*. Thomson Learning.

Pennycook, A. (2001). *Critical applied linguistics: A critical introduction*. Lawrence Erlbaum.

Seburn, T., Finegan, K., Greene, S., Howard, R., Lam, N., Petrie, D., & Veigga, T. (2016). *Parsnips in ELT: Stepping out of the comfort zone* (Vol. 3). Smashwords. https://www.smashwords.com/books/view/669186

Summer, T. (forthcoming). *Pop culture in English language education: From theory to practice*. ESV.

8 Taboos in Language Teacher Education
A Survey of Pre-Service Teachers' Attitudes

Theresa Summer and Christian Ludwig

Introduction

Pre-service teachers studying TEFL (Teaching English as a Foreign Language) to become teachers of English at primary or secondary schools commonly take part in a range of introductory, topic-specific, and practice-oriented seminars at university. Focusing on a variety of key aspects, central themes within these courses in Germany are language acquisition, skills and competence development, trans-/intercultural learning, differentiation, the use of different types of media and (literary) texts, lesson planning, and assessment. These central aspects typically feature in a range of introductory TEFL books (e.g., Gehring 2021; Grimm et al., 2015) that set the basis for many introductory seminars as well as more subject-specific seminars dealing with individual topics such as differentiation or literary texts in English language teaching (ELT). Addressing taboos might therefore seem like the odd-one out. Yet, scholars in Germany have recently turned to discuss the importance of integrating critical pedagogy into foreign language education (e.g., Gerlach, 2020). As for other countries such as the UK, lecturers have included concepts of critical thinking in degree programmes for non-native English speakers (Wharton, 2011). Despite these attempts, research within the field of pre-service teachers' attitudes towards the integration of taboo topics into TEFL seminars and ELT has been scarce. This contribution aims to fill this gap in the context of German teacher education of TEFL at universities.

In our university seminars, students have frequently expressed an interest in addressing controversial topics and asked questions about how to incorporate them into the classroom. This interest, for instance, emerged out of current political events such as the #MeToo debate, themes explored in (young adult) literary texts such as homosexuality or challenging situations students encountered in internships in which teenagers were bullied, confronted with sexting, or committed self-harm. Motivated by their curiosity as well as the importance of developing taboo literacy (see Ludwig & Summer, this volume), we decided to investigate the relevance of taboos in and for foreign language (teacher) education in an online survey. As such, after a short outline of the study, this contribution presents the main results while discussing implications for future teacher education programmes.

DOI: 10.4324/9781003220701-11

The Study

This study is part of a larger "Taboos in ELT" project that aims to identify the affordances and challenges related to an integration of different taboo topics in teacher education and English teaching practice. Using Dörnyei and Taguchi's (2009) guideline for constructing and administering questionnaires as a basis, data for this study were collected in a survey of 210 pre-service teachers studying English at German universities to become primary or secondary school teachers (n = 210). We piloted the survey in several stages by contacting the students at our universities (Würzburg and Berlin) as well as other universities through colleagues and professional networks across Germany. We used Google questionnaire and gathered data from June until October 2020. The participants, 77% of whom are female, 21.5% male, and 1.5% diverse, come from 11 different federal states in Germany. Consequently, the outcomes apply to this specific group only and they are not statistically representative. The predominance of female participants is, in our view, more or less representative of the gender distribution among students of TEFL in Germany.

The data source comprised a set of 16 closed questions and further questions on socio-demographics. In addition, the final open question asked students about their general opinion on integrating taboo topics into ELT, which is analysed elsewhere (Ludwig & Summer, 2022). A collection of 18 topics provided the basis for investigating different types of taboos related to gender (e.g., homosexuality, sex and dangers, sex and love) and conflicts (e.g., religious conflicts, radicalism, violence, self-mutilation), and as well as various other topics (see also Summer & Steinbock, this volume). For the design of the survey items, we included this list of topics in only six questions and included a range of other questions, which we discuss below, to avoid monotony (Petersen, 2014). Given the great diversity of the taboo topics included in the survey, each of which poses different challenges for classroom practice, our interest was to investigate whether (and, if so, how), teacher education can stay up-to-date with current needs of today's society while identifying general trends in pre-service teachers' attitudes towards taboos in ELT. More specifically, the study addressed the following research questions:

1 To what extent do university students perceive a mismatch between the presence of taboo topics in their lives and the topics dealt with at university?
2 To what extent are university students interested in addressing taboo topics and related pedagogic frameworks in TEFL seminars?
3 Which aspects do university students consider crucial for ELT practice when dealing with taboo topics (e.g., materials, challenges, guidelines)?

Importantly, the study focused on a pre-given set of taboo topics (see Summer & Steinbock, this volume); identifying pre-service teachers' perspective on other taboo topics would evidently require a further study. The following section presents an analysis of the main study results and discusses various implications focusing particularly on teacher education programmes.

Data Analysis and Discussion

This section summarises and discusses the general findings of the descriptive analysis concerning pre-service English teachers' perception of taboos. The findings relate to three main aspects: (1) university students' general perception of and experiences with taboo topics, (2) their perspective on the potential of taboos for ELT, and (3) challenges related to taboos in ELT – discussed in this order in the following sections.

Pre-Service Teachers' Experience with Taboos

This section discusses data related to pre-service teachers' experience with taboos in their everyday lives as well as their university studies of TEFL and their school experiences. To identify pre-service teachers' interests among multiple taboos, the first question examined pre-service teachers' interests in taboo topics in their spare time (see Figure 8.1).

Participants are mostly interested in the topic racism, which 83% of pre-service teachers are either "very interested" or "interested" in; this item also had the lowest standard deviation ($SD = 0.87$). Political developments and frequent media reports in 2020 related to the Black Lives Matter Movement and police violence against PoC might offer one explanation for this strong interest. The second most popular topic is illnesses (78% are "very interested" and "interested" [combined] in this topic), followed by environmentally destructive behaviour (68% are "very interested" and "interested" [combined] in this topic). Again, the Coronavirus pandemic, its impact on people's mental health and their COVID-19-related psychological stress (Wang et al., 2020) as well as media reports on and young people's interest in climate change (Deetjen & Ludwig, 2021) might explain this comparably high interest. In contrast to these top three topics, participants are least interested in the topics drugs and self-mutilation. Clearly, these topics, especially self-mutilation, are more specific than the other topics (compared to, for instance, the topics violence and radicalism also listed in the study), and this might therefore explain the lower level of interest. Nonetheless, we can conclude that currently relevant topics frequently addressed in the media and social media channels seem to be met with the greatest interest. For teacher education, this suggests that fostering critical literacy through a consideration of course participants' current interests is important as this might increase their intrinsic motivation in dealing with a topic and different texts on that topic.

When asked through which formats participants encounter different taboo topics, they referred to a number of different formats. They clicked racism most frequently in combination with different formats – a topic they encounter mostly through personal conversations, followed closely by videos and pictures or photos

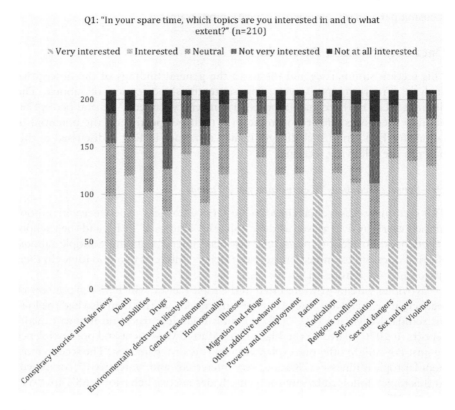

Figure 8.1 Taboo Topics Pre-Service Teachers Show Most Interest in.

(see Figure 8.2). This item has an important implication for educational practice: If university students encounter a topic they show great interest in through a multi-text approach, i.e. a variety of different textual formats in their real lives, this should be reflected in classroom practice. In the context of integrating queer perspectives into ELT, Merse (2017) also stresses the importance of working with text ensembles, allowing students to explore a given topic through different modes and from different perspectives. What is more, using texts that students encounter in their everyday lives such as videos and online chats, can provide authentic insights into the presence of taboos in everyday discourse. Further, it can influence the power dynamics in the classroom if teachers give learners a chance to include text types and media channels of their own. If this succeeds in improving social justice and raising the status of marginalised groups such as people with disabilities, for instance, as emphasised by Wharton (2011), we can fulfil one major goal of critical pedagogy.

Further items focused on pre-service teachers' experiences as learners at school. One major finding is that, generally, participants reportedly dealt with taboos

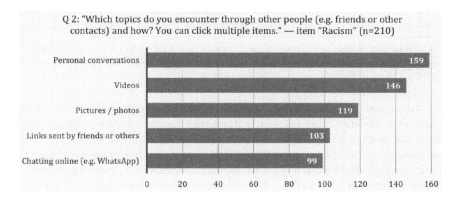

Figure 8.2 Formats Through which Pre-Service Teachers Encounter the Topic Racism.

in school education. Regardless of the subject English, they noted that violence is the topic they dealt with most frequently (32% "very often" and "often", combined) followed by illnesses, racism, and religious conflicts. Taboo topics in the literal sense were gender reassignment, self-mutilation, conspiracy theories, and homosexuality. Concerning homosexuality, 49% of participants noted that they "never" dealt with homosexuality; 40% "rarely" dealt with this topic. As various studies show that a considerable number of teenagers reject traditional gender terms such as man or woman or identify as transgender or gender fluid statistically (Hammack et al., 2021), this is an eye-opening result. It seems as though hardly anyone in school education feels responsible for dealing with this topic. This invisibility and underrepresentation can have devastating effects on adolescents if they do not feel represented – neither in classroom discourse nor in teaching materials. As concerns the latter, textbooks are often characterised by a traditional heterosexual representation of characters, as found in a recent study of grade 9 English textbooks in Germany (Alter et al., 2021).

When we asked participants which topics they felt were neglected at schools, and they could tick all that apply, the following emerged as the five top neglected topics: Illnesses, homosexuality, gender reassignment, sex and dangers, and racism (see Table 8.1).

The high number of clicks for these overall illustrates that various topics are literally tabooed in education. Concerning sex and dangers, for instance, this is an important topic that could be addressed in ELT, especially with the aim of protecting adolescents as sexual practices are moving online and sexting can result in personal conflicts (see Haskins & Ludwig, this volume). Overall, this disregard of taboo topics is also confirmed by students' agreement over the fact that taboos were not dealt with enough in their English lessons. In sum, 79% stated that they "fully agree" (62 out of $n = 187$) and "agree" (85 out of $n = 187$) with the given statement that "Taboo topics were marginalised in my English lessons at school" (Q 9).

Table 8.1 Top Five Neglected Taboo Topics at Schools

1. Illnesses	2. Homosexuality	3. Gender reassignment	4. Sex and dangers	5. Racism
172 clicks	164 clicks	150 clicks	148 clicks	139 clicks

Note. n = 210.

Focusing on their studies at university, the subsequent part of the study found that students most frequently dealt with the two topics of racism, and migration and refuge. Topics such as self-mutilation, sex and love, sex and dangers, and drugs were least covered in TEFL seminars. Given the dominance of these themes in public discourse and popular culture, this is a surprising result. The majority of students (79%), however, agree that taboo topics are not covered sufficiently in education at university (79 "fully agree"; 87 "agree" out of n = 210). This suggests that university lecturers should try to consider taboos and integrate these more and systematically into their teacher education programs. Importantly, also, 94% stress the importance of dealing with taboos in teacher training courses (133 "fully agree"; 65 "agree" out of n = 210). This is an indication of pre-service teachers' interest in finding out more about the practical dimension of handling taboos in educational settings. Furthermore, this suggests, in accordance with Bonnet and Hericks (2020), that critical foreign language pedagogy is less about thematic decisions, but more a question about teacher-student interaction (see Gardemann, this volume). Whereas this is true to a large extent, we would argue that thematic decisions are closely related to teacher-student interaction and can play a key role in establishing a trustworthy atmosphere – for instance, if teachers give learners a say in which taboos they wish to discuss and which ones they wish to keep private.

Pre-Service Teachers' Attitudes towards the Potential of Taboos for ELT

This section focuses specifically on pre-service teachers' attitudes towards the potential of taboos for teaching English. Regarding participants' openness to discuss taboo topics in ELT, 41% describe their attitude as "very open" and 42% as "open". Strikingly, none of the participants stated they are "not open at all" and only four (2%) said they were "not very open"; 15% "more or less open". We can conclude, therefore, that future teachers' open attitude towards addressing taboos in practice exemplifies the need to integrate critical foreign language pedagogy into teacher education programmes.

A further item introduced eight adjectives describing taboos in ELT: *frightening, important, emotionally disturbing, challenging, motivating, exciting, embarrassing*, and *interesting*. When asked, "To what extent do you agree with the following statements?" (Q 9, see Table 8.2) participants responded as follows:

Overall, respondents most frequently indicated three adjectives: challenging (98% "strongly agree" and "agree", combined), interesting (99% "strongly

Table 8.2 Pre-Service Teachers' Opinion on Dealing with Taboos in the English Classroom

In my opinion, dealing with taboo issues in the English classroom is …	Strongly agree	Agree	Neither agree nor disagree	Disagree	Strongly disagree
… interesting	155	52	3	0	0
… embarrassing	1	19	39	78	73
… exciting	45	99	57	9	0
… motivating	48	105	50	5	2
… challenging	128	77	3	2	0
… emotionally disturbing	16	62	76	44	12
… important	181	25	4	0	0
… frightening	9	70	78	37	16

Note. $n = 210$.

agree" and "agree", combined), and important (98% "strongly agree" and "agree", combined). Some discrepancies arise out of these findings: Whereas participants value taboo topics for ELT due to their importance and the interest they seem to evoke, they are also aware of the fact that they are challenging. This generates tension in a pedagogic sense because an enormous interest is confronted with an enormous challenge to handle the complexity and trickiness of certain topics. This may lead to a situation where, despite their open attitude towards taboo issues, teachers may refrain from discussing delicate and sensitive issues with their students as they fear not to know enough about these topics and, even more importantly, do not trust themselves in being able to guide students through discussing them in the classroom.

As the previously analysed data above indicate, a multi-text approach seems to be most suitable for dealing with some taboo topics. Interestingly, when asked, "Which formats do you generally consider most suitable for dealing with taboo topics in ELT? Tick the top five", pre-service teachers consider short films most suitable for dealing with taboos. Among a list of various formats (see Figure 8.3), they clicked short films most frequently along with inviting people personally affected by a topic. With regard to the former, we assume that this underlines the fact that we live in an audio-visual age. The latter, however, is less realistic in EFL education in Germany because people personally affected would obviously not typically be native or proficient speakers of English. Yet, this illustrates that pre-service teachers consider it crucial to offer opportunities for learners to meet people who can talk to them about their personal experience with regard to, for instance, physical abuse, drug use, or self-mutilation. Given the common practice at many German schools to invite experts such as police officers or former alcoholics to talk about cybercrime or alcohol addiction, our data suggest that participants would welcome an increase in such projects. As such, for school development generally, we can conclude that a closer cooperation with

88 *Theresa Summer and Christian Ludwig*

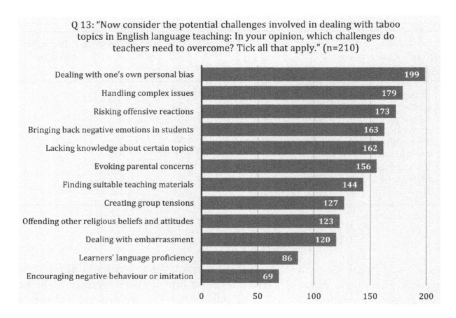

Figure 8.3 Potential Challenges when Dealing with Taboos.

individuals or organisations focusing on adolescents' healthy development could be beneficial.

Among the formats considered least suitable for addressing taboos, picturebooks and textbooks received fewest clicks. Only 20 out of 210 participants, 9.5%, consider picturebooks to be suitable; least participants, 7%, added textbooks. The former statistic might be related to the fact that most participants studied English for secondary school teaching; only 51 out of 201 (24%) studied English for primary education. As picturebooks are typically suggested for storytelling approaches in primary school education and scholars have only recently turned their attention to the use of picturebooks for more advanced learners (Alter & Merse, in press), we can assume that participants had little contact with picturebooks in the context of secondary ELT and, therefore, consider these texts less suitable.

The results generally indicate that participants consider non-pedagogic materials more suitable for developing taboo literacy than pedagogic materials – the English textbook of which is a central example. Among non-pedagogic texts, they rate digital and audio-visual media as more suitable. Although literary texts as a general category received 109 clicks and are thus considered suitable by 52% of participants, participants seem to underestimate the motivational and learning potential of multimodal texts such as picturebooks as well as comics and graphic novels. This is an indication of the fact that teacher education should include a greater range of multimodal texts (see Ludwig, this volume) to illustrate their broad range of topics to future teachers and pupils. Given the difficulties involved in categorising different text types, however, and the resulting imprecise categorisation in the examples listed in this item, this question would need to be addressed individually in a further study. We can say, however, that the outcomes provide substantial data highlighting the importance of Bland's recent call for more children's literature in teacher education (Bland, 2019). It implies that we need to include aspects related to the teaching of literature into TEFL teacher education programmes; we could even extend this with a call for more young adult's literature. It seems that pre-service teachers underestimate the enormous potential of working with literary (multimodal) texts, which have in recent years continued to be highlighted by various scholars (e.g., Bland, 2015; Delanoy et al., 2015). At the same time, this indicates a possible area for future research that could focus on the potential of literature to foster taboo literacy in teacher education programmes and in ELT practice.

Pre-Service Teacher Perceptions of Challenges Related to Taboos in ELT

The challenges teachers need to overcome when dealing with taboos in ELT were addressed in a following question (see Figure 8.3). From a list of 12 challenges, dealing with one's own personal bias, such as one's personal background and attitudes, is considered the biggest challenge followed by handling complex issues and risking offensive reactions. This illustrates the importance of incorporating taboo issues into university education as well as in-service teacher training, which should particularly emphasise approaches that help trainees overcome their personal biases and deal with potential challenges.

A further item, in which we asked pre-service teachers to rate various statements some of which were integrated into the discussion above, allows us to draw further conclusions with regard to challenges related to the practical dimension of integrating taboos in practice. Even though 91% of participants "fully agree" and "agree" (combined) that practical guidelines are required for dealing with taboo topics through pop culture artefacts, 99% (207 out of 210) of students reported that they do not know any specific approaches for dealing with taboo topics in educational practice. Only two respondents clicked "yes" indicating that they are familiar with such approaches. In their open responses, they listed two approaches: "Task based approach and, in addition, intercultural communicative competence" (P76) and "Critical media literacy" (P120). Given that only two pre-service teachers were able to link existing models such as task-based learning and critical media literacy to taboos, we need to find more transparent and systematic ways of integrating critical foreign language pedagogy not only into ELT practice, but also into teacher education programmes.

Implications for Teacher Education

The results of the study allow us to infer some preliminary implications for teacher education at university. First, teacher education should integrate taboo topics more systematically – both terms of methodology and materials. When university teachers deal with teaching methods and approaches, for instance, it is advisable to relate these to the development of critical literacy – thus integrating critical foreign language education bottom-up and making its importance transparent to pre-service teachers very early on. In addition, our data indicate that addressing currently relevant topics is important as well as connecting them to TEFL theory. Using multi-text approaches and focusing on media formats that are relevant to students' lives such as short films, for instance, is also central. For example, when talking about migration and refugees, written texts could be read together with analysing graphic novels and watching films as these different modes of input can support students in seeing different perspectives and gaining a better understanding of how different text and media convey information. This includes equipping future English teachers with necessary tools to critically analyse textbooks and other published teaching resources; or possibly use them as a starting point to develop an understanding of what a critical engagement with texts is all about. Finding ways of overcoming personal biases is crucial in this context, which furthermore calls for interdisciplinary courses and the integration of action research as an integral element of teacher education to help teachers investigate their students' media use and interests.

Conclusion

The present survey provides an insight into pre-service teachers' perceptions on the potential of taboos while also suggesting challenges and illustrating future pathways for teacher education. In sum, we can identify four key areas that summarise university students' attitudes towards taboo topics: (1) University students show a clear interest in currently relevant taboo topics; (2) they are open to address taboo topics in ELT, which means that we need to address them in both teacher education at university level as well as during pre- and in-service teacher training. The third and fourth aspects, however, are more complex. Whereas pre-service teachers (3) recognise the importance of addressing taboo topics in education, they are also (4) aware of the numerous challenges involved in addressing taboos in ELT. This has important implications for teaching practice and teacher education dealt with in this contribution. As pre-service teachers in Germany belong to a rather privileged social group studying to become English teachers in a country in which, to date, the teaching profession still enjoys some form of prestige, it seems that an exploration of social justice issues could be situated well into the context of addressing different taboo topics. By reflecting upon their own role in society and the privileged opportunities many will enjoy as future teachers, university students can be encouraged to acknowledge and critically reflect upon existing social and political inequities. This goes hand in hand with Wharton's call for social justice education that encourages "people in all social positions to understand the relationships between language and ideologies" (Wharton, 2011, p. 229). We can assume that, as taboos change or even disappear over time, future university students will be confronted with different taboos than today's students. Thus, an open attitude among teacher educators and university lecturers towards their students' interests in and experiences with taboo topics can offer rewarding opportunities for the development of taboo literacy – both among university students as well as their future learners. Having said that, of course, caution is required in terms of the specific taboo topic lecturers or teachers may deal with in practice as each taboo brings with it specific challenges among different groups of students.

References

Alter, G., König, L., & Merse, T. (2021). All inclusive? Eine kritische Lehrbuchanalyse zur Repräsentation von Diversität in Englischlehrbüchern der Klassenstufe 9. *Zeitschrift für Fremdsprachenforschung, 32*(1), 81–104.

Alter, G., & Merse, T. (Eds.). (forthcoming). *Re-thinking picturebooks for intermediate and advanced learners.* Narr.

Bland, J. (Ed.). (2015). *Teaching English to young learners: Critical issues in language teaching with 3–12 year olds.* Bloomsbury.

Bland, J. (2019). Teaching English to young learners: More teacher education and more children's literature! *Children's Literature in English Language Education, 7*(2), 79–103.

Bonnet, A., & Hericks, U. (2020). Fremdsprachendidaktik pädagogisch denken – oder: Was ein Staatsanwalt mit Englischunterricht zu tun hat. In D. Gerlach (Ed.), *Kritische Fremdsprachendidaktik: Grundlagen, Ziele, Beispiele* (pp. 165–180). Narr.

Deetjen, C., & Ludwig, C. (Eds.). (2021). *The world beyond: Developing critical environmental literacies in EFL.* Winter.

Delanoy, W., Eisenmann, M., & Matz, F. (Eds.). (2015). *Learning with literature in the EFL classroom.* Peter Lang.

Dörnyei, Z., & Taguchi, T. (2009). *Questionnaires in second language research: Construction, administration, and processing.* Taylor & Francis Group.

Gehring, W. (2021). *Englische Fachdidaktik: Forschung, Vermittlung, Unterricht.* ESV.

Gerlach, D. (Ed.). (2020). *Kritische Fremdsprachendidaktik: Grundlagen, Ziele, Beispiele.* Narr.

Grimm, N., Meyer, M., & Volkmann, L. (2015). *Teaching English.* Narr Francke Attempto.

Hammack, P. L., Hughes, S. D., Atwood, J. M., Cohen, E. M., & Clark, R. C. (2021). Gender and sexual identity in adolescence: A mixed-methods study of labeling in diverse community settings. *Journal of Adolescent Research,* 1–54. https://doi.org/10.1177/07435584211000315

Ludwig, C., & Summer, T. (2022). Integrating taboo topics into ELT: Investigating future English teachers' points of view. *Teacher Development Academic Journal, 2*(2), 42–48. https://tdsig.org/tdaj-v2n2/

Ludwig, C., & Deetjen, C. (Eds.). (2021). *The world beyond: Developing critical environmental literacies in EFL.* Winter.

Merse, T. (2017). *Other others, different differences: Queer perspectives on teaching English as a foreign language* [Dissertation, LMU München]. Elektronische Hochschulschriften der LMU München. https://edoc.ub.uni-muenchen.de/20597/1/Merse_Thorsten.pdf

Petersen, T. (2014). *Der Fragebogen in der Sozialforschung*. utb.

Wang, Y., Kala, M. P., & Jafar, T. H. (2020). Factors associated with psychological distress during the coronavirus disease 2019 (COVID-19) pandemic on the predominantly general population: A systematic review and meta-analysis. *PLoS One, 15*(12), Article e0244630. https://doi.org/10.1371/journal.pone.0244630

Wharton, S. (2011). Critical text analysis: Linking language and cultural studies. *ELT Journal, 65*(3), 221–229.

9 Teaching "13 Reasons Why"
A Study on the Importance of a Pedagogical Alliance in ELT

Christine Gardemann

Introduction

The EFL classroom traditionally familiarises learners with the histories and cultures of English-speaking countries. This includes introducing them to different perspectives that are supposed to help them critically evaluate their own points of view and expand their horizons (Volkmann, 2010). Works of fiction have the potential to facilitate these processes. Learners can be guided to put themselves into a fictional character's shoes to comprehend somebody else's actions, motives and emotions (Bredella, 2012). They can also be encouraged to discuss whether or not they would behave in the same way as the characters do in a story and notice similarities or differences between themselves and the characters, as well as between themselves and their fellow learners. This step requires learners to leave the fictional world and talk about their own experiences and opinions. While some will be open to freely sharing personal thoughts, others might feel uncomfortable doing so. What generally applies to fictional works is even more important when it comes to works that deal with controversial topics. In those cases, the fictional space can be understood as a "safe" space for learners. To honour this, teachers might allow learners to limit their contributions to discussing the fictional characters' views and actions, rather than revealing their personal opinions or experiences. Such a limitation, however, contradicts the conviction underlying the inclusion of controversial topics that by involving learners' personal opinions and experiences, meaningful learning can take place and critical thinking can be encouraged (Gerlach, 2020). Insights from professionalism research can help teachers navigate the challenge of wanting to critically engage learners while at the same time acknowledging learners' boundaries. In this context, it is particularly worthwhile to consider structural theory, the strand of professionalism research that focuses most on the complexities of the teacher-learner relationship that is particularly important when it comes to dealing with controversial topics sensitively.

This contribution first presents a brief introduction to structural theory and the idea of a pedagogical alliance, a concept by Helsper (2011), referring to a reciprocal relationship of mutual trust in the classroom. The contribution then uses an excerpt from a case study that I conducted to analyse how a well-intended

DOI: 10.4324/9781003220701-12

lesson on bullying in a Year 9 grammar school class falls flat when the learners reject the teacher's offer to contribute their personal opinions. It shows how the learning objective is not achieved due to a missing pedagogical alliance. The contribution concludes by suggesting practical implications for teaching and possible consequences for teacher education.

Theoretical Background: The Teacher-LearnerRelationship in Structural Theory

Since the 1980s, professionalism research in Germany has been dominated by structural theory, which since has been complemented by a competence-oriented and biographical approach to understanding teacher beliefs and actions (Terhart et al., 2011). Especially the sociologist Oevermann and the educationalist Helsper must be credited for applying structural theory to educational research. When teaching new subject matter, teachers present previously unknown problems to learners that they will not be able to solve unless they broaden their knowledge or apply a skill they have not yet learnt (Helsper, 2011). Every time learners face such a new problem, they are also confronted with the risk of failing. This is why structural theory describes every learning experience as a potential crisis: the initial uncertainty associated with tackling new challenges can be perceived as threatening (Oevermann, 1991). The teacher's role in structural theory is thus to both initiate a potential crisis and assist learners in overcoming this crisis. It becomes clear here why the teacher-learnerrelationship is at the centre of structural theory. Oevermann (1991) believes that learning can only successfully take place when both teachers and learners contribute to the learning process. In order to confidently tackle new challenges, learners need to trust their teachers when it comes to choosing appropriate materials and assignments and providing necessary scaffolding that allows them to solve a problem or master a new skill. To do that, teachers need to trust their learners to be open and honest about their knowledge, skills and struggles. It is this reciprocal relationship of mutual trust that Helsper (2011) refers to as "pedagogical alliance". In the following, excerpts from a case study with an experienced secondary school English teacher in Germany will illustrate the challenges teachers face in this context.

Research Methodology and Introduction to the Case Study

In a large-scale study that investigated the use of literary texts in secondary school EFL lessons (Gardemann, 2021), almost 400 teachers in Hamburg were asked about their text choices, the learning goals they aim at and the methods they make use of in Years 5–10. Based on the results of this survey, four teachers representing contrastive cases were approached for semi-narrative interviews, in which they were asked about their understanding of literature, their convictions and beliefs when it comes to choosing and teaching literary texts in the secondary EFL classroom and their roles as teachers in the literature classroom. The interviews were analysed using the Documentary Method that requires researchers to consider *what* is being said but pay particular attention to *how* things are said (Nohl, 2017). The overall aim of this approach is to reconstruct the interviewee's implicit knowledge, that is, the convictions, beliefs and attitudes that shape their actions to a higher degree than their explicit knowledge (cf. Caspari, 2003). In this contribution, I will use selected quotes from the interview with Mrs Wichmann who has 20 years of experience teaching English and Religious Studies at a German grammar school.

While talking about novels she had recently used in class, Mrs Wichmann mentioned her decision to discuss Jay Asher's (2017) youth adult novel *13 Reasons Why* with her Year 9. She was asked to elaborate on why she had chosen that particular novel and on how she had taught it. For readers to understand the interview excerpt discussed later, I will start with a brief summary of the novel and the critical debate surrounding it. The novel's main character is high school student Hannah, who has committed suicide by the time the novel begins. We learn about her story through cassette tapes which she has recorded and sent out to the 12 people named as the reasons for her suicide (one person is mentioned twice). While the novel gained popularity among its intended audience, psychologists were quick in criticising the author's portrayal of teenage suicide. The main focus of critics lies on the fact that Hannah's suicide is presented as being an overall comprehensible consequence of the bullying she experienced (Santana de Rosa et al., 2019). While the author emphasises that he intended to educate teenagers on the drastic consequences that seemingly harmless jokes can have on a sensitive person (e.g., Schulze, 2014), Hannah's decision to send accusatory tapes could be misunderstood as the ultimate revenge she could exact on her bullies. It has also been found that detailed, personalised reporting on suicides leads to a significant increase in both suicide attempts and suicides (for an overview of research on the Werther effect, cf. Brosius & Ziegler, 2001). Indeed, according to a National Institute of Health study, teenage suicide attempts significantly spiked after Netflix broadcast the first season of its series based on the novel (Bridge et al., 2019). In the light of these findings, the novel the series is based on should also be evaluated very carefully before being considered cannot be recommended for use in class.

Interview Analysis: "How Would You Feel Then?"

Mrs Wichmann is aware of the novel's theme being "hard fare" (Gardemann, 2021). However, she claims that as a teacher of English and Religious Studies, she is able to deal with possibly difficult topics "sensitively" (Gardemann, 2021). While Mrs Wichmann does not clarify what she means by "sensitively", this statement seems to be an indication of her belief that discussing difficult topics requires a safe and trusting atmosphere in the classroom, and as such, a working pedagogical alliance between herself and her learners. In the interview, Mrs Wichmann gives three reasons for choosing the novel for her Year 9. An unspecified time ago, she learnt about a suicidal girl in one of her other classes. While she says that she was happy learners trusted her enough to tell her about their classmate being in danger, she mainly describes feeling rather overwhelmed by the situation. She talks about how this experience made her realise that generally speaking, young people lack information on the topic of teenage suicide since it is "wonderfully hushed up and tabooed" (Gardemann, 2021, p. 238). Her goal in bringing the novel to her current class thus lies in providing learners with information about the broader context of teenage suicide and bullying. Since Hannah refers to the bullying she experienced at high school as one of the main reasons for her suicide, Mrs Wichmann says she also planned to discuss bullying to hopefully make her learners understand the dire consequences it can have.

Asked to elaborate on how she taught the novel, Mrs Wichmann talks about how she skipped an extensive pre-reading phase since she was pressured for time. Thus, she only asked her learners to complete a research assignment as homework, expecting them to look for information on teenage suicide online and report their findings to the class. Mrs Wichmann describes this approach as having "kind of ambushed" (Gardemann, 2021, p. 241) her class. This approach contrasts strongly with her previous assertion that she would deal with the topic of suicide "sensitively" (Gardemann, 2021, p. 237). Remarkably, Mrs Wichmann chooses the word "ambush" to describe the assignment, framing the homework as a surprise attack. This could indicate that looking back, she evaluates her approach critically. However, the qualifier "kind of" (Gardemann, 2021, p. 241) minimises the attack and so it seems that even in retrospect, Mrs Wichmann believes her approach to having been justified or appropriate. It is difficult, though, to reconcile her chosen approach with the concept of the pedagogical alliance: a teacher who, in her own words: ambushes her class does not build a trusting relationship with her learners.

Later in the interview, Mrs Wichmann describes a situation that happened in her class after the learners had just completed reading the second chapter, in which the main character Hannah describes a specific moment of feeling upset after being bullied at school. Mrs Wichmann recounts her attempts at starting a conversation about bullying with her learners.

> [I asked them] 'What do you think of her reaction now? Hannah's reaction? Is that exaggerated or do you think it's appropriate that she jumps at it like that? Or: How would you feel then?' [Hannah's] name appears in the second chapter on a Who's-hot-who's-not list as 'best ass of the year'. And that's something where many people would think: So? That's a compliment? But Hannah thought it was totally outrageous, because afterwards everyone felt obliged to grab her ass or stare at her ass. But that was a really cool point to get into a conversation with the learners: 'How would you like to have a list like that going around?' And then there were very clear statements by many of them. 'That wouldn't happen here. But it would happen in other classes.' And I thought okay, if they feel that they have a safe space in their class, then that's really great.
>
> (Gardemann, 2021, pp. 241–242)

Mrs Wichmann tries to make her learners connect to the fictional situation described in the novel. First, she asks them to comment on Hannah's reaction, for which they could keep an outsider's perspective. Mrs Wichmann does not state what the class' reaction to this first question was, but immediately adds a second question, aiming at a different level of engagement: "How would you feel then?" Here, she's asking the learners to put themselves into Hannah's position, which still allows them to comment on the situation without necessarily revealing their own thoughts. Again, Mrs Wichmann does not mention any learner reactions at this point. She then adds context information for the interviewer. Mrs Wichmann assumes that "many people" (Gardemann, 2021, p. 241) would consider being included on such a list to be a compliment rather than an instance of bullying. Mrs Wichmann then poses a third question to her learners. Outlining a hypothetical scenario in which such a list exists at their school, she asks them about their personal opinions. It is impossible to tell whether Mrs Wichmann asked these questions in such quick succession in class as well, or whether she is rather summarising the questions for the interviewer here. It is striking though that she exclusively recounts the learners' reaction to the very last question: asked to share their reactions to such a list going around in their own class in the form of teacher-studenttalk, the learners seemingly refuse to give any personal statements whatsoever and reject even the hypothetical possibility of such a scenario.

There are several possible explanations for the learners' reaction. It is impossible to tell whether these particular learners have had any direct experience with bullying, but it is striking that they even refuse to discuss the topic in a thought experiment. I would like to argue that one reason for the learners' refusal to share their thoughts and opinions might lie in the way in which Mrs Wichmann chose to introduce her learners to the novel.

By "ambushing" her learners with a research assignment on teenage suicide, Mrs Wichmann might very well have shocked them. Instead of accompanying her Year 9, she decided to leave her learners alone in the open space online in which they would have found facts and figures, but might also have read or seen unreliable and maybe even unsafe sources. By choosing this approach at the very beginning of the unit, Mrs Wichmann has in some way refused to uphold her part in the pedagogical alliance, in which learners expect their teachers to make appropriate choices for lessons. Since it is indeed likely that this Year 9 has found information on teenage suicide online overwhelming and possibly shocking, their refusal to share personal opinions on the bullying incident in the novel could be interpreted as them, in turn, refusing to play their part in the pedagogical alliance: they do not share what they think openly and honestly. The learners' rejection of the attempted conversation about bullying could thus be understood as an expression of mistrust.

While Mrs Wichmann describes the recounted part of the lesson as "a cool point to get into a conversation with the learners" (Gardemann, 2021, p. 242), such a conversation does not seem to have taken place. Based on what Mrs Wichmann shares about the lesson in the interview, she acknowledges the learners' quick dismissal of the hypothetical situation that apparently puts an immediate stop to the attempted discussion. It is commendable that Mrs Wichmann acknowledges learners' boundaries at this point, but at the same time, neither her previously stated goals were reached nor did this EFL lesson exploit the potential that controversial issues can offer. The failure of reaching the intended lesson goal seems to lie mainly in a lack of a pedagogical alliance between Mrs Wichmann and her Year 9. While Mrs Wichmann seems to trust her learners with tackling a novel she describes as "hard fare", one cannot help but wonder whether she might have underestimated their emotional response to the events in the novel and/or overestimated their willingness to engage with the topic on a more personal level. Earlier in the interview, Mrs Wichmann mentions that death, dying and suicide are topics that come up in Religious Education lessons and that teenagers in general are interested in. It is worth noting here that this Year 9 was not involved in choosing the novel; this was entirely the teacher's decision, based on her assumption that just like other teenagers, they would be interested in the topics explored in the novel. Given the challenges involved in teaching controversial issues that become apparent in Mrs Wichmann's lesson sequence, the following section discusses implications for teaching practice that can be deduced from the case study.

Implications for Teaching Practice

There are three major practical implications of this case study for teaching practice. They are all related to Bonnet and Hericks' (2020) idea that the key to achieving teaching goals connected to critical literacy might not lie in the choice of topics but in how teachers and learners interact. One, the first step in dealing with controversial issues should be to find out what learners already know or believe about them. This enables teachers to identify missing information as well as decide on appropriate teaching methods. In the case of potentially taboo(ed) topics, an anonymous survey (e.g., online) can be used to find out what learners feel comfortable sharing and will allow teachers to plan their lessons accordingly rather than having to rely on insufficient knowledge of learners' views and experiences (Jones & Carter, 2012). Even when pressed for time, such pre-reading activities should not be omitted or cut short. Two, the appropriateness of plenary discussions can be questioned when it comes to teaching controversial topics. Learners might feel more comfortable sharing thoughts in pair or group work, especially if they can choose their partner(s). Three, the case study shows that tasks that require learners to leave the safe space of the fictional world can become problematic. It might be worth considering alternative tasks that allow learners to remain vague, for example, asking them to write an email to a character that they can choose to write from their own or another character's point of view. This complies with the idea of a "(re)consideration of learner-centredness" (see Ludwig & Summer, this volume). Role-playing could be another way to explore different perspectives, for example, "What would a counsellor say?" or "What would a sibling say?".

Conclusion

In this contribution, a case study with an experienced teacher illustrates that negotiating controversial topics in the EFL classroom can entail pitfalls. In particular, neither a chosen text's potential nor the learners' willingness to discuss controversial topics in class should be overestimated. It becomes clear that if such issues are discussed, it is vital to not only consider topics that teachers find relevant but to also give learners a say in the choice of topics and acknowledge them as co-constructors of their educational processes. The analysis of Mrs Wichmann's case study both highlights and impressively emphasises the importance of establishing a solid pedagogical alliance between teachers and learners. It seems to be an indispensable necessity when dealing with potentially controversial topics. Without such an alliance, lessons easily become entirely teacheroriented in a way that prevents learners from actually engaging with topics on a personal level. There is much to be said then in favour of addressing and reflecting more intensively on our discipline's understanding of teachers' and learners' roles in EFL lessons and incorporating such discussions into foreign language teacher education.

References

Bonnet, A., & Hericks, U. (2020). Fremdsprachendidaktik pädagogisch denken – oder: Was ein Staatsanwalt mit Englischunterricht zu tun hat. In D. Gerlach (Ed.), *Kritische Fremdsprachendidaktik. Grundlagen, Ziele, Beispiele* (pp. 165–180). Narr.

Bredella, L. (2012). *Narratives und interkulturelles Verstehen – Zur Entwicklung von Empathie-, Urteils- und Kooperationsfähigkeit*. Narr.

Bridge, J. A., Greenhouse, J. B., Ruch, D., Horowitz, L. M., Kelleher, K. J., & Campo, J. V. (2019). Association between the release of Netflix's 13 reasons why and suicide rates in the United States: An interrupted time series analysis. *Journal of the American Academy of Child and Adolescent Psychiatry, 59*(2), 236–243.

Brosius, H.-B., & Ziegler, W. (2001). Massenmedien und Suizid: Praktische Konsequenzen aus dem Werther-Effekt. *Communicatio Socialis, 34*(1), 9–29.

Caspari, D. (2003). *Fremdsprachenlehrerinnen und Fremdsprachenlehrer. Studien zu ihrem beruflichen Selbstverständnis*. Narr.

Gardemann, C. (2021). *Literarische Texte im Englischunterricht der Sekundarstufe I. Eine Mixed Methods-Studie mit Hamburger Lehrer*innen*. Metzler.

Gerlach, D. (Ed.) (2020). *Kritische Fremdsprachendidaktik. Grundlagen, Ziele, Beispiele*. Narr.

Helsper, W. (2011). Lehrerprofessionalität – der strukturtheoretische Ansatz zum Lehrerberuf. In E. Terhart, H. Bennewitz, & F. Rothland (Eds.), *Handbuch der Forschung zum Lehrerberuf* (pp. 149–170). Waxmann.

Jones, C., & Carter, R. (2012). Literature and language awareness. Using literature to achieve CEFR outcomes. *Journal of Second Language Teaching and Research, 1*(1), 69–82.

Nohl, A.-M. (2007). *Interview und dokumentarische Methode. Anleitungen für die Forschungspraxis*. Springer VS.

Oevermann, U. (1991). Genetischer Strukturalismus und das sozialwissenschaftliche Problem der Erklärung der Entstehung des Neuen. In S. Müller-Doohm (Ed.), *Jenseits der Utopie. Theoriekritik der Gegenwart* (pp. 267–336). Suhrkamp.

Santana da Rosa, G., Santos Andrades, G., Caye, A., Paz Hidalgo, M., Alves Braga de Olieveira, M. K., & Pilz, L. (2019). Thirteen reasons why: The impact of suicide portrayal on adolescents' mental health. *Journal of Psychiatric Research, 108*, 2–6.

Schulze, B. (2014, October 23). *Jay Asher discusses thirteen reasons why | 50 states against bullying*. The Children's Book Review. https://www.thechildrensbookreview.com/2014/10/jay-asher-discusses-thirteen-reasons-why-50-states-against-bullying

Terhart, E., Bennewitz, H., & Rothland, M. (2011). *Handbuch der Forschung zum Lehrerberuf.* Waxmann.

Volkmann, L. (2010). *Fachdidaktik Englisch: Kultur und Sprache.* Narr.

Part III
Specific Taboos and Practical Examples

10 Swear/Taboo Words in English Rap Lyrics
Linguistic Analysis and Implications for Foreign Language Education

Valentin Werner

Introduction

It is evident that "communities do not just have taboo topics, they also have taboo words and expressions, which can be used in swearing" (Dewaele, 2019, p. 219). The use of swear/taboo words (STWs) can be associated with linguistic taboos and thus the broader domain of cultural taboos (see Ludwig & Summer, this volume). Traditionally, swearing has been viewed as an instance of "verbal violence" (Stapleton, 2010, p. 291), linked to anti-social and offensive behavior, concomitant with vernacular usage and low socioeconomic standing of those who swear. Given this negative evaluation, the question arises why educators should bother about swearing in foreign language education (FLE) at all.

In response, educators have pursued several lines of argumentation. For instance, from a sociocultural perspective Jay (2009) proposes that swearing is ubiquitous and notes that STWs occur around half as often as personal pronouns, which are among the most frequent items in spoken language. Swearing thus possesses a central relevance in all kinds of cultures and is increasingly socially acceptable or even normalized and commodified in target societies like the USA, reflected in STW presence in public domains like the mass media, for instance (e.g., Beers Fägersten & Pereira, 2021; Claire, 1998; Dewaele, 2015; Spears, 1998). Second, from a pragma-linguistic point of view, it has been submitted that swearing is an inherently complex and dynamic phenomenon with central relevance for the larger issues of emotional language use, relational work and (im)politeness (Pizziconi, 2015). On a related note, it has been emphasized that STWs are an effective device to "communicate emotion information (anger, frustration) more readily than non-taboo words, allowing speakers to achieve a variety of personal and social goals with them" (Jay, 2009, p. 153). Third, and this view apparently is central from a language-educational perspective, it has been argued that due to the real-life relevance and ubiquity of rudeness (see above), learners simply cannot avoid encountering pertinent structures and should therefore be made familiar with them as part of their (pragma-)linguistic repertoire (e.g., Félix-Brasdefer & Mugford, 2018; Horan, 2013; Mugford, 2008; see further Section "Relevance for Foreign Language Education"). The

DOI: 10.4324/9781003220701-14

present contribution addresses several of the aforementioned issues and explores whether and how to exploit rap lyrics as an allegedly STW-prone register in FLE.

Theoretical Background

Defining and Categorizing STWs

While there is a multitude of definitional attempts, STWs are commonly viewed as a special form of taboo language, which, in turn, can be conceptualized as

> any (string of) words whose production is transgressive of the norms which operate in interaction between people who are not intimates or close friends and in situations where the language produced is accessible, at least potentially, to limitless numbers of people.
>
> (O'Driscoll, 2020, p. 41)

STWs as "recognizable lexical items" (O'Driscoll, 2020, p. 45) thus have the potential to offend, "are sanctioned or restricted on both institutional and individual levels" (Jay, 2009, p. 153), and are used in swearing to express attitudes and emotions (Dewaele, 2019). Formally, STWs may variably occur as nouns (*You're an **asshole**!*), verbs (***Fuck** yourself!*), adjectives (*What a **shitty** party!*), or adverbs (*This was **fucking** awesome!*). From a semantic point of view, there are various STW categorizations, summarized under six broader (and partly overlapping) labels in Figure 10.1.

Empirical research (e.g., Dewaele, 2015; Jay, 2009) has further shown (i) that there is a relatively stable inventory of central STWs in English (*fuck, shit, hell, damn, goddamn, Jesus Christ, ass, oh my god, bitch, sucks*), making up 80% of all STW usage, (ii) that there are gender- and ethnicity-specific STW patterns, and

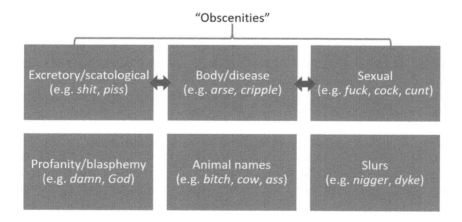

Figure 10.1 STW Categories (Synthesized from Claire, 1998; Jay, 2009; Stapleton, 2010).

(iii) that the level of perceived offensiveness of STWs may vary across contexts, with strongly offensive words (such as *cocksucker* or *nigger*) occurring rarely in public discourse.

While the expression of (negative) attitudes and emotions is arguably central for STWs, they are by no means restricted to this aspect, as illustrated in Figure 10.2. Notably, STWs also carry positive connotations, for instance, when "a speaker replaces physical violence with speech or feels a sense of relief or catharsis after swearing" (Jay, 2009, p. 155) or when social/strategic/interpersonal functions are fulfilled (Guo et al., 2016; see also Delis, 2022). STW usage thus is more complex and context-sensitive than folk-linguistically perceived (Beers Fägersten & Pereira, 2021) and possesses both "social and psychological significance" (Mercury, 1995, p. 31). This fact should be conveyed in FLE, involving a sociopragmatic perspective on the situational appropriateness of STW usage in different communicative contexts (Dewaele, 2019; Jay & Janschewitz, 2008).

STWs in Rap Lyrics: Corpus-Based Views

In addition to the aforementioned observations on STWs, the following passages rely on the findings of a recent linguistic analysis of rap lyrics (Werner, 2019). This may serve (i) to illustrate the salience of STWs in this genre and thus to motivate teachers to use relevant material (see also Section "Relevance for Foreign Language Education") and (ii) to set the empirical ground for the presentation of practical work (Section "Practical Example: *Nigga* and *Fuck* in Rap Lyrics").

In this study, I used the LYRAP corpus (c. 4,000 songs, c. 2 million words), which contains "classic" US rap. I employed keyness analysis, which identified words that are salient in LYRAP compared to a reference corpus of pop lyrics, as well as qualitative concordance analyses. A general result emerging from the keyness analysis was that rap lyrics indeed are characterized by a high incidence of STWs, a finding that is broadly reflective of comparable work (e.g., Beers Fägersten, 2008; Tegge & Coxhead, 2021). The STWs were found to come from

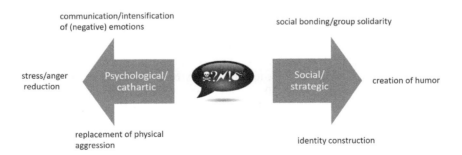

Figure 10.2 Multiple Functions of STWs (following Claire, 1998; Dewaele, 2004, 2015; Horan, 2013; Liyanage et al., 2015; Stapleton, 2010).

a variety of semantic domains (see Section "Defining and Categorizing STWs"), including excretory, sexual, slurs and animal names.

While corpus studies highlight the salience of STWs in rap, the quantitative perspective does not offer any information on what individual STWs actually mean when used in context. Therefore, the practical example presented (see Section "Practical Example: *Nigga* and *Fuck* in Rap Lyrics") will concentrate on two high-frequency (and presumably high-offensiveness) items, the lemmas *nigga* and *fuck*. The aim is to illustrate the inherent complexities of STW usage in rap with a special focus on their social/strategic functions, the area with which learners are least familiar.

Relevance for Foreign Language Education

The abovementioned issues (see Section "Introdution") connected to the disregard of STWs in FLE are complemented by (i) empirical evidence that pragmatic aspects need to be explicitly taught (Félix-Brasdefer & Mugford, 2018), (ii) a discontent with current teaching practices when it comes to impoliteness features (on which see further below), as well as (iii) observations on current learner patterns as regards their usage of emotional language, including STWs.

For instance, there is converging evidence from experimental studies that learners show weak physiological reactions to foreign-language STWs (e.g., Garrido & Prada, 2021). Learners also appear to have an undifferentiated conceptualization of STWs. Therefore, they tend to underuse emotion vocabulary in general and STWs specifically and may under- or, more likely, overestimate the offensiveness of STWs (Dewaele, 2004, 2019; Finn, 2017; Jay & Janschewitz, 2008; Register, 1996). However, research is also suggestive of learners' appropriate use of FL STWs correlating with increasing proficiency (Dewaele, 2017; Jay & Janschewitz, 2008).

Further, it has been argued that learners' underuse and misapplication of STWs is largely teaching-induced. Pizziconi (2015), for example, laments an underrepresentation of linguistic impoliteness research and a reductive conceptualization of impoliteness in central pedagogical frameworks such as the CEFR, which may lead to an "overtraining of polite to the expense of non-polite or impolite forms" (Pizziconi, 2015, p. 125). In addition, others have diagnosed (i) a persistent standard-orientedness in FLE, which leads, among other aspects, to an exclusion of STWs (Guo et al., 2016) and (ii) a general "red flag" (Dewaele, 2019, p. 225) approach toward STWs. This is reflected in the omission from or at least underrepresentation of the topic in textbooks and materials (Holster, 2005; Talebzadeh & Khazraie, 2021), and insecurity of learners, materializing as avoidance of STWs to evade alleged "devastating social consequences" (Dewaele, 2004, p. 204), as well as insecurity of teachers, who are reluctant to introduce STWs as an inherently complex and potentially contentious issue (Guo et al., 2016; Liyanage et al., 2015). This leads Liyanage et al. (2015) to synthesize that "taboo language has been taboo at all levels of language teaching, neglected by language teaching institutions, teacher education programmes and researchers" (p. 113).

However, the negligence of emotional language and STWs does not seem warranted. Besides the sociocultural and (pragma-)linguistic arguments provided in the introduction, and the general fact that emotion and ways of expressing them are crucial aspects of human life (Dewaele, 2004; Jay, 2009), there have been repeated calls that FLE should provide access to authentic communication and avoid the representation of a "Pollyanna" (Mugford, 2008, p. 375), that is an "idealized" (Holster, 2005, p. 45) or "sanitised" (Guo et al., 2016, p. 237) version of the target language and culture. For the area of emotional language, this implies not just looking at harmonious ways of expression but also at how negative attitudes and feelings such as revulsion, anger, pain, or frustration can be conveyed. This is connected to a pragmatic learner need in terms of a "right to be impolite" (Mugford, 2008, p. 382) and the ability to communicate emotion as important part of becoming a proficient speaker (Horan, 2013; Liyanage et al., 2015). It has further been suggested that introducing STWs in FLE offers an opportunity for the contextualized discussion of a complex linguistic issue (Horan, 2013; Mercury, 1995), which could eventually serve to foster overall language awareness (Mugford, 2008) and the development of sociopragmatic competence (Félix-Brasdefer & Mugford, 2018; Finn, 2017; Liyanage et al., 2015). Lastly, there also seems to be substantial fascination on part of the learners to learn about appropriate reactions to STW use (Dewaele, 2004; Wedlock, 2020).

To add an applied and learner-centered dimension to the broader arguments for the relevance of teaching emotional language and impoliteness, the present contribution suggests that using rap lyrics is a suitable approach to introduce STWs as one specific aspect of such endeavors. While lyrics have been widely used in FLE for various purposes (e.g., Summer, 2018; Werner, 2020), the choice of rap lyrics is motivated in the first place by the fact that rap as a genre is characterized by a defiant attitude. From a practical point of view, it has repeatedly been stated that learners unavoidably are exposed to STWs in pop culture media in general, and rap music specifically (Finn, 2017; Guo et al., 2016; Horan, 2013; Liyanage et al., 2015; Mercury, 1995). This is supported by recent surveys, which for instance found that 75% of the age group 14–19 in Germany "like to listen (very much)" to rap (German Music Information Centre, 2020). Further, it has been suggested that FLE classrooms should prepare for social interactions in target language communities of practice (Guo et al., 2016). Arguably, the rap/hip-hop sphere constitutes a relevant community of practice, and notably a community of practice characterized by a high incidence of STWs (Beers Fägersten, 2008; Spears, 1998; Tegge & Coxhead, 2021; Werner, 2019) as an in-group ritual. Finally, the as-yet-underrepresented social/strategic uses of STWs should be considered (see Section "Defining and Categorizing STWs"), which will be possible through a look at the importance of social bonding, authenticity and identity functions of rap language (Alim, 2012; Stapleton, 2010).

Practical Example: *Nigga* and *Fuck* in Rap Lyrics

This section illustrates at a general level how zooming in on selected high-frequency STWs can serve to highlight the complexities of STW usage in rap and their context-sensitivity in general. The topic of the lesson outline is STWs in rap lyrics, focusing particularly on the lemmas *nigga* and *fuck*. The aim is for learners to develop language awareness by gaining an insight into the different uses and meanings of STWs. To this end, I will first highlight linguistic/semantic properties of the two STWs and then provide some ideas for a possible lesson sequence.

As a starting point, Table 10.1 offers an overview of usages of *nigga* and *fuck* in rap lyrics, exemplifying the various shades of meaning the items can take. This table could serve as a basis for teachers that want to engage with the topic as well as a resource for learners that informs related activities (see below).

Overall, it emerges from Table 10.1 that the usages presented are mostly social/strategic and in some cases psychological/cathartic (see Figure 10.2). In the following, I will sketch ideas for a possible three-phase lesson that makes use of the linguistic/semantic categorization just presented.

A potential point of departure could be a lead-in activity in which learners are first asked to collect English STWs they know. Then several (excerpts from) rap songs are played, asking learners to name words frequently used in rap. It is likely that they will list several STWs, with *nigga* and *fuck* featuring prominently. A crucial follow-up step would then be to consider individual examples of the two STWs in rap lyrics. This could be done within the scope of an analysis phase in which learners are asked to explore and interpret the usage of *nigga* and *fuck* in various rap songs, based on the table with the explanations (see above). Concretely, based on the explanations of how STWs can be used in rap songs

Table 10.1 Usages of *Nigga* and *Fuck* in Rap Lyrics

Example	Meaning/usage
Told another **nigga**, so he told another **nigga** and it got around (Ludacris, 2011)	Generic neutral usage, meaning '(Black) man'/'person'
Look I don't give a fuck **nigga** (50 Cent, 2002)	Discourse marker, meaning "man"
Me, my **niggaz**, and my girl - livin the good life! (Tupac, 2001)	Explicitly positive connotation, meaning 'close friends' (cf. *homies*)
Y'all tryna **fuck me over**, y'all always tryna **fuck me over** (50 Cent, 2015)	Prepositional verb, non-literal, emotional (cf. *I don't give a fuck* in Table 10.1)
Then text that man to **fuck off** (Lil Wayne, 2015)	Prepositional verb, non-literal, emotional
Who the fuck you really wanna be with besides me? (Nicki Minaj, 2014)	Non-literal, emotional
Life is such a **fucking** roller coaster then it drops (Drake, 2009)	Adjectival usage, intensification
It's **fuckin'** deadly (Notorious B.I.G., 2005)	Adverb, intensification

to learners (e.g., on a poster or on the whiteboard), learners could be asked to work in pairs and to match the STWs they encounter in the lyrics with the right explanation, respectively. Next, the learners could be presented with provocative or biased statements about STWs in rap lyrics (e.g., taken from the media) to critically reflect upon the manifold usages of STWs. The overall aim of such activities would be to foster sociopragmatic competence and language awareness, specifically to make learners aware of the importance of usage contexts of STWs and the versatility of the items in question, which are not necessarily meant to offend in the lyrics.

In order to further enable learners to go beyond the "red flag" approach toward STWs (see Section "Relevance for Foreign Language Education"), a third teaching phase could involve discussion. Instructors could introduce a context, for instance a scenario with potential real-life relevance for the learners ("Your favorite radio station has just announced that due to complaints they'll now bleep all STWs when playing songs"). Based on the information they gained in the analysis phase, and assuming that learners will oppose the "red flag" policy of the radio station, they could be asked to choose one of the following options: (i) to prepare a written statement they could mail to the radio station or (ii) to formulate a list of arguments potentially usable in a phone call to the responsible editor/DJ, which (iii) could additionally be acted out in a role-play. As a concrete outcome emerges this way, learners will also train their communicative competence (either writing or speaking skills).

Conclusion

Overall, engagement with STWs in rap lyrics was presented as a viable choice to introduce the underrepresented topics of emotional language and impoliteness. The present contribution argued for a guided introduction of STWs as worthwhile activity in FLE to pursue the overarching aims of (i) introducing emotional language and linguistic impoliteness and (ii) developing language awareness and sociolinguistic competence (Guo et al., 2016; Liyanage et al., 2015), as well as of sociopragmatic competence (Dewaele, 2015, 2019). Even though the (selected) examples presented all stemmed from rap discourse and thus a restricted social domain, these aims nicely tie in with, or are even an inherent part of, taboo literacy, one of the central concerns of this volume.

Arguably, rap lyrics serve well as authentic material to encounter STWs in a contextualized fashion and may lead learners (and educators) to go beyond a "red flag" approach to STWs. Engaging with STWs in rap (not in the sense of "teaching to swear" but "teaching about swearing"; see Horan, 2013) may foster the demystification of STWs and may help to present their usage as a complex, context-sensitive phenomenon, serving a variety of functions.

While rap music and their lyrics have certainly been normalized, at least in Western societies, there are a few potential challenges of the approach presented. Above all, it is evident that, ideally, talking about STWs in rap has to be embedded into broader discussions (i) about linguistic conventions and cultural practices in African-American English (Alim, 2012; Spears, 1998) and (ii) about language representation in pop cultural media (Guo et al., 2016), with the aim of establishing the purposes of the salient STW usage in rap specifically. It is obvious that STW usage in rap due to genre conventions is an inherent feature rather than one of choice. This, in turn, will involve some additional discussion of the fact that rap discourse (unlike STW usage in general) is not a spontaneous communicative activity, problematizing the issue of transferability of STW usage from a performed domain to everyday usage. However, it is argued here that if learners understand how STWs work in one specific social context (and for one specific discourse community), this will arguably prepare them for encounters of STWs in various contexts outside of the classroom as well (see Dewaele, 2004).

Further, as STW usage emerged as a highly complex phenomenon and given that rap places high grammatical as well as lexical demands on the learners (Tegge & Coxhead, 2021), it is clear that relevant activities are more suitable for advanced learners. Another practical question may arise in terms of how to integrate the topic into extant curricula. However, many modern FLE curricula offer opportunities to connect it to either linguistic (e.g., reflecting on social and regional varieties, relevance of registers in different communicative situations) and cultural aspects (e.g., African Americans in the USA, music and society, regional and social identities, urban societies) or broader competences (e.g., text and media competence, intercultural competence). Finally, it goes without saying that treating STWs in a classroom may, comparable to other taboo topics, meet with resistance from headmasters and parents or may even be scandalized by journalists. Therefore, the potential consequences of introducing STWs have to be assessed on an individual basis, highlighting the slippery nature of appropriateness in specific educational and social contexts (see also Dewaele, 2008).

An aspect largely ignored is the overall content of rap lyrics. However, it is conceivable to specifically choose rap lyrics that allow an integration of STW-related activities into longer sequences problematizing taboo topics such as racism (see Stadelmann, this volume), sexism (see Haskins, this volume), homophobia, and others. Further, it is clear that there are several advanced topics not treated in the present chapter, such as cultural appropriateness, semantic inversion, internal variation of STW usage across time, region, cultures, and individuals (Dewaele, 2015; Horan, 2013; Liyanage et al., 2015) or the delineation of STWs from slang and informal idioms (see Register, 1996), another issue where situational appropriateness and social functions of language usage are prevalent.

Acknowledgments

I would like to thank Kristy Beers Fägersten, Jean-Marc Dewaele, Indika Liyanage, and the editors for commenting on earlier versions of the manuscript.

References

50 Cent. (2002). Get out the club [Song]. On *Guess Who's Back?*. Full Clip.
50 Cent. (2015). Tryna fuck me over [Song]. On *The Kanan tape*. G-Unit.
Alim, H. S. (2012). Hip hop nation language. In E. Finegan, & J. R. Rickford (Eds.), *Language in the USA* (pp. 387–409). Cambridge University Press.
Beers Fägersten, K. (2008). A corpus approach to discursive construction of hip-hop identity. In A. Ädel, & R. Reppen (Eds.), *Corpora and discourse* (pp. 211–240). Benjamins.
Beers Fägersten, K., & Pereira, G. M. (2021). Swear words for sale: The commodification of swearing. *Pragmatics and Society*, *12*(1), 79–105.
Claire, E. (1998). *Dangerous English 2000! An indispensable guide for language learners and others*. Delta.
Delis, P. (2022). Impoliteness in hip-hop music: African American and White artists' racist and sexist rhetoric. *Journal of Language Aggression and Conflict*, *10*(1), 197–218.
Dewaele, J.-M. (2004). The emotional force of swearwords and taboo words in the speech of multilinguals. *Journal of Multilingual and Multicultural Development*, *25*(2–3), 204–222.
Dewaele, J.-M. (2008). "Appropriateness" in foreign language acquisition and use: Some theoretical, methodological and ethical considerations. *International Review of Applied Linguistics in Language Teaching*, *46*(3), 245–265.
Dewaele, J.-M. (2015). British "Bollocks" versus American "Jerk": Do native British English speakers swear more – or differently – compared to American English speakers? *Applied Linguistics Review*, *6*(3), 309–339.
Dewaele, J.-M. (2019). Linguistic taboos in a second or foreign language. In K. Allan (Ed.), *The Oxford handbook of taboo words and language* (pp. 218–232). Oxford University Press.
Drake. (2009). Forever [Song]. On *More than a game*. Boi-1da.
Félix-Brasdefer, J. C., & Mugford, G. (2018). (Im)politeness: Learning and teaching. In J. Culpeper, M. Haugh, & D. Z. Kádár (Eds.), *The Palgrave handbook of linguistic (im)politeness* (pp. 489–516). Palgrave Macmillan.
Finn, E. (2017). Swearing: The good, the bad & the ugly. *ORTESOL Journal*, *34*, 17–26.
Garrido, M. V., & Prada, M. (2021). Comparing the valence, emotionality and subjective familiarity of words in a first and a second language. *International Journal of Bilingual Education and Bilingualism*, *24*(2), 275–291.
German Music Information Centre. (2020). *Appreciation of various music genres by age group*. http://www.miz.org/downloads/statistik/242/31_EN_Appreciation_music_genres_by_age_group.pdf
Guo, X., Liyanage, I., Bartlett, B., Walker, T., & Díaz, A. (2016). Uncertainty and reluctance in teaching taboo language: A case study of an experienced teacher of English as an additional language. In S. O'Neill, & H. van Rensburg (Eds.), *Global language policies and local educational practices and cultures* (pp. 232–243). Deep University Press.
Holster, D. (2005). *An investigation of ESOL teachers' attitudes towards teaching about taboo English in the second language classroom* [Master's thesis, Auckland University of Technology]. CORE. https://core.ac.uk/download/pdf/56360907.pdf
Horan, G. (2013). "You taught me language; and my profit on't/Is, I know how to curse": Cursing and swearing in foreign language learning. *Language and Intercultural Communication*, *13*(3), 283–297.
Jay, T. (2009). The utility and ubiquity of taboo words. *Perspectives on Psychological Science*, *4*(2), 153–161.

Jay, T., & Janschewitz, K. (2008). The pragmatics of swearing. *Journal of Politeness Research, 4*(2), 267–288.

Lil Wayne. (2015). Back 2 back [Song]. On *No ceilings 2*. Lil Wayne.

Liyanage, I., Walker, T., Bartlett, B., & Guo, X. (2015). Accommodating taboo language in English language teaching: Issues of appropriacy and authenticity. *Language, Culture and Curriculum, 28*(2), 113–125.

Ludacris. (2011). Say it to my face [Song]. On *Back to the first time*. INDEPENDENT.

Mercury, R.-E. (1995). Swearing: A "bad" part of language, a good part of language learning. *TESL Canada Journal, 13*(1), 28–36.

Mugford, G. (2008). How rude! Teaching impoliteness in the second-language classroom. *ELT Journal, 62*(4), 375–384.

Nicki Minaj. (2014). Only [Song]. On *The Pinkprint*. Young Money; Cash Money; Republic.

Notorious B. G. (2005). Watchu want [Song]. On *Duets: The final chapter*. Bad Boy; Atlantic.

O'Driscoll, J. (2020). *Offensive language: Taboo, offence and social control*. Bloomsbury.

Pizziconi, B. (2015). Teaching and learning (im)politeness: A look at the CEFR and pedagogical research. In B. Pizziconi, & M. A. Locher (Eds.), *Teaching and learning (im)politeness* (pp. 113–151). Mouton de Gruyter.

Register, N. A. (1996). Second-language learners and taboo words in American English. *English Today, 12*(3), 44–49.

Spears, A. K. (1998). African-American language use: Ideology and so-called obscenity. In S. S. Mufwene, J. R. Rickford, G. Bailey, & J. Baugh (Eds.), *African-American English: Structure, history, and use* (pp. 226–250). Routledge.

Stapleton, K. (2010). Swearing. In M. A. Locher, & S. L. Graham (Eds.), *Interpersonal pragmatics* (pp. 289–306). Mouton de Gruyter.

Summer, T. (2018). An analysis of pop songs for teaching English as a foreign language: Bridging the gap between corpus analysis and teaching practice. In V. Werner (Ed.), *The language of pop culture* (pp. 187–209). Routledge.

Talebzadeh, H., & Khazarie, M. (2021). "Ignoring the elephant in the room": (Under-)representation of impoliteness phenomenon in popular ELT textbooks. *Language Teaching Research*, 1–33. https://doi.org/10.1177/13621688211029028

Tegge, F., & Coxhead, A. (2021). Exploring the vocabulary of rap lyrics. In V. Werner, & F. Tegge (Eds.), *Pop culture in language education: Theory, research, practice* (pp. 71–84). Routledge.

Tupac, S. (2001). Good life [Song]. On *Until the end of time*. Amaru Entertainment.

Wedlock, J. (2020). Teaching about taboo language in EFL/ESL classes: A starting point. *ORTESOL Journal, 37*, 33–47.

Werner, V. (2019). Assessing hip-hop discourse: Linguistic realness and styling. *Text & Talk, 39*(5), 671–698.

Werner, V. (2020). "Song-advantage" or "cost of singing"? A research synthesis of classroom-based intervention studies applying lyrics-based language teaching (1972–2019). *Journal of Second Language Teaching & Research, 8*(1), 138–170.

11 Disability Awareness Education in ELT
Addressing Disability through Short Animation Films

Katrin Thomson

Introduction

Intolerance, prejudices, stereotypical thinking and any form of marginalization and discrimination clearly undermine the core values of democratic societies, which appreciate diversity, recognize the uniqueness of the individual and protect human rights and the dignity of all citizens. Promoting and defending core values such as fairness, respect, politeness, empathy, open-mindedness, solidarity and equality thus is and continues to be of utmost importance in democratic societies (Schubarth, 2019). Formal education from primary to tertiary level plays a key role in this endeavor. In the European context, this is reflected, for instance, in the adoption of the *Charter on Education for Democratic Citizenship and Human Rights Education* (Council of Europe, 2010). More specifically, in Germany, value-oriented and diversity-sensitive education are considered core principles of formal schooling and teacher education and have therefore been implemented in educational policies on both the national and federal state level (e.g., Kultusministerkonferenz (KMK) & Hochschulrektorenkonferenz (HRK), 2015; Staatsinstitut für Schulqualität und Bildungsforschung München (ISB), 2013). These and other documents emphasize that embracing diversity is a democratic value in itself and that it is the responsibility of all schools, subjects and teachers not only to promote value education (Matthes, 2008) but also to "create an environment in which diversity is acknowledged and appreciated" (KMK & HRK, 2015, p. 2). Diversity, like inclusion, is defined here as a complex concept that encompasses many different aspects – disability being one of them (KMK & HRK, 2015). In 2008, the ratification of the *UN Convention on the Rights of Persons with Disabilities* gave the initial impetus for creating such learning environments on the macro-structural, institutional level of formal education. It is in this context that, in countries like Germany, scholarly discussions on the scope and implications of concepts such as diversity, heterogeneity, individual differences and inclusive education have intensified – not only in the field of general pedagogy but increasingly so in specific domains such as foreign language education (FLE) (e.g., Burwitz-Melzer et al., 2017; Gerlach and Schmidt, 2021; Roters et al., 2018). In order to sensitize students to diversity and to promote the above-mentioned values, diversity itself and disability as one

DOI: 10.4324/9781003220701-15

aspect of it in particular, must also be addressed on the micro-level of English language teaching (ELT). Researchers stress that there is a strong need for Disability Awareness Education (DAE) across all school subjects and learner levels, arguing that students' limited knowledge about disability and disability issues can lead to negative attitudes, stereotypical thinking and misconceptions of people with disabilities (McGrail & Rieger, 2013). DAE aims at overcoming bias, stigma and social barriers and fosters the development of acceptance and empathy. Educating learners about disability contributes to diversity awareness and helps to create inclusive societies. However, in spite of its importance, disability as a topic has remained on the sidelines of ELT so far, and suitable materials and teaching concepts to facilitate DAE are rare.

Disability: A Sensitive and Challenging Topic

The neglect of disability as a topic is somewhat surprising because the EFL classroom lends itself to diversity-sensitive education: experiencing diversity/pluralism in societies, reflecting on similarities/differences between Self/Other, as well as developing empathy and the ability to change perspectives are key issues within the TEFL paradigms of (inter-/trans-)cultural and literary learning (Hallet & Königs, 2010; Küchler & Roters, 2014). Yet, the topic of disability is either absent or misrepresented in ELT coursebooks (Hodgson & Kirmeliene, 2019), which are still the main teaching resources in FLE. Recent empirical studies in the field of critical ELT coursebook analysis in Germany confirm these findings (Alter et al., 2021; Heinemann, 2020). They found that visual representations of persons with disabilities (e.g., in photos, illustrations) are rather one-sided, stereotypical and disproportional compared to the actual percentage of people with disabilities in society. Hence, opportunities for EFL learners to delve into the topic of disability in reflected, more differentiated ways in coursebooks are currently quite limited. Coursebook publishers, though, are aware of their responsibilities and acknowledge the ever-increasing importance of the topics diversity and inclusion in materials development (Barthold, 2021). But still, if foreign language teachers wish to address disability issues, they usually need to look for suitable resources outside the boundaries of published material.

Though incorporating more (authentic and appropriate) visualizations would certainly be a desirable step toward more diverse teaching materials, merely increasing visibility might however foster disability awareness only implicitly, if at all. Students' (visual) encounters with disability, especially when "unguided" and lacking pedagogic rationale, might lead to feelings of awkwardness and even bear the risk of causing negative, unacceptable reactions in students (such as laughter, hurtful words and discriminating comments). This is arguably more likely to happen in classes whose students have little or no contact with persons with disabilities in their social environments and everyday life (e.g., siblings, parents, relatives, friends), which is often still the case (Jeffress, 2022). While all learner groups are heterogeneous in several ways, the category of disability as one dimension of diversity is not necessarily represented in every class. Learner group composition and the presence/absence of peers with disabilities in a particular class are thus extremely important and highly context-specific factors for teachers to consider in the process of lesson planning, text selection and task design (Reckermann, 2020). With the implementation of inclusive (language) education, interpersonal contacts between learners with and without disabilities have certainly increased in countries like Germany, but this concept has not yet been implemented to the same extent in every school/classroom, due to demographic, geographical, institutional, infrastructural and attitudinal differences between Germany's 16 federal states (Hollenbach-Biele & Klemm, 2020). Thus, explicitly addressing the topic of disability on the level of lesson content is crucial, if *all* learners are to be provided with opportunities to develop disability awareness.

DAE is important because it helps students become more understanding and empathic. It helps eliminate prejudices, promotes positive attitudes towards persons with disabilities and supports students in developing an appreciation of diversity and individual differences in general (Nasatir & Horn, 2003; Williamson, 2014). Several studies have shown that these goals can be achieved, if suitable learning environments and materials are provided (Nasatir & Horn, 2003). In ELT, texts of all kinds – but literary/fictional texts and films in particular – are especially important in this context (Hallet & Königs, 2010). They provide teachers and learners with ample opportunities to address and explore different aspects of diversity, including disability, on the level of lesson content. A small body of TEFL publications on this topic has focused on specific genres (such as picturebooks, young adult novels, feature films) and suggested specific texts for various learner levels (Küchler & Roters, 2014; Reckermann, 2020). For different reasons, teaching full-length novels such as Palacio's *Wonder* (2012) or feature films like *The King's Speech* (Hooper, 2010), however, is not always feasible. Hence, teachers might wish to opt for shorter formats. Within the context of film-based language education, short animation films that address disability issues are highly valuable, yet mostly still untapped resources. Although animation films in general have recently received slightly more attention in FLE (Henseler et al., 2011; Kuty, 2020; Lütge, 2017), its potential for DAE is to be unlocked still.

Short Animation Film and Disability Awareness Education in ELT

Short animation films (with/without spoken language) in general are a valuable teaching resource for FLE and film literacy development. They offer a multitude of possibilities to explore characteristic genre features such as internal/external brevity, minimalistic narration, a low number of characters and settings and the limitation to usually only one plot line. They also provide ample opportunity to examine the use of metaphors and symbols, the high density of cinematic devices and the important role of editing, lighting and the musical score in the storytelling process (Rössler, 2009). Interestingly, there seems to be a close affinity between (short) animation film and the topic of disability (Greenberg, in press), which makes this audio-visual format a useful resource to promote disability awareness. Three aspects are particularly relevant to DAE in film-based ELT: (1) methodological issues, (2) language awareness and (3) curricular progression.

First, as concerns methodological issues, addressing a sensitive topic like disability requires "a (re)consideration of learner-centeredness" as well as methodological approaches "in which the topic rather than the learners' personal views or experiences is in the foreground and in which different texts and perspectives are investigated critically" (Ludwig & Summer, this volume). The use of short animation film takes account of this because in this format, the topic itself is of central importance, and viewers are more likely to deeply ponder on the implied topic (Rössler, 2009) rather than on how a specific story/character affects or relates to their own experiences. Moreover, animation films usually tell *fictional stories* and depict *fictional characters*, and even if students might relate to, empathize or possibly even identify with those characters, these narratives still "create a distance between the viewer and the film's protagonists" (Lütge, 2017, p. 70). Lütge emphasizes that it is the very fact that short animated films "do not feature 'real' people" that "helps pupils to maintain a certain 'viewer distance', which is sometimes all the more helpful for engaging in lively and productive communication about certain topics" (Lütge, 2017, p. 67). One of the assets of short animation film thus is their potential for dealing with challenging topics such as disability in educational settings.

Second, using short animation films about disability issues in ELT provides meaningful contexts for raising students' awareness of diversity-sensitive language. Since the actual theme or meaning of a short film is usually not spelled out explicitly but solely implied, language learners are required to literally find the right words in order to verbalize and address disability issues and to negotiate possible film meanings with their peers. Acquiring knowledge of and competence in disability-inclusive language use is crucial because inappropriate or derogatory language can "make people feel excluded" and "amount to discrimination and impinge on the enjoyment of human rights" (UN Geneva, 2019, p. 1). Thus, educating students in the general principles of disability-inclusive language use (e.g., using people-first language as in "people with disabilities" instead of "disabled person"; avoiding victimization by using, e.g., "has cerebral palsy" instead of "suffers from/is stricken by cerebral palsy"; UN Geneva, 2019) is essential in DAE and to the development of students' diversity-sensitive discourse competence and language awareness.

The third point to consider concerns the aspect of curricular progression both in regard to film literacy development and DAE. Dealing with the topic of disability in film-based ELT requires a clear understanding of how to increase students' knowledge and competence gains at different language proficiency levels. The aspect of curricular progression has recently received greater attention in ELT film education. There is growing consensus that film education can and should start at an early stage of ELT (e.g., Becker & Roos, 2016) and continue at secondary level (e.g., Blell et al., 2016; Henseler et al., 2011). While in primary

EFL classrooms the focus should be on very basic aspects of audio-visual literacy (e.g., understanding the storyline and character constellation; responding to a film with the help of simple phrases), more complex and increasingly sophisticated approaches to critical film analysis, reflection and evaluation need to be taken at the secondary level (this includes, e.g., critical reflection on film perceptions; analyzing/interpreting content-form relationships and functions of cinematic devices). This (here only roughly mapped out) progressive approach to film literacy development can be linked with the objectives of DAE at various learner levels.

As regards the early stages of FLE (A1/A1+/A2), young learners usually neither have the linguistic means nor the cognitive-affective capacities to process or respond to complex audio-visual representations of disability in (short) films. Teachers might therefore opt for (silent) short films with simple, straightforward, well-structured storylines whose topic can be easily identified by young learners. If short films about disability contain levels of meaning other than the literal, these should not be foregrounded, since learners at that stage are usually not yet able to identify and decode abstract, symbolic or metaphorical meanings. A short animation film like *Pip* (Simões, 2018), which features a young puppy who wants to become a trained guide dog to people with visual impairments, would be a suitable choice for beginners. *Pip*'s easy-to-follow storyline, the film's familiar school setting, the portrayal of the puppy dog, the optimistic outcome, the absence of spoken language, the congruence between visually presented contents and musical score – all of these aspects appeal to young language learners and allow for an age-/level-appropriate approach to the topic of disability and diversity. Since the film clearly focuses on the character of Pip, but still embeds her story in the wider context of assistance requirements of people who are visually impaired, teachers can address the topic of vision loss more directly. This is to say that *Pip* is actually more complex than it may seem at first glance and would therefore also be suitable for level B1/B1+, if learning objectives and task designs are adjusted accordingly. The focus of DAE at that stage could be moved to the more abstract issues addressed in *Pip*. These include: the notions of diverse classrooms and inclusive education (Pip is smaller than her classmates and it takes her longer to learn and make progress); the importance of believing in yourself/ others (Pip never gives up and stays positive; Pip's supportive dog trainer encourages her to keep learning); the (questionable) role of stringent educational standards (Pip does not meet the school's standards at the beginning but proves that she can live up to those in her own way and time); and the (somewhat problematic) aspect of pretending-to-be-blind versus actual vision loss (Simões, 2018).

Thus, as learners proceed from initial to intermediate and advanced stages of language learning (up to B1+/B2+/C1), short animated films with more abstract, symbolic or metaphorical representations of disability issues can be used. Films such as *The Present* (Frey, 2014) and *Ian* (Gorali & Campanella, 2018) are easy to follow but challenge learners to explore the topic's inherent complexity, analyze the use/effects of cinematic devices and negotiate possible film meanings. *The Present*, for instance, features a teenage boy with limb loss who prefers playing shooter games alone in the darkened living room. When, one day, his mother gives him a three-legged puppy, he first rejects this unwanted present, but eventually changes his mind and goes outside to play with the dog after all. Among other options, classroom activities at level B1/B1+ could focus on: the portrayal of the three-legged dog; its role in the boy's gradual transformation; the relationships between lighting, camera shots, musical score and the depiction of the boy's/dog's disability; and the mother's motives to get her son this particular dog (Thomson, in preparation). *Ian*, a short animated film about a boy with cerebral palsy, is suitable for more advanced learners at level B2/B2+/C1, because analyzing/interpreting the film's metaphorical leitmotif and visual effects in relation to disability issues requires considerable cognitive and linguistic skills (see Section "Practical Example" for teaching suggestions). At those stages, dealing with representations of disability in short animation films should clearly move beyond mere plot/character description and basic film analysis/interpretation. Rather, students also need to approach such films from different socio-cultural and critical perspectives in order to develop sensitivity to the more abstract, hidden subtext meanings and possible implicatures of portraying disability issues in those ways.

Practical Example: Using *Ian* (Gorali & Campanella, 2018) in the Advanced EFL Classroom

Drawing on the theoretical considerations above, this section focuses on *Ian* (Gorali & Campanella, 2018) and provides specific teaching ideas that help promote both DAE and film literacy at more advanced levels. This film features Ian, a young boy who has cerebral palsy and uses a wheelchair. Ian often comes to a playground where he watches the other children play through a chain-link fence. Whenever he tries to play or sit with them but does not have the physical strength to do so, the other children start staring and make fun of him. Every time this happens, Ian – by an invisible force – is pulled from the playground and through the fence. His body disintegrates into thousands of little pieces as he is being pulled through the fence, only to be put back together piece by piece on the other side of it, where he finds himself back in his wheelchair. And every time this happens, his mother dries off his tears, comforts him and then sadly pushes him away from the playground. One day, however, just as his mother is pushing him away again, Ian suddenly slams on the brake, turns his wheelchair around and, going faster and faster, takes himself back through the fence in to the playground. At first, the other children are astonished and stare at him, but when Ian is about to be pulled back through the fence yet again, a girl quickly runs after him, grabs his hand and tries to keep him on her side of the playground. The other children soon join in to help her, and although they all try hard, they are not strong enough to succeed. It is not until they, too, are being pulled through the fence (with their bodies falling apart and being put together in the same manner like Ian's before) that the children realize that they are actually all made the same way and that Ian's disability is no reason to exclude him from playing. Having come to this realization, the fence suddenly dissolves completely and all the children, including Ian, return to the playground together, Ian's wheelchair being pushed by the girl who had previously taken his hand.

Considering the heterogeneity and uniqueness of learner groups, the teaching suggestions (see Table 11.1) cannot simply be transferred but need to be adapted to fit the needs of a specific learner group. Whether or not *Ian* would be appropriate at all for a certain classroom is a question only teachers can answer individually. Since the aspect of learner group composition is an extremely crucial one, it might be entirely inappropriate to use this film if the respective learner group includes a student/students with exactly this (or, for that matter, any other) form of disability or impairment.

Table 11.1 Overview: Teaching Sequence on *Ian*

Topic	*Cerebral palsy, disability, inclusion, exclusion, resilience, bullying*
Goals	Students analyze and discuss an animation film about exclusion/inclusion and reflect on the social-emotional impact of bullying and discrimination against people with disabilities
	Students learn about different forms of disability, gain a deeper understanding of assistance requirements of people with disabilities and can self-reflect on their own attitudes toward people with disabilities/impairments
	Students reflect on and discuss the importance of DAE
Outcome	Recorded audio description of *Ian* for people with visual impairments; flyer for the school's Disability Awareness Day, announcing the film screening of *Ian* and a follow-up panel discussion
Level	B2/B2+/C1 (grade 11/12)
Time	Minimum of 3 lessons (45min each)
Materials	Pictures of playground equipment (pre-viewing); video of *Ian*, selected screenshots/film stills, worksheets (while-viewing), computer, internet, audio-recording device (post-viewing)
Activities	**Pre-viewing:** sharing childhood memories about playground experiences; vocabulary work: activating playground-related vocabulary
	While-viewing: students' personal responses to the film; in-depth analysis and discussion of plot, characters, cinematic devices, functions and metaphorical meanings of visual effects, the film's overall topic
	Post-viewing: online research on backstory (pair work); class discussion on online user comments and the need for DAE; options: producing an audio description (group work); creating a flyer (group work)

At first glance, it may seem odd to use a short film depicting playground motifs in advanced learner groups. Yet, while the playground images as such are easy to read, the storyline and VFX (i.e., the dissolve and disintegration effects in particular) add an artistic, abstract level to it, rendering some elements of the film's story-world unrealistic despite its realistic playground setting (see Figures 11.1 and 11.2). Thematically and aesthetically, *Ian* is rather challenging since students have to decipher the metaphorical meanings of both the fence and

Figure 11.1 Adding an Abstract Level of Meaning: Ian Is Being Pulled through the Fence.
Note. Courtesy of TheCGBros/Mundoloco CGI/Fundación IAN (www.thecgbros.com).

Figure 11.2 Dissolve and Disintegration Effect in *Ian* (2018).
Note. Courtesy of TheCGBros/Mundoloco CGI/Fundación IAN (www.thecgbros.com).

the disintegration effect in order to understand the film's topic and meaning. *Ian* entirely dispenses with spoken language. Thus, the cognitive and linguistic demands of decoding, analyzing, describing and interpreting not just the action but the film's overall meaning are quite high.

Considering the age/grade level, pre-viewing activities could be aimed at establishing a connection between the film setting and students' childhood memories and playground experiences. General questions such as *What did you like best/the least on playgrounds?, What playground activities did you enjoy the most/least? How much did you enjoy going to playgrounds? Who did you play with?* are not yet related to disability issues but serve to activate learners and retrieve (or introduce) lexical items/phrases required later on (e.g., *to play soccer, to go up and down on a seesaw, to go down a slide, to climb on a jungle gym, to go on the swings, to have a picnic, to play in the sandbox*). While play-and-pause approaches might be suitable for other short films, presenting the main film (Gorali & Campanella, 2018, 0:00–7:31 min) straight-through seems more appropriate here in order to give students the opportunity to experience the film as such. Thus, the film should not be interrupted during the first viewing, so that students can perceive the film's story and aesthetic design in its entirety and are not disturbed in the complex process of perception and meaning-making.

Students' individual receptions of and personal responses to *Ian* should then be the first focus in the while-viewing phase. Straightforward questions such as *What do you think of this film? How does it make you feel? What thoughts or questions were running through your mind while watching?* prompt students to not only describe their subjective reactions to the film, but also invite them to voice any aspects they personally may find difficult to understand and/or worth exploring (such as the meaning of the fence and disintegration effects). This, in turn, could initiate in-depth discussions in which students negotiate possible readings of this film. Teachers, in anticipation of these aspects, are able to structure and moderate such a discussion through film stills and worksheet tasks/questions that relate to: Ian's disability; his exclusion from the playground; the emotional effects of bullying; Ian's wish to belong; his resilience and determination to make the other children understand that he also just wants to play like they do; and the fact that sometimes one person, who reaches out and understands, is all it takes to break down barriers and make a difference.

In the post-viewing phase, teachers could return to a screenshot/film still at 0:33 min, which reveals that this film was actually inspired by a true story. The very last part of this video (Gorali & Campanella, 2018, 7:32–9:51 min) not only contains the film credits but, what is more, also includes video snippets of the real Ian playing with other children, as well as pencil drawings of the animated film characters. Students could watch this part, discuss its relation to the animated film with regard to the concept of inclusion, think of motives for making such a film and then research the backstory of this film production using appropriate online resources (e.g., Campbell, 2018 at www.respectability.org). In the user comments on this website, some commentators expressed their wish to have an audio description added to the film, so that people with low vision or vision loss would be able to access and understand it, too. This aspect could be made the focus of the post-viewing phase: students could be asked to produce an audio description for *Ian*. This rather complex project would enable learners to draw on content-/language-related issues dealt with in previous lessons and sensitize students to the requirements of people with low vision – thereby turning students' attention to another form of disability. Alternatively, students could be asked to reflect on the fact that among the commentators on this website are also many teachers stating to have used this film in their classrooms. Students could be invited to discuss why teachers might consider *Ian* a valuable resource, and by doing so, reflect on both the film's relevance and the importance of DAE on a meta-level. Based on those reflections, students can then create a flyer for their school's (perhaps even real) Disability Awareness Day, announcing the film screening of *Ian* and a follow-up panel discussion prepared and moderated by students of this EFL class. Teachers should establish criteria for the sort of information the flyer needs to include (e.g., teaser summary of *Ian*, purpose/goals of this event, possible topics for the panel discussion). The idea of having a Disability Awareness Day at school is inspired by the actually existing "Disability Awareness Month", which is celebrated in the USA in March every year to sensitize the public to disability issues and the concerns of people with disabilities. On a smaller scale, an interdisciplinary project day in the context of DAE could be organized at school: a Disability Awareness Day program could be put together with contributions coming from all school subjects and classes. Those could include, for instance, disability awareness activities, role plays/staged performances, talks and workshops prepared and conducted by students with the support of their respective subject teachers. An advanced EFL class could contribute to a Disability Awareness Day in the way suggested above. If such an event/day were to take place, the best flyer(s) could be chosen and printed for in-school advertisement, and this hypothetical part of the concept could be turned into practice as well. In any case, it has the potential to support the development of positive attitudes towards people with disabilities and to foster disability awareness.

Conclusion

Moving a sensitive topic like disability into the focus of FLE is extremely challenging. It "requires", as Ludwig and Summer (this volume) emphasize, "careful anticipation on the part of the teacher, as well as support, feedback, and guidance". This challenge, however, needs to be taken on if the call for diversity-sensitive and value-oriented education is not only to be heard but also answered. This contribution has discussed possible approaches to addressing the topic disability in ELT using short animation films. Selected methodological aspects of film-based DAE were examined, and various implications of using short animation films on disability at different language levels were discussed with regard to a curricular progression in both DAE and film literacy development. *Ian* (2018) was explored in more detail, and practical teaching suggestions were offered, strongly emphasizing though that these need to be carefully examined by teachers as regards their suitability for a specific learner group.

The theoretical and conceptual considerations in this chapter draw on current research and discourses in the fields of film education, diversity awareness and inclusive education, critical media studies and critical disability studies. It has become apparent that approaches to teaching challenging topics such as disability need to be informed by interdisciplinary perspectives. Moreover, practical implementation and empirical classroom research are needed to better understand in what ways film-based approaches can promote the objectives of DAE in the context of language learning. Also, the scope of this contribution is limited to the use of short animation film, and the examples discussed here depict only selected forms of disability and impairment. Thus, in order to widen the scope and allow for more *diversity within this topic*, other short film genres (such as infomercials and narrative music video clips) and other forms of disability (such as cognitive and social-emotional impairments) need to be taken into consideration as well.

Acknowledgment

Permission to use the screenshots from *Ian* (2018) for reproduction in this contribution (Figures 11.1 and 11.2) was granted by TheCGBros, Chula Vista, California, USA.

References

Alter, G., et al. (2021). All inclusive? Eine kritische Lehrbuchanalyse zur Repräsentation von Diversität in Englischbüchern der Klassenstufe 9. *Zeitschrift für Fremdsprachenforschung, 32*(1), 81–104.

Barthold, S. (2021). Diversität beginnt im Team. Wo fängt kulturelle Aneignung an, und wo hört sie auf? *Transparent: Das Cornelsen Magazin,* [*Diversity & Inclusion. In Lehrwerken und im Unternehmen: Wie Cornelsen Vielfalt fördert und sichtbar macht*], 2, 3–5.

Becker, C., & Roos, J. (2016). Film im Englischunterricht der Grundschule. In G. Blell, A. Grünewald, M. Kepser, & C. Surkamp (Eds.), *Film in den Fächern der sprachlichen Bildung* (pp. 79–95). Schneider Verlag Hohengehren.

Blell, G., Grünewald, A., Kepser, M., & Surkamp, C. (2016). Film in den Fächern Deutsch, Englisch, Französisch und Spanisch: Ein Modell zur sprach- und kulturübergreifenden Filmbildung. In G. Blell, A. Grünewald, M. Kepser, & C. Surkamp (Eds.), *Film in den Fächern der sprachlichen Bildung* (pp. 11–61). Schneider Verlag Hohengehren.

Burwitz-Melzer, E., et al. (Eds.). (2017). *Inklusion, Diversität und das Lehren und Lernen fremder Sprachen*. Narr.

Campbell, V. (2018, December 12). *Short film about playground inclusion wins international acclaim*. RespectAbility. https://www.respectability.org/2018/12/short-film-about-playground-inclusion-wins-international-acclaim/

Council of Europe. (2010). *Charter on education for democratic citizenship and human rights education*. Council of Europe. https://www.coe.int/en/web/edc/charter-on-education-for-democratic-citizenship-and-human-rights-education

Frey, J. (Director). (2014). *The Present* [Film]. Filmakademie Baden-Württemberg. YouTube. https://www.youtube.com/watch?v=WjqiU5FgsYc

Gerlach, D., & Schmidt, T. (2021). Heterogenität, Diversität und Inklusion: Ein systematisches Review zum aktuellen Forschungsstand der Fremdsprachenforschung in Deutschland. *Zeitschrift für Fremdsprachenforschung, 32*(1), 11–32.

Gorali, G., & Campanella, J. J. (Producers). (2018). *Ian* [Film]. Mundoloco CGI Ian Foundation. YouTube. https://www.youtube.com/watch?v=Hz_d-cikWmI&t=475s

Greenberg, S. (in press). *Animated film and disability. Cripping spectatorship*. Indiana University Press.

Hallet, W., & Königs, F. G. (2010). Fremdsprachendidaktik als Theorie und Disziplin. In W. Hallet, & F. G. Königs (Eds.), *Handbuch Fremdsprachendidaktik* (pp. 11–17). Klett Kallmeyer.

Heinemann, T. (2020). *Die Darstellung von Menschen mit Behinderung in Schulbüchern für den Englischunterricht. Eine Schulbuchanalyse.* [Doctoral dissertation, PH Ludwigsburg]. Pädagogische Hochschulbibliothek Ludwigsburg. https://phbl-opus.phlb.de/frontdoor/index/index/docId/663

Henseler, R., Möller, S., & Surkamp, C. (2011). *Filme im Englischunterricht: Grundlagen, Methoden, Genres*. Klett Kallmeyer.

Hodgson, E., & Kirmeliene, V. (2019). The cry for inclusiveness and diversity: Can there be light at the end of the tunnel? *Humanising Language Teaching, 21*(4), n.p. https://www.hltmag.co.uk/aug19/cry-for-inclusiveness-and-diversity

Hollenbach-Biele, N., & Klemm, K. (2020). *Inklusive Bildung zwischen Licht und Schatten: Eine Bilanz nach zehn Jahren inklusiven Unterricht*. Bertelsmann Stiftung.

Hooper, T. (Director). (2010). *The King's Speech* [Film]. UK Film Council; Momentum Pictures; Aegis Film Fund; Molinare; FilmNation Entertainment; See-Saw Films; Bedlam Productions.

Jeffress, M. S. (2022). Introduction. In M. S. Jeffress (Ed.), *Disability representation in film, TV, and print media* (pp. 1–9). Routledge.

Kultusministerkonferenz (KMK) & Hochschulrektorenkonferenz (HRK). (2015). *Educating teachers to embrace diversity*. https://www.kmk.org/fileadmin/veroeffentlichungen_beschluesse/2015/2015_03_12-KMK-HRK-Empfehlung-Vielfalt-englisch.pdf

Küchler, U., & Roters, B. (2014). Embracing everyone: Inklusiver Fremdsprachenunterricht. In B. Amrhein, & M. Dziak-Mahler (Eds.), *Fachdidaktik inklusiv. Auf der Suche nach didaktischen Leitlinien für den Umgang mit Vielfalt in der Schule* (pp. 232–248). Waxmann.

Kuty, M. (2020). Dustin: A story about two unusual friends. *English 5 bis 10, 52,* 8–11.

Lütge, C. (2017). Amazing short animation: 'Must see/teach' films for the EFL classroom. In E. Thaler (Ed.), *Short films in language teaching* (pp. 65–72). Narr.

Matthes, E. (2008). Werteorientierter Unterricht. In Bayerisches Staatsministerium für Unterricht und Kultus (Ed.), *Werte machen stark. Praxishandbuch zur Werteerziehung* (pp. 38–44). Brigg Verlag.

McGrail, E., & Rieger, A. (2013). Increasing disability awareness through comics literature. *Electronic Journal for Inclusive Education, 3*(1), 1–21.

Nasatir, D., & Horn, E. (2003). Addressing disability as a part of diversity through classroom children's literature. *Young Exceptional Children, 6*(4), 2–10.

Palacio, R. J. (2012). *Wonder*. Knopf.

Reckermann, J. (2020). Dealing with diversity in English children's books in the heterogeneous EFL classroom. *Zeitschrift für Schul- und Professionsentwicklung, 2*(4), 134–157.

Rössler, A. (2009). Überraschende Begegnungen der kurzen Art: Zum Einsatz von Kurzspielfilmen im Fremdsprachenunterricht. In E. Leitzke-Ungerer (Ed.), *Film im Fremdsprachenunterricht* (pp. 309–326). ibidem Verlag.

Roters, B., Gerlach, D., & Eßer, S. (Eds.). (2018). *Inklusiver Englischunterricht: Impulse zur Unterrichtsentwicklung aus fachdidaktischer und sonderpädagogischer Perspektive.* Waxmann.

Schubarth, W. (2019). Wertebildung in der Schule. In R. Verwiebe (Ed.), *Werte und Wertebildung aus interdisziplinärer Perspektive* (pp. 79–96). Springer.

Simões, B. (Director). (2018). *Pip* [Film]. Southeastern Guide Dogs. YouTube. https://www.youtube.com/watch?v=07d2dXHYb94

Staatsinstitut für Schulqualität und Bildungsforschung München (ISB). (2013). *Werte bilden. Impulse zur wertbasierten Schulentwicklung.* https://www.isb.bayern.de/download/20675/werte_bilden.pdf

Thomson, K. (in preparation). Different does not mean inferior: Mit einem Animationsfilm für den Umgang mit Behinderungen sensibilisieren (working title). *Englisch 5–10* (planned to be published in issue no. 63, 2023).

United Nations. (2008). *Convention on the rights of persons with disabilities.* https://www.un.org/disabilities/documents/convention/convoptprot-e.pdf

United Nations Geneva. (2019). *Diversity-inclusive language guidelines.* https://www.ungeneva.org/sites/default/files/2021-01/Disability-Inclusive-Language-Guidelines.pdf

Williamson, C. (2014). Effects of disability awareness educational programs on an inclusive classroom. *Honors Projects: Bowling Green State University*, 134. https://scholarworks.bgsu.edu/cgi/viewcontent.cgi?article=1138&context=honorsprojects

12 #mentalhealthmatters – Exploring Borderline Personality Disorder in ELT through Poetry Slams

Christian Ludwig and Veronika Martinez

Introduction

Adolescence is a critical period of life as teenagers frequently face drastic physical and social changes as well as emotional turmoil. These formative years confer particular vulnerability to a variety of mental health problems, which often go hand-in-hand with other adverse childhood experiences and health risks such as substance abuse, violence, and social discrimination.

Contrary to public opinion, mental illnesses are in fact alarmingly common among teenagers and can have a significant impact on their daily lives (Collishaw & Sellers, 2020). The World Health Organization (WHO) estimates that globally about "one in seven 10–19-year-olds experiences a mental disorder" (WHO, 2021, para. 1), with most cases being undetected and untreated. Yet, teenage mental health issues often continue to be shrouded in stigma and taboo also in many classrooms. As Madeline Halpert and Eva Rosenfeld, two high-school teenagers and school newspaper journalists who in their widely acclaimed article *New York Times* "Depressed, but Not Ashamed":

> MOST of our closest friends didn't know that we struggled with depression. It just wasn't something we discussed with our high school classmates. We found that we both had taken Prozac only when one of us caught a glimpse of a prescription bottle in a suitcase during a journalism conference last November. For the first time, we openly discussed our feelings and our use of antidepressants with someone who could relate. We took a risk sharing our experiences with depression, but in our honesty, we found a support system. We knew we had to take the idea further.
>
> (2014, para. 1)

This is particularly problematic as mental disorders among teenagers may influence their physical and mental health at higher ages (Kutcher & Wei, 2020), often resulting in lifelong damage and limiting their opportunities to lead a fulfilling and purposeful life. Thus, it seems mandatory to address mental disorders in schools, supporting students' mental well-being, raising their awareness about potential mental health crises, and creating spaces for those affected to

DOI: 10.4324/9781003220701-16

open up about their problems and seek help from professionals. As Kutcher and Wei emphasise:

> Approximately 70% of cases of mental disorder have their onset prior to 25 years of age. Globally, most young people spend much of their day in schools, and they can be more easily reached there than through any other single public health or clinic-based intervention. Resultingly, effectively addressing mental health and early onset of mental disorders in schools must be an essential component of youth-focused mental health policy.
>
> (2020, p. 174)

Taking this as a starting point for our contribution, we argue that mental disorders should be openly addressed in all subjects, including English language teaching (ELT). We first clarify some key terms. Following this, we explore the potential of ELT to address mental disorders through a variety of texts, particularly highlighting the fact that the foreign language classroom can provide a unique space for encouraging open discussions about mental health issues with adolescents. Against this background, we provide a practical classroom example of how to address and destigmatise one specific mental condition, namely borderline personality disorder (BPD). To illustrate how poetry slam videos can both help students understand the causes and symptoms of BPD and trigger productive conversations about mental disorders in general and BPD in particular.

Mental Health and Mental Disorders

Mental ill-health is more visible than ever. An increasing number of people have personal experiences with mental illnesses (Fuhrer & Keyes, 2019), more and more celebrities, including Adele, Wentworth Miller, Sinéad O'Connor, Miley Cyrus, Trevor Noah, and Emma Stone, publicly open up about their mental health problems, while anti-stigma initiatives and campaigns, such as the WHO *Mental Health Day* and the *Heads Together* campaign by The Duke and Duchess of Cambridge, promote open discussions about the topic. Moreover, social media platforms prove to be an effective tool for mental health campaigns as hashtags such as #mentalhealthmatters, #FundaMentalSDG, or #moveformentalhealth vividly illustrate. Last but not least, the Coronavirus has also put the spotlight especially on children and adolescents' mental health. As the UNICEF *The State of the World's Children 2021* report poignantly puts it, "the pandemic may [only] represent the tip of the mental health iceberg – an iceberg we have ignored for far too long" (UNICEF, 2021, p. 262).

In contrast to physical health, the well-being of the body, mental health refers to one's cognitive, behavioural, and emotional well-being and the ability to effectively function in daily life (see Figure 12.1). However, there is research that emphasises the reciprocal effects of physical and mental health (e.g., Lindwall et al., 2012). While one's mental health can be impacted by different biological and genetic factors, environmental factors seem particularly important. One of

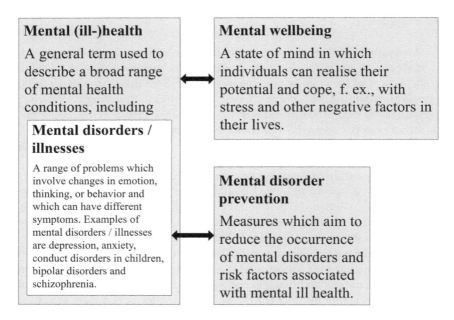

Figure 12.1 Key Terms Explained (based on American Psychiatric Association, n.d.; WHO, n.d.).

the main factors to negatively influence one's mental health is (chronic) stress, e.g., caused by traumatic events, social isolation, (cyber) bullying, domestic violence, substance abuse, or loss.

Physical health literacy comprises "the cognitive and social skills which determine the motivation and ability of individuals to gain access to, understand and use information in ways which promote and maintain health" (Nutbeam, 2015, p. 451). Based on this, mental health literacy describes the "knowledge and beliefs about mental disorders which aid their recognition, management or prevention" (Jorm et al., 1997, as cited in Jorm, 2000, p. 396). According to Jorm, mental health literacy consists of several components (Figure 12.2). While low levels of mental health literacy can lead to the misperception of one's own mental health needs (Miles et al., 2020), high levels of mental health literacy help affected individuals to seek help and undergo treatment (McCance-Katz & Lynch, 2019).

Grappling with mental health, however, should not be confused with suffering from a mental illness (also referred to as mental health disorder or ill mental health) which refers to a wide range of diagnosable mental health conditions such as depression, obsessive-compulsive disorder, or schizophrenia (see Telles-Correia et al., 2018, for a critical discussion of existing definitions of mental disorder). While low levels of mental health over a longer period of time can lead to serious mental illnesses, the mental health of individuals with a diagnosed

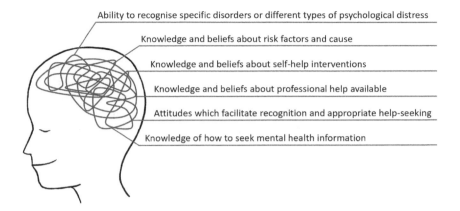

Figure 12.2 Components of Mental Health Literacy (based on Jorm, 2000, p. 396).

mental illness can fluctuate as they may experience moments or periods of good mental health. Although the exact causes are unknown, research suggests that mental disorders can be caused by a combination of different biological, psychological, and environmental factors (see Uher & Zwicker, 2017).

There are different systems used to classify mental disorders, including the DSM-5 by the American Psychiatric Association (2013) and the International Classification of Diseases (ICD-11) by the WHO (2019). Both include a broad range of different categories of disorders, e.g., neurodevelopmental disorders, anxiety disorders, sleep-wake disorders, or gender dysphoria. Although mental illnesses are not always easy to diagnose and numbers may vary from country to country (Chabrol et al., 2001; Zaranini & Frankenburg, 1997), anxiety, obsessive-compulsive, and disruptive behavioural disorders appear to be some of the most common disorders among adolescents (Kieling et al., 2022). Yet, not all teenagers are equally at risk. For example, in the United States Latino children and teenagers are at greater risk of suffering from mental health issues which is driven by the lack of access to basic care in some communities but also by the fact that mental ill-health remains a taboo in many Latino households (see De Silva et al., 2020). Overall, there seems to be a "complex array of internal and external factors" (Radez et al., 2021, p. 183) when it comes to teenagers not opening up about their mental health problems and seeking (professional) help. Teenagers, for example,

- have limited (or a lack of) knowledge about mental health (Radez et al., 2021),
- feel embarrassed and reject to recognise the fact that they have problems, or the desire to deal with them themselves (Gulliver et al., 2010),

- see systemic/structural obstacles such as financial costs (Radez et al., 2021),
- fear discrimination, stigmatisation, and social exclusion, or
- have negative attitudes towards the service providers and psychological treatment.

To sum up, despite the growing awareness of different forms of mental health conditions, youth mental health and mental disorders often remain a taboo as teenagers fear negative consequences when opening up about their problems or seeking help and support. This requires all subjects, including ELT, to address mental health and disorders more openly (see Kutcher & Wei, 2020) which we discuss in the ensuing section.

Addressing Mental Health in ELT

Despite the fact that the mental health crisis among adolescents has reached a critical point, mental health remains a sensitive issue in the classroom. While teachers can provide students with positive role models who are open to talk about mental health, they may (i) feel uncomfortable about dealing with taboo topics, (ii) not have the tools, resources, and (foreign) language skills to have mental health conversations with their students, (iii) have to cope with negative reactions from students, or (iv) even make the situation of those affected worse.

Yet, despite these perceived challenges, there are a number of compelling reasons for discussing mental health conditions with students as ELT can help

- raise awareness about mental health and mental conditions,
- increase knowledge about mental disorders,
- recognise warning signs and symptoms,
- provide self-care and coping strategies,
- offer insights into what it is like to live with a mental illness in different cultural and social contexts, and
- discuss where to go for support.

At first glance, some of these goals, many of which form important components of mental health literacy (see Figure 12.2), may be easier to link to ELT than others. As we discuss in the following with reference to the pedagogic framework for taboos presented in the introduction to this volume (see Ludwig & Summer, this volume), mental health can be connected to ELT on at least three different levels: curricular guidelines, approaches and methods, and materials, all of which will briefly be discussed in the following.

Competence-oriented curricula identify a number of competences and skills which students should acquire, most of which relate to the overall goal of being able to communicate effectively in the foreign language in authentic situations. One way of promoting students' communicative competence is to address authentic topics from outside the traditional realm of (conversation) topics. In other words, ELT should address topics that are close to the lived realities of the students, allowing them to relate to these topics and engage in real-life-related conversations about them. Many aspects of mental health would qualify as real-life related and student oriented and could elicit genuine responses from students, including the environmental factors that can have a negative effect on one's well-being (e.g., stress, bullying, excessive internet use, loss, sleep deprivation, major life changes, problems with family or friends, changes in their body, negative feelings about themselves) as well as common indicators of mental health problems (e.g., frequent illness, social withdrawal, changes in eating and sleeping habits, anger).

Closely related to this, discussing mental health in the classroom may well enhance students' inter- and transcultural as well as global competences (Becker, 2021), especially as mental health conditions are closely related to the social and cultural norms, values, and practices of a society or group (see, Fernando, 2015). First, as Gopalkrishnan points out, "health and illness are perceived differently across cultures" (2018, para. 7). Furthermore, in some cultures mental health challenges may be considered a weakness, which makes it harder or even impossible for affected individuals to open up about their mental health problems and seek help. Even worse, in some cultural contexts, people affected by mental health issues may even be said to be bewitched or possessed by evil spirits, which may prevent those affected from medical treatment but instead be pushed into the arms of traditional healers or exorcists.

Moreover, mental health can also be linked to critical foreign language pedagogy as defined in the introduction to this volume (see Ludwig & Summer, this volume; Seyi-Oderinde, 2021). Members of gender, sexual, ethnic, and other minority groups are more vulnerable to mental ill-health. For example, in the United States, teenagers of colour have higher rates of suicide than white teenagers (Price & Khubchandani, 2019; see Romanelli et al., 2022, for a more detailed study of the factors associated with suicide among Black adolescents). These numbers underline the importance of openly addressing teenagers' mental health needs.

Last but not least, supporting students in becoming digitally literate individuals has become an explained aim of ELT (Bündgens-Kosten & Schildhauer, 2021). With regard to the mental health of adolescents (and adults), digital technology may not only have positive but also negative effects. While social media may help teenagers to stay in touch with peers and feel connected, they may also cause negative feelings such as a fear of missing out (FOMO) or loneliness. Furthermore, cyberbullying, online grooming, and self-absorption, i.e., an increased self-centredness through posting selfies, are further negative effects of an uninformed use of social network sites. Avoiding health risks and protecting one's psychological health while using digital technology are thus important elements of digital literacy (see Vuorikari et al., 2016).

Textbooks and other materials seem to be moving towards explicitly addressing mental health and well-being as they have come to include topics such as stress and stress management, feelings of inadequacy about one's own life, and depression (e.g., the 6th edition of *Crossover* by Cornelsen; see Gussendorf et al.,

2021). Yet, especially the topic of mental (ill-)health offers numerous opportunities for incorporating authentic, real-life-related materials, including literature, films, comics and graphic novels, songs, and born-digital texts. These texts portray mental health (disorders) in different ways, from depicting those affected in a more realistic way to demeaning them. Obviously, these materials require student-centred and differentiated approaches to learning English, which can help students to make positive social connections, build positive peer-peer relationships, and experience what it is like to have both a voice and a choice.

In the following, we provide a practical example of how to approach a mental disorder in ELT, explicitly linking it to the three dimensions discussed in this section and illustrating how students of English can learn more about the daily struggles of adolescents who cope with mental health challenges while, at the same time, increasing their own mental health awareness. The classroom example focuses on BPD as one of many examples, a mental health disorder which influences both how those affected feel and think.

Exploring BPD in ELT: A Classroom Example

Schools provide a more than suitable opportunity for early detection of and intervention for children and adolescents with difficult mental health issues, such as BPD. However, teachers often report that they do not know enough about adolescent mental disorders or do not feel sufficiently competent to react adequately and thus feel rather stressed when confronted with cases of BPD (Townsend et al., 2018).

However, there are top-down attempts, such as the one by the WHO, which try to raise young people's awareness to different kinds of mental disorders – among them, BPD, which is considered one of the most severe mental illnesses of our time. BPD has a lifetime prevalence of approximately 3% and often starts during adolescence. BPD is associated with often severe consequences such as "low occupational and educational attainment, lack of long-term relationships, increased partner conflict, sexual risk-taking, low levels of social support, low life satisfaction, and increased service use" (Bohus & Reicherzer, 2020). Moreover, psychological and social stress, chronic suicidal tendencies and self-mutilation as well as the substantial chronification tendency pose great challenges to affected persons, relatives, and the healthcare system (Bohus, 2019). The fact that BPD symptoms can already be identified at an early age renders schools in general and the ELT classroom in particular an ideal place for detecting BPD in a timely manner and helping raise students' awareness of BPD symptoms and the stigma around the illness.

Borderline Disorder (BPD): A Short Overview

The term borderline personality was coined by Adolf Stern in 1938 in the United States. Until well into the 1960s, BPD was often considered a type of schizophrenia. However, in the mid-1960s, a deeper awareness of BPD developed.

Psychoanalysts like Otto Kernberg positioned BPD somewhere between psychosis and neurosis. In other words, BPD was used to describe the blurred line between two disorders.

Since BPD was first included in the Diagnostic and Statistical Manual of Mental Disorders III or DSM-III in 1975, criteria have been subject to change. The latest versions of the manuals, the DSM-V and the ICD-11 by the WHO, have largely adopted the criteria listed in the DSM-IV. While in the 1980s BPD was considered very difficult to be treated, this changed in 1991 with the introduction of DBT (dialectical behaviour therapy) (Bohus, 2019), a treatment which combines different strategies and techniques in order to increase patients' mindfulness, interpersonal skills, and emotional regulation.

It is assumed that the lifetime prevalence of BPD lies between 3 and 6% (Trull et al., 2010), with a prevalence rate for adolescents between 3 and 18% (Zanarini & Frankenburg, 1997; Chabrol et al., 2001). With 70–80%, self-harming behaviour is frequent among people suffering from BPD and 7–10% of the cases result in suicide (Skodol et al., 2002). As the number of suicide attempts is very high (66%), therapists are often reluctant to accept BPD patients (Bohus & Höschel, 2006).

Affect dysregulation is another core component of BPD. This includes excessively strong and long-lasting emotional conditions, which can be triggered very easily. For example, those affected may no longer be able to differentiate between positive and negative emotions or even experience a loss of control over their emotions. Patients also report dissociative experiences (Stiglmayr et al., 2005) which they perceive as highly distressing and often try to compensate with self-mutilation (Wolf et al., 2009). Impulsive behaviour such as excessive alcohol or substance abuse, binge eating, or high-risk behaviour might be consequences of affective dysregulation as well. Some people also show intense anger or difficulty controlling their anger, while others show more auto-aggressive behaviour (Bohus, 2019).

Moreover, those affected may see themselves confronted with identity disturbances such as an unstable self-image or sense of self (Wilkinson-Ryan & Westen, 2000). For example, they can get absorbed by one single social role. They may also suffer from an inner struggle due to a lack of sense of coherence. Additionally, they can experience a painful inconsistency as they adapt their identity according to the contact person or figure of attachment. Last but not least, they might have difficulties accepting a social role with all its requirements because they fear becoming absorbed by it.

Interpersonal problems of people with BPD are complex. Empirical data indicate that patients have pronounced difficulties to recognise positive social signals and process such signals (Liebke et al., 2018). Furthermore, there is a distinctive anxiety of social rejection and the expectation of being devalued by others. Even if they are deliberately included in groups, people affected feel ostracised. Consequently, they often show uncooperative and suspicious behaviour. BPD patients are particularly sensitive towards emotional reactions of other people. What is more, their ability to trust other people is very poorly pronounced. This also heavily influences their behavioural pattern. Whereas they are initially willing to invest emotions in relationships, they are not ready to tolerate or forgive breaches of trust. Another frequently targeted problem is the regulation of distance and proximity. As patients with BPD feel a deep fear of getting abandoned, they get unhealthily attached to people. Simultaneously, it is especially the feeling of intimacy that triggers anxiety, shame and guilt in people suffering from a BPD (Bohus, 2019). In the following, we put theory into practice by outlining how BPD can be addressed in the classroom through slam videos in which those affected open up about their emotional and often daily struggles.

Exploring BPD through Poetry Slams: A Practical Example

BPD largely remains in the shadows. Thus, the overall aim of this lesson sequence is to enable students to learn more about BPD and critically reflect their own behaviour and attitudes towards mental disorders in general and BPD in particular. In more detail, the sequence aims to (i) raise students' awareness of BPD, (ii) reduce the stigma around the illness, and (iii) improve help-seeking behaviour among potentially affected students.

This should be achieved by poems which are written to be read aloud and performed not to be read in silence. Slam poetry, which emerged in bars and youth centres in Chicago in the 1980s, has found its way into global popular culture. Slams are a subgenre of performance poetry, a mixed genre which combines elements of theatre, poetry, storytelling, and performance. Thus, they bring poetry to the stage as instead of just reading a poem, a standing poetry-slammer performs the text in a creative and engaging way, using the stylistic devices of poetry, intertextual references, and rhythm and voice.

Usually, slammers compete in contests in which the audience votes for their favourite performer, making them an active part of the performance. In the following, we argue that poetry slams, as a modern and creative form of poetry, are a suitable format to learn more about BDP, especially as slam poems usually deal with emotional topics and carry a deep emotional impact.

In her slam poem, uploaded in 2016, Nayo Jones talks about the journey with her illness, sharing the emotional instability, intense mood swings, and incapability of self-love she has experienced from an early age on (SlamFind, 2016; see Figure 12.3). The way she opens up about herself in an increasingly dramatic monologue, chooses and uses her words carefully, e.g., through repeating certain words such as love and hate, and plays with her vocal skills makes this performance unique and increasingly draws the viewer into the emotional rollercoaster of someone suffering from BPD (a short ride for the audience but a lifetime ride for those affected). One can almost feel what it is like to be in a never-ending spiral into self-hatred (notice how she reaches out to the audience). She loves and hates herself, longs for the love of others, while fearing to be abandoned. As Jones puts it:

#mentalhealthmatters 135

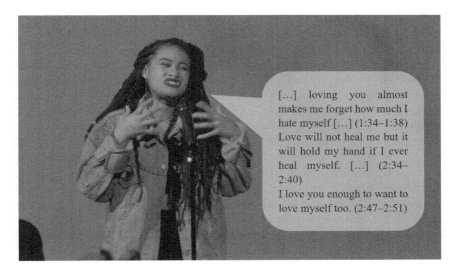

Figure 12.3 Screenshot from Nayo Jones' Performance of "Healing" (SlamFind, 2016), Including Quotes.

> I remember hating myself at the age of seven. Journals filled to the brim with criticisms by eight, I had enough pages to stitch them into wings. To fly close enough to the sun to see my tears turn to steam. Felt the wax burn on my shoulders and mold into thick skin. I was nine when I wanted to die.
> (SlamFind, 2016, 00:32–00:48)

The images Nayo Jones uses to describe her self-hatred are an obvious allusion to the myth of Icarus who falls into the sea and drowns when his wings made of wax melt in the sunlight, losing control over her emotions as Icarus does in the mythological tale.

Another focus of her performance is her incapability of loving herself but her desire to be healed through loving someone. Alluding to the nature of love poetry, she says:

> So when I told you that loving you almost makes life worth it, I was not joking. When I tell you that loving you almost makes me forget how much I hate myself, it is not poetry. Loving you is taking all the love I could never give myself and putting it to good use.
> (SlamFind, 2016, 01:28–01:45)

Closely related to this, she also describes her hope that loving someone and being loved by someone can "absorb the bad days" (SlamFind, 2016, 02:41) and save her. She states: "[...] if someone can love a dying thing this way, can hold the

Lazarus of my body and give thanks for the way it holds back" (SlamFind, 2016, 01:47–01:55). Here, the reference to Lazarus, who died and was risen from the dead by Jesus himself not only emphasises the intensity of her emotions but also the severeness of her illness.

Despite the overt allusions to self-harm and suicide ("Your love be the drawers that hide all the sharp things" [SlamFind, 2016, 2:13–2:16]), which would have to be addressed in the classroom, Jones' slam performance provides an engaging opportunity for students to find out more about the struggles that BPD go through.

Slam performances often deal with emotional, critical or even tabooed issues. Their performative dimension offers numerous anchor points for engaging learner-centred activities, encouraging students to explore how to get a message across to the audience. With slam poetry videos, students listen to the poem, see the performance, and, as in the case of the video by Jones, can even read the lyrics. Verbal and non-verbal language, lightening, special effects, camera angles, music, and reactions by the audience all contribute to the performance. Furthermore, language (e.g., different varieties of English, colloquial language, or figurative language) itself can be analysed.

The following sequence of activities illustrates in an exemplary fashion how slam poems can be used in ELT, offering students the opportunity to find out more about poetry slams as a genre and BPD. First, the key characteristics of a slam are introduced, then students analyse the main symptoms of BPD, and finally think of strategies to communicate and help people with BPD (see Table 12.1).

Table 12.1 A Sample Lesson Sequence on BPD

Pre-viewing	Trigger warning: Make sure to inform parents and students that you are about to discuss a mental disorder in your lessons. Arrange "time outs" with alternative activities for students who are personally affected or do not feel comfortable talking about BPD. Introducing BPD: The teacher • projects an image of a sad teenager and asks the students to name some emotions the teenager may feel in that particular moment (e.g., angry, furious, sad, lonely, dejected, hopeless). Depending on the group, a mood meter could be used to let the students collect their ideas individually before sharing them with the whole class, • shows a short quote from a poetry slam about BPD and asks the students to identify emotions conveyed in the performance, • asks the students in which situation people may have such feelings and if they know certain conditions in which those feelings may be more intense than usual, • writes borderline personality disorder (BPD) on the whiteboard, gathering some first reactions from the students, and • asks the students to think about why poetry may be a suitable genre to talk about mental illnesses such as BPD.

While-viewing 1	Talking about poetry slams:
	In order to find out more about the main characteristics of a poetry slam, the students watch a slam video about BPD, e.g., from YouTube or TikTok. In groups they are given guiding questions which help them to identify some of the key features of an engaging slam performance:
	Slammers don't just read their poem, they perform it.
	• How do they do this?
	• How do they use their voice, face and body?
	• How do they create rhythm or flow for their poems?
	Students collect their answers in the form of a (digital) placemat and agree on four key characteristics which they would like to share with the whole class. Based on the groups' results, the whole class puts together a list of characteristics of a slam performance.
While-viewing 2	Analysing a poetry slam for BPD symptoms.
	The students
	• get a pictogram-only infographic (which are available on Google), showing various symptoms of the disorder (no written descriptions). This helps the students to already think of terms that they might encounter in the video,
	• watch the same poetry slam again to collect the key symptoms of BPD (fear of abandonment, extreme mood swings, unstable relationships, impulsive self-destructive behaviour, feelings of emptiness, paranoia, unstable self-image, self-harm),
	• write the expressions below the corresponding pictograms,
	• share their findings in class and fill in gaps if necessary, and
	• evaluate in how far a poetry slam is an adequate medium for expressing one's BDP condition.
Post-viewing	1. Reflecting (own) preconceptions about the disorder
	With the help of the infographic the students compare their first reactions from the beginning of the lesson. By doing this, they reflect their previous attitude towards the disorder. In the next step, they think about other potential preconceptions that might come up when people are confronted with certain symptoms.
	In this way, the students become aware of their own prejudices and of those others might hold.
	2. Appreciating and evaluating poetry slams as a form of art through which emotions can be expressed and mental ill-health can be talked about. The students reflect
	• their slam experiences,
	• aspects of language learning such as new words they learned,
	• talk about how slam poems can encapsulate (difficult) emotions, and pull emotions to the surface,
	• the severity of the disorder and the sensitivity it should be dealt with, and
	• how we can help those affected to speak more freely and openly about their emotions and experiences and encourage them to seek professional help.
	The teacher encourages students to share their questions in an open discussion.

Conclusion

ELT seems to be ideal to create open discussions about mental health and the many stigmas around mental health conditions. It can potentially provide a supportive environment which students may not find in their families and peer groups and help both those affected and those not affected to enter into an open dialogue about mental health issues. As the discussed example illustrates, poetry slams are one of many ways of encouraging students to find out more about mental disorders such as BPD, one of the most common mental illnesses among adults and adolescents alike.

References

American Psychiatric Association. (n.d.). *What is mental illness?* https://www.psychiatry.org/patients-families/what-is-mental-illness

American Psychiatric Association. (2013). *Diagnostic and statistical manual of mental disorders* (5th ed.). American Psychiatric Publishing.

Becker, D. (2021, November 26–27). *Global, competent…and healthy? Dimensions of mental health education in English language teaching* [Conference presentation]. Symposium on Mental Health in Foreign Language Education, University of Würzburg, Germany.

Bohus, M. (2019). *Borderline-Störung* (2nd ed.). Hogrefe.

Bohus, M., & Höschel, K. (2006). Psychopathologie und Behandlung der Borderline-Persönlichkeitsstörung. *Psychotherapeut, 52*(4), 261–270.

Bohus, M., & Reicherzer, M. (2020). *Ratgeber Borderline-Störungen: Informationen für Betroffene und Angehörige* (2nd ed.). Hogrefe.

Bündgens-Kosten, J., & Schildhauer, P. (Eds.). (2021). *Englischunterricht in einer digitalisierten Gesellschaft*. Beltz Juventa.

Chabrol, H., Montovany, A., Chouicha, K., Callahan, S., & Mullet, E. (2001). Frequency of borderline personality disorder in a sample of French high school students. *The Canadian Journal of Psychiatry, 46*(9), 847–849.

Collishaw, S., & Sellers, R. (2020). Trends in child and adolescent mental health prevalence, outcomes, and inequalities. In E. Taylor, F. C. Verhulst, J. Wong, & K. Yoshida (Eds.), *Mental health and illness of children and adolescents: Mental health and illness worldwide* (pp. 63–73). Springer.

De Silva, L. E. D., Ponting, C., Ramos, G., Guevara, M. V. C., & Chavira, D. A. (2020). Urban Latinx parents' attitudes towards mental health: Mental health literacy and service use. *Children and Youth Services Review, 109*, Article 104719. https://doi.org/10.1016/j.childyouth.2019.104719

Fernando, S. (2015). *Race and culture in psychiatry*. Routledge.

Fuhrer, R., & Keyes, K. M. (2019). Population mental health in the 21st century: Aspirations and experiences. *American Journal of Public Health, 109*(S3), 150–151.

Gopalkrishnan, N. (2018). Cultural diversity and mental health: Considerations for policy and practice. *Frontiers in Public Health, 6*, Article 179. https://doi.org/10.3389/fpubh.2018.00179

Gulliver, A., Griffiths, K. M., & Christensen, H. (2010). Perceived barriers and facilitators to mental health help-seeking in young people: a systematic review. *BMC Psychiatry, 10*, Article 113. https://doi.org/10.1186/1471-244X-10-113

Gussendorf, M., Hine, E., & Köpf, A. (2021). *6th edition Crossover 1.* Cornelsen.

Halpert, M., & Rosenfeld, E. (2014, May 22). *Depressed, but not ashamed.* The New York Times. https://www.nytimes.com/2014/05/22/opinion/depressed-but-not-ashamed.html

Jorm, A. F. (2000). Mental health literacy: Public knowledge and beliefs about mental disorders. *British Journal of Psychiatry, 177*(5), 396–401.

Kieling, C., Salum, G. A., Pan, P. M., & Bressan, R. A. (2022). Youth mental health services: The right time for a global reach. *World Psychiatry, 21*(1), 86–87.

Kutcher, S., & Wei, Y. (2020). School mental health: A necessary component of youth mental health policy and plans. *World Psychiatry, 19*(2), 174–175.

Liebke, L., Koppe, G., Bungert, M., Thome, J., Hauschild, S., Defiebre, N., Izurieta Hidalgo, N. A., Schmahl, C., Bohus, M., & Lis, S. (2018). Difficulties with being socially accepted: An experimental study in borderline personality disorder. *Journal of Abnormal Psychology, 127*(7), 670–682.

Lindwall, M., Ljung, T., Hadzibajramovic, E., & Jonsdottir, I. (2012). Self-reported physical activity and aerobic fitness are differently related to mental health. *Mental Health and Physical Activity, 5*(1), 28–34.

McCance-Katz, E., & Lynch, C. (2019). *Guidance to states and school systems on addressing mental health and substance use issues in schools.* Substance Abuse and Mental Health Administration, Center for Medicaid & Chip Services. https://store.samhsa.gov/sites/default/files/d7/priv/pep19-school-guide.pdf

Miles, R., Rabin, L., Krishnan, A., Grandoit, E., & Kloskowski, K. (2020). Mental health literacy in a diverse sample of undergraduate students: Demographic, psychological, and academic correlates. *BMC Public Health, 20*(1), 1–13. https://doi.org/10.1186/s12889-020-09696-0

Nutbeam, D. (2015). Defining, measuring and improving health literacy. *Health Evaluation and Promotion, 42*(4), 450–455.

Price, J. H., & Khubchandani, J. (2019). The changing characteristics of African-American adolescent suicides, 2001–2017. *Journal of Community Health: The Publication for Health Promotion and Disease Prevention, 44*(4), 756–763.

Radez, J., Reardon, T., Creswell, C., Lawrence, P. J., Evdoka-Burton, G., & Waite, P. (2021). Why do children and adolescents (not) seek and access professional help for their mental health problems? A systematic review of quantitative and qualitative studies. *European Child & Adolescent Psychiatry, 30*(2), 183–211.

Romanelli, M., Sheftall, A. H., Irsheid, S. B., Lindsey, M. A., & Grogan, T. M. (2022). Factors associated with distinct patterns of suicidal thoughts, suicide plans, and suicide attempts among US adolescents. *Prevention Science, 23*(1), 73–84.

Seyi-Oderinde, D. R. (2021). Rethinking mental health literacy programmes for enhanced help-seeking behaviour among young male adults. *Interdisciplinary Journal of Rural and Community Studies, 3*(2), 41–51.

Skodol, A. E., Gunderson, J. G., Pfohl, B., Widiger, T. A., Livesley, W. J., & Siever, L. J. (2002). The borderline diagnosis I: psychopathology, comorbidity, and personality structure. *Biological Psychiatry, 51*(12), 936–950.

SlamFind. (2016, November 27). *Nayo Jones – 'Healing'* [Video]. YouTube. https://www.youtube.com/watch?v=8YzIGoonIrE

Stiglmayr, C. E., Grathwol, T., Linehan, M. M., Ihorst, G., Fahrenberg, J., & Bohus, M. (2005). Aversive tension in patients with borderline personality disorder: A computer-based controlled field study. *Acta Psychiatrica Scandinavica, 111*(5), 372–379.

Telles-Correia, D., Saraiva, S., & Gonçalves, J. (2018). Mental disorder – The need for an accurate definition. *Frontiers in Psychiatry, 9*, Article 64. https://doi.org/10.3389/fpsyt.2018.00064

Townsend, M. L., Gray, A. S., Lancaster, T. M., & Grenyer, B. (2018). A whole of school intervention for personality disorder and self-harm in youth: A pilot study of changes in teachers' attitudes, knowledge and skills. *Borderline Personality Disorder and Emotion Dysregulation, 5*, Article 17. https://doi.org/10.1186/s40479-018-0094-8

Trull, T. J., Jahng, S., Tomko, R. L., Wood, P. K., & Sher, K. J. (2010). Revised NESARC personality disorder diagnoses: Gender, prevalence, and comorbidity with substance dependence disorders. *Journal of Personality Disorders, 24*(4), 412–426.

Uher, R., & Zwicker, A. (2017). Etiology in psychiatry: Embracing the reality of polygene-environmental causation of mental illness. *World Psychiatry, 16*(2), 121–129.

UNICEF. (2021). *The state of the world's children 2021: On my mind – Promoting, protecting and caring for children's mental health*. UNICEF. https://www.unicef.org/media/114636/file/SOWC-2021-full-report-English.pdf

Vuorikari, R., Punie, Y., Carretero Gomez, S., & Van Den Brande, L. (2016). *DigComp 2.0: The digital competence framework for citizens. Update phase 1: The conceptual reference model*. Publications Office of the European Union.

World Health Organisation (WHO). (n.d.). *Key terms and definitions in mental health*. WHO. https://www.euro.who.int/en/health-topics/noncommunicable-diseases/mental-health/data-and-resources/key-terms-and-definitions-in-mental-health

World Health Organisation (WHO). (2019). *Eleventh revision of the international classification of diseases*. WHO. https://cdn.who.int/media/docs/default-source/classification/icd/icd11/a72_29-en_icd-11-adoption.pdf

World Health Organisation (WHO). (2021). *Adolescent mental health*. WHO. https://www.who.int/news-room/fact-sheets/detail/adolescent-mental-health

Wilkinson-Ryan, T., & Western, D. (2000). Identity disturbance in borderline personality disorder: An empirical investigation. *American Journal of Psychiatry, 157*(4), 528–541.

Wolf, M., Limberger, M. F., Kleindienst, N., Stieglitz, R. -D., Domsalla, M., Philipsen, A., Steil, R., & Bohus, M. (2009). Kurzversion der Borderline-Symptom-Liste (BSL-23): Entwicklung und Überprüfung der psychometrischen Eigenschaften. *Psychotherapie, Psychosomatik, medizinische Psychologie, 59*(8), 321–324.

Zanarini, M. C., & Frankenburg, F. R. (1997). Pathways to the development of borderline personality disorder. *Journal of Personality Disorders, 11*(1), 93–104.

13 Let's Talk about Sexting

Discussing Erotic and Sexually Explicit Messaging in Foreign Language Education

Charlotte Haskins and Christian Ludwig

Introduction

In the heat of the moment, we have all said and done things that we regret – sometimes as soon as we have said or done them. Smartphones and other devices we take with us everywhere ensure that we can communicate with a large number of people with only a few swipes of a finger. However, this also means we risk making our mistakes in apparently safe situations and in front of a much larger audience as messages can quickly become pitfalls if used unwisely. Also, it can be very difficult to remove all trace of content from the internet once one has posted something. Therefore, in the digital age, it is important to encourage young adults to think about their own actions online and make them aware of possible (often life-long) consequences that may follow from them: essential skills in the digital skills landscape.

With the global digital transformation underway, social situations, as Brosnan and Gavin (2015) point out, increasingly occur online. Even sexual socialisation is increasingly reshaped and "sexual development itself is technologically mediated" (Lemma, 2021, p. 118). For example, pornographic content is available everywhere, cyberstalking and online sexual harassment have become part of our lived experiences in the digital world (Kalish, 2020) and new (and often manipulative) dating trends such as love bombing, ghosting, benching, or breadcrumbing, which threaten our mental well-being, have evolved. The perceptions of sexuality, intimacy, and love of the teenage generation are increasingly shaped by technology. Despite these problems, the internet, to put a more positive spin on it, "provides an important medium for the exploration and elaboration of adolescents' sexuality" (Kalish, 2020, n.p.).

One online behaviour that is becoming increasingly common among adults and adolescents alike but is hardly talked about is sexting. While a recent meta-analysis by Madigan et al. (2018) across 39 studies from different countries with 110,380 participants roughly between 12 and 17 found that only a minority of youth engage in sexting (1 in 7 sends texts, while 1 in 4 receives texts), the high prevalence of non-consensual sexting in adolescents is alarming (cf. also Budde et al., 2022; Döhring, 2014), with 1 in 8 adolescents already having forwarded a sext.

DOI: 10.4324/9781003220701-17

With this contribution, we by no means want to insinuate that sexting is per se bad or illegal, as engaging in consensual sexting has become a normal way of exploring one's own sexuality and building (sometimes lasting) relationships. Yet, teenagers should also learn about the potential dangers and (real-world) negative consequences that may result from sexting, not only if it is non-consensual. This may be difficult, however, if sexting continues to be considered a taboo, a sign of the moral decay of the teenage generation, or the disintegration of moral values of digital society. As Budde et al. point out, "[i]n international publications, sexting is generally classified as a deviant behavior, and accordingly it is discussed from the perspective of the risks it entails" (2022, n.p.). In contrast to condemning sexting, we need to raise young people's awareness of risks and possible effects of sexting to avoid unhealthy and risky sexting behaviour. Admittedly, talking about sex-related topics with teenagers in the (foreign language) classroom can be a very awkward experience, yet it is detrimental to skip them completely as, by doing so, we deny adolescents the opportunity to make their own informed choices. In tackling this topic, we do not suggest that teachers discuss the latest sexting trends with their students. Quite the contrary, we advocate for approaching sexting as an important phenomenon of the digital age. This also means that teachers would need to inform themselves about sexting as a phenomenon of the digital age and the potential risks that come with it. In other words, we consider the knowledge of different categories of sexting, signs of sexting "gone wrong", and protective strategies against involuntary sexting as integral components of a critical digital literacy which empowers students to handle digital communication responsibly and protect themselves, while maintaining ethical and moral standards. If we take this as a starting point, sexting as a topic in the EFL classroom, we argue in the following, can help to bring the students' real-life experiences into the classroom and initiate authentic, meaningful discourses while, at the same time, also supporting them in acquiring the necessary skills and competences needed to lead a safe and healthy digital life (cf. Carretero et al., 2017).

The contribution begins with an explanation of what sexting is and how it has become an important part of teenage digital life. It then discusses the relevance of sexting for foreign language education, particularly focusing on why sexting is an important point on the digital education agenda. A short video about sexting created for adolescents is explored and a lesson sequence based on the video is examined.

Sexting and the Teenage Generation

When it is not possible for lovers to be together, it has long since been common that trinkets are exchanged to help remind the partners of each other. Modern digital photography, however, is a far cry from the painted portrait miniatures of the 16th century. Nowadays, it is easy to send a photo or video of anything to anyone with your smartphone or other digital devices, providing you have the other person's contact details. This also means that couples can quickly and easily send each other messages of a more intimate nature and thus what we now know as sexting, a portmanteau created by putting together the words "sex" and "texting", came into the digital world (for a more detailed history of sexting see Courtice & Shaughnessy, 2021).

The term sexting is difficult to define as sexting can take different forms, happen on different devices and through different channels, and can also rely on different interaction dynamics (Courtice & Shaughnessy, 2021). As Del Rey Rosario et al. put it, "sexting definitions vary much depending on the behavior in question, the type of material, and whether sexting is restricted to sexual content or also encompasses erotic content" (2019, n.p.). For example, a sext may consist of a combination of various modes of representation. In its text-based form, sexting is usually supported by small pictures known as emojis that have started to become available on all modern smartphones since 2010. As phone companies do not have lewd images as a standard in their devices, a number of emojis are widely used to symbolise other things. The most famous of these is the aubergine/eggplant emoji, which is used in lieu of an erect penis to show arousal, though bananas, hot dogs and corn may also be used. Others include a peach instead of a bottom and the three drops of water to symbolise sexual fluids. It is clear that the attempt to describe this topic in its totality cannot avoid those aspects that touch on the explicit. For the purpose of this contribution we understand sexting as the act of receiving or sending erotic or sexually explicit messages (cf. Crofts et al., 2015).

Moreover, sexting may not only be looked at from the perspective of who is involved, as individuals can take on different roles in sexting; they can be "the sender of a sext, a receiver of it, or can engage in reciprocal sexting behaviour (i.e., both sending and receiving sexts)" (Bradley et al., 2020, p. 2). An important distinction has to be made between primary and secondary sexting, the former referring to consensual situations in which two persons receive or send an image of themselves and the latter meaning that sensitive, intimate content, such as images of another person, is forwarded without consent (Wicks, 2017). While primary sexting may simply be a form of romantic, intimate communication, for example, between partners in a relationship or people who date, secondary sexting is an attack on a person's self-worth, potentially resulting in humiliation, harassment, and bullying (Wicks, 2017). Figure 13.1 offers one possible categorisation of (youth) sexting, including a wide range of different behaviours.

Experimental sexting refers to all voluntary sexting behaviour that does not include any criminal behaviour and in which "youth took pictures of themselves to send to established boy – or girlfriends, to create romantic interest in other youth, or for attention-seeking or other reasons that did not appear to involve elements of the Aggravated cases" (Wolak & Finkelhor, 2011, p. 3). Aggravated sexting behaviour, in contrast, includes abusive or criminal elements such as soliciting images from underage youth, extortion, threats, or forwarding sexual images without consent.

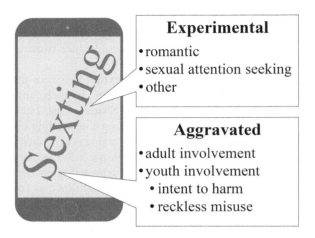

Figure 13.1 Types of Sexting.
Note. Figure based on Wolak and Finkelhor (2011, p. 1).

Despite the risks involved, it is important to note that sexting, no matter on which device and in which form it may occur, even among teenagers, is not per se a bad thing as it may "represent a developmentally appropriate exploration of sexuality" (Bradley et al., 2020, p. 3), which is used for sexual expression among adolescents and is important for the development of their sexual agency (Bradley et al., 2020). The fact that sexting is illegal in so many places and that adolescents' parents may disapprove can make sexting an even greater thrill for young adults. It is very likely, however, that because of the thrill of sexting students may not be aware of the emotional or social consequences and legal implications of sexting (Aldridge et al., 2013). While primary sexting is generally considered harmless, even the act of sexting itself may sometimes lead to serious mental health issues such as depression (cf., Jasso Medrano, 2018). Secondary sexting, i.e., if nudes are shared without consent or misused for illegal purposes such as cyberpornography, can lead to embarrassment or worse. For example, a spurned former lover may share intimate images without the consent of the other party after a relationship has ended in an attempt to humiliate their former significant other (revenge porn) or people are blackmailed with the threat that their sensitive images will be sent to others (sextortion). Although these practices are sordid, not talking about them in education inadvertently protects those who commit them and silences the devastated victims.

There are quite a number of (large-scale) studies available that investigated the sexting behaviour of adolescents in different countries. A recent study by Widman et al. among high school students in the United States found that 89% of the participants had either viewed pornography, sexted, or started a relationship online, with 35% having engaged in all three activities (2021). A survey in the

Netherlands among over 20,000 young adults between 12 and 15 showed that in the six months before the study over 13% of the boys and 12% of the girls had shared nude photos or sex videos of themselves with someone else (Naezer & van Oosterhout, 2020). Last but not least, a study in Spain with over 3,000 adolescents found that "more than 2 in 25 teenagers send or forward sexual content, while more than 1 in 5 receive it directly from the creator, and more than 1 in 4 teenagers receive it via an intermediary" (Ojeda et al., 2020, p. 14 as cited in Budde et al., 2022, n.p.). These studies show that research on (adolescent) sexting behaviour, as Steinberg et al. point out, is burgeoning (2019). Yet, existing data on teenage sexting should be interpreted with care. As Courtice and Shaughnessy contend: "Despite over ten years of empirical studies examining sexting among adolescents and adults, little is known about the predictors, correlates, outcomes, or even the prevalence of sexting" (2021, p. 415). A comprehensive discussion of the reasons for that would go beyond the scope of this contribution. Suffice it to say that studies on sexting among youth so far have mostly focused on engaging in sexting as a risk behaviour, draw on broader or more narrow understandings of what sexting is, use different sampling methods, or study different sample demographics, for example with regard to age, gender, and ethnicity (cf. Steinberg et al., 2019). What we do know, however, is that sexting behaviour is becoming commonplace among youth, increases with age (Steinberg et al., 2019), and that non-consensual sexting is more prevalent than consensual sexting (Ojeda et al., 2020).

With regard to the legal consequences, "a sext dispersed to an unintended audience" (Bretscher, 2021, p. 23) is pornography (cf. Amundsen, 2019). Laws on sexting when done by minors vary from country to country. German law, for instance, permits the sending and receiving of intimate images of those who are 14 or above as long as it is consensual and not shown to anyone else. In the UK and Ireland, it is illegal as the laws have not been adapted and so it is still categorised as child pornography. The punishments for those convicted can also be very different.

By the very nature of the topic, it is difficult to decide which school subject sexting should be included in, as to many, it is a delicate subject and talking to teenagers about sex in general can be challenging. Pretending that sexting is something that teenagers do not engage in, however, will not make it go away and as it can have such dire consequences for young people's lives it should not be swept under the rug. Quite in contrast, the figures available clearly signal that it is time to address the problem face on also in the classroom. It is an important and widespread phenomenon and thus it is important that students are able to talk about it in English. Furthermore, students can only protect themselves online if they are, for example, familiar with the language possibly used to attack them sexually online. In other words, if combined with digital citizenship education, sexting may provide a suitable example of digital communication which illustrates that it is vital to always engage in online communication responsibly and respectfully and with one's (on- and offline) safety concerns in mind as discussed in the ensuing section.

The Relevance of Sexting for the Foreign Language Classroom

In today's digital world, we use our mobile devices for almost everything so it does not come as a surprise that sexting is very common. However, while sexting is widespread, it continues to remain a taboo in many parts of society. Part of the reason for this may be that sexting is still far away from being considered a digital normality or form of (sexual) liberation but rather a deviant form of flirty, erotic, or sexual behaviour. Closely related to this, there may also be a lack of understanding of why people sext.

Instead of being shunned, sexting should be treated for what it is – a real and authentic topic that comes from students' lives and can lead to authentic discussions and provocative questions in the classroom, especially as students of all age groups should be encouraged to speak about their lives, their friendships and peer groups, gender relations and stereotypes as well as social media use, some of which are factors often involved in sexting. Sexting should not be tabooed but discussed in different subjects as it is important and reassuring for young adults to learn how to cope with difficult and sometimes threatening situations and whom they can confide in when they need help. It allows teachers to tackle a real-world issue in the classroom, which potentially engages students and illustrates how "sexuality takes shape via highly individual, socially and historically mutable sexual norms and values" (Budde et al., 2022, n.p.).

As already mentioned, countries, and, for instance, religious groups may differ in attitudes towards and motives for sexting as well as the "moralistic stereotypes" (Lordello et al., 2021, n.p.) that they build around sexting. In other words, sexting is not only a social taboo but may also be a cultural one. Yet, as Naezer and van Oosterhout (2020) point out, contemporary norms and taboos regarding gender and sexuality pave the way for the non-consensual image sharing and contribute to the normalisation of this form of sexual violence. Thus, critically discussing different sexting practices and learning how to set rules of engagement but also accepting the other person's boundaries help to normalise sexting and make it less easy for predators to find and manipulate their potential victims.

While "it is still unclear to what extent digital sexual communication restores stereotypical gender roles and restrictive sexuality norms or, alternatively, enables new spaces of possibility" (Budde et al., 2022, n.p.), sexting can also be discussed in the context of gender roles and gender stereotypes, especially with regard to the sexualisation and exploitation of the (female) body as, to our own surprise, research is inconclusive regarding possible gender imbalances in sexting behaviour. For example, in Madigan et al.'s meta-analysis, results regarding sex differences are inconsistent (2018, p. 328). Some studies found that female adolescents are more likely to sext than males (e.g., Mitchell et al., 2012; O'Connor et al., 2001); other studies have not found any sex differences (Dake et al., 2012; Temple et al., 2012), or suggest that boys are more likely to sext than girls (Strassberg et al., 2013) (for a more detailed overview and discussion, see Madigan, 2018).

It is not possible here to extensively discuss the different motives for sexting in male and female adolescents or the gender norms attached to gendered aspects of sexting. Suffice it to say that traditional (self-perceived) gender norms play an important role in digital sexting. For example, girls who engage in sexting may be considered immoral while the same behaviour will increase the status of boys (who will always be boys) (Peskin et al., 2013). Furthermore, females may find themselves bound to traditional gender norms more than males (Springston, 2017) and send sexts to please the male receiver (Van Ouytsel et al., 2016), while some may find two-way sexting to be the norm (Gordon-Messer et al., 2013). It is clear though that a "simple narrative of the male predator who coerces the female victim into sending sexts as proof of their love" (Bretscher, 2021, p. 32) may be too simple.

In an age in which our lives are increasingly shaped by digital communication technologies, however, sexting should not only be discussed in the foreign language classroom because it interests students and is a contemporary cultural phenomenon but also because dealing with erotic and sexual interaction in digital contexts and its potential risks and consequences are important components of both critical citizenship and digital competence. Digital competence, in very simple terms, means to be able to benefit from digital opportunities but also to mitigate the many possible risks related to them (Carretero et al., 2017). Mitigating the possible risks of digital interaction also includes erotic and sexual interaction (sexting), especially as it "carries specific risks for boundary violations" (Budde et al., 2022, n.p.). In other words, in an age in which sexual socialisation as well as erotic and sexual communication and interaction increasingly take place in digital spaces (Budde et al., 2022; Wachs et al., 2021) and the boundaries between healthy and unhealthy behaviour are often blurred, it is important that young adults are able to identify potentially harmful behaviours. For instance, someone may be coerced into primary sexting in the first place or may even have given their consent to primary sexting and suddenly find themselves in a situation in which their texts, images, or videos have been shared for mere entertainment, revenge, or blackmailing. These examples illustrate that a sex- and sexuality-related digital media competence is important for adolescents who regularly encounter situations in which they have to protect themselves from harmful and disinhibited behaviours such as cyberbullying, cyber grooming, and blackmailing.

The Digital Competence Framework 2.1 (DigComp) was developed by the European Commission to conceptualise the digital competences citizens of the European Union should have in the digital age. Each of the components in the five areas of the framework can be directly linked to sexting and consensual/non-consensual sharing as the overview in Table 13.1 shows.

To sum up, talking about risk factors and consequences related to sexting with teenagers is of paramount importance as they can learn how to use chat and (dating) platforms appropriately and how to deal with unexpected pressure, their rights as individuals, and ultimately how to protect themselves. A suggestion of how this could be done will be described in the following section.

Table 13.1 Relating Selected Components of the DigComp 2.1 to Sexting

Component	Description	Sexting
2.1 Interacting through digital technologies	To interact through a variety of digital technologies and to understand appropriate digital communication means for a given context.	To understand that sexting is a form of media production or an act of media authorship (Hasinoff 2012: 449–465) and that sexting can happen on different platforms and through different channels.
4.1 "Protecting devices"	To protect devices and digital content and to understand risks and threats in digital environments. To know about safety and security measures and to have due regard for reliability and privacy.	To be aware of the risks of sexting and adjust device settings accordingly and account for one's own but also the privacy rights of others.
4.2 Protecting personal data and privacy	To protect personal data and privacy in digital environments. To understand how to use and share personally identifiable information while being able to protect oneself and others from damages.	To be mindful of which sexts to send and when, e.g., to make sure to frame photos in a way that identifiable features like one's face are out of the shot. Safely storing one's sensitive photos and videos after they are sent so that they do not, for example, end up in shared clouds.
4.3 Protecting health and well-being	To be able to avoid health risks and threats to physical and psychological well-being while using digital technologies. To be able to protect oneself and others from possible dangers in digital environments (e.g. cyber bullying). To be aware of digital technologies for social well-being and social inclusion	To understand that while sexting may bring us closer to the other person and, for example, help relieve stress, it may also have negative consequences which bring harm. To make sure that both parties involved are comfortable with how the conversation develops.
5.4 Identifying digital competence gaps	To understand where one's own digital competence needs to be improved or updated.	To understand the fact that sexting may be uncharted waters and that one needs to learn more about how to sext safely and with whom.

Talking about Sexting in ELT – A Sample Lesson Sequence

One of the reasons why (foreign language) teachers may shy away from discussing the topic of sexting with their students is that they feel that they do not have enough experience in managing potentially controversial classroom discussions. Fortunately, there is a wealth of easy to find websites and carefully compiled teaching material about sexting available. A well-researched example of this is Klicksafe, an awareness campaign promoting media literacy and adequate handling of the internet based in Germany and co-funded by the European Union.

The following lesson sequence is designed for students that are 16 or over. This age restriction is based on the legal age of consent in most countries. In the lesson, students are given the opportunity to explore the possible risks and consequences of sexting, not least encouraging them to critically think about their own opinion on the subject. Closely related to this, it also intends to develop students' language competences, allowing them to critically discuss the benefits and risks of sexting. More specifically, the unit encourages students to learn more about different aspects of sexting such as

- different forms of sexting (e.g., primary and secondary sexting, erotic or sexually suggestive/explicit texts, photos, videos),
- who is involved (sender, receiver, intermediary),
- motives for engaging in sexting behaviour (e.g., attracting attention, seeking sensations, expressing sexual curiosity, maintaining one's relationship, expressing affection, or reinforcing one's body image),
- rules and boundaries (e.g., right to say no, consent, sexual agency),
- dangers, risks, and consequences of sexting (e.g., grooming, harassment and sexual abuse, blackmailing, bullying, and victim blaming),
- illegal aspects of sexting (e.g., secondary sexting, sexual violence), and
- emotional, social, and legal consequences of sexting (substance abuse, lower self-esteem, fines, or jail) (based on Burkett, 2015; Hornor, 2020; Madigan et al., 2018).

This unit on sexting is divided into three lessons; depending on the learners' level of proficiency this can be adjusted accordingly. The lessons follow a progressive sequence where each part builds upon the previous one. Part 1 begins by defining sexting. In the second part, learners watch a short video by an Irish charity about sexting and answer questions about it. A creative writing activity follows designed to let the students imagine they are one of the protagonists from the video. In the final part, learners are asked to create memes about sexting.

Many young adults not only well know what sexting is but are also well aware of the potential implications of sexting practices (Walker et al., 2013). Thus, the aim of the following activities is by no means to convince adolescents not to sext but to empower them to make their own informed choices regarding their participation in sexting and raise their awareness of possible warning signs of and protective strategies against unsafe sexting.

The sequence begins by defining the term sexting. Before starting the actual discussion, students should be informed that they will deal with a sensitive issue which requires everyone to follow basic discussion guidelines. After that, the lesson starts with showing the students the image depicted in Figure 13.2.

After the students have looked at the image, they talk to a partner about what they think is happening there. Ideally, students come up with the idea that two people are cautiously sexting with each other. Alternatively, the lesson could also begin by asking a more general question such as "Do you think a message, photo, or video sent to another person will remain anonymous and private forever? If not, in which situations may this be problematic?". After that, ideas about what counts as sexting are collected. To conclude, the teacher shares a simple definition of sexting with the students and emphasises the fact that sexting is a term which can be understood differently by different people, including or excluding certain media types or communication channels, the form (text, emojis, photos, videos), the nature and explicitness of the content, sexual or non-sexual intention, and the degree to which participants voluntarily engage in sexting (Budde et al., 2022).

During the second part of this lesson sequence, the students watch a short video about the consequences of sexting. The video "Just for fun" is part of the educational resource "Lockers", which deals with the problems connected with the creating and sharing of intimate images of and by minors (PDST Technology in Education, 2016). It tells the story of popular student Seán passing on his girlfriend Bronagh's intimate image during a sexting conversation. He does this due to peer group pressure from his football team-mates and a selection of

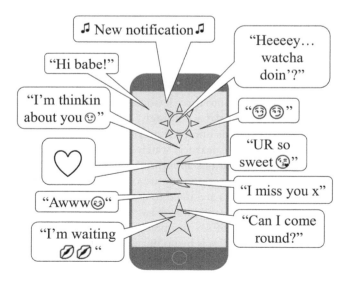

Figure 13.2 Example of a Sexting Situation.

objects in his locker are used to tell the story. "Just For Fun" is suitable for the foreign language classroom as it has an easy plot and the simple English used is supported by clear multimodal elements to aid understanding. As it is only just over three minutes long it can be watched several times during a lesson.

In the pre-viewing phase, the previous lesson is briefly summarised and discussed. Before watching the video the students can be asked to speculate about the title of the video. In the first while-viewing phase, the students should just watch the video and make notes on what they think the video is about ("What happens in the video?"). After this has been discussed, the video is shown again and following this, the students are put into small groups and asked to discuss questions such as "What leads to the sexting situation?, "At which point does the situation get out of hand?", or "What are the consequences of the non-consensual sexting for the different parties involved?" A word list with expressions which are mentioned in the video, e.g., nude, FYEO (for your eyes only), and HOT PIC XXX, can be provided for the students. In addition to this, the student should also discuss how the different elements of the video contribute to the mood or tone of the video, including, for example, the animation, music, colours, action, special effects, etc. They should particularly focus on the roles of the different items and people that appear in the film, such as the football trophy, the team-mates, the books, the newspaper clippings stuck to the inside of the locker or the photo of Seán and Bronagh, which all add to the story and serve to illustrate the complex reasons for and consequences of (non-consensual) sexting. For example, students could be asked to list all the people, activities, and objects in the video and write down which role they play. This can lead to interesting and controversial discussions, for example, as Seán, the football player of the year, is depicted as a golden trophy which looks like him, symbolising the successful and happy life he had before he shared the intimate images of his girlfriend. From this, a discussion of other motives for engaging in sexting behaviour, the rules and boundaries as well as the dangers, risks, and consequences of sexting can evolve. Finally, in the post-viewing phase, the students are asked to work in pairs and imagine what happens next from the perspectives of Seán and Bronagh, the parents, or the football team. A possible homework task would be to write a diary entry from Seán's or Bronagh's point of view talking about what they want to do next or looking back on the situation after six months have passed.

In the final lesson, the students create a meme about sexting based on the video. According to Shifman (2014, p. 41), internet memes can be defined "as (a) a group of digital items sharing common characteristics of content, form, and/or stance, which (b) were created with awareness of each other, and (c) were circulated, imitated, and/or transformed via the Internet by many users". Their use of photos and messages usually consisting of only a few words mean that memes of current events can be created and distributed very quickly. Making and sharing memes with friends is a popular activity for teenagers and a lot of the meme templates and punchlines are instantly recognisable to digital residents. There are a lot of sites like *Meme Generator* (Imgflip, 2022) that have the most popular photos used in memes on them, where you can add a text of your choice to create a personalised meme. By doing that, students need to create short and humorous sentences in English, while also taking into account that memes rely on both the text and the picture that comes with it to convey meaning. Thus, students not only engage in making meaning through a combination of text and image but also develop skills in areas such as the creation and integration of digital content as well as aspects of copyright and licencing as outlined in the DigComp 2.1 (Carretero et al., 2017). With a partner, the students are asked to design and create memes about the reasons for as well as risks and consequences of sexting. The results can then be displayed on a Padlet wall.

Through this lesson, students have not only used their listening and comprehension English skills to follow the storyline of the video and be able to summarise but also engaged in discussing a critical topic of the digital age related to protecting one's privacy and well-being. Moreover, and closely related to this, they have also trained their digital competences in all areas of the DigComp as they have not only interacted and communicated through digital technologies but also developed digital content themselves.

Conclusion

Digital media have the potential to empower teenagers. Yet, if the perils of an unreflected digital media use are not discussed openly with students, digital technology may also disempower them as they are potentially victimised. Sexting is a reality of teenagers' lives and should not be treated as a taboo subject. Instead, the social and cultural taboos around (adolescent) sexting should be lifted. As Best and Bogle (2014) point out, it is not a new thing for the media, parents, and teachers to assume that the current generation of young adults is up to far more nefarious things than they themselves could have. It is an inherent part of being a teenager to experiment, test boundaries, and so learn about the world they live in. Openly discussing sexting in English language teaching can help students to understand sexting as a social phenomenon and also develop those digital media competences they need in order to communicate successfully and mindfully in protecting their own well-being and health in the digital age.

References

Aldridge, M. J., Arndt, K. J., & Davies, S. (2013). You found the sext, what to do next? How school psychologists can assist with prevention, policy, and intervention. *The Ohio School Psychologist, 58*(2), 5–10.

Amundsen, R. (2019). "Kind of like making porn of yourself": Understanding sexting through pornography. *Feminist Media Studies, 19*(4), 479–494.

Best, J., & Bogle, K. A. (2014). *From rainbow parties to sexting – Kids gone wild.* New York University Press.

Bradley, N., Gliea, B., Overton, S., & O'Neill, R. (2020). Sexting between minors: Ethical, legal, and clinical considerations. *Journal of Counselor Practice, 11*(2), 1–20.

Bretscher, M. (2021). *The role of sexting in the development of romantic relationships* [Master's thesis]. University of South Carolina. https://scholarcommons.sc.edu/etd/6219

Brosnan, M., & Gavin, J. (2015). Are "Friends" electric? Why those with an autism spectrum disorder (ASD) thrive in online cultures but suffer in offline cultures. In L. D. Rosen, N. A. Cheever, & L. M. Carrier (Eds.), *The Wiley handbook of psychology, technology, and society* (pp. 250–270). Wiley-Blackwell.

Budde, J., Witz, C., & Böhm, M. (2022). Sexual boundary violations via digital media among students. *Frontiers in Psychology, 12*, 1–15. https://doi.org/10.3389/fpsyg.2021.755752

Burkett, M. (2015). Sex(t) talk: A qualitative analysis of young adults' negotiations of the pleasures and perils of sexting. *Sexuality & Culture, 19*, 835–863.

Carretero Gomez, S., Vuorikari, R., & Punie, Y. (2017). *DigComp 2.1: The digital competence framework for citizens with eight proficiency levels and examples of use*. Publications Office of the European Union.

Courtice, E. L., & Shaughnessy, K. (2021). Four problems in sexting research and their solutions. *Sexes, 2*(4), 415–432. https://doi.org/10.3390/sexes2040033

Crofts, T., Murray, L., McGovern, A., & Milivojevic, S. (Eds.). (2015). *Sexting and young people*. Palgrave Macmillan.

Dake, J. A., Price, J. H., Maziarz, L., & Ward, B. (2012). Prevalence and correlates of sexting behavior in adolescents. *American Journal of Sex Education, 7*(1), 1–15.

Del Rey Rosario, O., Mónica, C., José, A., Mora-Merchán, J. A., & Paz, E. (2019). Sexting among adolescents: The emotional impact and influence of the need for popularity. *Frontiers in Psychology, 10*, 1–11. https://doi.org/10.3389/fpsyg.2019.01828

Döring, N. (2014). Consensual sexting among adolescents: Risk prevention through abstinence education or safer sexting?. *Cyberpsychology: Journal of Psychosocial Research on Cyberspace, 8*(1), Article 9. https://doi.org/10.5817/CP2014-1-9

Gordon-Messer, D., Bauermeister, J. A., Grodzinski, A., & Zimmerman, M. (2013). Sexting among young adults. *Journal of Adolescent Health, 52*(3), 301–306. https://doi.org/10.1016/j.jadohealth.2012.05.013

Hasinoff, A. A. (2012). Sexting as media production: Rethinking social media and sexuality. *New Media and Society, 15*(4), 449–465.

Hornor, G. (2020). Online sexual solicitation of children and adolescents. *Journal of Pediatric Health Care, 34*(6), 610–618.

Imgflip. (2022). *Meme generator*. https://imgflip.com/memegenerator

Jasso Medrano, J. L., Lopez Rosales, F., & Gámez-Guadix, M. (2018). Assessing the links of sexting, cybervictimization, depression, and suicidal ideation among university students. *Archives of Suicide Research, 22*(1), 153–164.

Kalish, R. (2020). *Young adult sexuality in the digital age*. IGI Global.

Lemma, A. (2021). Introduction – Becoming sexual in digital times: The risks and harms of online pornography. *The Psychoanalytic Study of the Child, 74*(1), 118–130.

Lordello, S. R., Silveira, I., Deamici da, P., S. dos Santos, & Souza, L. (2021). Sexting in Covid-19 times: should we care?. *Estudos de Psicologia (Natal), 26*(2), 197–206. https://dx.doi.org/10.22491/1678-4669.20210019

Madigan, S., Ly, A., Rash, C. L., Van Ouytsel, J., & Temple, J. R. (2018). Prevalence of multiple forms of sexting behavior among youth: A systematic review and meta-analysis. *JAMA Pediatrics, 172*(4), 327–335.

Mitchell, K. J., Finkelhor, D., Jones, L. M., & Wolak, J. (2012). Prevalence and characteristics of youth sexting: a national study. *Pediatrics, 129*(1), 13–20.

Naezer, M., & van Oosterhout, L. (2020). Only sluts love sexting: Youth, sexual norms and non-consensual sharing of digital sexual images. *Journal of Gender Studies, 30*(1), 79–90.

O'Connor, T. G., Dunn, J., Jenkins, J. M., Pickering, K., & Rasbash, J. (2001). Family settings and children's adjustment: Differential adjustment within and across families. *The British Journal of Psychiatry, 179*(2), 110–115.

Ojeda, M., del-Rey, R., Walrave, M., & Vandebosch, H. (2020). Sexting en adolescentes: Prevalencia y comportamientos [Sexting in adolescents: Prevalence and behaviours]. *Comunicar, 28*(64), 9–19. https://doi.org/10.3916/C64-2020-01

PDST Technology in Education. (2016, March 23). *Just for fun* [Video]. Vimeo. https://vimeo.com/160080883

Peskin, M. F., Markham, C. M., Addy, R. C., Shegog, R., Thiel, M., & Tortolero, S. R. (2013). Prevalence and patterns of sexting among ethnic minority urban high school students. *Cyberpsychology, Behavior, and Social Networking, 16*(6), 454–459.

Shifman, S. (2014). *Memes in digital culture*. The MIT Press.

Springston, K. M. (2017). Gender differences in participation in and motivations for sexting: The effects of gender role attitudes, masculinity, and femininity. *Butler Journal of Undergraduate Research, 3*, Article 9.

Steinberg, D. B., Simon, V. A., Victor, B. G., Kernsmith, P. D., & Smith-Darden, J. (2019). Onset trajectories of sexting and other sexual behaviors across high school: A longitudinal growth mixture modeling approach. *Archives of Sexual Behavior, 48*(8), 2321–2331.

Strassberg, D. S., McKinnon, R. K., Sustaíta, M. A., & Rullo, J. (2013). Sexting by high school students: An exploratory and descriptive study. *Archives of Sexual Behavior, 42*(1), 15–21.

Temple, J. R., Paul, J. A., van den Berg, P., Le, V. D., McElhany, A., & Temple, B. W. (2012). Teen sexting and its association with sexual behaviors. *Archives of Pediatrics & Adolescent Medicine, 166*(9), 828–833.

Van Ouytsel, J., Van Gool, E., Walrave, M., Ponnet, K., & Peeters, E. (2016). Sexting: Adolescents' perceptions of the applications used for, motives for, and consequences of sexting. *Journal of Youth Studies, 20*(4), 1–25. https://doi.org/10.1080/13676261.2016.1241865

Van Ouytsel, J., Walrave, M., Ponnet, K., & Heirman, W. (2015). The association between adolescent sexting, psychosocial difficulties, and risk behavior. *The Journal of School Nursing, 31*(1), 54–69. https://doi.org/10.1177/1059840514541964

Wachs, S., Wright, M. F., Gámez-Guadix, M., & Döring, N. (2021). How are consensual, non-consensual, and pressured sexting linked to depression and self-harm? The moderating effects of demographic variables. *International Journal of Environmental Research and Public Health, 18*(5), 2597.

Walker, S., Sanci, L., & Temple-Smith, M. (2013). Sexting: Young women's and men's views on its nature and origins. *Journal of Adolescent Health, 52*, 697–701.

Wicks, E. P. (2017). *Secondary sexting: A restorative framework for understanding and addressing the harms of sexting behaviour among secondary school students* [Master's thesis]. Victoria University of Wellington. https://researcharchive.vuw.ac.nz/xmlui/bitstream/handle/10063/6223/thesis_access.pdf?sequence=1

Widman, L., Javidi, H., Maheux, A. J., Evans, R., Nesi, J., & Choukas-Bradley, S. (2021). Sexual communication in the digital age: Adolescent sexual communication with parents and friends about sexting, pornography, and starting relationships online. *Sexuality & Culture, 25*, 2092–2109.

Wolak, J., & Finkelhor, D. (2011). *Sexting: A typology*. America University of New Hampshire.

14 Making the Unseen Seen

Exploring Human Trafficking through Comics and Graphic Novels in ELT

Christian Ludwig

Introduction

As I am writing this chapter, thousands of people are waiting at the gates of Kabul airport to leave Afghanistan as the Taliban have regained control of almost the entire country. As the last evacuation flights are taking off, the international community fears that the Afghan crisis may trigger a mass exodus with millions having been forced to flee within Afghanistan or settling in neighbouring countries, many of which have now shut down their borders. This latest refugee crisis narrative powerfully illustrates that, as the BBC poignantly put it in a 2015 article, "[t]oday's map of the world is a complex spider's web of movement" (Adams, 2015, para. 6). Yet, not all parts of this metaphorical spider web are visible. There are also hidden forms of migration, such as human smuggling and other illegal migration flows, which are also an integral part of contemporary global migration patterns. One example is human trafficking, the trade of humans to exploit them and make profit, which has become one of the largest crime industries not only in Afghanistan, where children are recruited as child soldiers or dancing boys (*bacha bazi*), but also in many other countries where people are being recruited to work in low price nail saloons or as domestic servants. International migrants are particularly vulnerable to trafficking practices, especially as certain migration-related factors may increase the vulnerability of migrants to human trafficking. However, (un)documented migrants are not the only one potential group to be trafficked, as human trafficking is more than a form of a migration. In contrast to, for example, human smuggling, individuals can be trafficked to neighbouring countries but also between countries or within their own country, e.g., from a poor suburb to economically wealthier parts of a city or simply from one household to another. Furthermore, other groups such as (teenage) runaways are likely victims of (sex) trafficking in countries of the global north such as the United States. For example, in the United States, most trafficked individuals are U.S. citizens (UNICEF USA, n.d.), exploited in legal and illicit industries such as commercial sex, massage parlours, religious institutions, domestic work, care for persons with disabilities, and many others (U.S. Department of State, n.d.).

DOI: 10.4324/9781003220701-18

At first glance, human trafficking may seem an unusual and uncomfortable subject for the EFL classroom. Yet, there are number of compelling reasons for addressing the issue in English language teaching (ELT). Human trafficking is not only a global phenomenon but also common practice in many English-speaking countries, especially as some of the goods that we consume from countries such as Pakistan or Bangladesh may have been the product of victims of trafficking. Moreover, traffickers may well use the internet and social media to recruit and control their vulnerable victims, which makes it vital to help learners recognise and avoid dangerous (online) trafficking situations (Fight the New Drug, 2021). Thus, talking about the topic may not only increase students' knowledge about human trafficking but also increase their language-specific competences such as their lexical and inter- and transcultural competences but also their digital competences as they, for example, learn how to navigate safely online.

One way to approach this sensitive issue with learners is using comics and graphic novels which have a long history of exploring "counter-cultural issues like experimental drug use, racism, sexual taboos, and alternative communities" (Dycus, 2012, p. 16). Although there is still some controversy about the medium, which is surprising considering the fact that today's generation of students is surrounded by multimodal representations of information, comics and graphic novels are slowly finding their way into the (foreign language) classroom (Abel & Klein, 2016; Elsner et al., 2013; Hassett & Schieble, 2007; Ludwig & Pointner, 2013). For a long time, comics and graphic novels have been criticised, censored, or even banned for tackling taboo issues, to put it more bluntly, they have been taboo(ed) themselves. An early example of this is the Comics Code of 1954, which enforced rules of acceptable content until 2011. However, the recent ban of the Pulitzer Prize-winning graphic novel *Maus* by Art Spiegelman (1980) by a school in Tennessee due to the book's use of rough language as well as depiction of naked women and the fact that it may indoctrinate students illustrates that the tabooisation of the medium is not a thing of the past.

Yet, the popularity of graphic novels has made them a powerful medium of expression, covering a wide range of contemporary challenging, controversial, and tough topics such as disturbed eating habits or post-traumatic stress disorder (PTSD), which, as stated in the introduction to this volume, may be "perceived as taboo by some people or social groups in certain situations" (Ludwig & Summer).

As Abel and Klein (2016) point out, (post-)colonial heroes with migration experience have moved even more into the spotlight since Marjane Satrapi's autobiographic coming-of-age story *Persepolis* (2000–2003). However, voluntary and forced migration as well as related themes such as racism or exclusion have been common themes in the comic medium since its beginning. In Richard F. Outcault's *The Yellow Kid* (1895–1898), Mickey Dugan depicted the life of Irish-Americans in the immigrant ghettos of New York while the iconic superhero Superman, the only survivor of the destruction of the planet Krypton, tries to assimilate into American culture by hiding his superpowers behind his human identity.

Against this background of legal and illegal forms of migration, this contribution first provides a brief introduction to human trafficking which remains a topic that is hardly talked about not only in education. It then moves on to the depiction of human trafficking in comics and graphic novels, arguing that the medium provides the perfect platform for telling and examining experiences of modern slavery. The contribution concludes by demonstrating potential avenues of exploring the issue of human trafficking with secondary EFL learners, particularly concentrating on the potential of comics as an instructional medium for approaching the topic through authentic, real-world tasks and materials.

Human Trafficking

Stories of illegal immigrants suffocating in containers or lorries regularly make it into the news, of which the Essex lorry deaths are only one of many examples. Many of these "illegal" immigrants are victims of transnational human trafficking which involves the "recruitment, transportation, transfer, harboring or receipt of persons" by "the use of force or other means of coercion" (Everts, 2003, p. 150) and with the purpose of exploiting them. While there is a "human trafficking and migration nexus" (Duong, 2020, p. 1819), such as the similarities between migration and trafficking flows, human trafficking should not be confused with concepts such as migrant smuggling or illegal migration in general, especially as human trafficking can take place both domestically and across borders. Despite the fact that human trafficking generates billions of dollars every year, there are still many myths and misbeliefs around the trafficking of human beings, including the misconception that human trafficking is synonymous with illegal prostitution. Yet, trafficking is by no means restricted to the sex trade business as it also includes, for example, forced labour or services, slavery, begging, criminal activity, the removal of organs, and forced marriage (Bales, 1999). According to the United Nations 2020 *Global Report on Trafficking in Persons*, human trafficking can be "found in every country and every region" (United Nations Office on Drugs and Crime, 2021). The number of victims of human trafficking is difficult to estimate and varies greatly but sources estimate that "27 million people are exploited as slaves including exploitation through bonded labor, forced labor, forced child labor, and sexual slavery" (Benton & Peterka-Benton, 2013, p. 21). While human trafficking affects all sexes and genders, women and girls are more likely to be trafficked than, for example, male adults. Furthermore, members of marginalised groups of society, e.g., undocumented migrants, the unemployed, economically disadvantaged, or individuals with mental disorders as well as children from poor or dysfunctional families, are much more likely to be preyed upon than other groups of society. Closely related to this, human trafficking can easily go unnoticed although perpetrators may recruit their victims "publicly" through agencies and fishing strategies such as advertisements. Yet, with technological advancement and globalisation, "human trafficking has gone digital and dark" (Reid & Fox, 2020, p. 77; cf. also Latonero, 2011; Reid, 2016). According to the US-American charity organisation *Fight The New Drug*, more than two-thirds of underage victims recruited online in 2020 were recruited through Facebook, while 14% were recruited through Instagram, and 8% through Snapchat (Fight the New Drug, 2021). Yet, the (dark spaces of the) internet and social media are not only misused by traffickers for grooming and recruiting their victims but also by their clients who may use the anonymity of the internet book and pay for trafficking-related services (Latonero, 2011) or even the real-time abuse of children and teenagers (Reid & Fox, 2020).

Human Trafficking in Comics and Graphic Novels

Comics and graphic novels have a long tradition of demonstrating social and political awareness and, in fact, addressing issues which are considered taboos. Examples of this can be found in almost all genres of the medium, including the Superhero comic which has covered taboo issues such as the AIDS crisis, homophobia, and racism, attempting to provide "justice to those who have been marginalized and made powerless" (Benton & Peterka-Benton, 2013, p. 19). In fact, *Action Comics #1* (DC Comics), which established the genre of the Superhero comic, openly addressed the topic of domestic violence as early as 1938. Yet, addressing taboo(ed) issues is not something that is limited to the (Superhero) comic but also a generic feature of the graphic novel. Each month, new graphic novels which cover tough and delicate issues and traumatic events are published, providing a platform for those who cannot speak for themselves. This is largely due to the underground comic scene of the 1960s and 1970s, a counter-culture and anti-establishment movement, which gave comic writers the necessary freedom to tackle uncomfortable topics and address the unspeakable and unseen through both images and words (Boatright, 2010). While captions and speech balloons address the reader more directly, the images depict the interiority (memories, thoughts, and feelings) of characters, often narrating the story of one character, allowing readers to empathise with the affected subject.

With regard to human trafficking experiences, graphic narratives, as Oh (2007) points out, "have become important media in advancing dialogue on this important issue in new and innovative ways" (p. 316). This is mainly due to the medium's power to narrate, memorise, represent, and document bodily and emotional traumas (Davies & Rifkind, 2020). Famous examples of this are Art Spiegelman's *Maus: A Survivor's Tale* (1980), in which he tells the story of his father, an Auschwitz survivor, and the great number of comics which were published in response to the 9/11 terror attacks (see e.g., Eisenmann, 2013). With regard to human trafficking, also the Superhero comic has not been silent. To mention but one example, in *Wonder Woman: The Hiketeia* by Greg Rucka (2020), a girl asks Wonder Woman for protection after she killed the traffickers of her sister, as the eponymous title suggests. The sister's trafficking story showcases a common procedure of human trafficking as

> she received an offer by 'talent scouts' to join an 'entertainment group' that promised to make her a star. The trafficking group said that she

had to work to cover the cost of transportation from her hometown to the city. The work was posing for nude photos and ultimately coerced prostitution.

(Benton & Peterka-Benton, 2013, pp. 24–25)

In addition to the large body of Superhero comics, there is now a number of other representatives of the medium dealing with human trafficking such as *You're not for sale* by the Council of Europe (2006), *Audrey: A Story of Child Sex Trafficking* by H.E.A.T. Watch (2013), or *Abolitionista!*, a comic book series against human trafficking (Estler, n.d.). These works explore different aspects of the trafficking business such as ways of recruiting, transporting, and exploiting; thus depicting the brutal realities and traumatic consequences of being a transnational or domestic trafficking victim. In the following, one example of a comic which explicitly deals with human sex trafficking is discussed in more detail. The example serves to show how comics about human trafficking can be used in ELT to enhance students' content knowledge as well as their language competences and literacy skills. The sample lesson plan designed for students at B2/C1 level concentrates on excerpts from the H.E.A.T. *Watch Series* which makes the experiences of trafficking victims even more tangible than other graphic renderings of the topic.

The Representation of Human Trafficking in the H.E.A.T. Watch Series

In Volume I of the H.E.A.T. *Watch Series*, the protagonist Audrey has been lured into prostitution by means of false promises of a better life. Coming from a poor family, she frequently experiences hunger and domestic violence until she decides to get out: "I got out of there as fast as I could. I felt bad leaving my brother and sister, but I couldn't be my dad's punching bag any more. Anything was better than home" (H.E.A.T. Watch, 2013, p. 13). One night on the street, she is picked up by Mac, a nice and friendly boy. Mac seems to give her everything she has missed during her loveless childhood:

> Over the next few weeks, he gave me everything I ever wanted: love, affection and attention. I opened up to him and told him about my past. He made me forget the pain. He was like the dad I never had and the boyfriend I always wanted.
>
> (H.E.A.T. Watch, 2013, p. 15)

However, when Mac forces her into prostituting herself, Audrey is trapped into another vicious cycle of violence and emotional dependence, worse than what she experienced at home. The comic is held almost entirely in black and white, metaphorically conveying the grim reality of Audrey's life and evoking negative emotions related to the trafficking subject such as anger, disgust, fear, or sadness in the reader. The sequence depicted in Figure 14.1 shows the stops on Audrey's journey across the United States in eight panels, each of them being represented

160 *Christian Ludwig*

by an iconic landmark in the United States such as, not without irony, The Statue of Liberty.

With each stop, Audrey associates a specific memory of her suffering such when she got Mac's name tattooed on her back like cattle, a common practice in the trafficking business, indicating that the trafficking victim belongs to her trafficker.

The second excerpt (Figure 14.2) from the comic illustrates the medium's visual narrative power as it tells Audrey's story of physical and emotional abuse and trauma in just three panels. In contrast to her father, Mac beats her for no reason. While the left panel shows Mac, depicted as an oversized black shadow in the largest of the three panels, Audrey is depicted as helpless and full of fear in two much smaller and cramped panels, emphasising her subjection and powerlessness. The employed onomatopoetic elements add to the panels' tone of violence, terror and pain. One only has to look at the capitalised "SLAM!!" to almost feel the omnipotence of the pimp. To add to this, the sequence also shows how the medium plays with seeing and being seen (Oh, 2016). We look at the perpetrator through Audrey's eyes while, at the same time, seeing her. As these examples powerfully illustrate, comics and graphic novels provide a unique opportunity to go beyond public discourse and (inter-)national policy making around human trafficking, detabooing trafficking experiences as they explore the lived experiences of trafficked individuals.

Figure 14.1 A Panel Sequence from H.E.A.T. Watch Series.

Making the Unseen Seen 161

Figure 14.2 Excerpt from H.E.A.T. Watch Series.

Talking about Human Trafficking in ELT

For the EFL classroom, human trafficking provides an authentic and multifaceted topic for students of English as a foreign language, which can be looked at from different angles. These include, among others, root causes of human trafficking (in the context of global migration practices), recruitment types, vulnerable groups, types of transportation as well as national and global anti-trafficking policies. Thus, human trafficking can be connected to broader topics such as migration, racism, or domestic and gendered violence. These examples illustrate that exploring human trafficking can help to develop students' communicative as well as intercultural and global competences as the topic not only affects different groups of people but represents a global issue which can be looked at from different intercultural angles and perspectives (e.g., Lourenço & Simões, 2021). Last but not least, human trafficking can also be beneficial with regard to students' critical literacies (see Ludwig & Summer, this volume) as dealing with the topic involves detecting often hidden power structures such as gender (Eisenmann & Ludwig, 2018) or ethnicity as well as social and economic (in)justices.

A strong point has been made for employing pop-cultural artefacts such as TV series, songs, and video games in the foreign language classroom (Werner & Tegge, 2021), arguing that students can not only acquire the foreign language through engaging with pop culture but also learn about popular culture through language education. Pop culture artefacts not only provide an accessible vehicle through which to explore aspects of the English-speaking world but can also help students to make sense of the world (Summer, forthcoming). With regard to human trafficking, there are various pop culture artefacts that explicitly deal with the topic from different perspectives. The probably most prominent example is probably the music video to Lady Gaga's well-known song *Bad Romance* (2009), in which she is kidnapped from a bathhouse and sold into sexual slavery. Moreover, several literary texts exist on this topic, including picturebooks such as Nettles' *A Free Me: How Taylor Escaped Becoming a Victim of Human Trafficking* (2020) and young adult novels such as Kim Purcell's *Trafficked* (2012) about a girl from Moldova sold as a slave to a Los Angeles based family.

The lesson sequence described in the following introduces students to the phenomenon of human trafficking. It concentrates on developing their awareness of the topic through engaging with a comic, particularly focusing on enhancing students' visual literacy (Elsner et al., 2013; Fisher & Frey, 2008) as well as (critical) digital media literacy (Bündgens-Kosten & Schildhauer, 2021; Lütge & Merse, 2021) in that they learn to "participate and benefit from digital opportunities—but also to mitigate possible risks" (Vuorikari et al., 2016, p. 3). Thus, the sequence refers to different components of digital competence as defined by the Digital Competence Framework (DigComp 2.0) (Summer, 2021; Vuorikari et al., 2016). While the topic of human trafficking can provide a starting point to develop all five of the framework's major components, it is particularly suitable to enhance students' competences as defined in components two (e.g., to manage one's digital identity and reputation) and four (e.g., to protect physical and psychological health).

A Lesson Sequence on Human Trafficking

As pointed out above, children and teenagers are particularly vulnerable to being trafficked through social media, making it particularly important to educate them about the dangers of predatory practices online, with some potential victims never meeting their traffickers face-to-face. Taking this as a starting point, the following sample lesson sequence showcases how to approach the topic with advanced learners of English through the medium of comics. It concentrates on enhancing both students' visual literacy and digital media competence as they reflect their own digital media behaviour, learn about how social media are exploited for trafficking purposes, and consider their own inherent worth and right to emotional and physical integrity. The main goal of the sequence is to increase students' knowledge of what qualifies a person to become a trafficking victim, raise their awareness of different forms of human trafficking and how traffickers use social media to recruit and exploit their victims, and encourage them to reflect the dangers of becoming potential targets themselves.

Teachers could introduce the topic by helping students reflect what they already know about human trafficking and what they would like to learn about it, for example, by opening a word cloud, asking them to add everything that comes to their mind when hearing the term "human trafficking" (as a prompt students can be reminded of the word traffic in trafficking). The results of the word cloud are then discussed and a broad definition of the term, such as that human trafficking means trading and exploiting humans against their will, may be provided by the teacher. Following this, the teacher clarifies that the focus of the lesson sequence is to explore one possible form of human trafficking, i.e., domestic (sex-)trafficking, emphasising that although the type of abuse may vary, different forms of human trafficking work in very similar ways. With a partner, the students then think about how traffickers may use social media to groom their victims. They are then given typical (fake) social media posts, such as the one depicted in Figure 14.3, in which teenagers express their negative emotions such as being depressed, having problems at home, or being bullied (e.g., "Nobody gets me", "I am so fat", "I hate myself", "Life sucks", "I want to run away").

Following this, students talk about how these posts may be dangerous and how traffickers may misuse these posts to lure their victims into sex trafficking. As a form of differentiation, students could either be given possible trafficker initial responses or think of some themselves (e.g., "I feel you", "I know what you are going through", "I think you're beautiful", "I'll make you successful").

Figure 14.3 An Example of a Social Media Post in which a Teenager Is Cyber Groomed.

164 *Christian Ludwig*

In the main part of the sequence, students then individually or in groups work with the comic or excerpts from the H.E.A.T. *Watch Series*. The focus of the task may be to explore how the comic visualises power and control for example using an adapted version of the power and control wheel developed by Polaris (2010), an NGO that aims to combat human trafficking in North America. The wheel provides a categorisation of how power and control are exercised by the trafficker. In contrast to the original version of the wheel, the adapted version displayed in Figure 14.4 can encourage students in the classroom to engage with both the content as well as narrative forms and devices of the comic medium (McCloud, 1993; Mikkonen, 2017; Schüwer, 2008) as exemplified in the sample reading in Section "The Representation of Human Trafficking in the H.E.A.T. Watch Series".

If an individual reading approach is applied, the wheel can, for example, be used as a reading diary. As can be seen in Figure 14.4, the wheel allows students to make notes on how power is exercised in the trafficker/victim relationship through, for example, economic or physical abuse, isolation, or intimidation and on how these power dynamics are expressed through the language of comics as all aspects of a comic panel, including its design and layout, convey meaning. Thus, the wheel can be easily adapted for using any comic that deals with a similar topic. Students could then discuss the results of their readings in smaller groups, identifying both the main ways in which traffickers exercise power over

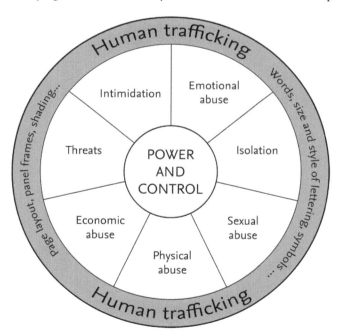

Figure 14.4 The Polaris Power and Control Wheel to Explore Comic and Graphic Novel Renderings of Human Trafficking.

their victims and which narrative devices the comic medium uses to represent them. Closely related to this, students could also discuss how Audrey's inner thoughts and emotions are expressed in the comic, e.g., through the use (or absence of) captions, thought bubbles, word balloons, colours, or onomatopoeia. The results of these discussions could well lead into further projects such as creating short trafficking prevention comic strips. Designing such comic strips allows students to actively use what they learned about social media trafficking and comic narratology. These examples illustrate that through working with human trafficking comics, students not only acquire important human trafficking-related vocabulary such as grooming, manipulating, abusing, exploiting, and drugging but also vocabulary to describe the (visual) language of comics.

Conclusion

Human trafficking is a phenomenon which is fostered by the global economy. Comics and graphic novels give a human face and voice to trafficking victims who often fall under the radar. As the example discussed in this contribution illustrates, the comic medium makes it possible to address this sensitive issue also with teenage students of English as a foreign language, especially if one aim is to foster students' critical literacies. The focus of the sequence on social media trafficking can help students to navigate safely online, protect themselves on social media and not become victims themselves, which represent important components of digital media competence.

References

Abel, J., & Klein, C. (Eds.). (2016). *Comics und Graphic Novels: Eine Einführung*. J.B. Metzler.
Adams, P. (2015, May 28). *Migration: Are more people on the move than ever before?* BBC. https://www.bbc.com/news/world-32912867
Bales, K. (1999). *Disposable people: New slavery in the global economy*. University of California Press.
Benton, B., & Peterka-Benton, D. (2013). When the abyss looks back: Treatments of human trafficking in superhero comic books. *The Popular Culture Studies Journal, 1*(1–2), 18–35.
Boatright, M. D. (2010). Graphic journeys: Graphic novels' representations of immigrant experiences: Graphic novels can be a provocative resource for engaging the complex issues surrounding immigration and immigrant experiences. *Journal of Adolescent & Adult Literacy, 53*(6), 468–476.
Bündgens-Kosten, J., & Schildhauer, P. (2021). *Englischunterricht in einer digitalisierten Gesellschaft*. Beltz Juventa.
Council of Europe. (2006). *You're not for sale*. Council of Europe.
Davies, D., & Rifkind, C. (Eds.). (2020). *Documenting trauma in comics: Traumatic pasts, embodied histories, and graphic reportage*. Palgrave Macmillan.
DC Comics. (Ed.). (1938). *Action comics #1*. DC Comics.

Duong, K. A. (2020). Human trafficking and migration: Examining the issues from gender and policy perspectives. In J. Winterdyk, & J. Jones (Eds.), *The Palgrave international handbook of human trafficking* (pp. 1819–1833). Palgrave Macmillan.

Dycus, D. J. (2012). *Chris Ware's Jimmy Corrigan: Honing the hybridity of the graphic novel.* Cambridge Scholars Publishing.

Eisenmann, M. (2013). Shadows and superheroes in 9/11 graphic novels. In F. E. Pointner, & C. Ludwig (Eds.), *Teaching comics in the English language classroom* (pp. 183–212). WVT.

Eisenmann, M., & Ludwig, C. (2018). *Queer beats – Gender and literature in the EFL classroom.* Peter Lang.

Elsner, D., Helff, S., & Viebrock, B. (Eds.). (2013). *Films, graphic novels & visuals: Developing multiliteracies in foreign language education – An interdisciplinary approach.* LIT-Verlag.

Estler, T. (n.d.). *Abolitionista! Comic books.* Abolitionista. https://www.abolitionista.org/comic-books

Everts, D. (2003). Human trafficking: The ruthless trade in human misery. *The Brown Journal of World Affairs, 10*(1), 149–158.

Fight the New Drug. (2021). *How sex traffickers use social media to contact, recruit, and sell children.* https://fightthenewdrug.org/how-sex-traffickers-use-social-media-to-contact-recruit-and-sell-children-for-sex/

Fisher, D., & Frey, N. (Eds.). (2008). *Teaching visual literacy: Using comic books, graphic novels, anime, cartoons, and more to develop comprehension and thinking skills.* Corwin Press.

Hassett, D. D., & Schieble, M. B. (2007). Finding space and time for the visual in K-12 literacy instruction. *The English Journal, 97*(1), 62–68.

H.E.A.T. Watch. (Ed.). (2013). *Audrey: A story of child sex trafficking.* Alameda County District Attorney's Office.

Lady Gaga. (2009, November 24). *Bad romance* [Video]. YouTube. https://www.youtube.com/watch?v=qrO4YZeyl0I

Latonero, M. (2011). *Human trafficking online: The role of social networking sites and online classifieds.* University of Southern California. http://doi.org/10.2139/ssrn.2045851

Lourenço, M., & Simões, A. R. (2021). Teaching and learning for global citizenship in the EFL classroom: Towards a pedagogical framework. In S. Saúde, M. A. Raposo, N. Pereira, & A. I. Rodrigues (Eds.), *Teaching and learning practices that promote sustainable development and active citizenship* (pp. 86–106). IGI Global.

Ludwig, C., & Pointner, F. E. (Eds.). (2013). *Teaching comics in the foreign language classroom.* WVT.

Lütge, C., & Merse, T. (Eds.). (2021). *Digital teaching and learning: Perspectives for English language education.* Narr.

McCloud, S. (1993). *Understanding comics: The invisible art.* Kitchen Sink Press.

Mikkonen, K. (2017). *The narratology of comic art.* Routledge.

Nettles, B. (2020). *A free me: How Taylor escaped becoming a victim of human trafficking.* Brodrick Nettles.

Oh, S. (2007). Graphical and ethical spectatorship: Human trafficking in Stanford graphic novel project's from Busan to San Francisco and Mark Kalesniko's mail order bride. In C. C. Choy, & J. T. -C. Wu (Eds.), *Gendering the trans-pacific world* (pp. 316–340). Brill.

Oh, S. (2016). Ethical spectatorship in Adrian Tomine's "Shortcomings." *Mosaic: An Interdisciplinary Critical Journal, 49*(4), 107–127.

Outcault, R. F. (1895–1898). *The Yellow Kid*. New York World.

Polaris. (2010). *Power & Control Wheel*. Human Trafficking Hotline. https://humantraffickinghotline.org/sites/default/files/HT%20Power%26Control%20Wheel%20NEW.pdf

Purcell, K. (2012). *Trafficked*. Penguin.

Reid, J. (Ed.). (2016). *Human trafficking: Contexts and connections to conventional crime*. Routledge.

Reid, J., & Fox, B. (2020). Human trafficking and the darknet: Technology, innovation, and evolving criminal justice strategies. In B. Fox, J. Reid, & A. Masys (Eds.), *Science informed policing* (pp. 77–96). Springer.

Rucka, G. (2020). *Wonder Woman: The Hiketeia*. DC Comics.

Satrapi, M. (2000–2003). *Persepolis*. L'Association.

Schüwer, M. (2008). *Wie Comics erzählen: Grundriss einer intermedialen Erzähltheorie der grafischen Literatur*. WVT.

Spiegelman, A. (1980). *Maus: A survivor's tale*. Pantheon Books.

Summer, T. (2021). Digital competence in a global world. In C. Lütge, & T. Merse (Eds.), *Digital teaching and learning: Perspectives for English language education* (pp. 185–206). Narr.

Summer, T. (forthcoming). *Pop culture in English language education: From theory to practice*. Erich Schmidt Verlag.

UNICEF USA. (n.d.). *Child trafficking in the U.S.* https://www.unicefusa.org/child-trafficking-us

United Nations Office on Drugs and Crime. (2021). *Global report on trafficking in persons 2020*. United Nations. https://www.unodc.org/documents/data-and-analysis/tip/2021/GLOTiP_2020_15jan_web.pdf

U.S. Department of State. (n.d.). *About human trafficking*. https://www.state.gov/humantrafficking-about-human-trafficking/#profile

Vuorikari, R., Punie, Y., Carretero Gomez, S., & Van Den Brande, L. (2016). *DigComp 2.0: The digital competence framework for citizens. Update phase 1: The conceptual reference model*. Publications Office of the European Union.

Werner, V., & Tegge, F. (Eds.). (2021). *Pop culture in language education: Theory, research, practice*. Routledge.

15 I'm Not Racist! – Addressing Racism in Predominantly White Classrooms with Cooperatively Designed Multimodal Text Ensembles

Silke Braselmann

Introduction

Developments such as the global impact of the Black Lives Matter protests or the gradual diversification of popular culture have led to increasing awareness of racism among young adults. However, the topic and its relevance to the learners' own lives and contexts remains to be frequently avoided, if not tabooed in many classrooms. Especially in predominantly white settings addressing racism causes a certain amount of unease since "the term is so forceful that most people react very defensively against any suggestion that they might possibly be involved in actions or processes that could conceivably be termed as 'racist'" (Gillborn, 2008, p. 4).

This defensive reaction is a product of an informed and increasingly liberal society in which most people would claim that they are not racist. As bell hooks (1995, p. 5) astutely observed, "overt racism isn't as fashionable as it once was". However, this self-proclaimed societal non-racism is part of the problem: Ignoring its covert, subtle, and institutional forms upholds racism. Understanding all its manifestations and effects should consequently be seen as a societal endeavor that can be kickstarted in classrooms. Especially English language teaching (ELT) offers many opportunities to do so, as it is concerned with language and its power, notions of "otherness", and transcultural or global issues. By working with a variety of perspectives, this contribution will show that English language education can promote self-reflexivity, enhance critical thinking skills, and enable learners to understand the structural and systemic nature of racism not only in the traditional "target cultures" of ELT but in their cultural context.

This contribution will outline the theoretical foundation of anti-racist ELT, namely critical race theory (CRT) and critical (whiteness) pedagogy, touch upon the specific challenges and emotive reactions that occur in predominantly white settings and suggest preliminary principles for addressing racism in the English language classroom. In the scope of this brief and practice-oriented contribution, it is not possible to consider all possible reactions, e.g., overtly racist utterances, to show sensible pedagogical reactions for specific scenarios. However, as a practical starting point for establishing an anti-racist teaching practice from a perspective of critical whiteness, this contribution can offer inspiration for addressing racism by exploring the potential of multimodal text ensembles. These ensembles present an opportunity to amplify marginalized voices, start critical debates and offer various participatory opportunities that can encourage self-reflexivity and critical debate in predominantly white classrooms.

Terms, Concepts, and Principles for Addressing Racism in ELT

Since positionality and self-reflexivity are essential to anti-racist teaching (Mihan, 2012), it is important to stress that the observations made in this contribution stem from a white perspective within a predominantly white society. As a privileged, white, middle-class woman who works in higher education at a University in the German state of Thuringia, I am mostly teaching predominantly white, middle-class students. When staying in Thuringia, they will also teach in predominantly white classrooms, as regional demographics suggest. Addressing racism in these settings presents specific challenges and risks that differ widely from those in more urban or multicultural ones. White people, as opposed to non-white people, can choose freely whether or not they want to think about their identities in relation to the concept of *race* – a privilege that is often taken for granted: "For most Whites, to think about what it means to *be* White is itself a radical move" (Cooks, 2003, p. 248). As a result of this perceived and mostly unquestioned normalcy, reflecting on whiteness in connection with the distribution of power and resources oftentimes leads to resistance ("Are you calling me racist?"), denial ("I don't see colors, only humans!"), or fear of "reverse racism" ("Now I am being judged for being white!"). For educators, reacting to these responses requires a great deal of preparation and willingness for discussion and dissent in the classroom – a hurdle that often appears to be too high to be taken.

Despite these challenges, countering racism in educational contexts needs to be understood as an interdisciplinary endeavor and professional obligation of teachers in democratic societies. After all, studies have shown that young adults experience racism in schools much more frequently and openly than they do outside of the educational setting, e.g., in their free time and after-school activities (Moffit & Juang, 2019). Racism experienced in schools, Moffit and Juang (2019) show, includes individual and "everyday racism" by teachers and peers (i.e., interpersonal discrimination, unconscious bias, othering) as well as structural or institutional racism within the school system (i.e., intentional and unintentional segregation, implicit curricula). Further, the centering of white and Eurocentric knowledge, epistemologies, and practices – also referred to as "epistemological racism" (Kubota & Lin, 2009, pp. 7–8) – remains prevalent in teaching materials. When addressed in ELT, specifically, racism is frequently taught as a historical or political phenomenon of the US or as a part of British colonial history.

Anti-racist language teaching requires a different approach: It uses these historical realities as conversation starters about racism as a transcultural, transversal and structural problem and explores their relevance to the learners' lives.

Focusing solely on language proficiency and communicative competencies might be the easier and less controversial task. However, since "language, culture, and community are inextricably connected, the language education classroom provides the ideal context for entering critical, transformative spaces of culture and community study informed by a social justice framework" (Randolph & Johnson, 2017, p. 101). Acknowledging this great potential and developing ideas for an anti-racist teaching practice does not only have consequences for in-service English language teachers but also calls for implementation in teacher education: The possibilities and challenges for dealing with racism in the classroom – from language issues to teaching materials – therefore need to be addressed in pre-service teacher education, and strategies for identifying and addressing racism in different learner groups need to be explored and developed with future teachers.

However, within the scope of this contribution and its focus on the English language classroom, one of the starting questions concerns the use of terminology and language: To be able to talk about racism, one needs to talk about *race* – this is one of the hallmarks of CRT. CRT supports an understanding of races as social constructs. Focusing on the interrelation of race, power, and policy through storytelling and narrative, the theoretical framework highlights that races are social constructs. As such, they "are products of social thought and relations. Not objective, inherent, or fixed, they correspond to no biological or genetic reality; rather, races are categories that society invents, manipulates, or retires when convenient", as Delgado and Stefancic (2017, p. 9) point out. Understanding these constructions and manipulations is key to critically reflecting on their violent and discriminatory effects – both on a global scale and in the learners' context. This focus on the structural rather than the individual level of racism helps to establish an anti-racist and critical teaching practice that is also based on the principles of critical pedagogy: By honing critical thinking skills, it strives to enable learners to question and actively and intellectually challenge any societal structure, belief or narrative that is related to the power of one group over another (see Ludwig & Summer, this volume). In connection to the issue of racism, subject positioning as required by critical pedagogy requires a reflection on one's privileges and (dis)advantages. Consequently, predominantly white classrooms call for a critical examination of the construct of whiteness and its effects on the distribution of resources and power – a challenging task.

Questioning, criticizing, and rearticulating whiteness to counter white supremacy, as proponents of critical whiteness pedagogy demand (cf. Giroux, 1997; Rodriguez, 2000), may seem challenging and overwhelming at first. However, the pedagogy of discomfort stresses that there can be great value in making learners feel *uncomfortable* "in their own skin": "discomforting feelings are valuable in challenging dominant beliefs, social habits and normative practices that sustain social inequities and thus create openings for individual and social transformation" (Zembylas, 2015, p. 8).

When learners are confronted with issues that make them uneasy, this response needs to be embedded in processes of thorough self-reflection – a complex task for both learners and teachers with a plethora of benefits: The reflection process can lead to a broadened horizon and help to discover the limits of perception that may prevent a multi-dimensional, enriching, truthful, and more accurate way of looking at the world (Boler, 1999). The initially uncomfortable process of understanding how societies actively construct and shape realities presents opportunities for navigating the "worlds that are 'supercomplex' [...] and require our active engagement" (Phipps & Guilherme, 2004, p. 1) – a notion that can also be transferred to many other issues of social injustice. Visualizing and analyzing the normative, socially constructed power of whiteness makes the issue of racism *personal* and *relatable* for learners who may not feel directly affected by racism, leading to a possible reconsideration of the learner's identity (Cooks, 2003).

Addressing Racism in ELT – Challenges and Principles

This challenging task of "nurturing the self-development and self-actualization" (hooks, 2013, p. iii) of learners is seldom or, as bell hooks finds, hardly ever met with cooperation. Yet, she also stresses that students "do not become critical thinkers overnight. First, they must learn to embrace the joy and power of thinking itself" (hooks, 2013, p. 2). To do so, encouraging controversial debates and allowing for discussions is essential. Regarding racism, teachers in predominantly white classrooms should be prepared to deal with the previously mentioned negative responses of denial and resistance. These are not only rooted in internalized worldviews but also closely related to a feeling of insecurity: Resulting from the fear to insult someone – especially in a foreign language – or to make unintentional hurtful or retraumatizing remarks can lead to avoiding the topic or nipping discussions about it in the bud. Yet, especially in ELT, these language-related insecurities should not be avoided but rather laid open. By openly discussing the use of language, changing perception of terminology, and how cultures create and negotiate meanings of words, an understanding of the power of language (cf. Ludwig & Summer, this volume) can be promoted. Further, learners can work toward a change of perspective that embraces vulnerability, ambiguity, and insecurities (Zembylas, 2015) when they are invited to ask: *Why was this hurtful?*, *Whom did it hurt?*, and *Why didn't it hurt me?* These reactions and resulting feelings of discomfort can be seen as essential for actual change driven by young adults.

To encourage a teaching practice that anticipates and draws on these emotive responses and insecurities, I want to outline heuristic principles that foster a better understanding of racism as a structural rather than an individual issue and promote self-reflexivity. Anti-racism is an attitude – it always requires a commitment by the teacher and thus cannot be reduced to simple guidelines. However, in the following points, I want to break down key aspects from critical (whiteness) pedagogy (Akbari, 2008; Cooks, 2003; Gillborn 2006; Mihan, 2012; Rodriguez, 2000, 2009) and CRT (Delgado & Stefancic 2017; Gillborn, 2008; Giroux, 1997) into practical principles that may serve as a guideline for addressing racism in ELT. Anti-racist lesson planning (1) begins with self-reflexivity and positionality of both teachers and learners (Kishimoto, 2018) and (2) is aware of potential experiences with racism in the learner group and of the difficulties of raising and addressing them. It consequently offers various opportunities for sharing or withholding these personal stories by presenting options and materials that allow for a more theoretical or abstract conversation (Braselmann, 2021). It also (3) addresses racism as a transnational and transversal problem rather than from an intercultural perspective and thereby (4) actively challenges binary categories of "us" versus "them". Further, it (5) identifies material, imagery, and narratives that uphold, reproduce, and reinforce racist knowledge and lastly (6) critically reflects on the power of language and the powerful role of the English language in the construction of social categories (Akbari, 2008).

These principles can also help to support teachers in their preparation and selection of materials for anti-racist teaching practice. All choices regarding the selection and design of materials – from questions, tasks, and visualizations on worksheets to selection of film, music, and literature used – can work toward identifying, describing, and, ultimately, dismantling racism. Taking the previously developed guiding principles for anti-racist ELT into consideration, materials, texts, and media used should

- make racist language, images, and narratives visible. Textbooks, narratives, and images are critically examined regarding these depictions and descriptions,
- engage in a transcultural comparison of contexts and phenomena rather than focusing on "target cultures" by using additional material that relates the topic to the learners' context (Akbari, 2008),
- be (partially) selected by the learners in cooperative processes, whenever possible, and thus encourage critical debate and controversy about the selection process,
- be complemented with ample scaffolding for analysis and critical discussion,
- include multiple perspectives on the same topic and favor multimodal materials that offer a wide array of participatory opportunities in different classroom settings (Matias & Mackey, 2016),
- foreground and amplify the voices of minorities and favor narratives of resistance and joy over those of victimization and suffering, and
- encourage learners to engage with perspectives that differ from their own (Gillborn, 2006).

Naturally, the application of these guidelines differs in each classroom – concrete suggestions for their implementation can therefore only serve as examples. Nevertheless, the following teaching suggestion can inspire applying these principles and guidelines by working with cooperatively designed multimodal text ensembles.

Practical Example: Addressing Racism with Cooperatively Designed Multimodal Text Ensembles

The great potential that the re-discovered concept of text ensembles (Delanoy, 2015) holds for critical ELT is discussed in several publications (e.g., Braselmann et al., 2021; Merse, 2018). Text ensembles refer to a selection and combination of various literary and non-fictional texts and materials. They can encourage critical comparisons of different perspectives on the same issue and shared topic and encourage negotiation of different perspectives and interpretations among learners (Merse, 2018). By doing so, they offer great potential for social justice and establishing equal visibility for minorities (Merse, 2018; Randolph & Johnson, 2017). Further, these ensembles help to solve a pedagogical double-bind, as they enable empathetic perspective-taking with oppressed peoples and minorities, hone analytical skills, and promote a critical understanding of different text forms and their ability to shape (and manipulate) one's understanding of the world (Braselmann et al., 2021).

An additional focus on creating *multimodal* text ensembles highlights the relevance of including different media and semiotic modes for various participatory opportunities within heterogeneous learner groups – this is especially relevant regarding racism, as experiences and understanding of the problem can differ widely between different classrooms. Additionally, the inclusion of social media and digital media is very important when it comes to race and racism: According to Matias and Mackey (2016), (white) learners should learn to analyze racism through a variety of texts – *especially* "social media, music, YouTube clips, art, and other symbolic representations of society" (Matias & Mackey, 2016, pp. 37–38) – so they can understand racism in all its facets and are encouraged to reflect on their own position within the discourse. Working with these different media types establishes a connection to the learners' lives and, at the same time, helps them engage with different cultural products that foreground marginalized perspectives. In addition, the selection process can encourage learners to search for media and texts outside of their own social media "bubble". This way, learners can become acquainted with media dynamics and learn how to research and critically assess different media products as they discuss the selection process and reflect upon it.

Discussion and reflection are an integral part of the *cooperative design* of text ensembles. The cooperative selection of texts and media is rooted in the principles of critical pedagogy and thus includes material that the learners have suggested, researched, and selected, taking into consideration the "localness of learning and learning needs" (Akbari, 2008, p. 280). The teacher as a guide and facilitator prepares language and genre scaffolding, using methods and activities that enable the learners to understand and work with their chosen texts. Learners are further encouraged to engage with perspectives that are different from their own. By doing so, the text ensemble amplifies marginalized voices in literature and media and highlights a diverse range of cultural products by minorities.

However, teaching with multiple perspectives may also come across as an "anything goes" approach that promotes a careless or indifferent stance toward subjective truths and politics (Braselmann et al., 2021). At worst, this may result in a reproduction of hurtful, discriminating, and even racist materials. Teachers thus need to be well-versed in the topic and prepared to engage in controversial

174 *Silke Braselmann*

Table 15.1 Overview of the Teaching Sequence on "Racism and Discrimination"

Topic	Racism, discrimination, and privilege
Goals	Students can self-reflect on their position within the discourse on racism and gain an understanding of racism as a structural problem. Students critically analyze a variety of text forms
Outcome	Creative response (poster, video, essay, image, montage/collage)
Level	Grade 11/12
Time	Minimum three 90-minute lessons
Materials	Word cards
	Worksheet with reflection questions
	Multimodal text ensemble: Digital or analog collection of materials/texts/videos/snippets as prepared by the learners, the teacher prepares alternatives/additions
Activities	Reflection questions
	Vocabulary work: Word fields privilege and discrimination (mind mapping)
	Research task: finding and selecting texts about racism, discrimination, and privilege
	Presentation and discussion of text ensemble
	Text analysis tasks in groups
	Creative response

debates on a controversial topic, equipped with several strategies to lead constructive and safe discussions. Agreeing upon certain communicative rules that center critical reflection of the power of language (Randolph & Johnson, 2017) at the beginning of a teaching unit (or school year) can help to ensure racism is problematized rather than reproduced. The following outline of a teaching sequence serves as a possible example of addressing racism, discrimination, and privilege with a cooperatively designed multimodal text ensemble (see Table 15.1). Importantly, the activities and materials chosen need to be carefully matched with the respective learner group. The suggestions and proposed outcomes are therefore only illustrative.

As a pre-activity that activates previous knowledge and includes vocabulary work, the learners could arrange and discuss word cards with terms and chunks that belong to the word fields *privilege* and *discrimination* and match them to either term – either on the floor, wall, or board to encourage movement during the task, or digitally. The word cards may include words and chunks such as *prejudice, being white, to have opportunities, advantages, to grant a privilege, racism, race, class, gender, sexism, ableism, framing, to belong to a majority*, etc. (see Figures 15.1 and 15.2 for practical examples of collaboratively created mind maps). Some cards need to be prepared twice (i.e., *race, class, gender*). Others may require explanation or dictionary work – this can be done in group or partner work. Here, the difference between "race" in the anglophone context and its possible translations into German need to be discussed critically. Other terms may stir controversial debate and require an openness for discussion. Some word cards should be left blank or invite completion (*being able to..., feeling...,*

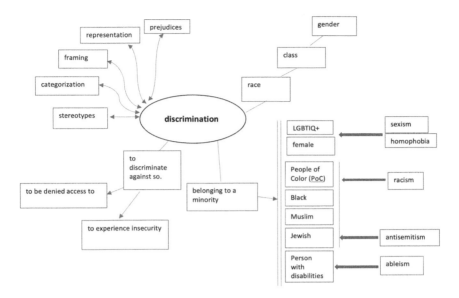

Figure 15.1 Practical Example of a Collaboratively Created Mind Map for the Word Field "Discrimination".

knowing that...). Arranging and discussing the cards can ignite processes of reflecting on structural modes of privilege and discrimination, as different levels and elements of discrimination and privilege are addressed. Questions such as "Who constitutes the majority (in this classroom, in our school in our town, in our country...)?" could also be discussed. The resulting mind maps provide important vocabulary and terminology and, most importantly, visualize the structural nature of privilege and discrimination. In advanced and motivated learner groups, the concept of intersectionality could be introduced by inviting the learners to identify and discuss the different connections and overlaps of discrimination and privilege in the mind maps.

The task at the center of this teaching unit is the cooperative creation of the text ensemble. As a first step of the while-phase, a "text pool" is created based on the teacher's material prepared (see Table 15.2 for suggestions). Each group rates and decides on a number of texts – either digitally by liking and commenting or physically by scanning materials in the room, selecting and grouping, depending on the material included. Learners can now suggest texts, videos, songs, photographs, and any other kind of material subsumed under the given topic.

In preparation for this step, some guiding principles and criteria should be discussed with the learners: To center a power-critical concern, Merse (2018) stresses, text ensembles should present a variety of positions, move beyond the "single story", and problematize and critically reflect on social constructs and their normative powers rather than confirming them. In practice, this can

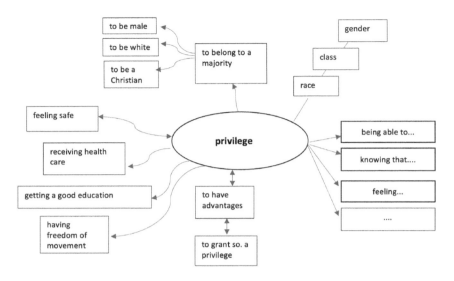

Figure 15.2 Practical Example of a Collaboratively Created Mind Map for the Word Field "Privilege".

be done by inspiring and encouraging the learners to include clashing and conflicting materials and perspectives that initiate debate. However, especially when it comes to tabooed issues, the teacher needs to ensure that no hurtful texts and media are included. To do so, learners and teachers can either agree on certain preferences and no-goes (i.e., language-use, content) or agree on methods to ensure the safe reception of texts (i.e., trigger warning or content notes). Further, the teacher needs to review the text pool and clarify issues regarding problematic choices. If the text pool is created digitally, the "like" and "comment" functions that most tools (e.g., *Padlet*) provide can offer a highly transparent option for the selection process. A teacher's (or, as teachers may miss certain aspects, learner's) comment on why a certain kind of text or material could be problematic can help to foster critical thinking and initiate reflective processes.

An accompanying self-reflexive task during the while-phase could be a written response to questions such as: "What is my perspective – who represents it in media and popular culture, and how?", "Am I seen as representative of a particular group – by whom?" or "Thinking back to my childhood, has race ever played a role in my community, family, or neighborhood?"

In the post-phase, each group can prepare a creative response – videos, posters, or other visualizations, montages, essays – to their text/material, work with analytical and reflective questions prepared by the teacher, and present the material and answers to the class. The presentation of the creative responses then leads to a cooperative phase of comparing, contrasting, and merging the different

I'm Not Racist! 177

Table 15.2 Suggestions for a Text Ensemble for Racism, Discrimination, and Privilege

Novels (excerpts)	Bernardine Evaristo. Girl, Woman, Other. pp. 65–66
	Excerpt. A group of girls discussing privileges.
Non-fiction	Reni Eddo-Lodge. *Why I'm no longer talking to white people about race.* p. 86
	Excerpt. Defining white privilege.
	Kendi, Ibram X. *How to be an anti-racist.* pp. 17–23.
	Excerpt. Autobiographical narrative with definitions of racism.
Newspaper article	Ruth Terry. *How to be an active bystander when you see casual racism.*
	https://www.nytimes.com/2020/10/29/smarter-living/how-to-be-an-active-bystander-when-you-see-casual-racism.html?
Song lyrics (excerpts)	Hip Hop songs that deal with different perspectives within the discourse about racism
	– Macklemore & Ryan Lewis. *White Privilege II* – song and web project by (white) hip hop artist Macklemore reflecting on his role in hip hop culture, cultural appropriation and white people's participation in the Black Lives Matter movement
	– Giant Panda. *Racist* – hip hop group Giant Panda raps about stereotypes from a Black, white and Asian perspective
Music videos	Music videos by hip hop artists
	Joyner Lucas. *I'm not racist* – Lucas raps about racism from a white and Black perspective
Tweets	Tweet by Ibram X. Kendi about white children's alleged discomfort when taught about discrimination in US history: https://twitter.com/DrIbram/status/1483812914821750788
Photography	Photographs from the Black Lives Matter Protests (2020) by Black photographers (Hill, 2020)
Video	*The Daily Show* with Trevor Noah. *DiscrimiNATION*
Transcultural perspective	Video *Racism in Germany* by Deutsche Welle (Douglas, 2020)

perspectives that are represented in the text ensemble. Posters, presentations, videos, collages/montages, or other artifacts should serve as conversation starters. Linking the examples to terms and concepts from the two word fields and mind maps can be done by exploring the discursive elements presented by or contested in the different samples. As a follow-up or additional task, an anonymous essay about the personal reaction to the text ensemble could be a feasible option: Writing anonymously can make learners feel safe to describe their emotive responses and share their thoughts about positionality, perspectives, privilege, and racism without fear of being judged. A pedagogical challenge that would require further consideration that goes beyond the scope of this contribution is the teacher's response to these texts. Especially when racist sentiments are reproduced or racist statements are made, teachers have to carefully decide whether or not they feel it is a safe option to openly address these sentiments – this, of course, is highly dependent on the learner group, the experiences with racism, and the classroom atmosphere.

Conclusion

Planning and teaching a unit that addresses racism and reflects on privilege, whiteness, and discrimination in predominantly white settings is a challenge that teachers need to be prepared for. Instead of summarizing the previous pages, I therefore want to underline the necessity to promote anti-racist teaching in teacher education. Establishing an anti-racist teaching practice, as mentioned above, requires a teacher's commitment to standing up against any form of discrimination. Especially in predominantly white settings, a willingness to engage in controversial debate, to accept shortcomings, and to openly address blunders is of the essence. Making the emotional effort to create a cooperative and open atmosphere, to be willing to "do the work" and stay on top of changes in terminology and discourse – and to adjust teaching activities accordingly and frequently on the go – requires flexibility, time, and nerves. Oftentimes, curricular frameworks, assessment, and lack of time are in the way of including new material or engaging in debate. Critical foreign language education may always be challenging, but it is also rewarding and highly important. To prepare teachers for addressing racism and for being able to deal with different perspectives as well as emotive responses, teacher education should encourage future teachers to be daring in this respect and equip them with tools and ideas that they can implement in their teaching. It should highlight the necessity to be committed and should present strategies for fostering critical thinking skills and for enduring discomfort in class. By doing so, ELT can actively promote a more just and open-minded society – and, at the same time, foster language proficiency required to address societal problems and speak up against them.

Preparing students for their different classroom settings and supporting them in naming and anticipating the challenges and risks that may come with addressing issues such as racism actively helps in establishing a teaching practice that is truly anti-racist, self-reflexive, and, ultimately, more just for everyone. For this, English language education can encourage future teachers to introduce a variety of voices and texts and offer explorations of the languages and cultures from which they stem. By highlighting the benefits of working with multiple perspectives and acquainting them with different modes for selection, cooperative design, and the planning of teaching units, teacher education can inspire pre-service teachers to see the value in a cooperative and self-reflexive teaching practice. Openly discussing reservations and concerns regarding critical thinking, activism, and political education in teacher education can thus promote an anti-racist and engaged teaching practice in the English language classroom.

References

Akbari, R. (2008). Transforming lives: Introducing critical pedagogy into ELT classrooms. *ELT Journal, 62*(3), 267–283.
Boler, M. (1999). *Feeling power: Emotions and education.* Routledge.

Braselmann, S. (2021). Activism or 'slacktivism'? Politisches Engagement im Internet am Beispiel von #BlackLivesMatter und #BlackOutTuesday reflektieren. *Der Fremdsprachliche Unterricht Englisch: Black Lives Matter*, Nr. 173, 26–31.

Braselmann, S., Glas, K., & Volkmann, L. (2021). Ecology, cultural awareness, antiracism and critical thinking: Integrating multiple perspectives in foreign language teaching. *Ecozon@, 12*(1), 8–24.

Cooks, L. (2003). Pedagogy, performance, and positionality: Teaching about whiteness in interracial communication. *Communication Education, 52*(3), 245–257.

Delanoy, W. (2015). Literature teaching and learning: Theory and practice. In W. Delanoy, M. Eisenmann, & F. Matz (Eds.), *Learning with literature in the EFL classroom* (pp. 19–47). Peter Lang.

Delgado, R., & Stefancic, J. (2017). *Critical race theory. An introduction*. New York University Press.

Douglas, E. (2020, August 28). *Racism in Germany*. Deutsche Welle. https://www.dw.com/en/germany-asylum-seeker-dessau-oury-jalloh/a-54727651

Eddo-Lodge, R. (2018). *Why I'm no longer talking to white people about race*. Bloomsbury.

Evaristo, B. (2019). *Girl, woman, other*. Hamilton.

Giant Panda. (2005). Racist [Song]. On *With It*. Tres Records.

Gillborn, D. (2006). Critical race theory and education: Racism and anti-racism in educational theory and praxis. *Discourse, 27*(1), 11–32.

Gillborn, D. (2008). *Racism and education: Coincidence or conspiracy?* Routledge.

Giroux, H. A. (1997). White squall: Resistance and the pedagogy of whiteness. *Cultural Studies, 11*(3), 376–389.

Hill, L. (2020, June 10). *3 black photographers on capturing the George Floyd protests*. The Wired. https://www.wired.com/story/black-photographers-george-floyd-protests/

hooks, B. (1995). *Killing rage: Ending racism*. Routledge.

hooks, B. (2013). *Critical thinking. Practical wisdom*. Routledge.

Joyner, L. (2017, November 28). *I'm not racist* [Video]. YouTube. https://www.youtube.com/watch?v=43gm3CJePn0

Kishimoto, K. (2018). Anti-racist pedagogy: From faculty's self-reflection to organizing within and beyond the classroom. *Race Ethnicity and Education, 21*(4), 540–554.

Kendi, I. X. (2019). *How to be an anti-racist*. Penguin.

Kubota, R., & Lin, A. M. Y. (2009). Race, culture, and identities in second language education: Introduction to research and practice. In K. Ryuko, & A. M. Y. Lin (Eds.), *Race, culture, and identities in second language education exploring critically engaged practice* (pp. 1–25). Routledge.

Macklemore & Ryan Lewis. (2016). White Privilege II [Song]. On *This Unruly Mess I've Made*. Macklemore LLC.

Matias, C. E., & Mackey, J. (2016). 'Breakin' down whiteness in antiracist teaching: Introducing critical whiteness pedagogy. *Urban Review, 48*, 32–50.

Merse, T. (2018). Creating queer text ensembles for the EFL literature classroom: Conceptual considerations and practice-oriented perspectives. In M. Eisenmann, & C. Ludwig (Eds.), *Queer beats – Gender and literature in the EFL classroom* (pp. 289–307). Peter Lang.

Mihan, A. (2012). Toni Morrisons 'Recitatif' als Gegenstand eines Diskurses zu Doing/Undoing Race. In J. Hammer, M. Eisenmann, & R. Ahrens (Eds.), *Anglophone Literaturdidaktik: Zukunftsperspektiven für den Englischunterricht* (pp. 193–207). Winter.

Moffit, U., & Juang, L. P. (2019). 'We don't do that in Germany!' A critical race theory examination of Turkish heritage young adult's school experiences. *Ethnicities, 19*(5), 830–857.

Phipps, A., & Guilherme, M. (2004). Introduction. In A. Phipps, & M. Guilherme (Eds.), *Critical pedagogy. Political approaches to languages and intercultural communication* (pp. 1–6). Multilingual Matters.

Randolph, L. J., & Johnson, S. M. (2017). Social justice in the language classroom: A call to action. *Dimension, 2017,* 99–121. https://eric.ed.gov/?id=EJ1207903

Rodriguez, D. (2009). The usual suspect: Negotiating white student resistance and teacher authority in a predominantly white classroom. *Cultural Studies – Critical Methodologies, 9,* 483–508.

Rodriguez, N. M. (2000). Projects of whiteness in critical pedagogy. In N. M. Rodriguez, & L. E. Villaverde (Eds.), *Dismantling white privilege: Pedagogy, politics, and whiteness* (pp. 1–24). Peter Lang.

Terry, R. (2020, October 29). *How to be an active bystander when you see casual racism.* The New York Times. https://www.nytimes.com/2020/10/29/smarter-living/how-to-be-an-active-bystander-when-you-see-casual-racism.html

The Daily Show with Trevor Noah. (2018, August 29). *DiscrimiNATION.* [Video]. YouTube. https://www.youtube.com/watch?v=0xK1DJ691sE

Zembylas, M. (2015). 'Pedagogy of discomfort' and its ethical implications: The tensions of ethical violence in social justice education. *Ethics and Education, 10,* 1–12.

16 Critical Animal Pedagogy and Global Education in the EFL Classroom

Maria Eisenmann

Introduction – Education for Sustainable Development and Animal Welfare

The constantly changing relationships between human and non-human animals, nature, and the environment have been subject to an enormous acceleration process since the 1950s, which has resulted in considerable ecological, social, economic, and cultural consequences. I define *human animals* as what is generally understood as human beings or persons. By non-human animals I mean the entire animal world, be it domesticated or zoo animals as well as animals in the wild. One of the challenges of the 21st century is to shape a transformation of the human–animal–nature relationship in such a way that both the ecological crises of the time and global injustice are contained. Especially against the background of an obviously growing political-social awareness of young people and their increasing interest in getting involved in society, the foundations must be laid in schools by establishing a critical discourse. In the sense of critical pedagogy (see Ludwig & Summer, this volume), one of the central tasks of schools is to introduce learners to such discourses and further enable them to participate actively in social and political decision-making (Gerlach, 2020).

Critical pedagogy views teaching as a political act where students are engaged to transform the world for *human as well as non-human animals* for the better. In the English language classroom, teachers should therefore constantly emphasise the importance of global as well as local contexts and encourage the inclusion of students' daily lives and interests in the classroom. This can happen by combining curricular requirements with the learners' genuine concerns and needs. At first glance, fundamental topics, especially from the field of Education for Sustainable Development (ESD), can be introduced in a general way but then have to be treated in a problem-oriented discursive mode on the basis of local or regional specificities in order to be able to promote transformational-reflective thinking and political action. Potential subject areas of a critically oriented EFL classroom can be topics that are fed by current (local) news, such as social classes, political power structures, violence, racism, and prejudices (Gerlach, 2020). The focus, however, can also be on global challenges from the climate crisis to urgent questions of animal ethics and animal rights.

DOI: 10.4324/9781003220701-20

Animal welfare is not yet a central topic in materials published within the field of global education, which mostly focus on the climate crisis and human-related aspects (see Küchler & Preiß, 2020). Yet, animal welfare should be addressed when discussing issues related to environmental sustainability, not least because improvements in animal welfare can be closely aligned with the three pillars of sustainable development – social, economic and environmental sustainability. It is the responsibility of teachers to integrate these important, often tabooed, topics into their classrooms, as they are also responsible for filling gaps by addressing topics that are typically excluded from teaching materials such as English textbooks.

Terrible daily processes such as factory farming and mass slaughter are ignored in our society. Due to the fact that Western societies tend to see animals as products they can consume, the killing of animals is a taboo subject inside and outside the classroom. The origins of taboos around killing animals and eating their meat seem to stem from three major historical developments: some meat types were not considered practical to prepare and store or even considered unhealthy, while other animals or parts of animals used to hold, and partly still do, a symbolic meaning (Harris, 1985). Thirdly, certain animals may be representative of a social or religious group of which the sacred cow in India, which represents Mother Earth, is one of many examples.

However, it should be noted that while eating meat is stagnating in Western societies, such as Europe or the United States, consumption is rising dramatically in Asian boom countries such as China and India as well as in many parts of Africa or South America, where it is a sign of growing prosperity (Destatis, 2021). The work of a butcher is an everyday activity, and what happens in a slaughterhouse is common knowledge and no secret. However, many meat eaters suppress the easy-to-follow formula of meat production: meat = animal + killing. This is not least because since the industrialisation of meat production and the killing of animals in huge slaughterhouses, most people are not confronted with the suffering of animals as it is hidden and can therefore easily be ignored. The products are ready in the butcher's shop or increasingly ready packaged in the supermarkets. The association between product and death is only weakly made by most people, if at all. Society not only approves of the killing of animals; the vast majority is even in favour of it because it ensures that the population will find plenty of affordable meat and sausage products on supermarket shelves. Although today there are many footages of slaughter for meat production, most meat eaters do not want to be confronted with them. They even find these images impertinent. It seems as if the killing and slaughtering should take place quite deliberately in secret, which reinforces their tabooing.

With regard to the classroom, some (image) materials, such as pictures of animals cramped together in barns, may be disturbing for students. Very often, the victims in the pictures or films are poultry animals, which are kept in terrible conditions by the thousands and are not able to move in a manner appropriate to their species. The horrifying footage shows how much the animals suffer in these barns: Turkeys or hens caught in coop bars and showing major injuries, including broken legs. There are often signs of painful feather pecking and inflamed footpads indicating that every step must cause pain. However, here the great importance of moments of irritation comes into play. Images that upset, irritate or disturb as well as facts which shake our self-image or our view of the (animal) world, are often given little space in our everyday lives, are ignored or marginalised. This also applies to the context of school and teaching. To my conviction, however, moments of irritation can form the basis of education. Precisely because irritations affect personally, broaden the students' views and bring them into contact with aspects that seem strange and incomprehensible, it seems meaningful from a pedagogic perspective to reflect on them in their complexity.

From early approaches in environmental learning to more recent ones, such as ESD or global environmental citizenship education, subsequent developments in ecocriticism at an international political level have underlined the significance of addressing environmental issues in the classroom. Similar to discussions surrounding global education and the development of global competence, Byram developed the concept of Education for Intercultural Citizenship (EIC). It aims to include a greater focus on political, social, and cultural issues in English language education (Byram et al., 2017). New or re-named concepts of global education, global learning and transcultural competence have become indispensable terms in ELT (e.g., Eisenmann, 2019; Ludwig & Deetjen, 2021; Lütge, 2015; Oxfam Education, 2015; Volkmann, 2015). In this context, it has become widely accepted that environmental issues should not only be a concern of the science classroom as environmental issues are, in fact, cultural issues. Hence, environmental education in the fields of language, literature, and culture is also of key significance for developing a sound understanding of the cultural roots of our environmental crisis and fostering the attitudes and skills necessary to critically assess and solve the problems we are facing. This is the key notion of global education, which emerged initially in the 1970s and found a more substantial place in foreign language education in the early 21st century (e.g., Bartosch & Grimm, 2014; Christensen, 2008; Garrard, 2012; Lopez, 2014; Mayer & Wilson, 2006; Misiaszek, 2018; Siperstein et al., 2017; Waage, 1985).

In the context of critical foreign language pedagogy, taboo and challenging topics related to animal welfare such as global warming, natural disasters or pollution might be especially interesting for young learners and adolescents. The clear majority of students is politically interested, ready to get involved and take action. They expect politics to do more for the climate and the environment, and they see potential in each individual to behave in a more environmentally friendly way. These are the results of the representative survey of more than one thousand young people between the ages of 14 and 22 *"Zukunft? Jugend fragen!"*, which was conducted by the Institute for Ecological Economy Research (Bundesministerium für Umwelt, Naturschutz und nukleare Sicherheit (BMU), 2018). In countries all around the world, recent youth climate strikes also indicate a growing concern among young people regarding environmental issues, and an increased awareness of the need to take urgent political action at a local and global scale. Hundreds of thousands of (young) people have joined the global "Fridays for Future" movement, striking for real climate protection and calling on political leaders to meet their targets and international climate agreements. They are concerned about their individual future as well as the planet's future, and they receive support for their commitment from scientific circles.

For ELT, this means that it is in the hands of teachers and educators to convey what sustainability means in concrete terms and how each individual can effectively commit to its common goals. The goal of global education is to develop learners' global awareness by confronting them with global problems and encouraging them to acquire knowledge about them. Global education and ESD as understood here can be implemented in practice in a variety of ways. In order to raise environmental, social and political awareness, the global goals can be dealt with and reflected upon in class and other global issues or problems such as animal rights can set the basis for topic-based ELT. In this context, students' awareness must be drawn to the cultural dimension of how animals are perceived in the society they live in. This view is influenced by how people in a society see themselves, what religious concepts and beliefs they have and how they, in consequence, treat their living environment.

Yet, the mere discussion or analysis of texts is insufficient and a focus on learner action is considered indispensable. Therefore, lessons should not only provide opportunities for students to participate in meaningful, socially relevant debates but also enhance students to ultimately develop an opinion and a voice of their own. Based on Patrick Geddes' motto "think globally, act locally" (1915), learners should become actively involved in solving global problems by fostering peace, living a sustainable life, and respecting their surroundings.

Critical pedagogy as well as ESD have always been responsive to the deepest problems and conflicts of our time and in the field of foreign language education, many political and environmental issues have found their way into conceptual developments and practical applications. However, in this context, considering urgent questions of animal ethics and animals' rights is often neglected in scholarly discussions as well as in teaching materials. As such, this contribution aims to address why animal rights should be included as a central challenging topic in ELT and foreign language education in general.

Critical Animal Pedagogy

Over the past few decades, the increase in public and scholarly attention to human–animal relations has inspired an animal turn in a number of academic disciplines including environmental education research (Bartosch, 2014, 2021; Russell & Spannring, 2019). The animal turn has led to an increasing interest in animals, in the relationships between human and non-human animals, and in the role and status of animals in society. In my view, critical animal pedagogy means education for an awareness of, for example, the extinction of species in nature, the outdated activity of recreational hunting, controversial animal experiments, industrial mass animal breeding with its fatal consequences for humans, animals and ecology, and last but not least, the critical questioning of animal protection laws. It should become clear to students that animal welfare always incorporates environmental protection. However, the focus of critical animal pedagogy should always be on the extremely deplorable situation of the animals themselves. In addition, the human–animal relationship in all its facets must be considered against an interdisciplinary background, which includes historical, philosophical, theological and scientific approaches.

In this context, Bartosch (2021, p. 146) lists three reasons why animals should "be a central concern in environmental education". Firstly, most students are fascinated by animals and quite a few have or would like to have a pet – a fact that can be observed in many children. And it is precisely because animals arouse emotions in many pupils that they can help develop empathy and get them excited about nature and its processes. Secondly, with a strong focus on the climate crisis, schools have been contributing to environmental education for quite some time and should pay even more attention to biodiversity loss in particular in the future. Animal rights and species extinction are equally urgent and directly interconnected, which is why these issues deserve more attention in school education generally. Thirdly, it makes sense to look at the human–animal relationship in the light of human-animal studies and therefore to examine interactions as well as the anthropocentric separation between human and non-human animals as the core of the current ecological crisis (Bartosch, 2021).

I consider the last point to be the most urgent one because we as a society do indeed have many reasons to rethink our relationship with non-human animals. In the preface to his political philosophy of animal rights, Bernd Ladwig (2020) lists many of these arguments. Industrial livestock farming, for instance, contributes more to the climate crisis than the entire global transport sector. Furthermore, the earth could feed more people if we consumed grains like wheat and corn ourselves instead of feeding them to animals. Liquid manure produced by animals and used as fertiliser puts harmful nitrates into drinking water. Also, antibiotics and other medicinal products administered to livestock endanger human health because bacteria are becoming increasingly resistant to antibiotics as a result (Umweltinstitut München e.V., n.d.). Therefore, reasons of self-interest and justice among humans alone speak against the current system of keeping, using, and killing animals.

As a result of the industrialisation of agriculture in the early 20th century, not only humans have been increasingly replaced by machine power but also animals are devalued to mere commodities (Hayer & Schröder, 2018). The resulting suffering is now present in the media. Again and again, journalists and animal rights activists have documented images of shredded chicks, the castration of piglets without anaesthesia (Deutscher Tierschutzbund e.V., n.d.), insufficiently anaesthetised cattle during slaughter, dehydrated pigs or pregnant cows on animal transports (Carstens, 2021), and all varieties of cruel forms of animal experiments and slaughter worldwide (Foer, 2009). On the Internet, the *Animal Kill Clock* shows a real time estimate of the number of animals killed for food, for example, in the United States, as well as the total number of animals killed each year (Animalclock, 2022). This abhorrent prevailing form of factory farming, which inflicts great suffering on animals, cannot be justified as humanity in most places in the world could feed itself with fewer or without any animal products at all.

Due to this shocking extent of mass torture phenomena in the history of livestock farming, or to use Albert Schweitzer's term "animal hell" (Schweitzer, 2006, p. 59), which is caused by price pressure and changes in the diet of an affluent society, the question of interspecies relations needs to be newly investigated. What can the humanities as well as educational institutions such as universities or schools contribute to this fundamental debate? Since this issue is about re-measuring and re-surveying the field of discourse, that offers a large spectrum of possibilities, it is particularly suitable for raising students' awareness in the foreign language classroom.

Discussing issues related to animal torture in the classroom cannot only help raise students' environmental, social, and political awareness towards human–animal relationship but also provide opportunities for them to engage in ecocritical and environmental discourses in order to prepare them for their (future) roles as responsible global citizens. Dealing with materials combined with hands-on activities allows students to critically reflect their everyday practices and encounters with treating and/or eating animals. By engaging in animal ethical topics in using a great variety of materials in the foreign language classroom, students acquire key multiliteracy skills as well as critical environmental literacies. This could be done, for example, through *language-sensitive teaching*, where students are asked for their spontaneous associations with terms such as *chicken*, *pigs* or *cows*. This way, teachers could find out whether learners see animals as fellow creatures or as food on the plate. In a further step, students can try to find answers as to why the English language differentiates between *cow* and *beef*, *pig* and *pork*, *sheep* and *mutton*, or *calf* and *veal*. Equally, they could compare words used for animals across other languages they are familiar with in a multilingual approach, e.g., the French words *bœuf*, *porc*, *veau*.

The most pressing issues discussed in animal ethics are the use of animals for food purposes as well as animal experiments. Other questions concern hunting, bullfighting, circus and zoo keeping as well as fur farming. Problems are also raised by the handling of so-called cultural followers (foxes, rats, etc.) – animals that gain advantages due to anthropogenic landscape-altering measures and therefore follow humans into their cultural landscape (forests, fields, meadows, traffic routes, settlements, and cities) – and the conflict with wild animals over limited resources. If a serious ethical consideration of animals requires the granting of equal status, then many practices of animal use appear questionable. For then, human interests such as culinary enjoyment, aesthetic pleasure, and cultural preservation cannot serve as justification for inflicting significant suffering on animals in the form of pain, fear or deprivation of opportunities for activity and social contact. But how could it come to this?

Until early modern times, representatives of anthropocentrism insisted on the trait approach, i.e., postulated species-specific characteristics are used to undermine the principle of equality between human and non-human animals (Schmitz, 2014). This is a means of domination, because the most advantageous characteristics of one's own group or species are overweighed and generalised, and those of others – inferiors – are marginalised. So-called borderline cases that do not (or no longer) possess the "human" characteristics are indirectly assumed to be deficient as individuals. However, the culturally grown constructions of the supposed inferiority of non-human animals are increasingly and strongly questioned by behaviouristic and neuroscientific research results. Criteria such as the ability to speak, self-awareness or being aware of one's own dying and death can hardly be named as distinct characteristics (Hayer & Schröder, 2018). It would be better to distinguish between human and non-human animals because ultimately, all beings are products of the same evolutionary natural history whether that be worms, amphibians, fish, birds or mammals, all the way to our close relatives, the chimpanzees. Since all species are evolutionarily and biologically connected, the difference between human and non-human animals is only one of degree, but not of principle.

To develop an understanding of these fundamental interrelationships is the main task of foreign language teaching in a globalised world. Through creative participation tasks, students cannot only develop critical environmental literacies; they are also encouraged to explore issues such as human-animal relations, biodiversity, and environmental crisis. In view of this threat towards animals posed by human-induced cruelty and destruction, critical animal pedagogy on a local and global level is becoming increasingly important. It is a concept which is based on the cultural orientations of ecocriticism and provides an essential contribution to the discourse of inter- and transcultural learning as well as global foreign language teaching.

People's cultures are diverse, and these cultural differences can be very small or huge. Even among seemingly similar Western countries, there can be significant cultural differences in the relationship between human and non-human animals. A commonality is that almost all cultures eat animals and use them for scientific purposes, for work, and for entertainment. Thus, the use and exploitation of animals is culturally pervasive, and the universality of human violence against animals is remarkable. Despite the obvious similarities, cultural differences in attitudes towards and treatment of animals can be profound. Cultures have different views about the nature of animals, the value of certain species, moral and ethical obligations to animals, and how they should be treated.

However, globalisation can have a massive impact on the effectiveness of advocacy for animals. Attempts in one nation to protect animals may have unintended consequences in the globalised world. For example, bans on certain uses of animals in agriculture, experimentation, or entertainment in one country may cause those practices to move to another. Due to the consequences of globalisation, cultural differences and commonalities in advocacy for animal rights and welfare are now of paramount importance in determining a global strategy for animal welfare. Given the potpourri of human cultures and being aware that animal rights work has to be considered globally, the class can consider together how animal rights activists can advocate for animals most effectively and successfully. In order to do this, students can learn about the various animal welfare laws which, in recent years, have been tightened in most countries of the European Union and its neighbouring countries, but they have not been uniformly regulated yet.

From a cultural-historical point of view, the category "animal" was mostly seen in opposition to humans. Assigning a weaker value to animals because they are not considered equal incurs the reproach of speciesism, i.e., preference of one's own species, what Ryder (1971) already criticised in the 1970s. For we grant humans, for example, the newborn or the demented, a full moral status even if they do not have the capacities of human animals in the proper sense. According to Singer (1982), paying less respect to non-human animals that have similar or even higher intellectual abilities because they do not belong to the human species constitutes unfounded discrimination, which has structural similarities with other forms of discrimination such as racism or sexism (Tuider & Wolf, 2014). Ultimately, any artificially asserted dualisation – animalum versus humanum – is a product of discursive power relations established solely by human animals, privileging them as well as their chosen pets (Schröder & Hayer, 2016).

And here an ethical dilemma opens up, or, according to Garry Francione, a moral schizophrenia (Francione, 2014). While some are massively exploited, others are caressed and pampered. Humans' attitudes towards animals fluctuate between sentimentality and instrumentalisation. Some animals get names, others get numbers. People buy and eat cheap pork on the one hand and cuddle dogs and cats on the other. For some, tombstones are erected, whereas others are thrown away. Some animals are allowed to frolic freely, others are denied the right to turn on their own axis. Some are likely to be watched in the woods and meadows, others have to smell their own excrements through slatted floors. Many pets are trained to develop amazing abilities, others, in captivity, prevented from performing the simplest tasks, driving them into apathy or madness. For some, expensive surgeries are paid so that they can live a few months longer, others are killed long before their biological end (Ladwig, 2020).

Philosophers such as Tom Regan, Robert Spaemann, or Bernd Ladwig have long since pleaded for an institutionally and legally effective upgrading of animals. Ladwig's approach is directly linked to the question of the "dignity of creature" as enshrined in the constitutions of Switzerland (since 1992) and Luxembourg (since 2018). The concept of animals' dignity goes beyond common welfare approaches based on scientific grounds because besides avoiding suffering and pain it states that animals should also be protected from unjustified interventions on their appearance, from humiliation and from excessive instrumentalisation. Sue Donaldson's and Will Kymlicka's (2013) *Zoopolis* should be mentioned here because they also base their approach on elementary assumptions of the animal rights discourse. This states that animals do not exist to serve human ends and they are neither servants nor slaves of humans but have their own moral value and their own individual existence, on which their basic moral rights to life and freedom are based (Donaldson & Kymlicka, 2013). To this end, Donaldson and Kymlicka suggest that the long-term plan should not be to disconnect human and non-human animals further, but to explore and affirm the rich possibilities of coexistence. The aim is to build up new relations of justice through the specific design of different legal statuses between human and non-human animals (Donaldson & Kymlicka, 2013). In terms of EFL teaching, approaches of critical animal pedagogy in the context of ecological education may provide opportunities for students to develop their critical thinking skills, voice an opinion of their own and participate in meaningful discussions of relevant issues in the face of using non-human animals for human purposes.

Up to this point, a rough overview of central positions and discussions within animal ethics will suffice and the next section will focus on practical implications for ELT. In particular, immersive media such as literature, images and films can help to promote empathy and understanding for other creatures. In the following, some teaching ideas are presented with which critical animal pedagogy can be discursively designed in foreign language teaching with the aim of explicitly addressing taboo topics such as the animal torture and killing animals. The selected approaches are interdisciplinary and can easily be linked to subjects such as biology, geography, history, ethics, or religious education.

Interdisciplinary Teaching Ideas

In the following, some interdisciplinary teaching ideas for all levels of proficiency will be presented. They are designed across classes and can be modified according to the students' language proficiency and their general skills, readiness, abilities and learning profiles. The learning objectives are based on the concepts of critical pedagogy as well as critical animal pedagogy as a theoretical basis for exploring taboos. The overarching learning goal here is to develop taboo literacy as a component of critical literacy (see Ludwig & Summer, this volume). This is implemented through assignments on how animal-related taboos can provide opportunities to engage students in critical discussions about animal welfare and animal rights that they are likely to encounter in their daily lives outside the classroom.

In terms of ESD, as well as for global environmental citizenship, students should think about when and in what contexts they are confronted with animals and what role they play. They should reflect on why we distinguish between pets and farm animals and who is responsible for this categorisation. To discuss why we eat some and love others opens up a tabooed topic as industrial mass animal breeding and mass slaughter is probably not "on the table" in most families.

A promising way to start a teaching unit on the topic at hand is a survey of learners' food preferences. Learners are first asked to name two of their favourite dishes and then make menu proposals for a family feast. The survey is done orally, while, unobtrusively, the teacher notes the numbers of vegan, vegetarian, and meat dishes, separately for favourite foods and suggestions for a holiday such as Easter or Christmas celebrations. While it is to be expected that favourite meals will often include vegetarian dishes, the menu for family gatherings and celebrations will generally include meat. These findings serve as a starting point for a brief conversation about possible (historical) reasons. The following guiding questions for the ensuing discussion are conceivable:

- Why do human beings like to eat meat?
- Why do they consider meat a part of a celebratory meal?

Through this discussion, students are sensitised to the topic and gradually prepared to deal with it. To lead the students even more deeply into the field of animal welfare and animal rights, they create a list with two columns, in which pets are listed on one side and farm animals on the other. Following individual activity, the lists are compared and discussed based on the following questions:

- Are there animals that can be assigned to both columns? Guess which ones they could be.
- Describe, from your own personal point of view, what distinguishes the animals on the two lists. What do you have to do with pets? What do you have to do with farm animals? Which ones do you like the most? Why? How do you know each of them? How do they appear in your everyday life?
- Choose some animals that you know (from where?) and that are close to you. Pay attention to your associations with each animal: What are their characteristics? What ways of life do they have? What habitat? What connects you to each animal? What do you feel about each one – no matter where you know it from (maybe alive, maybe from a(n) (animated) film, maybe from an encyclopaedia or an animal book)?
- What actually makes animals livestock (= animals that are bred, exploited, killed and eaten) and who decides about it?

In a next step, based on these critical pedagogical questions, students can present their very personal experiences with individual animals in a written and/or drawn profile in a group or in the whole class and add their newly gained knowledge to their personal profiles.

In order to develop a deeper empathy for animals and understand how the exploitation of animals affects the environment and the lives of both humans and animals, students watch the short film (10 minutes) *Their Future in Your Hands* (Animal Aid, 2020), produced for Animal Aid by Environment Films in 2020. This is an educational film that can serve as an introduction to animal rights movements along with a discussion about the ethical and appropriate treatment of animals. By presenting facts about animals' rich emotional complexity and drawing parallels between the animal rights movement and other social justice movements in recent history, this video can help students use critical thinking skills to examine why and how the general exploitation of animals continues. While or after watching the film, students should be asked to evaluate inhumane uses of animals practiced throughout history as well as today that are both legal and standard procedures. Rather than simply describing the suffering of animals in laboratories and factory farms, the film supports students in learning how they can help to stop it for creating a better world for human and non-human animals as well as for the environment.

After watching the film, teachers need to provide learners with an opportunity to express their emotions and state their moments of irritation because some of the pictures might be disturbing for them. Hence, it is essential to give the students space to express their impressions. In groups or with a partner they discuss what particularly surprised and/or touched them while watching the film.

An alternative for introducing this topic could also be the trailer for the documentary *Gunda* (Filmwelt Verleih, 2021). Director Victor Kossakovsky tells the story of the breeding pig Gunda and the rearing of her piglets. The film is shot in black and white and manages without words. With the clear reduction to the perspective of farm animals that are allowed to grow up in a maximally species-appropriate husbandry, the film succeeds in making a plea for the importance of animal welfare and the right to life. Through its calm, carefully composed shots, the film communicates the sensations of animals. It presents them as creatures with their own perceptions, sensibilities and habits. It allows students to reflect on the mystery of animal consciousness and the role human beings play in it. Following this, students can be asked to formulate what they expect from the film based on the trailer.

As post-viewing activities, the following assignments are appropriate for both films:

Task "Farm Animal Husbandry"

What do you know about farm animal husbandry? In which places are farm animals kept? In small groups, collect the places in a mind map and organise them by species. Research typical characteristics, habitat, and social behaviour for each of the farm animals you selected. After researching, add which conditions of animal husbandry European laws prescribe. Create a podcast with factual information about the species and their habitats, and with a personal commentary on what you learned through the research. Post your podcasts on your school's website.

Task "Eating Animals"

- None of us would slaughter and eat their pets such as dogs, cats, or guinea pigs. But why chickens, rabbits and pigs? What is the difference?
- Discuss your findings in groups. Extend your arguments to the more general question: Do animals exist for humans? What speaks in favour, what speaks against this?
- Form at least two groups of different opinions. Research your arguments and compile them into a mind map or list. Discuss your different positions and arguments in groups/in class.
- Research on the Internet what a full Thanksgiving dinner should include. Create an alternative Thanksgiving meal that does not harm animals.

Task "Take Political Action"

- In small groups, conduct (online) research to find out which organisations and groups are particularly committed to animal rights. Introduce these organisations to the class in short presentations. Discuss the differences between the groups in terms of motivations and goals. Consider whether and in what way you could possibly participate as a class in one of them (e.g., sponsorships, fundraising run, toy or cake stand at the school festival, active local work during the holidays).
- Check the "Farm to Fork" strategy and write a letter to the European Commission's expert group on animal health in which you draw attention to the abuses in animal protection in your region. Then formulate your demands.

Farm to Fork: https://ec.europa.eu/food/horizontal-topics/farm-fork-strategy_de;

European Commission: https://ec.europa.eu/info/about-european-commission/contact_en#Contact-the-European-Commission

I am aware that the entire topic of animal welfare and the associated tasks bear potential challenges for those teachers who are not critical pedagogues and/or do not support ESD. Nevertheless, I hope that this task design is convincing and can thus contribute to a critical examination of how we want to treat non-human animals in the future and thus shape our world.

Conclusion

In the context of critical pedagogy, this contribution shows why it is important to include animal rights as a central challenging taboo topic (not only) in the foreign language classroom. In view of the human-animal relationship as well as the global threat posed by human-induced animal torture, global education and ESD are becoming increasingly important. They are concepts that are based on the literary and cultural orientations of ecocriticism and provide an essential contribution to the future discourse of animal well-being. Looking closely at the animals' disastrous situation is hard to bear, but simply looking away and carrying on as before is morally reprehensible. A "system change" supported by society is therefore urgently needed. It is therefore the teachers' task to work for a change in ecological awareness and for a rethinking of the human-animal relationship. This can only happen by educating the students with the help of facts and figures via suitable materials such as factual documentaries. Factually informative education can make a significant contribution to students rethinking and possibly changing their (consumer) behaviour. They are also educated to express their opinions, to participate in the discourse on animal rights, and to get involved in animal welfare.

References

Animal Aid. (2020, November 23). *Their future in your hands (2020 edit)*. [Video]. YouTube. https://www.youtube.com/watch?v=w-AUBaabXL8

Animalclock. (2022). *2022 U.S. Animal kill clock*. https://animalclock.org

Bartosch, R. (2014). Teaching a poetics of failure? The benefit of *not*-understanding the other, posthumanism, and the works of Shaun Tan and Wolf Erlbruch. In R. Bartosch, & S. Grimm (Eds.), *Teaching environments. Ecocritical encounters* (pp. 59–73). Peter Lang.

Bartosch, R. (2021). Augmented animality: Immersion and participation in digital environments. In C. Ludwig, & C. Deetjen (Eds.), *The world beyond. Developing critical environmental literacies in EFL* (pp. 143–162). Winter.

Bartosch, R., & Grimm, S. (2014). *Teaching environments. Ecocritical encounters*. Peter Lang.

Bundesministerium für Umwelt, Naturschutz und nukleare Sicherheit [BMU]. (2018). *Zukunft? Jugend fragen! Nachhaltigkeit, Politik, Engagement – eine Studie zu Einstellungen und Alltag junger Menschen*. https://www.ioew.de/publikation/zukunft_jugend_fragen/

Byram, M., Golubeva, I., Hui, H., & Wagner, M. (Eds.). (2017). *From principles to practice in education for intercultural citizenship*. Multilingual Matters.

Carstens, P. (2021, May 27). *Vom Emsland nach Nordafrika: Gericht erlaubt Transport von 500 schwangeren Kühen*. Geo. https://www.geo.de/natur/tierwelt/gericht-erlaubt-transport-von-500-schwangeren-kuehen-30546192.html

Christensen, L. (Ed.). (2008). *Teaching North American environmental literature*. The Modern Language Association of America.

Destatis. (2021). *Globale Tierhaltung, Fleischproduktion und Fleischkonsum*. https://www.destatis.de/DE/Themen/Laender-Regionen/Internationales/Thema/Landwirtschaft-fischerei/tierhaltung-fleischkonsum/_inhalt.html

Deutscher Tierschutzbund e.V. (n.d.). *Ferkelkastration*. https://www.tierschutzbund.de/information/hintergrund/landwirtschaft/schweine/ferkelkastration/

Donaldson, S., & Kymlicka, W. (2013). *Zoopolis. Eine politische Theorie der Tierrechte*. Suhrkamp.

Eisenmann, M. (2019). The potential of young adult dystopian fiction in the EFL classroom. In C. Ludwig, & N. Maruo-Schröder (Eds.), *'Tell freedom I said hello'. Issues in contemporary young adult dystopian fiction* (pp. 137–159). Winter.

European Commission. (n.d.a). *Contact*. https://ec.europa.eu/info/about-european-commission/contact_en#Contact-the-European-Commission

European Commission. (n.d.b). *Farm to fork*. https://ec.europa.eu/food/horizontal-topics/farm-fork-strategy_de

Filmwelt Verleih. (2021, June 4). *GUNDA – Offizieller Trailer*. [Video]. YouTube. https://www.youtube.com/watch?v=1a3dIFbKNb0

Foer, J. S. (2009). *Eating animals*. Little, Brown and Company.

Francione, G. L. (2014). Empfindungsfähigkeit, ernst genommen. In F. Schmitz (Ed.), *Tierethik* (pp. 153–174). Suhrkamp.

Garrard, G. (2012). *Teaching ecocriticism and green cultural studies*. Palgrave Macmillan.

Geddes, P. (1915). *Cities in evolution*. Williams and Norgate.

Gerlach, D. (Ed.). (2020). Einführung in eine Kritische Fremdsprachendidaktik. In D. Gerlach (Ed.), *Kritische Fremdsprachendidaktik: Grundlagen, Ziele, Beispiele* (pp. 7–31). Narr.

Harris, M. (1985). *Good to eat: Riddles of food and culture*. Simon & Schuster.
Hayer, B., & Schröder, K. (Eds.). (2018). *Tierethik transdisziplinär. Literatur – Kultur –Didaktik*. Transcript.
Küchler, U., & Preiß, J. (2020). *Schwerpunktthema Abitur Englisch: Green matters. Planet earth – language – culture*. Cornelsen.
Ladwig, B. (2020). *Politische Philosophie der Tierrechte*. Suhrkamp.
Lopez, A. (2014). *Greening media education. Bridging media literacy with green cultural citizenship*. Peter Lang.
Ludwig, C., & Deetjen, C. (Eds.). (2021). *The world beyond. Developing critical environmental literacies in ELT*. Winter.
Lütge, C. (2015). Introduction: Global education and English language teaching. In C. Lütge (Ed.), *Global education: Perspectives for English language teaching* (pp. 7–16). LIT.
Mayer, S., & Graham, W. (Eds.). (2006). *Ecodidactic perspectives on English language, literature and culture*. Wissenschaftlicher Verlag Trier.
Misiaszek, G. W. (2018). *Educating the global environmental citizen. Understanding ecopedagogy in global contexts*. Routledge.
Oxfam Education. (2015). *Education for global citizenship: A guide for schools*. https://www.oxfam.org.uk/education/resources/education-for-global-citizenship-a-guide-for-schools
Russell, C., & Spannring, R. (2019). So what for other animals? Environmental education after the animal turn. *Environmental Education Research*, 25(8), 1137–1142.
Ryder, R. D. (1971). Experiments on animals. In R. Godlovitch, S. Godlovitch, & R. Harris (Eds.), *Animals, men and morals. An enquiry into the mal-treatment of non-humans* (pp. 41–82). Taplinger.
Schmitz, F. (2014). Tierethik – eine Einführung. In F. Schmitz (Ed.), *Tierethik. Grundlagentexte* (pp. 13–73). Suhrkamp.
Schröder, K., & Hayer, B. (2016). Tierethik in Literatur und Unterricht. Ein Plädoyer. In K. Schröder, & B. Hayer (Eds.), *Didaktik des Animalen. Vorschläge für einen tierethisch gestützten Literaturunterricht* (pp. 1–14). WVT.
Schweitzer, A. (2006). Die zum Leiden verurteilte Kreatur. In E. Gräßer (Ed.), *Ehrfurcht vor den Tieren* (pp. 48–57). C.H. Beck.
Singer, P. (1982). *Practical ethics*. Cambridge University Press.
Siperstein, S., Hall, S., & LeMenager, S. (Eds.). (2017). *Teaching climate change in the humanities*. Routledge.
Tuider, J., & Wolf, U. (2014, January 14). *Tierethische Positionen*. Bundeszentrale für politische Bildung. https://www.bpb.de/gesellschaft/umwelt/bioethik/176364/tierethische-positionen
Umweltinstitut München e.V. (n.d.). *Keine Massentierhaltung ohne Medikamente*. http://www.umweltinstitut.org/themen/landwirtschaft/massentierhaltung/antibiotika-im-stall.html
Volkmann, L. (2015). Opportunities and challenges for transcultural learning and global education via literature. In W. Delanoy, M. Eisenmann, & F. Matz (Eds.), *Learning with literature in the EFL classroom* (pp. 237–262). Peter Lang.
Waage, F. O. (1985). *Teaching environmental literature: Materials, methods, resources*. The Modern Language Association of America.

17 Death, Extinction, and the Limits of Literacy

Roman Bartosch

Introduction: Taboos Everywhere

Educational conversations about death in the current climate of catastrophic environmental change touch, this contribution will argue, on a number of tabooed topics and thus challenge English language teaching (ELT) theories and practices in a variety of ways. First, "death" in modern societies is widely tabooed in a very general sense: It is little talked about and has been relegated to health and care institutions; it seems to have no real place in educational settings. The current pandemic and the new ubiquity of discourses of dying do not contradict but seem to underline this observation, as societal debates on public health frequently appear oddly unrelated to debates on educational practice, often framed as a technological, rather than an existential challenge. Second, while mortality and finitude may at least constitute philosophical concerns on which language and literature education in English could draw, dying in an age of looming climate catastrophe ups the ante: Articulations of climate anxiety, for instance in the context of Fridays for Future demonstrations, are less concerned with mortality as such but with the mostly unprecedented dread of large-scale extinctions of humans and other life forms. Understood this way, death touches on matters of intergenerational injustice, and it is often belittled, by educators and political or economic stakeholders alike, as hysteria, adding insult to tabooed injury. A third aspect concerns the day-to-day implications of dealing with death and extinction in current educational systems: Existential threat and dread may require pedagogic practices less concerned with standardised learning outcomes and small-scale improvements in individual competence and literacy, but with a new culture of learning and flourishing, or what Jem Bendell calls "doom and bloom" (2019, p. 137). Contemporary assessment and evaluation culture seem to be in the way of this – as it were, they seem to render such demands taboo. This contribution will address some of the taboos surrounding death, extinctions, and educational practices, and it will draw on findings from literary studies and literature pedagogy to make a case for the possibility, indeed: the necessity, to rethink literary learning as a practice of flourishing in the precarious present.

DOI: 10.4324/9781003220701-21

Death Writ Large: Learning to Die in an Age of Extinctions?

Recent years have seen an impressive increase, partly boosted by soaring biodiversity loss and growing recognition of the severity of climate threats for human flourishing and survival, in research on extinctions and the collapse of social and ecological systems. Social and cultural anthropology, and research on indigenous communities in the Global South more generally, have therefore suggested an "anthropology of extinction" (Rose et al., 2017; Sodikoff, 2012; van Dooren, 2014); it is here that we can find early articulations of the interconnection between human well-being and ecological health in a more encompassing frame. These concerns have by now been recognised by global policymakers such as the UNESCO and WHO that have adopted some of these insights in their "one health" framework which posits that "optimal health and well-being" requires an acknowledgement of "the interconnections between people, animals, plants and their shared environments" (UNESCO, 2020). The COVID-19 pandemic as well as better understandings of the links between consumption and dietary practices, urban and industrial development, and diseases transmitted between humans and other animals (zoonoses) alongside skyrocketing cases of species loss underline the urgency of such integrative viewpoints.

These viewpoints have also been developed and elaborated by research in the environmental humanities. Ursula Heise has analysed the "cultural meaning of endangered species" and argues for a better understanding of "multispecies justice" that "puts questions of justice for both humans and nonhumans front and center" (2016, p. 202). Her minute attention to narrative patterns, iconographies and imaginative templates helps to understand current debates on the geological, global human impact on climate and biodiversity as "speculative fiction" (Heise, 2016, p. 215). This, in turn, underlines the potential of the imagination for multispecies communities as well as possible educational leeway for discussing histories, cultures and values within more general concerns about sustainability and conservation (see Heise, 2016). In a similar manner, Rob Nixon (2011) has shown that environmental and social justice are inextricably connected, and he has suggested "slow violence" as a term for the incrementing yet hardly visible damage done to disenfranchised communities by neo-colonial, "unsustainable", and ecocidal economies. His case for the potential of fiction to write against the invisibilities of such injustices undergirds arguments for the importance of literature classrooms for transformative action, as does Kate Rigby's arresting natural and cultural histories of disaster with their cases for the role and potential of narrative "in perilous times" (Rigby, 2015). It is with an eye on the role of narratives – for dealing with, and for witnessing – the extent and implications of human-caused climate and biodiversity crises that I am reading Owain Jones, Kate Rigby and Linda Williams's work on the "inability to mourn" as well. They ask:

> Will we develop the capacity to stem and then reverse the unfolding destruction of our earthly home, the untimely death of evolutionary kin, and the

gradual erasure of a beauty so intrinsic to our sense of the world that its replacement by barrenness and ugliness seems inconceivable?
(Jones et al., 2020, p. 394)

Their call for greater attentiveness over and against a "not yet [...] commensurate relationship between the severity of the crisis we are facing and the collective (societal) anger and grief being expressed" (Jones et al., 2020, p. 394) points to the taboo surrounding appropriate emotional and political responses.

So far, this research has had little or no impact on educational theory and practice with the exception of work on pedagogy and the Anthropocene (as found in Lysgaard et al., 2019). To some degree, this is understandable; however, and as I will argue in the next section, it is also somewhat surprising, unwarranted, and problematic. As socioecological death writ large, extinction is twice tabooed and therefore difficult to address indeed in classroom situations where student well-being and environments conducive to learning are key. At the same time, education is widely understood to be a crucial factor when it comes to preparing young people for their adult life in this world. It might therefore be time to reconsider what it means to be(come) educated in what Roy Scranton calls "humanity's most philosophical age" (Scranton, 2015, p. 21), marked by existential dread over current and future loss. His book suggests that "learning to die in the Anthropocene" is a key societal challenge; I take this as my cue for a discussion of the potential role of education and the question which part the English language and literature classroom in particular can play in this regard.

Why Does It Matter?

Few people enjoy thinking of, let along talking about, death. The fact that tackling this taboo topic is challenging thus goes without saying; however, it also needs to be noted that addressing such existential questions in an environment conducive to reflection and care-filled communication can add to student health and well-being (Bartosch, 2021; Pennebaker, 1995) and that it potentially "facilitates emotional processing and problem-solving" (Berman, 2012, p. 5). In an age of increasing awareness of large-scale loss and ecological devastation, there might thus be more need than ever to provide spaces for the reflection of and engagement with questions of death and dying. It is therefore important to think about teaching methodologies as much as pedagogic justifications for discussions teachers might have "to defend and legitimize" their decision to address these issues in conversations with colleagues and students' parents. This is especially so because they know the topic "reflects students' reality, even as it makes adults uncomfortable and fearful about their inability to protect children from that very reality" (Linder & Majerus, 2016, p. viii).

Whereas the importance of educational work on the reality of death and dying is recognised in social and health work education as well as in medical and nursing schools (Berman, 2012), in other disciplines, including English, these topics seem to belong to a phenomenon that Kenneth Doka calls "disenfranchised grief"; that is, an experience of "a sense of loss" that people experience without "a socially recognized right, role, or capacity to grieve" (1989, p. 1, as cited in Berman, 2012, p. 10). This is surprising insofar as the English literature classroom knows many reasons to talk about death: "Death", Jeffrey Berman reminds us, "is often encountered in English courses – Hamlet's death, celebrity death, death from the terrorist attacks during 9/11 – but students rarely have the opportunity to write about their own experiences of death" (Berman, 2012, p. 10). Berman rightly stresses the importance of safe and empathic learning environments when it comes to changing that, to which I will return later. It is also critical to emphasise that English teachers are neither professional therapists nor counsellors, which means that while we are qualified to speak about writings about death – or "deaths writ large" in extinction scenarios, as discussed above – we are not trained to provide professional help to students whose mental health is seriously affected by these issues. This makes it all the more important to create learning scenarios that focus on literary learning first and foremost, and that offer means of negotiating the topic with care and sensitivity.

One way of achieving this might be by pointing to the literary dimension of representations of death. A cursory look at popular children's literature for instance reveals not only the frequency but also the creativity of thanatological narratives: Think of Peter Pan's Neverland and the explanation that he takes children who fell out of the perambulator flying across the sea to a place where they don't age – an afterlife scenario if ever there was one, but one that is cleverly interwoven with adventure and coming-of-age motifs. Or enter *The Secret Garden*: Frances Hodgson Burnett's 1911 classic is another topographical take on the topos of death – as well as of illness and eventual flourishing (the list of such meaningful connections could be extended, for instance, when including animals and even plants; see Höing, 2018, 2021). Depictions of and creative takes on death even take place "at species scale", as David Herman (2018, p. 249) calls it: Kurt Vonnegut's novel *Galápagos*, while presenting a narrative of evolution in the process of which cast-away human characters turn into human-animal hybrids, right from the start marks those characters soon about to die with little crosses and indicates in a footnote that this is meant as an aid for readers who do not have to concern themselves with those characters for too long. To add one more example, Shaun Tan's *The Rabbits* presents readers with the intricate connection between species death by invasive species, colonial violence towards Australian Aboriginal communities, and individual theriomorphic characters all in one go and in a single, both excitingly accessible and aesthetically rewarding, storybook.

The latter narrative is particularly interesting because of its intricate connection of the different forms and, if you will, different magnitudes of loss it describes. In bringing together different stories of loss, of individual, cultural ways of being in the world, and complete ecosystems, and thus combining postcolonial and ecological histories, it creates a rich semiotic texture that not only provides a fruitful space for aesthetic learning, which I have described as "semiodiverse environments" (Bartosch, 2022, p. 90). It thus offers numerous avenues for meaningful communication in the language and literature classroom and cleverly circumvents the divide between individual death and large-scale devastations by way of its aesthetic and narrative strategies. This is helpful on a variety of counts: It offers means of identification and emotional engagement (see Weik von Mossner, 2017); and its connection of these two scales of devastation speaks to the need of teachers to choose suitable texts for an English classroom for which it may be hard to find narratives "at species scale", while numerous texts that lend themselves to discussions of death of individuals are recognised by canons and curricula, as argued above. Lastly, the strategy of connecting (individual) death and (large-scale) extinctions helpfully challenges the quirky anthropocentrism underlying the assumption, sometimes found in philosophical and critical thought, that humans die as persons while animal populations die as statistical numbers (see Eisenmann, this volume). If we can cultivate grief in times of environmental and biodiversity catastrophe in order to make readers more attuned to the many dimensions of devastation in store for humans and nonhumans alike, the grief we are talking about has to be transspecies grief.

Such a notion of transspecies eco-grief lastly points to a challenge with which I want to conclude this section so I can turn to a literary example by means of which I will try to spell out some practical implications of a language and literature pedagogy of death and extinction: the limits of literacy. Like the concept of competences, literacy often suggests an ability to process information and act accordingly (see Bartosch, 2021). It thus places its emphasis on ideas of informed decision making grounded in agency and empowerment of individual students that might no longer hold, or will at least have to be readjusted, when it comes to loss and mourning and when we talk about learning environments that make necessary other forms of relating, such as paying witness, and ways of addressing our collective (in)ability to mourn (see Jones et al., 2020). Such an understanding of literacy moreover tends to suggest that teachers know which information and which resulting action is appropriate. John Parham has forcefully critiqued the tendency in environmental education to assume that teachers know best what is to be done and how learners might get there, describing this assumption as a stance of "environmental capital" (Parham, 2006). He rightly reminds us that an open, democratic pedagogy demands teachers are listeners as well as guides and that there are no simple answers to environmental catastrophe. This is even more so in the context of extinction and large-scale ecological devastation, the dire consequences of which will be felt by learners more than by teachers, simply because of the number of years both will be having in these changing times. There is, in other words, an additional challenge of intergenerational injustice in climate catastrophe and biodiversity loss that we need to consider and that calls into question age-old assumptions about the role and authority of teachers and their definitions of literacy. As Greg Garrard and I have written elsewhere, we see our jobs as educators in "encouraging [students] in their own search for answers" because this seems to us "the only real preparation imaginable for a risky, exciting and unprecedented future. Which is, after all, where our students will have to live" (Bartosch & Garrard, 2013, p. 5). I want to engage this insight for the educational guidelines (see Table 17.1, see

Table 17.1 Parsnippy Topics

Educational guidelines	Explanation
T Texts & artefacts	Selecting texts or text ensembles that engage creatively with individual, human death, animal death, or both provides linkage between large-scale loss and individual mourning, thus challenging the taboo of death and dying as well as the taboo of transspecies eco-grief.
A Advice & help	Creating an atmosphere of trust and space for meaningful communication is necessary when talking about aesthetics and ethics in an intergenerational community.
B Be fair!	Reminding learners that difficult topics require that everyone listens and pays true attention is important – and this includes teachers who have to learn from those actually inhabiting a changed and challenged future.
O Open: knowledge	Talking about death and extinction requires more than facts and figures about biodiversity loss and demands full recognition of the diversity of aesthetic and narrative ways to reflect on eco-grief and forms of mourning. Paying witness and processing are as important as pure knowledge.
O Open: views	Thinking about ecological and biological devastations can only be challenging. Teaching these issues cannot be about the "right" attitudes but is about valuing individual stories and viewpoints out of which a bigger picture of transspecies eco-grief can emerge.
S Student-centredness	Leaving space to think and reflect is even more important when it comes to loss and mourning; and these processes must be taken seriously and mobilised for shared and convivial learning. This means that personal attunement can come from all sorts of sources: a pet dying, a moving story, or the latest news report on extinction rates deserve equal consideration.

Ludwig & Summer, this volume), on which I will base my teaching suggestions in the last section of this chapter.

(How) Can I Teach That?

I want to draw together the various strands I have been concerned with in this contribution – the role of death and dying in literature as well as in literature pedagogy, an emerging awareness of extinction phenomena as part of learner's lifeworlds, the limits of literacy when it comes to paying witness and reflecting on these developments, as well as the nature and challenge of tabooed issues in the classroom – by briefly discussing a literary example and its educational affordances. Adam Silvera's *They Both Die at the End* (2017) will serve as this example and help to interrelate what has been said so far in order to find suitable pathways to literary learning.

They Both Die at the End is a young adult novel weirdly positioned at the intersection of dystopian future narrative (in which individual futures are waning) and coming-of-age romance (in which waning time expands intensely). It is set in a (near-future) society in which individuals learn about their exact date of death: By way of the digital media device "Death-Cast" and their perfected algorithms, these predictions are always correct and, in good and all-too realistic manner, always come with suggestions for services that will help those now called "Deckers" spend their last days, either by providing entertainment or by matching them with another person to share their remaining time. This is what happens to Mateo, who opts for the friendship service "Last Friend" and eventually meets what will be his last friend, Rufus. The two strangers first become friends and later lovers and, as the title makes unequivocally clear, they both die at the end.

The title and the whole novel are remarkable in a number of ways. Like the example of Vonnegut's *Galápagos*, mentioned above, it is not so much through the plot alone but through literary form that thinking about death is encouraged: What does it mean if a novel starts, is in fact titled with a spoiler? Like the crosses in Vonnegut, this narrative decision says as much about literary fiction's licence and inventiveness as it says about finitude more generally. And like *The Rabbits* and the other examples discussed previously, the novel succeeds in making meaningful connections between the theme of death and dying and other concerns, amongst them mental health (Mateo is anxious and depressed), sickness and loss (Mateo's father is in a coma and his mother and sister died in a car-crash years ago), and friendship, (queer) love and care in times of digital media and the pangs of adolescence.

It has to be noted, however, that it does *not* comment explicitly on (species) extinctions in the context of ecological disaster. As I will discuss below, my choice of this text has to do with the relative absence of such literary narratives of a certain quality and aptitude for young learners of English – but it likewise reflects my conviction that literary fiction is most effective when it circumvents this very distinction between individual, human death and large-scale extinctions. Dying in *They Both Die at the End* is, after all, also a large-scale matter; in that it turns human death into a matter of statistics while also focussing on the individual tragedy of its adolescent lovers however, the novel productively challenges the assumption that species death is not for *homo sapiens*.

A pre-reading task would of course have to be about readerly expectations arising upon reading the title. As said above, this spoiler seems to go against usual reading procedures while it at the same time provides reasons to discuss finitude as such. It is uncommon for a novel to explain who will ultimately perish, yet "dying at the end" is in another sense a fundamental truth of existence. A potential while-reading activity could consecutively be about noticing when dramatic arches and plot-lines lead us to assume the two will indeed have a great future together, although we know they won't: Even though this is the whole point of the novel, death eventually comes unexpected and as a shock. And yet, it has been hovering above characters and story alike, so it is by way of its literary form that the text offers spaces of reflection on death and dying as well as the function of storytelling in imagining futures.

Since the text is a rich resource of topics relevant to learners and an education geared towards tackling difficult and taboo issues, it is up to educators to either decide which of the many affordances will benefit a specific group of learners or to offer diverse avenues into the text in order for learners to decide for themselves. This is even more relevant in light of the above remarks about a changing teacher's role in the context of environmental or extinction education, where educators are well advised to foster learner autonomy by having students identify and choose thematic concerns they find relevant and want to engage with. It is this diversity of potential avenues for discussing the text that also helps to contextualise the difficult topic of death and integrate it into a larger social texture of growing up in a world of loss.

Given the difficulty of finding appropriate texts that allow for such learning processes *and* approaching head-on the issue of biodiversity loss, it seems advisable to tackle the topic of extinction more explicitly in the post-reading phase. It is here that findings from reading the literary text(s) can fuse into a productive engagement with individually produced extinction stories that draw on the analytical findings of prior phases and connect them with more creative work. This phase can link demands for creative work based on subjective experiences and needs with a necessary language focus by adding a more creative and critical form of language awareness through the engagement with narratives of (species) death. With the right form of storytelling in mind, the bleak encounter with narratives of death can be turned into an instance of agency and even an experience of flourishing. I am taking my cue for such an activity from David Quammen's oft-quoted excerpt from his 1996 book on extinction, *The Song of the Dodo*. In this short passage, Quammen narrativizes species death by focussing on the last specimen of the eponymous Dodo, merging scientific information with speculations about an individual animal and adding rhetoric strategies that invite analytical scrutiny. He writes:

> *Raphus cucullatus* had become rare unto death. But this one flesh-and-blood individual still lived. Imagine that she was thirty years old, or thirty-five, an ancient age for most sorts of bird but not impossible for a member of such a large-bodied species. She no longer ran, she waddled. Lately, she was going blind. Her digestive system was balky. In the dark of an early morning in 1667, say, during a rainstorm, she took cover beneath a cold stone ledge at the base of one of the Black River cliffs. She drew her head down against her body, fluffed her feathers for warmth, squinted in patient misery. She waited. She didn't know it, nor did anyone else, but she was the only dodo on Earth. When the storm passed, she never opened her eyes. This is extinction.
>
> (Quammen, 1996, p. 275)

A purely scientific take on extinction will have us contradict: This is *not* extinction, but a speculative, fictionalised account of the last specimen of the Dodo. The text's appeal lies in its combination of scientific nomenclature at the beginning and ecological interpretation at the end ("Raphus cucullatus"/ "extinction") with endearing, moving – and, not least, heavily gendered – imagery of a waddling animal going blind and exposed to the rain whose death has significance beyond the very biological realm it initially invokes. Language awareness will play a part in understanding this; creative work will invite learners to come up with their own, short extinction stories of those who will die at the end: dislocated earthlings, habitat-derived critters ending up as roadkill, and indeed whole generations whose futures are in peril.

Concluding Remarks

By way of conclusion, let me summarise some of the points made here and situate this contribution in the larger context both of taboo and literacy research. I have taken my initial cue from the observation that while death has been a taboo topic ever since, the current environmental and biodiversity crises add a new dimension of urgency and responsibility to what is now conceived as large-scale extinctions rather than individual processes of dying. This development challenges ELT practices and requires creative approaches that help students to cope and flourish, even and especially in calamitous times. The TABOOS chart (Table 17.1) summarises some of the key insights of my own research on ways and methodologies to foster such support and address what I have termed transspecies and intergenerational eco-grief. And yet, while I fully subscribe to the idea that literary learning can support educational approaches to tackling eco-grief, I am aware of two further challenges in this respect: the question of text selection and the notion of literacy underlying environmental learning in the literature classroom.

It has been a deliberate decision to work here with a text that features not species death but the tragic dying of two human protagonists. This decision, I have argued, has not only to do with the difficulty of finding appropriate texts that go beyond calls for climate action and animal protection but instead mobilise the potential of literary form. It moreover fruitfully challenges the very distinction between human death and animal extinction, as shown above. What is more, since the proposed task cycle includes creative (re-)writings of textual material, it helps to revise a problematic notion of literacy that focusses on action rather than reflection. In order to address the limits of such solution-oriented understandings of literacy, I suggest we probe the potential of creativity for engendering moments of sustained reflection and creative agency and thus do justice to the demands as well as specific potentials of literary learning in ELT contexts (see Bartosch, 2021). In fact, paying more attention to creative and collaborative work also does better justice to research on the "new literacies" (Gee, 2021) and its focus on learning relations beyond the level of the text alone as well as its acknowledgement that "meaning emerge[s] from interaction in unforeseen ways that cannot be textually explained" and that is always "on the move and [...] is [...] socially, historically, and culturally rooted in processes of production" (Stornaiuolo, 2021, p. 563; see also Pahl, 2009). There are limits to designing learning spaces in times of existential crisis but hardly any limits to the creative imagination. And it is the creative imagination that might be needed more than ever. It is thus not only about time we tackled the taboo issue of death and extinction but to make a stronger case for the unique potential of the English literature classroom for meaningful engagement in these times of unprecedented loss.

References

Bartosch, R. (2021). What *if* we stopped pretending? Radical interdisciplinarity, applied literary studies, and the limits of "education for sustainable development". *Anglistik: International Journal of English Studies, 32*(3), 157–171.
Bartosch, R. (2022). Dying to learn: Teaching human-animal studies in an age of extinction. In A. Hübner, M. Edlich, & M. Moss (Eds.), *Multispecies futures: New approaches to teaching human-animal studies* (pp. 77–94). Neofelis.
Bartosch, R., & Garrard, G. (2013). The function of criticism: A response to William Major and Andrew McMurry's editorial. *Journal of Ecocriticism, 5*(1), 1–6.
Bendell, J. (2019). Doom and bloom: Adapting to collapse. In Extinction rebellion (Eds.), *This is not a drill: An extinction rebellion handbook* (pp. 73–80). Penguin.
Berman, J. (2012). *Death education in the writing classroom*. Routledge.
Doka, K. J. (1989). *Disenfranchised grief: Recognizing hidden sorrow*. Lexington Books.
Gee, J. P. (2021). The new literacy studies. In J. Rowsell, & K. Pahl (Eds.), *The Routledge handbook of literacy studies* (pp. 35–48). Routledge.
Heise, U. K. (2016). *Imagining extinction: The cultural meaning of endangered species*. University of Chicago Press.
Herman, D. (2018). *Narratology beyond the human: Storytelling and animal life*. Oxford University Press.
Höing, A. (2018). Animalic agency: Intersecting the child and the animal in popular British children's fiction. In I. E. Castro, & J. Clark (Eds.), *Representing agency in popular culture: Children and youth on page, screen, and in-between* (pp. 65–84). Lexington Books.
Höing, A. (2021). Vegetal individuals and plant agency in twenty-first century children's literature. In M. Duckworth, & L. Guanio-Uluru (Eds.), *Plants in children's and young adult literature* (pp. 159–170). Routledge.
Jones, O., Rigby, K., & Williams, L. (2020). Everyday ecocide, toxic dwelling, and the inability to mourn: A response to geographies of extinction. *Environmental Humanities, 12*(1), 388–405.
Linder, S., & Majerus, E. (Eds.). (2016). *Can I teach that? Negotiating taboo language and controversial topics in the language arts classroom*. Rowman and Littlefield.
Lysgaard, J. A., Bengtsson, S., & Laugesen, M. H.-L. (2020). *Dark pedagogy: Education, horror and the anthropocene*. Palgrave Macmillan.
Nixon, R. (2011). *Slow violence and the environmentalism of the poor*. Harvard University Press.
Pahl, K. (2009). Interactions, intersections and improvisations: Studying the multimodal texts and classroom talk of six- to seven-year-olds. *Journal of Early Childhood Literacy, 9*(2), 188–210.

Parham, J. (2006). The deficiency of "environmental capital": Why environmentalism needs a reflexive pedagogy. In S. Mayer & G. Wilson (Eds.), *Ecodidactic perspectives on English language, literatures and cultures* (pp. 7–22). Wissenschaftlicher Verlag Trier.

Pennebaker, J. (Ed.). (1995). *Emotion, disclosure, and health.* American Psychological Association.

Quammen, D. (1996). *The song of the dodo.* Scribner.

Rigby, K. (2015). *Dancing with disaster: Environmental histories, narratives, and ethics for perilous times.* University of Virginia Press.

Rose, D. B., van Dooren, T., & Chrulew, M. (Eds.). (2017). *Extinction studies: Stories of time, death and generations.* Columbia University Press.

Scranton, R. (2015). *Learning to die in the Anthropocene: reflections on the end of a civilization.* City Lights.

Silvera, A. (2017). *They both die at the end.* HarperTeen.

Sodikoff, G. M. (Ed.). (2012). *The anthropology of extinction: Essays on culture and species death.* Indiana University Press.

Stornaiuolo, A. (2021). Literacy as worldmaking: Multimodality, creativity and cosmopolitanism. In J. Rowsell, & K. Pahl (Eds.), *The Routledge handbook of literacy studies* (pp. 561–571). Routledge.

UNESCO. (2020, September 18). *Preventing the next pandemic: The one health approach.* https://en.unesco.org/news/preventing-next-pandemic-one-health-approach

van Dooren, T. (2014). *Flight ways: Life and loss at the edge of extinction.* Columbia University Press.

Weik von Mossner, A. (2017). *Affective ecologies: Empathy, emotion, and environmental narrative.* Ohio State University Press.

18 Cultural Taboos from a Sri Lankan Perspective
Developing Taboo Literacy with Feature Films

Anchala Amarasinghe and Susanne Borgwaldt

Introduction

Learning a new language requires exposure to novel cultures and societies, as their values, traditions, customs and norms are key factors that influence a language (Premawardhena, 2009). Thus, language learners must expand their existing cultural boundaries and open up to topics in foreign cultures that are tabooed in their own culture(s). Taboos can be regarded as cultural byproducts. They are part of the socialization process, learned from an early age and often not particularly reflected upon. Studies on taboos in foreign language teaching are mainly found in the context of teaching English as a foreign language in the Arab world and are therefore often confined to PARSNIP topics (see Ludwig & Summer, this volume, Figure 1.1). Most of the literature on PARSNIP taboos discusses which culture-sensitive topics should be avoided (and why) when teaching in Muslim societies (e.g., El-Sakran, 2017; Etri, 2021; Gobert, 2015; Helms, 1984; Hudson, 2013). Yet, it is to be expected that taboos exist on a multicultural level and may therefore appear in authentic materials or textbooks from the target culture, regardless of the measures that are taken to avoid them. It is thus sensible to find ways of integrating content that might be perceived as taboo in the learner culture in the foreign language classroom, instead of skipping or substituting culture-sensitive topics (see Becker, this volume).

In the following sections, we first give an overview of cultural taboos in Sri Lanka and subsequently show how taboo topics can be dealt with in the foreign language classroom via feature films and how working with films can contribute to the development of taboo literacy.

Cultural Taboos in Sri Lanka

Sri Lanka (formerly Ceylon) is an island nation that is renowned for its amalgamation of ethnic and cultural diversity. Its inhabitants practice a variety of religions with Buddhism being the main religion. According to the Central Intelligence Agency (2021), in 2012, 70.2% of its population identified as Buddhist, 12.6% as Hindu, followed by Muslims (9.7%) and Christians (7.4%). Sri Lankan culture, values, opinions and traditions are strongly influenced by the

DOI: 10.4324/9781003220701-22

Cultural Taboos from a Sri Lankan Perspective 207

heritage of Theravada Buddhism, as is apparent in local art, architecture, cuisine and the indigenous medicine Ayurveda. Although most Sri Lankans welcome modernity, they still highly respect traditional values, for example the notion of *karma*, beliefs like the existence of *reincarnation* and customs such as the obligation to *enter a temple barefoot*. Buddhism as the main religion is generally respected, regardless of the citizens' religious identities. Therefore, commonly respected cultural values among Sri Lankans are not limited to only Buddhists.

Figure 18.1 depicts some prominent cultural taboos of Sri Lanka that will be elaborated upon in this section.

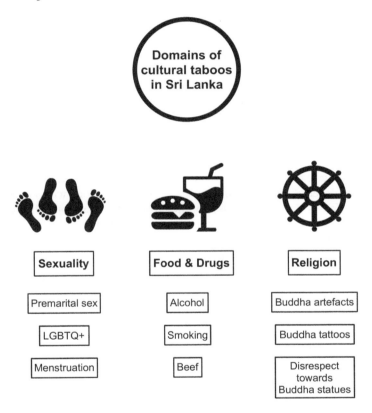

Figure 18.1 Domains of Cultural Taboos in Sri Lanka.

Sex and nearly every facet associated with sexuality is perceived as a major taboo in Sri Lankan society in general. In many Sri Lankan classrooms, sex education is narrowed down to biological diagrams of female and male reproductive systems and a medical depiction of sexual reproduction. Therefore, many youngsters have a below average knowledge of sex-related topics (Rajapaksa-Hewageegana et al., 2015). In the same vein, the perception of nudity is often associated with sex and sex-related acts. Nudity is interpreted as being shameless and immoral, particularly among older generations. Therefore, nudity is censored in most films that are played at cinema halls, regardless whether it is of a sexual nature or otherwise.

The first menstruation of a girl is perceived as a significant turning point in her life; it is celebrated as an auspicious event with an array of puberty rituals, especially in Sri Lankan villages. However, girls are frequently taught by elders to maintain secrecy, when they are menstruating, as this is considered an embarrassing occurrence. Due to the misconception that menstrual blood is impure, some believe that they are polluted when menstruating. There is no direct claim in Buddhist teachings that women on periods cannot attend religious ceremonies, but often women refrain from participating in religious rituals and events when they are menstruating. As an outcome of deeply etched cultural norms, premarital sex is often considered taboo in Sri Lanka. Conservative Sri Lankans, particularly from older generations deem sex as an act that should only be explored after marriage. The concept of virginity is correlated with purity, especially for females. Girls who are born to conservative families are raised to value the culture-based idealistic view of premarital virginity (Jordal et al., 2015; Rajapaksa-Hewageegana et al., 2015). In Sri Lankan society, sexual minorities (LGBTQ+) often experience social stigma and are subjected to multiple forms of oppression. Homosexuality is, on paper at least, criminalized by Sri Lankan law. According to the sections 365 and 365A of Penal Code "carnal intercourse against the order of nature" and "any act of gross indecency with another person" are offenses. In other words, non-heterosexual acts are punishable by law (Ellawala, 2019), however, a conviction against an individual belonging to the LGBTQ+ community is rarely heard of. Sri Lankan society displays a certain degree of homophobia due to the lack of knowledge about sexual orientations and gender identities. According to Adikaram and Liyanage (2021) and Priscilla et al. (2021), LGBTQ+ individuals face discrimination and harassment in the workplace, unemployment due to workplace prejudices, domestic violence, inadequate mental health support and bullying.

The religious teachings of Theravada Buddhism discourage consumption of alcohol irrespective of one's gender. Yet, it is tolerated among men in contemporary society. However, when women consume strong alcoholic beverages, it is generally frowned upon, especially by older generations. Consequently, many women abstain from hard liquor. According to Hettige and Paranagama (2005), the 2002 GENACIS survey showed that only 13.7% of females had ever consumed an alcoholic beverage. Also, with 0.1%, the prevalence of smoking among females is extremely low (Katulanda et al., 2011). Sri Lankan females who do smoke tend to keep it to themselves as they fear social backlash and rejection. Many Buddhists and almost all Hindus in Sri Lanka refrain from consuming beef. Although consuming beef is not perceived as a major taboo for Buddhists, it is traditionally looked down upon as an unethical practice. In a study exploring socio-cultural parameters of meat purchasing and consumption pattern, de Silva et al. (2011) reported that out of 183 Buddhist respondents none of the females and only 12% of the males consumed beef. Antipathy for killing animals (82%) and religious beliefs (74%) are the central motives for not being meat consumers. As Stewart (2014) explains, Buddhism advocates a position of total nonviolence, which comprises all forms of violence towards humans and animals. This is the foundation of Buddhist ethics.

Buddha statues have a high and sacred status in Sri Lankan culture. They can be seen at Buddhist homes, in every Buddhist temple and at most street junctions, especially under bo trees. This tree (Ficus religiosa) is sacred for Buddhists, as it is believed that Buddha (Siddharta Gautama) attained enlightenment under a bo tree. It is disrespectful to turn one's back at a Buddha statue, have tattoos related to Buddhism or wear attire or have ornaments that feature Buddha (Berkwitz, 2006).

It is apparent that Sri Lankan culture diverges in many aspects from Western culture(s). Therefore, some characteristics of Western culture may be perceived as culture-sensitive topics in Sri Lanka. When learning a new language, the cultural dimension cannot be separated from linguistics. In the area of foreign language teaching both intercultural (e.g., Byram, 1997; Kramsch, 2013) and transcultural (e.g., Baker, 2021; Bhabha, 1994; Slimbach, 2005) approaches hold prominent positions.

Transcultural approaches to language learning are intrinsically linked to concepts of *cultural hybridity* and *fluid identities*. As Baker (2021, p. 7) notes, "culture and identity are seen as fluid and changing concepts". In this line of argument, binary notions of *self and other*, typical for intercultural models, might seem too simplistic, when observed from a transcultural perspective. Bhabha (1994, pp. 35–36) points out that "cultures are never unitary in themselves, nor simply dualistic in the relation of Self to Other". This signifies that culture(s) can neither be perceived in a homogeneous nor a binary perspective. Every cultural identity is unique in their own way and is shaped by various factors, for example, an Indian-Polish couple working at an American company in Cairo may develop their own unique cultural identities. Their interaction styles may change and evolve according to the context. For instance, the communication style of the Polish partner will be drastically different when visiting their Indian in-laws, compared to a casual chat with their American colleague at a nightclub.

For the purpose of developing taboo literacy, an intercultural perspective such as the one in Byram's (1997) model of intercultural communicative competence may work well. When interacting with other cultures, knowledge of one's own culture is crucial, as this aids in comparing, interpreting, relating and empathizing with foreign cultures. Byram (1997, p. 34) calls this component "savoir étre". In this sense, understanding one's own cultural taboos paves a way to make it easier to empathize with other cultures. Moreover, attitudes of relativizing self and valuing others (Byram, 1997) lead to open communication. With an unbiased attitude, one can perceive taboos of other cultures beyond one's own cultural biases, thus relating one's self to other people. In the context of intercultural learning, Byram (1997, p. 34) argues that the goal of foreign language teaching is to "prepare learners to communicate and interact with foreigners who are 'other' and accepted as such, rather than being reduced to people assumed to be (almost) 'like us'".

Identities are perceived to be less fluid with regard to taboos than with regard to other cultural elements such as hairstyle, choice of music or tipping habits. A Sri Lankan-Australian student might throw together a mean jackfruit curry for lunch and participate in an Anzac biscuit baking competition in the afternoon. However, they will not be able to focus only on aesthetics, when viewing their neighbours' sunroom that is decorated with Buddha head flower pots, as the respect for Buddha is deeply ingrained in their cultural identity, regardless of their religious identification. Therefore, the notion of cultural fluidity in transcultural approach may be less applicable with regard to taboo literacy, as learners may find it difficult to transcend the boundaries of their culture(s).

Thus, we suggest taking a predominantly intercultural stance, when using foreign feature films to address culture-specific aspects of the target culture and expose learners to topics that are considered taboo in their home culture(s). It is expected that this will allow learners to reflect and discuss such topics while developing respect and tolerance towards other foreign cultures.

Addressing Cultural Taboos in Foreign Language Feature Films

There is a vast array of literature about how to use films in foreign language teaching (e.g., Donaghy, 2017; Herrero & Vanderschelden, 2019; Viebrock, 2016). While there are some materials dealing with teaching taboo topics (see Ludwig & Summer, this volume), the use of films in this regard has not been particularly reflected upon.

Based on the CEFR descriptors for audio-visual competences, "Watching film, TV and video" (Council of Europe, 2020), we recommend incorporating film activities into the classroom from the CEFR-level B1 onwards. In order to keep lessons varied and interactive, films are often shown in segments and learning activities take place at intervals, i.e., pre-viewing, (while) viewing and post-viewing (Donaghy, 2017). In the following section, we use two taboos, i.e., *smoking among females* and *eating with hand* to showcase how teaching with films or video clips can develop taboo literacy.

The symbolic function of smoking in films and its changing nature has been discussed in detail (e.g., Szczepaniak-Gillece, 2016), memorable smoking scenes in films from the last century depict actors such as Marlene Dietrich in *Der blaue Engel* [The Blue Angel] (von Sternberg, 1930), James Dean in *Rebel Without a Cause* (Ray, 1955), Audrey Hepburn in *Breakfast at Tiffany's* (Edwards, 1961) and Sharon Stone in *Basic Instinct* (Verhoeven, 1992). While in Western countries women smoke less than men (Ritchie, 2019), women in Sri Lanka rarely smoke at all (Katulanda et al., 2011). The knowledge of facts, functions and the historical development of smoking in Western societies and Western films might help students from non-Western cultures to be less biased and avoid stereotyping when encountering smokers in reality or fiction. Table 18.1 showcases how the cultural taboo of smoking among females can be addressed with feature films.

This teaching suggestion can be adopted to different classroom settings and cultural contexts. It allows both students from non-Western countries such as Sri Lanka as well as students from Western cultures to develop an awareness of gender-related aspects of smoking. Reflecting on the cultural taboo of smoking among females can reduce learners' prejudices and help them not to label women who smoke as "immoral" or "less-cultured".

As a pre-viewing activity, stills and/or film posters with smoking scenarios can be shown to discuss the symbolic or stylistic functions cigarettes play in the depicted scenes. In *The Maltese Falcon* (Huston, 1941), cigarettes accentuate Humphrey Bogart's "toughness and masculinity" (Harmetz, 1992, p. 13), in other films they might stand for power or dominance, seduction or courtship, or simply be a fashion statement. Students might correctly observe that the depiction of a character's smoking can add to the character portrayal, as for example often "smokers tend to be major characters, white, male, and mature. They tend to play leadership roles" (Dozier et al., 2005, p. 8).

For while-viewing activities, we recommend observation-based tasks involving questions such as, "What could be the purpose of smoking here?" Discussions might reveal answers such as "to reduce stress", "to relax after a meal", or "to rebel". This opportunity can be used to draw parallels with the learners' cultures by asking questions like "What would a woman in your country do in this situation instead of smoking?" as a plenary activity.

Feature films might convey unrealistic pictures of the target culture and even strengthen cultural stereotypes. In order to avoid one-dimensional viewpoints, it is important to reflect on exaggerated portrayals of characters or situations in films and to combine film material with other sources, like newspaper articles, documentaries, interviews or film reviews.

As a post-viewing activity, we suggest comparing current statistics of gender-related prevalence of smoking in one's own country with the target countries. For example, in Serbia 40% of men and slightly more than 41% of women smoke tobacco, in the United States somewhat more than 31% of men and almost 19% of women smoke tobacco. However, in Sri Lanka slightly more than 43% of men but less than 3% of women smoke tobacco, which reveals a significant difference between genders (Ritchie, 2019). After examining the present-day statistics, students can explore the historical development of smoking. These activities might ultimately result in learners realizing that smoking tobacco is relatively common in the Western world, also among women, but has been declining in the last decades, due to an increased awareness of its harmfulness. This realization might lead to a discussion about other psycho-active substances, such as alcohol, betel leaves or opiates and focus on cultural patterns of drug use.

Table 18.1 Teaching Suggestion: Dealing with the Cultural Taboo of Smoking among Females

Topic	Taboo: women who smoke tobacco
Goal	Creating awareness of gender-related aspects of smoking in different cultures (e.g., Serbia, Sri Lanka and the United States)
Outcome	Students are able to relate gender-related smoking prevalence to historical developments of smoking in different cultures
Level	From B1 onwards
Time	90 minutes or more
Materials	Video clips, stills and/or film posters with smoking scenes, statistical information about the current prevalence and historical development of smoking in different countries

Working with films also provides opportunities to develop awareness of taboos in one's own culture: Film scenes where people are having a meal can be used to draw parallels between eating habits in one's own culture(s) and eating habits in other cultures, e.g., Sri Lanka. Sri Lankans eat with their right hand. This is considered the proper manner of eating and it is believed that the warmth of the fingertips helps spices to release their aroma which enhances the flavour of the food. Eating with hand is an art in cultures that eat with hand; in Sri Lanka only the cleaned fingertips are used to mix the food with condiments and make small bite-sized mounds; the thumb is used to push the food into the mouth. It is common for Sri Lankans to eat by hand, even at local restaurants, especially when rice and curry is served.

In Western countries, however, eating a meal by hand is – apart from street food (e.g., hot dogs, burgers, French fries, etc.) – a taboo. Babies are taught very early in their life to eat properly, i.e., with a spoon. Eating with cutlery is perceived as the civilized option. A comparison between eating habits and traditions in one's own culture and Sri Lanka (or other cultures that eat with hand, e.g., India and Ethiopia) can help learners reflect the *eating with hand taboo* in their own culture(s), as shown in Table 18.2.

Table 18.2 Teaching Suggestion: Dealing with the Cultural Taboo of Eating with Hand

Topic	Taboo: eating with hand
Goal	Sharing knowledge about different eating habits
Outcome	Students are able to understand, respect and reflect on eating habits in their own and other culture(s)
Level	From B1 onwards
Time	90 minutes or more
Materials	Video clips, informative texts, food items

As food is a predominant theme in films, there are plenty of scenes where people are eating together, in both formal and informal settings, for example, at family get-togethers and celebrations or at restaurants. Showing video clips from different cultures such as Denmark: *Babettes Gæstebud* [Babettes Feast] (Axel, 1987), France: *Le charme discret de la bourgeoisie* [The Discreet charm of the bourgeoisie] (Buñuel, 1972), the United States: *Titanic* (Cameron, 1997), Philippines/United States: *American Adobo* (Guillen, 2002), India: *Hum Dil De Chuke Sanam* [Straight From the Heart] (Bhansali, 1999), Sri Lanka: *Saroja* (Dissanayake, 2000), Japan: *Tampopo* (Itami, 1985) and Taiwan: *Yǐn shí nán nǚ* [Eat drink man woman] (Lee, 1994), will allow students to see different practices of eating food. Some characters eat with the hand, while others use chopsticks or cutlery, such as fork and knife in Western countries or fork and spoon in the Philippines and other Southeast Asian countries. This will lead to post-viewing discussions, which – in a group of Western students – might reveal the perceived superiority of using utensils compared to eating with hand.

In order to help students realize that there is a dining etiquette in every culture, regardless of whether one eats with hand or with utensils, teachers can present materials informing about both the historical development of eating culture in Europe and difficulties of properly eating with hand (e.g., Mindess, 2012; Yorke, 2019) and discuss the implications.

Moreover, to let students discover, reflect and discuss different sensory experiences, food items such as fruit, cheese, pickles or small pieces of cake can be brought into the classroom and offered to students, who are divided into two groups: One group eats with hand and the other group with a toothpick or fork (Madzharov, 2019). Students from the first group should be asked to wash their hands before touching the food and this instruction can be used to discuss cultural and religious aspects of body hygiene, such as the ritual of hand washing.

The activities suggested above can be taught in a variety of settings, ideally in a class where language learners are from different cultures. Some will discover that their culture-based eating habits may not be well received in some cultures, whereas others will realize that their "civilized" way of consuming food may not be the only accepted way of eating. The above mentioned suggestions (for more ideas see Borgwaldt & Amarasinghe, in press) aid language teachers to use films as authentic cultural material in order to address taboo topics. However, it is possible that learners might feel pressured to respond in a socially desirable manner when sensitive topics appear in classroom settings. One way to reduce such tendencies is creating activities that might offer an insight into diverse opinions related to a specific topic. For example, one could compare film reviews of *Bend it like Beckham* (Chadha, 2002) from "family value"-promoting websites, e.g., Pluggedin (n.d.), with more progressive reviews, e.g., AfterEllen (2021). Such activities will allow learners to perceive and compare different beliefs without having to directly express their own opinions in the classroom (for more suggestions regarding gender awareness in the foreign language classroom, see e.g., Heß & Ludwig, 2018; Lohe & Viebrock, 2018).

Conclusion

The use of films in foreign language teaching allows bringing foreign cultures into the classroom with relative ease, which can improve on the one hand language learners' intercultural competence, motivate them to develop understanding and respect and to cultivate independent, unbiased opinions about other cultures. Language teachers on the other hand can address taboo topics through "the lens of the film makers".

In some classroom environments, such topics might become the starting point for lively discussions, in other classrooms it will be important not to force learners to openly express their opinions, but provide food for thought and opportunities for critical reflection. Sometimes, learners might just need time to open themselves up to other points of view and perspectives because discussing provocative topics contradicts their usual mechanism of dealing with controversiality, which is avoidance. Thus, it is important to be patient and to gradually introduce controversial topics. As a result of their perception of politeness, some learners, especially from Asian cultures, believe that it is rude and disrespectful to openly argue with a teacher (Rao, 1996). However, they might open up fairly well in group settings because they feel safer than when questioned individually.

Apart from addressing and reflecting upon taboo topics in the classroom, we recommend creating opportunities to allow learners to obtain first-hand cultural experience via exchange opportunities (face to face or digital). As a result, language learners can hone their social interaction skills, cultivate intercultural awareness and develop willingness to relate and accept cultural differences (Byram, 1997). This might lead to developing an empathetic attitude towards others that may enable individuals from different cultural settings to put themselves in others' shoes and to see things from their points of view. It is essential to offer learners glimpses into different worlds, cultures and mindsets and feature films have the potential to do that. However, it is equally important to identify and take learners' cultures into account when dealing with feature films depicting culture-sensitive topics in the classroom. When encountering taboo topics learners might feel threatened if they were forced to transcend into a novel identity, as they could feel "tortured by the conflict of their own sets of values and the newly acquired ones" (Yue, 2019, p. 199). Teaching sensitive topics should help learners understand unique characteristics of their own cultures and realize that what is normal for them might be a taboo for someone from another culture. This realization about their own culture and acceptance of other cultures often materializes after teachers and learners compare different cultures and become aware of their taboos.

To sum up, all cultures have their different sets of taboos. How challenging it may be, addressing cultural taboos in the foreign language classroom offers ample opportunity to explore cultural differences and similarities but needs careful scaffolding as cultural taboos are often closely intertwined with the learners' beliefs, values and, ultimately, identities.

References

Adikaram, A., & Liyanage, D. (2021). Undisclosed reality: Harassment of gay male employees in Sri Lankan heteronormative workplaces. *Culture and Organization*, 27(6), 1–17. https://doi.org/10.1080/14759551.2021.1919894

AfterEllen. (2021, February 08). *Bend it like Beckham: It's time for a lesbian sequel.* https://afterellen.com/bend-it-like-beckham-its-time-for-a-lesbian-sequel/
Axel, G. (Director). (1987). *Babettes Gæstebud* [Babette's feast] [Film]. Nordisk Film.
Baker, W. (2021). From intercultural to transcultural communication. *Language and Intercultural Communication*, 1–14. https://doi.org/10.1080/14708477.2021.2001477
Berkwitz, S. (2006). Buddhism in Sri Lanka: Practice, protest, and preservation. In S. Berkwitz (Ed.), *Buddhism in world cultures: Comparative perspectives* (pp. 45–72). ABC-CLIO.
Bhabha, H. (1994). *The location of culture.* Routledge.
Bhansali, S. (Director). (1999). *Hum Dil De Chuke Sanam* [Straight from the heart] [Film]. Bhansali Films.
Borgwaldt, S., & Amarasinghe, A. (in press). Interkulturelles Lernen durch Spielfilme im DaF-Unterricht: Tabus [Intercultural learning through feature films in German as a foreign language class: Taboos]. In K. Böhnert, M. Maataoui, & H. Slutas (Eds.), *Tabuthemen aus deutsch-tunesischer Perspektive* [Taboo topics from a German-Tunisian perspective]. Peter Lang.
Buñuel, L. (Director). (1972). *Le charme discret de la bourgeoisie* [The discreet charm of the bourgeoisie] [Film]. Greenwich Film Production.
Byram, M. (1997). *Teaching and assessing intercultural communicative competence.* Multilingual Matters.
Cameron, J. (Director). (1997). *Titanic* [Film]. Paramount Pictures.
Central Intelligence Agency. (2021). *Sri Lanka.* Central Intelligence Agency. https://www.cia.gov/the-world-factbook/countries/sri-lanka/#people-and-society
Chadha, G. (Director). (2002). *Bend it like Beckham* [Film]. Kintop Pictures.
Council of Europe. (2020). *Common European framework of reference for languages: Learning, teaching, assessment – Companion volume.* Council of Europe. www.coe.int/lang-cefr
de Silva, P., Atapattu, N., & Sandika, A. (2011). A study of the socio-cultural parameters associated with meat purchasing and consumption pattern: A case of Southern Province, Sri Lanka. *Journal of Agricultural Sciences – Sri Lanka, 5*(2), 71–79.
Dissanayake, S. (Director). (2000). *Saroja* [Film]. Rupareka Productions.
Donaghy, K. (2017). *Film in action: Teaching language using moving images.* Delta.
Dozier, D., Lauzen, M., Day, C., Payne, S., & Tafoya, M. (2005). Leaders and elites: Portrayals of smoking in popular films. *Tobacco Control, 14,* 7–9.
Edwards, B. (Director). (1961). *Breakfast at Tiffany's* [Film]. Paramount Pictures.
Ellawala, T. (2019). Legitimating violences: The 'gay rights' NGO and the disciplining of the Sri Lankan queer figure. *Journal of South Asian Development, 14*(1), 83–107.
El-Sakran, O. (2017). *Teachers' perspectives on the discussion of culturally sensitive topics in the United Arab Emirates* [Master's thesis, University of Sharjah]. American University of Sharjah Digital Repository. https://dspace.aus.edu/xmlui/bitstream/handle/11073/8862/29.232-2017.09%20Omnia%20Tharwat%20El-Sakran.pdf?isAllowed=y&sequence=1
Etri, W. (2021). Strategies for withstanding the inevitable at ground zero. *Open Journal of Modern Linguistics, 11,* 34–48. https://doi.org/10.4236/ojml.2021.111003
Gobert, M. (2015). Taboo topics in the ESL/EFL classroom in the Gulf region. In R. Raddawi (Ed.), *Intercultural communication with Arabs: Studies in educational, professional and societal contexts* (pp. 109–126). Springer.
Guillen, L. (Director). (2002). *American Adobo* [Film]. ABS-CBN Film Productions.
Harmetz, A. (1992, November 08). History is written in smoke. *The New York Times,* 13.

Helms, A. (1984). *Cultures in conflict: A handbook for ESL teachers of Arab students* [Master's thesis, San Francisco State University]. CORE. https://core.ac.uk/download/pdf/48498469.pdf

Herrero, C., & Vanderschelden, I. (2019). *Using film and media in the language classroom*. Multilingual Matters.

Heß, N., & Ludwig, C. (2018). 'Look at that baby with those cream-puffs' – Exploring LQBTQ life through American TV series in the EFL classroom. In M. Eisenmann, & C. Ludwig (Eds.), *Queer beats: Gender and literature in the EFL classroom* (pp. 359–385). Peter Lang.

Hettige, S., & Paranagama, D. (2005). Gender, alcohol and culture in Sri Lanka. In I. Obot, & R. Room (Eds.), *Alcohol, gender and drinking problems in low and middle income countries* (pp. 167–188). World Health Organization. https://apps.who.int/iris/bitstream/handle/10665/43299/9241563028_eng.pdf?sequence=1&isAllowed=y

Hudson, P. (2013). *Tiptoeing through the minefield: Teaching English in higher educational institutes in the United Arab Emirates* [Doctoral dissertation, Canterbury Christ Church University]. Canterbury Christ Church University.

Huston, J. (Director). (1941). *The Maltese falcon* [Film]. Warner Bros. Pictures.

Itami, J. (Director). (1985). *Tampopo* [Film]. Itami Productions.

Jordal, M., Wijewardena, K., Öhman, A., Essén, B., & Olsson, P. (2015). 'Disrespectful men, disrespectable women': Men's perceptions on heterosexual relationships and premarital sex in a Sri Lankan Free Trade Zone – A qualitative interview study. *BMC International Health and Human Rights*, 15(3), 1–11.

Katulanda, P., Wickramasinghe, K., Mahesh, J., Rathnapala, A., Constantine, G., Sheriff, R., Matthews, D., & Fernando, S. (2011). Prevalence and correlates of tobacco smoking in Sri Lanka. *Asia Pacific Journal of Public Health*, 23(7), 861–869.

Kramsch, C. (2013). Culture in foreign language teaching. *Iranian Journal of Language Teaching Research*, 1(1), 57–78. https://ijltr.urmia.ac.ir/article_20453.html

Lee, A. (Director). (1994). *Yin shí nán nǚ* [Eat drink man woman] [Film]. Central Motion Pictures.

Lohe, V., & Viebrock, B. (2018). Deconstructing gender stereotypes in EFL classrooms through contemporary movies. In M. Eisenmann, & C. Ludwig (Eds.), *Queer beats: Gender and literature in the EFL classroom* (pp. 413–436). Peter Lang.

Madzharov, A. (2019). Self-control and touch: When does direct versus indirect touch increase hedonic evaluations and consumption of food. *Journal of Retailing*, 95(4), 170–185.

Mindess, A. (2012, February 22). *Eat with your hands for a sensuous, intimate, mindful meal*. KQED. https://www.kqed.org/bayareabites/39132/eat-with-your-hands-for-a-sensuous-intimate-mindful-meal

Pluggedin. (n.d.). *Bend it like Beckham*. https://www.pluggedin.com/movie-reviews/benditlikebeckham/

Premawardhena, N. (2009). *Foundations in language learning*. Pelican Printers.

Priscilla, D., Mendis, M., & Jayasinghe, P. (2021, June 29). *One country, many arbitrary laws – Rethinking laws and policies that leave LGBTQ+ Sri Lankans behind*. Westminster Foundation for Democracy. https://www.wfd.org/what-we-do/resources/rethinking-laws-and-policies-leave-lgbtiq-sri-lankans-behind

Rajapaksa-Hewageegana, N., Piercy, H., Salway, S., & Samarage, S. (2015). Sexual and reproductive knowledge, attitudes and behaviours in a school going population of Sri Lankan adolescents. *Sexual & Reproductive Healthcare*, 6(1), 3–8.

Rao, Z. (1996). Reconciling communicative approaches to the teaching of English with traditional Chinese methods. *Research in the Teaching of English, 30*(4), 458–471.

Ray, N. (Director). (1955). *Rebel without a cause* [Film]. Warner Bros. Pictures.

Ritchie, H. (2019, September 02). *Who smokes more, men or women?* Our World in Data. https://ourworldindata.org/who-smokes-more-men-or-women

Slimbach, R. (2005). The transcultural journey. *Frontiers: The Interdisciplinary Journal of Study Abroad, 11*(1), 205–230. https://doi.org/10.36366/frontiers.v11i1.159

Stewart, J. (2014). Violence and nonviolence in Buddhist animal ethics. *Journal of Buddhist Ethics, 21*, 623–655. https://blogs.dickinson.edu/buddhistethics/2014/08/30/violence-and-nonviolence-in-buddhist-animal-ethics/

Szczepaniak-Gillece, J. (2016). Smoke and mirrors: Cigarettes, cinephilia, and reverie in the American movie theatre. *Film History, 28*(3), 85–113. https://doi.org/10.2979/filmhistory.28.3.05

Verhoeven, P. (Director). (1992). *Basic instinct* [Film]. Carolco Pictures.

Viebrock, B. (Ed.). (2016). *Feature films in English language teaching.* Narr.

von Sternberg, J. (Director). (1930). *Der blaue Engel* [The blue angel] [Film]. UFA.

Yorke, E. (2019). The science, folklore and joy of eating with one's hands. *MOLD Magazine,* (4). https://thisismold.com/process/materials/the-science-folklore-and-joy-of-eating-with-ones-hands#.XuOnmmqpEWp

Yue, J. (2019). Use of foreign films in cultivating intercultural communicative competence in ELT – A case study. *Theory and Practice in Language Studies, 9*(2), 198–203.

19 *La pobreza, las drogas y el sida*
Using Series Like Élite as a Means of Making the Unspeakable Speakable

Janina Reinhardt

Introduction

The use of video streaming has increased steadily in Europe over the last ten years (Statista, 2021). Video streaming also has become more and more common among teenagers (Medienpädagogischer Forschungsverbund Südwest (mpfs), 2020), with Netflix being the fourth most popular online site (after YouTube, Instagram and WhatsApp). Interestingly, teens also seem to have adopted new habits concerning the choice of language: In Germany in 2017, one in four 12- to 19-year-olds watched English-speaking series in the original version at least once a week (mpfs, 2017), and in 2020, 43% watched YouTube videos in another language – mostly, but not exclusively in English – at least several times a week (mpfs, 2020). Audio-visual material in foreign languages has thus become an integral part of young people's everyday lives and may be used in foreign language classes to appeal to pupils' media habits, motivate them, and make subject content more memorable.

In the context of teaching Spanish as a foreign language, the series Élite (Montero et al., 2018–2022), which has been an enormous international success, is particularly interesting for several reasons. First, it is set in a school setting with 16-year-old protagonists, and cinematic as well as narrative techniques are used in quite a sophisticated way. Hence, a variety of tasks can be developed to discuss these noteworthy artistic elements of the series. Moreover, perhaps even more importantly, the series deals with numerous taboo topics, such as drug abuse, homosexuality, and HIV. Consequently, by exploring this piece of fiction in the classroom, taboo topics can be made accessible to students in an educational context.

In the following, I will discuss the series and its pedagogical potential in greater detail. I will begin by outlining the plot of the first season, showing which taboo topics are addressed. Subsequently, I will highlight the relevance of discussing fiction for making tough topics accessible to teenage foreign language learners. Finally, I will present a teaching unit based on the first season of Élite with concrete suggestions for the selection of key scenes and the development of learning activities. More precisely, I will explain how a key scene of the fifth episode can be used as a hook for a research and creative writing task on HIV.

DOI: 10.4324/9781003220701-23

Exploring Taboo Topics in *Élite*

Three working-class students get a scholarship for *Las Encinas*, a (fictional) elite school in Spain. The differences between the wealthy students and the newcomers lead to several conflicts, which culminate in a murder. During the eight episodes (each about 50 minutes) of the first season (Montero et al., 2018), investigations are carried out, mixing interrogation scenes with scenes that take place between the arrival of the newcomers at *Las Encinas* and the murder. Several storylines are interwoven, and with each episode, the constellation of characters becomes more complex. As a multiplicity of alternative lifestyles is presented, several clashes of cultures and social groups become evident, and various important issues are addressed, such as poverty, sexually transmitted diseases, and homicide. Throughout the series, different taboo topics are tackled (see Figure 19.1 for an overview in Spanish): One of the most frequently recurring topics is drugs and addictions. To give an example, a punch bowl is spiked, some pupils take/sell marijuana, and several affluent adults take cocaine. Likewise, different personal convictions and social conventions continuously play a role and lead to religious and class conflicts. For example, one of the poor pupils feels forced to buy an expensive suit when he is invited to an upper-class party. As his schoolmates discover that he left the price tag on the suit to return it after the party, he earns scorn and condescension. These and other taboo topics (such as gender/sex/sexuality, relations, health and illnesses, crimes and violence, consumerism, human rights, and social injustice) are discussed throughout season one. With regard to teacher education, it might be interesting to discuss why these topics may be challenging to talk about in the classroom, why they should be addressed, and how Élite may serve as a starting point for doing so.

As Figure 19.1 shows, the series consists of a smorgasbord of controversial issues that are combined with a compelling coming-of-age story. *Tabooness* – that is, the fact of not being acceptable to say (out loud) or do (in public), is even addressed as a topic itself as the plot revolves around what one says openly and what one prefers to keep to oneself. For example, Marina – one of the rich students – only speaks about her HIV infection when her classmates have already found out about her disease, and she accuses her parents of never saying out loud that their 16-year-old daughter is HIV positive (Salazar, 2018a, 43:47–44:17). In addition, Ander – another wealthy student and son of the school headmaster – keeps his homosexuality hidden from his parents, but when they find out about it, they advise him not to make his sexual orientation public, as they fear it could affect his tennis career. In the case of Omar – Ander's boyfriend and one of the poor students – the situation is even more complicated. His father is a traditional Muslim with strict rules, and it is out of the question that his son could be "queer" (as his father puts it in the English translation of the series; Salazar, 2018b, 34:00). Consequently, even when asked directly, Omar denies his homosexuality. As these examples show, the whole story is about what is concealed or revealed, as well as (not) said and (not) spread. Against this background, the

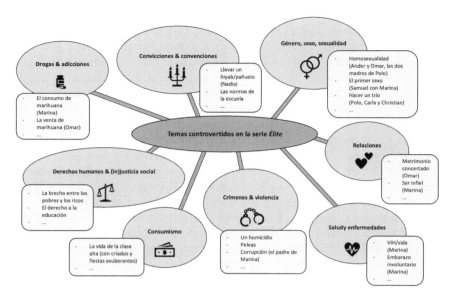

Figure 19.1 Controversial Topics in the First Season of Élite (following Figure 1.2 in Ludwig & Summer, this volume).

following section will show why films and series that contain taboo issues or treat tabooness itself – and hence Élite in particular – can be a useful means to integrate controversial topics in foreign language courses.

The Relevance of Series Like *Élite* for the Foreign Language Classroom

In the following, it will be argued that fiction like Élite (Montero, 2018–2022) provides spaces for diverse linguistic and cultural experiences. These experiences include encounters with several uses, application contexts and varieties of Spanish as well as with different personalities, lifestyles, and levels of society that most pupils would not come into contact with otherwise. By talking about such encounters, one can initiate meaningful discussions and even address taboo issues that would be hard to tackle on a purely factual level. As Ludwig and Summer point out, students today tend to be more open to exchanging views on topics that used to be considered challenging, so "the time seems to have come to push the boundaries of what can be discussed in the foreign language classroom" (Ludwig & Summer, this volume). However, addressing real problems can be unpredictable and do more harm than good – and certain topics are simply inaccessible or inadequate for an open discussion in class. To give an example, many young people have no qualms about talking about sex in general, but they will probably not want to share their own sexual experiences in class, and most teachers would certainly not want to listen to that kind of disclosure. Likewise, pupils may voluntarily discuss the potential legalisation of the consumption of marijuana, but if they have had experiences with drugs, the discussion of these encounters would pose them at (social) risk. For sharing one's own experience on taboo topics, the classroom has never been and is likely to never become an appropriate place – and even less so if the pupils are supposed to communicate in a foreign language.

As these instances show, many taboo topics are mainly taboo when talking about oneself. Unlike in many other cases, teachers will thus not try to make students talk about their own experience when it comes to these topics. They may attempt to get pupils (emotionally) involved, but they will certainly not aim to make them engage in private gossip. Instead, they want to sensitise them to certain issues and make them gain knowledge and skills that can help them to make reflected decisions. Hence, students should be encouraged to think critically (cf. Freire, 2008; Gerlach, 2020). Here, audio-visual fiction proves to be very useful: Films and series open up protected spaces, which include authentic language use, target-cultural practices as well as various alternative lifestyles (cf. Borgwaldt & Amarasinghe, this volume). They allow an (almost direct and truly individual) experience that is clearly separated from the real world. The discussion of these experiences can lead to authentic questions, real answers, and meaningful discussions, which are essential for the promotion of discourse literacy (KMK, 2012) and symbolic competence (Kramsch, 2006, 2018) as they offer opportunities to negotiate meaning and to engage in power plays. As Kramsch (2006, p. 251) explains, students need "the ability to produce and exchange symbolic goods in the complex global context in which we live today", and this ability "has to be nourished by a literary imagination". According to Kramsch, literature can help to show "the full meaning making potential of language" (2006, p. 251) by producing complexity, fostering a certain tolerance of ambiguity, and putting special emphasis on form. In line with this idea, fictional series (as a modern literary text type) can bring together a diversity of forms and meanings and make them more accessible to foreign language learners. Linguistic variation (e.g., varying speech styles of characters from different places and classes), other living practices (e.g., the school rules in a fictive *colegio*), or new perspectives (e.g., different ways of dealing with someone who has HIV) are brought into a concrete context in which they can be discussed.

At any rate, films and series represent textual forms that young people are used to consuming and can engage with (Azadian, 2017). This is crucial for learning, as Freire (2008, p. 21) points out: "Cualquier texto necesita de una cosa: que el lector o la lectora se entreguen a él de forma crítica, crecientemente curiosa". To put it in English, readers must engage with a text in a critical, increasingly curious way. According to Nieweler (2019), films are prone to move pupils emotionally, and if learners experience something affectively, they are more likely to participate in discussions. In other words, audio-visual texts can pave the way for successful language learning by creating spaces where pupils can take stances without having to fear real consequences. By discussing fictional actions and mindsets, learners get to know other creeds, learn to assess which opinions are (un)likely to gain majority support, and practise forming and articulating informed opinions by speaking about their own views and supporting them with arguments. Therefore, Élite (Montero et al., 2018–2022) can serve to develop linguistic skills and orientation knowledge as well as discourse and critical literacy.

Practical Example

This section offers a practical example of working with the first season of Élite (Montero et al., 2018–2022) in the foreign language classroom. As shown above, this series covers many interesting topics and can be a good starting point for discussions. However, teachers should also consider the demanding linguistic level of this authentic text. Aesthetic and emotional experiences should also be taken into account, and learners should be encouraged to reflect critically upon films and topics. Thus, teachers must ensure that listening and viewing comprehension activities do not degenerate into mere language exercises but are used for deeper discussions and the acquisition of real-life knowledge.

In the following, I describe some ideas for such learning activities. First, I give an overview of topics and key scenes that could be covered in a teaching unit. After that, an example of a lesson on Marina's HIV outing is given, presenting a scaffold for a pre-while-post sequence with two concrete post-viewing activities.

Overview of the Topics and Key Scenes of the First Season

Key scenes of the eight episodes of the first season of Élite (Montero et al., 2018) are listed in Table 19.1. In each episode, various taboo topics are addressed, but there is usually one critical issue that is particularly highlighted. Teachers can use this selection of scenes for developing a teaching unit on Élite and taboo topics. In addition to comprehension tasks targeting these scenes, I would suggest providing more in-depth tasks focussing on the critical issues.

For each episode (and thus each critical issue), I planned one lesson of 90 minutes. As the series is very complex, I would advise against reducing it any further, but it would be possible to focus on only one topic if relevant context information is given. Another challenge is to focus on specific topics without diminishing the aesthetic and emotional experience of watching a series as a piece of art. Hence, it may be sensible to mix different presentation modes (see Azadian, 2017; Lütge, 2020; Nieweler, 2019) by watching only segments (in sequential order) in class and making students watch whole episodes during a film night or at their own pleasure.

To illustrate how these scenes and critical issues can be tackled in the English classroom, an exemplary lesson is given below. The critical issue selected is the topic of HIV/AIDS. After presenting the plot of the corresponding key scene, a sequence of activities will be described. A special focus is placed on the creation of concrete tasks for the teaching of English as a foreign language.

Table 19.1 Overview of Selected Key Scenes and Themes of the First Season of the Series Élite

Episode	Lesson topics and critical issues Key scenes and further texts
1	**Introduction to series in general and *Élite* in particular** Film poster, opening scene (00:00–02:33), and first school day (05:46–09:03)
2	**Search for identity, self-presentation, and tabooness** The project task (00:49–02:38) and Marina's profile (46:18–47:21)
3	**Autonomy and heteronomy of the individual in society** The invitation (00:00–01:13), party preparations (08:13–09:40), and party conversations (18:54–20:18)
4	**Power plays in school and (high) society** The grading system (01:44–03:15), Lu's corruption attempt (13:28–15:25), and party scenes (18:20–26:35)
5	**HIV and AIDS** Marina's outing (15:09–17:31) and conversation with Samuel (20:01–21:30)
6	**Drug abuse and teenage pregnancy** Marina getting caught with marijuana (07:26–09:32) and Marina's pregnancy (27:05–30:27)
7	**Homosexuality and arranged marriages** Omar and Ander (18:17–21:50), Ander's conversation with his parents (22:44–25:24) and Omar's father in school (29:32–31:55)
8	**Bringing the season to a conclusion** The escaping plan (01:26–2:37), the award ceremony (17:02–19:12), the interrogation (00:00–00:48), and guessing the murderer, https://www.youtube.com/watch?v=9D28artKyDY

Lesson on HIV

The topic of HIV and AIDS is addressed in episode five. The key scene for this topic is Marina's HIV outing (de la Orden, 2018b, 15:09–17:31), which takes place in school. When Samuel, one of the three poor students and Marina's boyfriend, is caught texting in class, the teacher takes the phone from him and has Nadia read the message out loud. It is thus made public that Marina does not have AIDS ("Marina no tiene sida") but is just HIV positive ("es VIH") (de la Orden, 2018b, 15:45). The situation almost escalates as Guzmán wants to protect his sister, verbally attacking Samuel and accusing the teacher of abusing his position of power. In the end, Marina decides to say a few clarifying words, explaining that she contracted the virus about a year ago and has been taking medication and blood tests since then. As she states, the virus in her blood is undetectable and there is no risk of passing it on. While most of the students are supportive, Nadia obviously disapproves of Marina's behaviour. When the teacher asks her if she does not think that it is brave to share such information, she refuses to answer in order to not "hurt anyone's feelings" (de la Orden, 2018b, 17:28).

From a critical pedagogy and taboo literacy perspective, this scene comprises several noteworthy aspects: It illustrates power structures (i.e., the teacher takes away Samuel's phone and forces Nadia to read the message), it shows different viewpoints (e.g., Christian expresses his agreement by clapping, while Nadia explicitly prefers not to speak her mind), and it takes up the taboo topic of HIV and puts it centre stage (de la Orden, 2018b). The strong emotions in this scene help to arouse genuine interest in the difference between HIV and AIDS and in prevention measures to avoid the disease.

The following sequence of activities (see Table 19.2) is an attempt to scaffold the comprehension and discussion of this scene by using not only the pre-while-post model, but also separating the visual/non-verbal from the audio/verbal input.

As the comprehension of this scene will be challenging for most learners (due to the rapid development of action, high speech rate, strong emotional reactions, overlapping speech, challenging wording, the difficult topic), particular attention should be paid to providing sufficient language support. Knowing that a focus on non-verbal communication can help comprehension, I suggest watching the scene first without sound. In the second step, pupils can try to get the gist of the scene. In the last step, it may be a good idea to offer them a transcription in which some key words (e.g., "Marina no tiene (sida), animal. Tiene VIH"/"Me (contagié) hace un año más o menos") are left out. As such a gap-filling activity will be difficult for some of the learners, the missing words can be presented in alphabetical order in a box above the text. Once the scene is decoded on a factual level, pupils can evaluate the behaviour and reactions of the different characters. For example, it can be discussed whether the teacher had the right to make Nadia read out the message, what pupils think of Marina's decision to come clean, and Nadia's reasons for being so disdainful.

Table 19.2 Sequence of Activities on Marina's HIV Outing

Number of activity	Viewing/listening phase	Learning activity => Goals of learning phases
1	Pre viewing	Characterisation of the protagonists => Activate prior knowledge on the characters
2	While viewing (without sound)	Observation of body language => Foster visual literacy
3	Post viewing (without sound)	Hypotheses on the content => Facilitate listening comprehension
4	While viewing (with sound) 1	Global comprehension task => Identify the key topic
5	While viewing (with sound) 2	Selective comprehension tasks => Discover key terms
6	Post-viewing activity 1	Reflection on the characters' reactions => Arouse interest in the topic and foster critical thinking
7	Post-viewing activity 2a	Research on HIV and AIDS => Gain knowledge and foster research competence
8	Post-viewing activity 2b	Processing of research results in a creative-writing task => Empathise with Samuel and transfer of knowledge

La pobreza, las drogas y el sida   225

Finally, the topic of HIV should be dealt with in more detail. Especially the difference between "having AIDS" and "being HIV positive", which is mentioned but not explained in the scene, should be clarified. To this purpose, students can conduct an Internet search, using official websites of international (e.g., WHO) as well as Hispanic (e.g., the Argentine or Spanish Ministry of Health) institutions (see Table 19.3). By doing so, they not only train their reading-comprehension skills, but also get to know reliable sources for finding information on health issues.

In the second step, they process their acquired knowledge and write the text message Samuel could have written if he had not been interrupted. This creative writing task can be medially supported by the web-based tool *Fake Chat App* (n.d.), which allows students to have their texts look like authentic WhatsApp messages (see Figure 19.2). Instead of simply writing down their researched

Table 19.3 Sources for Internet Research on AIDS and HIV

La página de la Organización Mundial de la Salud	 https://www.who.int/es
La página del Ministerio de Sanidad, Consumo y Bienestar Social de España	 https://www.mscbs.gob.es
La(s) página(s) de otro(s) ministerio(s) de salud	Escribe "ministerio de salud" (en español o en otra lengua) en un buscador como Escosia (https://www.ecosia.org/) o Google.

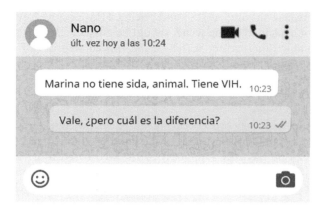

Figure 19.2 Fake Chat in Text Messenger for Creative Writing (Fake Chat App, n.d. [Screenshot taken 10 July 2022]).

knowledge, they cast it into a particular text form of everyday language. In this way, the taboo topic of AIDS is made accessible for more informal discussions – and this may be a good way to show that this is not just some technical discussion but a real-life issue that concerns young people.

Conclusion

Teachers might avoid taboo issues because they lack confidence, methods, or time to tackle them. However, teaching – and teaching languages in particular – implies entering into a critical dialogue with students (Freire, 2008). For such conversations, controversial topics are essential if one does not want to speak about platitudes and truisms. Discussing controversial topics can be a promising way to talk about opposing interests and value systems as well as strategies for conflict resolution and avoidance. As a responsible adventurer (Freire, 2008), teachers should, nonetheless, respect students' privacy and provide (protected) spaces where discussions can take place without pillorying individuals. To this end, the series Élite (Montero et al., 2018–2022) seems to be a suitable text: Not only is it an exciting teenage story that will captivate students, but it also addresses challenging issues that might go unspoken if not dealt with in fiction.

Hopefully, students will never encounter problems like drug dealing, AIDS, or homicide in real life, but it is more than likely that they are interested in them, especially when they are addressed in a contemporary series with protagonists of their own age. Why should we not use Élite to foster critical and taboo literacy? How could we miss the opportunity to enable our students to form informed opinions, discuss crucial issues, and learn how to prevent problems from arising in the first place? Let me conclude with a quote from the series: "*We can demonise* [taboo topics and teen shows], *or we can use them as tools – for learning*" (de la Orden, 2018a, 01:11–01:18; spoken text).

References

Azadian, R. (2017). *Erste Hilfe für das Referendariat und die Berufseinstiegsphase Spanisch.* Schmetterling.

de la Orden, D. (Director). (2018a, October 5). Deseo [Desire] (Season 1, Episode 2) [TV series episode]. In C. Montero, D. Madrona, D. Betancor, & I. Juaristi (Executive Producers), Élite. Zeta Producciones.

de la Orden, D. (Director). (2018b, October 5). Todos mienten [Everyone lies] (Season 1, Episode 5) [TV series episode]. In C. Montero, D. Madrona, D. Betancor, & I. Juaristi (Executive Producers), Élite. Zeta Producciones.

Élite Netflix. (2018, October 15). Élite. ¿Quién es el asesino? El cast de Elite adivina. Élite Netflix [Video]. YouTube. https://youtu.be/9D28artKyDY

Fake Chat App. (n.d.). *Fake Chat App.* https://www.fakechatapp.com/

Freire, P. (2008). *Pedagogía de la autonomía: saberes necesarios para la práctica educativa.* Siglo XXI.

Gerlach, D. (2020). Einführung in eine Kritische Fremdsprachendidaktik. In D. Gerlach (Ed.), *Kritische Fremdsprachendidaktik: Grundlagen, Ziele, Beispiele* (pp. 7–32). Narr.

Kramsch, C. (2006). From communicative competence to symbolic competence. *The Modern Language Journal, 90*(2), 249–252.

Kramsch, C. (2018). Symbolische Kompetenz. In S. Schiedermair (Ed.), *Deutsch als Fremd- und Zweitsprache. Zugänge zu sozialen Wirklichkeiten.* iudicium.

Kultusministerkonferenz (KMK). (2012). *Bildungsstandards für die fortgeführte Fremdsprache (Englisch/Französisch) für die Allgemeine Hochschulreife* (Decision of October 18, 2012). https://www.kmk.org/fileadmin/Dateien/veroeffentlichungen_beschluesse/2012/2012_10_18-Bildungsstandards-Fortgef-FS-Abi.pdf

Lütge, C. (2020). Die Arbeit mit Filmen. In W. Hallet, F. G. Königs, H. Martinez (Eds.), *Handbuch Methoden im Fremdsprachenunterricht.* Klett Kallmeyer.

Medienpädagogischer Forschungsverbund Südwest (mpfs). (2017). *JIM 2017: Jugend, Information, (Multi-) Media.* https://www.mpfs.de/fileadmin/files/Studien/JIM/2017/JIM_2017.pdf

Medienpädagogischer Forschungsverbund Südwest (mpfs). (2020). *JIM 2020: Jugend, Information, Medien.* https://www.mpfs.de/fileadmin/files/Studien/JIM/2020/JIM-Studie-2020_Web_final.pdf

Montero, C., Madrona, D., Betancor, D., & Juaristi, I. (Executive Producers). (2018–2022). Élite [TV series]. Zeta Producciones.

Nieweler, A. (2019). *Fremdsprachen unterrichten. Ein Ratgeber für Studium und Unterrichtspraxis.* Ernst Klett.

Salazar, R. (Director). (2018a, October 5). Bienvenidos [Welcome] (Season 1, Episode 1) [TV series episode]. In C. Montero, D. Madrona, D. Betancor, & I. Juaristi (Executive Producers), Élite. Zeta Producciones.

Salazar, R. (Director). (2018b, October 5). Todo estalla [Everything explodes] (Season 1, Episode 7) [TV series episode]. In C. Montero, D. Madrona, D. Betancor, & I. Juaristi (Executive Producers), Élite. Zeta Producciones.

Statista. (2021). *Video streaming in Germany.* https://www.statista.com/study/74108/video-streaming-in-germany/

20 Addressing South African Perspectives on Taboos and Tricky Topics in European Literature Classrooms

Sandra Stadler-Heer

Introduction

The below quote provides insights into a meeting that has taken place at a South African university between students and teachers concerning how to decolonize a university's curriculum.

> It is 2016 – a time of heightened student protests here in South Africa. In response to these protests, my academic department has invited our senior students to give us some honest advice about how we might go about decolonizing our curriculum. The students welcome the opportunity and we have a robust but mostly cordial discussion. As the discussion is ending, a student seated next to me, who took an African Studies course with me the previous year, turns to me and says, with quite some anger, that I should not be teaching the African Studies course. "I need a black body in front of me!" she says and points to one of my black colleagues saying something like "Why doesn't she teach the course rather than you?".
>
> (Matthews, 2021, p. 2)

In "Decolonizing while white?", Matthews (2021), herself a white female South African scholar, addresses a formerly tabooed yet universal topic and its implications for teaching young learners in South Africa and beyond: As white bodies still represent most academic and educational personnel and are living and breathing "reminder[s] of the long history of white dominance in educational spaces in South Africa", how can they become agents of debate? How can they discuss the fact that "the bodies in which we dwell affect how others respond to us and interpret what we say" (Matthews, 2021, p. 2) without reinforcing white supremacist and hegemonic curricular thinking? The publication of Matthews' (2021) article and research in further disciplines, such as South African young adult literature in English (Stadler, 2017), shows that debates about specific aspects of whiteness, gender norms, and language use are no longer taboo in the South African educational context. Having entered public discourse, they are now recognized as "threshold concepts", or "tricky topics" – a term used by practitioners to refer to "transformative", "irreversible", "integrative",

DOI: 10.4324/9781003220701-24

"bounded", or "troublesome" knowledge and core topics that affect learners' individual development (Sharples et al., 2014, p. 32; see also Pike et al., 2019). This contribution is a first attempt to bring selected South African perspectives on discussing topics that are no longer taboo but recognized as tricky to European literature classrooms and teacher education. Despite a lack of official statistics on the ethnic diversity among teachers in European classrooms, we can assume that most educators arguably have white bodies just as in South Africa. How can they become agents of debate despite Europe's white supremacist legacy? How can they address issues of whiteness, gender, or the politics of language use with language learners? One way of addressing these issues is through establishing knowledge bases of threshold concepts feeding supremacist discourses in educational settings and teacher education. Adapting a teaching concept by Pike et al. (2019), I present selected avenues into knowledge bases needed to engage in critical debates about whiteness, gender norms, and language use in foreign language classrooms.

Theoretical Background

Given that debates on whiteness, gender, and language use continue to represent a major source of both societal upheaval and silence not only in South Africa, presenting only a small selection of South African perspectives on these topics might be a taboo in itself. Indeed, South African citizens, scholars, and critics continue to struggle in normalizing decolonization discourses related to gender, socioeconomics, and space (Stadler, 2017) despite massive attempts to "rewrite the nation" (Verbeeck, 2006). Moreover, this is a contribution written by a white, German, female teacher educator appearing in a volume edited by two white German scholars. By naming credentials, I deliberately place this contribution in an emerging body of research that addresses the dilemma of knowledge production, which has historically been dominated by white cultures, and is crucially aware of the "ethical concern that the labour of deconstructing the centering of whiteness should not be seen as the sole responsibility of academics of colour" (Roberts, 2021, p. 6).

Due to the challenges tricky topics like whiteness, gender, and language use pose, reading up on and discussing contemporary writings on these often silenced and neglected subjects is of pivotal interest to both teachers and learners. To develop learners' content- and context-specific skills as well as critically debate existing South African ideologies and practices while responding to them in their own contexts, (European) teachers must become knowledgeable in the following discourses.

Addressing Whiteness

Importantly, if white people want to contribute to the decolonization of educational curricula, they "should try to do so, but not assume their ability to do so or their right to participate in decolonial projects" (Matthews, 2021, p. 4).

Indeed, there is very little research that addresses the effects of race on white academics' classroom experience (Matthews, 2021). Given the sensitivity of the topic, only few video data, audio data, or transcripts on actual classroom talk exist allowing us to analyze how white educators address race in their heterogeneous classrooms (Roberts, 2021). Matthews, for instance, thematized her whiteness in her classroom by "de-center[ing]" (2021, p. 6) herself and introducing a black postgraduate student as moderator of small group discussions.

When teaching literature, white scholars need to revisit their understanding of knowledge production and the role they play in developing knowledge in the first place, particularly as they are the ones selecting and telling stories. Inggs (2021) was able to show that the socioeconomic background of storytellers vitally influences their retellings of folktales. In the case of South Africa,

> [b]lack storytellers [of folktales] commonly belong to the indigenous communities where the tales were passed down in an oral tradition, while the white writers narrate the tales from a different perspective, influenced by their own background and their prior experience of tales from both Africa and the rest of the world.
>
> (Inggs, 2021, p. 343)

If we transfer Inggs' findings to the classroom, literature teachers should be aware of factors influencing their teaching of South African texts to contribute to ongoing debates about decoloniality. Importantly, instead of trying "to produce 'decolonized' knowledge" in the classroom, which is in danger of being overly "moralistic and potentially narcissistic" (Matthews, 2021, p. 6), results of learning about decoloniality and whiteness should be seen as situated and selective; an attempt "to assess with some degree of plausibility various intuitions about what is going on, what is possible, and the odds against it" (Mbembe, 2012, p. 22). Acknowledging the partiality and incompleteness of both insights to be gained from literary texts and the influence of one's own ethnicity and socioeconomic background on responses to the text are a first essential step in debating South African perspectives on tricky topics.

Addressing Language Use and Gender Norms

Teachers play a crucial role in the formation of learners' identities. If their classroom language is characterized by, for instance, "categorical constructions around bodily markers such as race, gender and religion [and how these] play in who is privileged to inclusion or problematised as different" (Roberts, 2021, p. 3), they may unconsciously perpetuate preconceived notions and beliefs. Thus, in their pedagogical attempts to include students from multiple backgrounds, genders, and languages in classroom discourse, teachers must pay attention to their choice of words when moderating content-specific classroom interaction. Formulations like "'different from' can be conflated with 'less than'" (Roberts, 2021, p. 3) and carry notions of deservingness and degeneration and perpetuate power relations. Indeed, if "[d]iscourses of difference and diversity" (Roberts, 2021, p. 3) continue to focus on those not at the center, those already at the center remain the powerful and privileged in local social frameworks.

The topic of language use is particularly delicate in South African contexts. The lack of codification of African languages and the simultaneously continued dominance of publishing in Afrikaans is one instance exemplifying the "social value placed on Afrikaans whiteness" (Roberts, 2021, p. 2) even after the end of apartheid. The significance of the languages one speaks and their impact on identity formation cannot be underestimated. If Afrikaans is the language associated with power and privilege, non-Afrikaans-speaking students may feel the urge "to align with expectations of dominant white culture" due to "implicit suggestions that their own cultural practices and aesthetics are somehow deficient" (Roberts, 2021, p. 2).

Regarding gender norms, recent ethnographic studies, for instance, report that progressive masculinity is still a taboo in African countries (Agozino & Agu, 2021). Presently, the absence of strategic educational programmes for boys leads to the reinforcement of tropes that equate education with femininity and trouble with masculinity (Agozino & Agu, 2021). Interestingly, positive examples "of nurturing fathers in the Caribbean and Africa who work hard to provide for their children and support their wives or partners when women are the main breadwinners" (Agozino & Agu, 2021, p. 81) are also seldom found in English South African texts written in the realist mode (Stadler, 2017). However, if fictional texts do not include communicative negotiations of gender norms, fictionalized examples of such debates are missing from cultural products and cannot serve as sample conversations to be critically reflected on in educational contexts. The language used in texts selected for in-class reading, viewing, and listening or included in teaching materials contributes to constructing individual identities along specific lines and consequently may be tabooed or at least remain silent toward the development of alternative individualities. Ultimately, as I clarify in the next section, it is the (foreign language) teachers' responsible and professional use of language, choice of teaching materials, and insight into thematic gaps in texts that can help break up the centering of topics by making the very discourse of power relations in educational settings and in language use a topic of classroom discussion.

Relevance for the Foreign Language Classroom

Not only each society but each school subject or academic discipline has uncomfortable and uneasy topics as well as concepts that are notoriously difficult to understand and talk about. As a result, such tricky topics are often misunderstood, neglected, or silenced altogether. Given the tendency to avoid critical engagement with these topics, misconceptions can easily arise and may even lead to flawed intuitive beliefs (Coley & Tanner, 2012). Given the potential of the aforementioned South African perspectives on whiteness, masculinity, and use of language to irreversibly transform a person's conceptualization of their individual worldview and their influence on individual development and beliefs, they can be called "threshold concepts" (Meyer & Land, 2006, p. xv).

Threshold concepts are "akin to a portal, opening up a new and previously inaccessible way of thinking about something" (Meyer & Land, 2006, p. xv). For learners to progress and arrive at "a transformed way of understanding, or interpreting" (Meyer & Land, 2006, p. xv), they require professional educators to guide their development in a critically reflective and task-oriented manner. Since 2018, preparing teachers to teach, talk about, and critically evaluate topics that are uncomfortable, difficult, or tricky has been the topic of a free online professional development course for teachers and educators (Pike et al., 2019). As threshold concepts "focus on the cognitive (thinking) domain of learning rather than the affective (feelings, moods and emotions) or behavioral (physical/kinaesthetic) domains of learning" (Pike et al., 2019), they can help to counter misconceptions that may hinder communicative exchange between different groups of people.

The following lesson sequence adapts the Open University's learning design (Pike et al., 2019) to integrate debates about some of South Africa's tricky topics in European foreign language classrooms. As I teach in Germany, EFL classrooms in this country are chosen as a setting. The German Standards of Education call the engagement with topics of global relevance access points in foreign language teaching to develop learners' intercultural communicative competence (Kultusministerkonferenz (KMK), 2012). Examples of such globally relevant topics are, for instance, race, gender, and language.

At the end of secondary education, according to the German Standards of foreign language education (KMK, 2012), learners should be able to

- recognize, question, put into perspective, and, if necessary, revise their perceptions and (pre-)judgments;
- change perspectives and compare and weigh up different perspectives;
- recognize the values, attitudes, and positions of their target language communication partners and classify them taking into account their foreign cultural background;
- understand, interpret, and evaluate foreign language texts and discourses in their foreign cultural dimension;
- classify their own and other people's values, attitudes, and behavior in relation to international conventions (e.g., human rights) (KMK, 2012, p. 20).

Thus, a lesson sequence developing learners' competences in gathering facts about South Africa's context-specific tricky topics is in line with the German educational standards. Especially so if they ask learners to reflect on their own context-specific values, attitudes, and positions about these topics. Ultimately, the following practical example aims at promoting interactional competences (Galaczi & Taylor, 2018) through engagement with authentic texts, classroom debates, and presenting the gathered facts and opinions to others (see Table 20.1).

Table 20.1 Lesson Sequence: Debating Selected South African Tricky Topics (B2+ to C1)

Topic	South African perspectives on tricky topics
Goals	• Learners train interactional competences • Learners gain insights in a selected set of South Africa's tricky topics as represented in literary texts • Learners recognize, question, put into perspective and, if necessary, revise perceptions and (pre-)judgments about tricky topics (see KMK, 2012, p. 20)
Outcome	Depending on the teaching context and the technical resources available: oral presentations, optional: presentation of materials on school website or local news platform
Level	B2+ to C1
Time	180 minutes (up to 4×45 minutes)
Materials and activities	Rubrics for (peer-)feedback and (self-, peer-) assessment, combination of individually selected literary texts (from the online FunDza Mobi Library, https://live.fundza.mobi/home/library/) and scientific facts (e.g. South Africa's Publishing Association Reports)
Differentiation	Outcomes: • Oral presentations can be presented alone, in teams of two to three students or entire groups either live or pre-recorded • A public debate could be performed live orally in class or in writing via chat

Practical Example

The following example (Table 20.1) addresses whiteness, gender, and the use of language from South African perspectives with the help of (fictional and factual) texts in the foreign language. Learners read, discuss, and summarize these texts, for instance, in oral presentations, that should ideally be made available to a larger public in a gallery walk or public debate. As students' roles would change from learner to expert, they could test their interactional competence and debating skills gained in the classroom context with members of their local communities.

The teacher can use the following key questions adapted from Matthews (2021) to introduce the lesson sequence (see Table 20.2):

1 Can white people play a genuine role in decolonizing how we speak about tricky topics?
2 If so, is their role different to that of black or colored scholars? Can white people find words to describe that difference?
3 Which language can white people use when talking about tricky topics?

These complex questions contain several previously mentioned threshold concepts: whiteness, gender, the power of language, and of pedagogy. The questions hold the opportunity for learners to decide on individual access points and to highlight concrete problems they see in their own private lives in their responses.

Table 20.2 Suggested Activities for a Task Cycle (Tasks in Part II are Adapted from Poelzleitner, 2010)

Pre-task and needs analysis (15 minutes)	Presenting the projects questions (see above) as a silent impulse, students are encouraged to utter individual responses in pair work. Possible follow-up questions could be: • Are the following questions or elements of them relevant to you personally? • Which associations arise when reading these questions? • Have you already passively or actively experienced or witnessed conversations about whiteness, gender, or language? • In which contexts are these questions relevant to you personally?

Task (105 minutes)	The starting point: Written texts, fictional or factual, open new worlds and allow us to change perspectives. FunDza Mobi Library (https://live.fundza.mobi/home/library/) is our access point to South Africa. We want to get to know South Africa from as many perspectives as possible and not just read a single story. Only then can we begin to understand local ideas about tricky topics, avoid misconceptions, or feed our false intuitive beliefs.
	Task overview: Work in groups of three. Exchange your ideas about the text and how it makes you feel; ask yourself how your own upbringing and living situation influences your thoughts and feelings. Then, prepare a ten-minute oral presentation (supported by visual aids and quotes from texts) about a South African tricky topic of your choice. Be smart about organizing who does what in your group presentation.
	Input: Consult these websites for inspiration for your (online) presentations (creative book presentations: https://epep.at/?page_id=1075; presenting books online: https://readingiscool.xyz/rc/):
	Task steps:
	1. Pick a story/essay/poem/play of your choice from the following online library: https://live.fundza.mobi/home/library/
	2. Read an excerpt of the text of your choice and think about the following two questions. Structure your group's ideas with the help of a collaborative writing tool
	   a) What kind of **TOPIC and IDEA** does your text promote?
	   b) How are **WHITENESS/GENDER/LANGUAGES** represented as topics in the text you have read?
	   c) **Facts about South Africa's publishing industry**: Ask your teacher for an overview of South African young adult literature (Stadler, 2015) and current statistics on publishing in different languages in South Africa (https://publishsa.co.za/publishing-industry-survey-2019-2021/). How important is publishing in the English language in South Africa?
	3. Present your results as part of a (virtual) gallery walk
	* Optional, 90 minutes: Make your knowledge accessible to the public by organizing a (public) debate on your chosen topic in the context of your hometown
	* Optional, 90 minutes: Prepare a documentation of materials and projects on your school's website (inspiration: https://readingiscool.xyz/rc/). Promote it on your local digital news platform

Post-task (30 minutes)	Critical reflection on the different stages of the task cycle in relation to the degree of engagement with tricky topics Discussion: What can you do to help normalize tricky topics like whiteness, gender norms, or the use of language?

Student answers to the above questions are likely to change over the course of the lesson sequence. This ambivalence can be reflected in students' working process when narrowing down topics suitable for oral presentations. A task-based cycle and principles of critical pedagogy, both of which aim to transfer learning from pedagogic tasks to real-life tasks, were chosen due to the former's effectiveness (Bryfonski & McKay, 2019) and the latter's conviction that "beliefs and practices in society, which are related to power and domination of certain groups over others, should be questioned and challenged" (see Ludwig & Summer, this volume). The following sequence (Table 20.2) makes the ambiguous role that European foreign language literature teachers play when debating South Africa's tricky topics apparent.

The project places non-canonical literary texts in dialogue with pressing societal discourses with the goal to normalize discourses related to tricky topics (Stadler, 2017). One way of catering to individual learner differences is by letting learners choose their preferred text type in Part I of the task cycle. FunDza's open online library helps provide these individual avenues into the engagement with tricky topics and opportunities to develop one's own story of negotiating the implications of whiteness, gender norms, and the language then used to talk about these topics in the context of a presentation. From my own teaching experience, I know that this approach is likely to not only heighten reading motivation and self-esteem but also reduce fears of not understanding texts, concepts, and speaking publicly about tricky topics. The project's outcome depends on student's topic-specific language competence and the degree to which students and teachers can reflect critically on their own attitudes toward tricky topics.

Conclusion

This contribution identified former taboos that have entered public discourse and become recognized as threshold concepts with the help of South African studies and literary texts. A lesson sequence was designed to help European language teachers in addressing controversial topics with their learners. As teachers tend to include in their teaching only those topics that they feel confident about, university-based teacher education needs to include critical engagement with taboos and tricky topics in curricula and offer training in moderating student interactions (Boughey & McKenna, 2021). For that purpose, more content- and skill-specific continuous professional development and explicit teaching materials subscribing to critical pedagogy and power in pedagogy (Roberts, 2021) are still required to promote learning about taboos and tricky topics. Lastly, more qualitative research on the implications of teaching local perceptions on tricky topics in classrooms as well as teacher language used to introduce such topics is required.

References

Agozino, B., & Agu, A. (2021). Taboos of masculinity: Positive and progressive masculinities. *Taboo: The Journal of Culture and Education, 20*(1). https://digitalscholarship.unlv.edu/taboo/vol20/iss1/5

Boughey, C., & McKenna, S. (2021). *Understanding higher education: Alternative perspectives.* African Minds.

Bryfonski, L., & McKay, T. H. (2019). TBLT implementation and evaluation: A meta-analysis. *Language Teaching Research, 23*(5), 603–632. https://doi.org/10.1177/1362168817744389

Coley, J. D., & Tanner, K. D. (2012). Common origins of diverse misconceptions: Cognitive principles and the development of biology thinking. *CBE—Life Sciences Education, 11,* 209–215. https://doi.org/10.1187/cbe.12-06-0074

Galaczi, E., & Taylor, L. (2018). Interactional competence: Conceptualisations, operationalisations, and outstanding questions. *Language Assessment Quarterly, 15*(3), 1–18. https://doi.org/10.1080/15434303.2018.1453816

Inggs, J. (2021). Weak or wily? Girls' voices in tellings and retellings of African folktales for children. *Children's Literature in Education, 52,* 342–356.

Kultusministerkonferenz (KMK). (2012). *Bildungsstandards für die fortgeführte Fremdsprache (Englisch/Französisch) für die Allgemeine Hochschulreife* (Decision of October 18, 2012). https://www.kmk.org/fileadmin/Dateien/veroeffentlichungen_beschluesse/2012/2012_10_18-Bildungsstandards-Fortgef-FS-Abi.pdf

Matthews, S. (2021). Decolonising while white: Confronting race in a South African classroom. *Teaching in Higher Education, 26*(7–8), 1113–1121. https://doi.org/10.1080/13562517.2021.1914571

Mbembe, A. (2012). Theory from the Antipodes. Note on Jean & John Comaroffs' TFS. *The Johannesburg Salon, 5,* 18–25.

Meyer, J., & Land, R. (2006). Overcoming barriers to student understanding: Threshold concepts and troublesome knowledge. In J. Meyer, & R. Land (Eds.), *Overcoming barriers to student understanding: Threshold concepts and troublesome knowledge* (pp. 19–32). Routledge.

Pike, A., Adams, A., Clough, G., Sargent, J., Hartnett, L., McFarlane, R. Anastasiou, P. & Hart, J. (2019). *Teaching and learning tricky topics, Week 1.* The Open University. https://www.open.edu/openlearn/ocw/mod/oucontent/view.php?id=72094&section=__acknowledgements

Poelzleitner, E. (2010, March 19). *Upper school literature projects.* Elizabeth Poelzleitner's English Pool. https://epep.at/?page_id=275

Roberts, J. S. (2021). Power in pedagogy: Legacies of apartheid in a South African school. *Whiteness and Education, 6*(2), 130–146. https://doi.org/10.1080/23793406.2021.1917305

Sharples, M., Adams, A., Ferguson, R., Gaved, M., McAndrew, P., Rienties, B., Weller, M., & Whitelock, D. (2014). *Innovating pedagogy 2014: Open university innovation report 3.* The Open Universy.

Stadler, S. (2017) *South African young adult literature in English, 2000–2014.* Winter.

Stadler, S. (2015). Debating equal representation in South African youth literature written in English (2000–2013) – A statistical assessment. *Bookbird, 53*(2), 47–58.

Verbeeck, G. (2006). Anachronism and the rewriting of history: The South Africa case. *The Journal for Transdisciplinary Research in Southern Africa, 2*(1), 181–200. https://doi.org/10.4102/td.v2i1.314

21 Addressing Taboo Topics in Translator and Interpreter Training

Eva Seidl

Introduction

Throughout this chapter, and in line with Massey and Kiraly (2019), I will use the terms interpreter training and education synonymously. Critically analysing the last 25 years of research in language teaching for prospective interpreters and translators, Cerezo Herrero and Schmidhofer (2021) argue that language education for this specific target group has yet to be positioned as a vital part of translator and interpreter (T&I) training. In addition, together with other researchers in the emerging field of *Translation and Interpreting-Oriented Language Learning and Teaching* (TILLT), they advocate a tailor-suited pedagogical approach and the establishment of TILLT as a specific academic branch within modern Translation Studies. Recent research in the field of TILLT highlights the importance of firmly grounding language learning and teaching in T&I principles in order to help students with the transition from the language classroom to the actual T&I classroom (Stachl-Peier & Schwarz, 2020). Of course, linguistic accuracy, a critical approach to texts and theories, and intercultural sensitivity are relevant for both future language teachers and future translators or interpreters. Another point in common, as Sinclair (2021) notes, is the fact that the sphere of language teaching, especially in the sector of adult education, represents a common professional activity for translation graduates.

In translator education, however, it is of utmost importance – for teachers and students alike – to be clear about the differences between such a study programme and general modern language programmes. T&I students, first and foremost, must develop a translator identity in addition to a foreign language learner identity. Another essential distinction, for example, is that students' very own communicative goals are not at the heart of their studies. Rather, translation students learn how to act communicatively on behalf of others, or, put differently, how to use their knowledge and skills concerning language, culture, and communication for the communicative goals of others (Schmidhofer & Ahmann, 2015). In the words of Siever (2019, p. 86), the translator, thus, can be described as a cognitive and emotional nomad who transcends boundaries in order to enable communication where there was none before. Neither with their thoughts nor feelings can translators stick to the culture of the source text nor

DOI: 10.4324/9781003220701-25

to the one of the target text. They are obliged to, cognitively and emotionally, wander between the two (Siever, 2019, p. 81).

In terms of the relationship between language and culture, Kadrić et al. (2019) state that "the translation process is the place where language becomes visible as culture" and where translators, in their minds and for the purpose of a specific communicative situation, make critical comparisons between cultures, languages and discourse (p. 38, own translation). This resonates with Blell's and Doff's (2014) definition of transculturally competent learners as being able to "consciously and skillfully [interpret] culture(s) (race, class, gender, religion, *language included*) in which insider/outsider status is replaced by blurring the borders and recognizing multiplicities or identity and group affiliation" (p. 90). This definition lends itself particularly well for the case of undergraduate students of Transcultural Communication who lay the foundation for a master's degree in Translation Studies in the years of their bachelor's degree and whose experience with and thoughts on taboo topics in language education will be given attention to in this chapter. By means of giving voice to the student perspective, I wish to make a case for the language teachers' and students' shared responsibility to learn how to address taboo topics in T&I training competently.

Theoretical Background

The relevance of addressing taboo topics in T&I training has its foundation in Freire's call "never to dichotomize cognition and emotion", since "we learn, we teach, we know with our entire body", with emotions, with doubts, with passion, but also with critical reasoning (2018/2005, p. 5). According to bell hooks (1994), teachers' unwillingness to include an "awareness of race, sex, and class is often rooted in the fear that classrooms will be uncontrollable, that emotions and passions will not be contained" (p. 39). However, if we do incorporate these issues and, concurrently, help our students appreciate difficulty as part and parcel of intellectual development, they can learn that "there is integrity to be found in grappling with difficult material, [e.g.,] confessional narratives, books, or discussions" (hooks, 1994, p. 154).

For prospective translators and interpreters, it is of paramount importance not to regard their linguistic and cultural frames of reference as natural but to distance themselves from the all-too-familiar in order to recognise cultural values in linguistic expressions (Kadrić et al., 2019, p. 37). When it comes to taboo literacy, the language classroom, which is underpinned by engaged, critical language pedagogy, as proposed by hooks (1994), can gain valuable stimuli from the pedagogical approach of shared vulnerability. Brantmeier (2013) asserts that such an approach promotes a climate of mutual trust and the practice of critical self-reflection. Teachers and students examine the origins of their worldviews and question the assumptions of their values and behaviour while also scrutinising comparative and contrasting frames of reference.

This is in line with a transformative approach to learning, based on the teacher's efforts to create a safe classroom that encourages risk-taking and rewards openness in order to facilitate the expression of new awareness (Prado et al., 2021). Prado and her colleagues underscore the crucial importance of an educational environment of trust and support for learners – and here, I would like to add teachers – to have "emotional and intellectual space to challenge previously held assumptions or perspectives" (Prado et al., 2021, p. 123). This is all the more critical when taboo topics are addressed in the language classroom since it might not be easy for everyone involved to give up long-held beliefs and convictions.

For Killick (2015), a transformative approach requires and enables students "to engage with curriculum content in ways that involve them not only critically engaging *with* texts and theories but also taking a critical stance *towards* texts and theories *per se*" (p. 141, original emphasis). In addition, the *lived curriculum* could also be reflected through a lively exchange of lived and observed experiences. Brantmeier (2013) defines such a curriculum as the content of each person's life, and their past lived experiences, which are the foundation of learning new concepts, skills or values, and which are "just as important as the book content" (p. 97).

By means of a reflection on their lived curriculum and how it might intersect with the curriculum content of the classroom or the study programme, students can experience "transformative personal and professional growth that can lead to a sense of agency to create change in broader society" (p. 104). Enhancing their taboo literacy, the next generation of interpreters and translators can develop an "enlivened sense of agency in personal and professional domains" (Brantmeier, 2013, p. 104), which might be crucial amidst the turmoil of our changing world.

Relevance for the Translation-Oriented Foreign Language Classroom

This section suggests a number of reasons why language educators should address taboo topics in TILLT. According to Kadrić and Kaindl (2016), the primary purpose of higher education lies in civic education and advocacy for democracy. Students should be inspired to critically reflect on their responsibilities towards themselves and towards society as well as on their roles in it. Against this backdrop, it is even more important to emphasise the crucial relevance of high-quality translations in order to actively support democracy, the rule of law and social justice (Kadrić & Kaindl, 2016, p. 7). Translation service delivery has to be impartial and unbiased by engaging in anti-racist and anti-discriminatory behaviour and following a professional code of conduct and code of ethics, not least because, as Kadrić and Kaindl (2016, p. 7, author's translation) assert:

> The quality of a translation might determine the outcome of an asylum application or a criminal proceeding and, thus, have an impact on the trajectory of somebody's life. A similar situation applies to interpreter-mediated communication in healthcare settings. Mistranslations or misinterpretations could lead to a wrong diagnosis and to dramatic consequences.

Consequently, these authors advocate the integration of not only practical skills and methodological competence in T&I programmes but also of socio-political, affective and ethical aspects, together with social communication skills (Kadrić & Kaindl, 2016). Nixon (2008) argues in a similar vein by defining teaching as a moral endeavour. He posits that "students and teachers have a responsibility to think about the moral implications, for themselves and others, of what they are learning: what kind of persons they want to become and what kind of society they wish to create" (Nixon, 2008, p. 126). T&I graduates can therefore be expected to act responsibly and to be highly competent professionals who are not only familiar with digital media but also with taboo topics.

These skills are needed, for example, in audio-visual translations of taboo words in the field of interlingual film subtitling (Ben Slamia, 2020). In her analysis of translation strategies for expressions concerning death, sexuality, and religion from English into Arabic, Ben Slamia (2020) underlined the relationship between taboo words and morality. Since taboo words (see also Werner, this volume) are culture-bound and specific to language and context, it cannot be emphasised enough that "[n]othing is taboo for all people under all circumstances for all time" (Allan, 2018, p. 14). The fact that Ben Slamia (2020) investigated taboos in film subtitling of American and British films for an Arabic television audience of popular TV channels supports the idea that "every taboo must be specified for a particular community of people for a specified context at a given place and time" (Allan, 2018, p. 16). This particularly applies to cultural taboo topics (see Amarasinghe & Borgwaldt, this volume).

Furthermore, this is especially the case for community interpreting, i.e., interpreter-mediated public service encounters in settings such as courts, hospitals or schools (Grbić & Wolf, 2021). If not handled appropriately, taboos in such contexts may negatively, if not drastically, impact communication and communicative goals. This is why this field poignantly reveals that interpreting requires much more than linguistic competence. For interpreters to live up to professional standards, they should be aware of the fact that

> [t]aboo is relative in two senses: cultural group (what is taboo for some cultures may not be so for others) and intensity or offensiveness (the *same* topic or word may be taboo for different cultures, but the face (cultural) threat, risk, or offensiveness associated with it may vary from one culture to another.
> (Taibi & El-Madkouri Maataoui, 2016, pp. 72–73, emphasis added)

This also has an important implication for language education in T&I training, namely that "the word itself is only part of the picture, the taboo value depends on the use of intensifiers or hedges, on the tone of voice or the facial expression" (Dewaele, 2018, p. 231). To help translation students transition from foreign (or LX) language *learners* to LX *users*, teachers can foster the acquisition of the affective meaning and the emotional power of taboo words. As a matter of fact, because of more prolonged, often more varied, and intense exposure from birth, L1 users have undeniable advantages over LX users (Dewaele, 2018).

In this light, the growing scholarly interest in emotions and nonverbal communication (cf. Gregersen & MacIntyre, 2021) or in embodied cognition (cf. Witte, 2021) is very promising for the enhancement of taboo literacy. Witte (2021, p. 35) convincingly argues that "[t]he involvement of the whole body in the process of foreign language/culture learning facilitates unmediated corporeal experiences and resulting insights for learners in the process of interacting with their felt selves, and their cultural and linguistic identities". This "affective-corporeal dimension of engagement with the world" (Witte, 2021, p. 46) resonates with Gregersen and MacIntyre (2021). They contend that we continuously experience feelings, even if we are often not fully aware of such background emotions or how they affect our behaviour.

This means that the LX classroom should promote attentiveness to corporeal resonances and responses, to the proximity of the interlocutors, olfactory dimensions, gestures, posture, touching behaviour, facial expressions, eye contact, or the exchange of glances (Witte, 2021, p. 30). This could support aspiring interpreters in the judgement of acceptability or appropriateness of words and behaviour with respect to taboos for a particular communicative encounter while taking into consideration the influence of space, time and interpersonal relationships.

Practical Examples and Student Voices

In what follows, I will present key findings of empirical data from 16 bachelor's students of Transcultural Communication (ten female, six male) at the Department of Translation Studies at an Austrian University. In this very diverse, multilingual and multicultural environment, I have been teaching German as L1 and LX for almost two decades now. Similar to Dobutowitsch's (2020) depiction of the lived, plurilingual reality of the current student body in many German universities, the majority of students of German as LX at this Austrian university are bilinguals with a migration background. These young adults can best be described as having non-stereotypical, hybrid identities, which they strive to express through various senses of belonging.

They study two foreign languages at the Department for Translation Studies, where they can choose between 12 languages, including Austrian sign language. In the summer semester of 2020 (March to June), due to the COVID-19 pandemic, the German as LX course was held online, using BigBlueButton as a conference tool embedded in the learning management system Moodle. In April, I uploaded the call for papers for an online conference on taboo topics in foreign language education at the University of Würzburg, Germany. In the call, the conference organisers listed ten taboo topics, i.e., more than the taboos of the acronym PARNSIP (see Ludwig and Summer, this volume). Using the forum activity in Moodle, which allows learners and teachers to exchange ideas by posting comments as part of a thread, I asked the students (1) to carefully read the call for papers and (2) to comment on the listed taboos and on their experience with taboo topics, in particular as regards language learning and teaching.

Three of 16 students openly shared their personal, painful familiarity with exposure to discrimination (as regards racism, linguistic discrimination, and chronic illness). Two students mentioned that in their home countries, it was dangerous, or even life-threatening, to discuss politics publicly. With regard to Banegas' and Evripidou's (2021) contention that it is possible that some language learners and teachers might be non-heterosexual or non-binary in a given class and that sexual identity should be approached as potentially relevant to anyone and not just to a minority, it is telling that the students expressed mixed feelings about gender, non-traditional relationships and sexual identities.

For one thing, some raised concerns about whether they would be comfortable discussing these issues with their peers in the language classroom, not to mention the difference in age between them and their teachers. Interestingly, however, one student stated that it is a challenging endeavour to acquire and reinforce language and social communication skills to address issues related to sexuality appropriately if the LX classroom does not provide such opportunities. This concern is reflected in the literature on taboo and swear words in the sense that LX users are described as "vulnerable in social interactions [because of] [un]certainty about meaning, offensiveness, and appropriateness of taboo words [...], which is why they tend to refrain from using them, or prefer less offensive ones" (Dewaele, 2018, p. 232). The author further argues (Dewaele, 2018, p. 226),

> As the LX learners become LX users and socialise in the LX, they get more opportunities to hear the words and deduce the pragmatic value of their prosody and intonation contours before starting to use the words themselves. It is a long and gradual process because their avoidance of taboo words in the LX limits the feedback they receive on their appropriateness of use.

If the TILLT foreign language classroom promotes diversity and recognises the multiplicity of identities, "explorations of sexual identities can allow language learners to become equipped with the necessary communicative competences needed to perform their identities in appropriate ways [...] [and for] respectful communication with LGBTQ+ individuals" (Banegas & Evripidou, 2021, p. 128). For translator education, it is interesting that less than half of the respondents (6 out of 16 students) mentioned the relevance of taboo literacy to their studies. The taboo topics that were found to be of particular interest were sexual LGBTQ+, anxieties, addictions and depression, environmental risks, terrorism, and human rights.

The comments generally revealed a heightened awareness "of both the options and limitations of plurality and diversity of human beings" (Blell & Doff, 2014, p. 84). A significant finding is that several students identified mutual trust

Table 21.1 Practical Examples for the Translation-Oriented LX Classroom

Topic	Material	Activity
Racism, prejudice	• http://www.eycb.coe.int/edupack/31.html (ideas to challenge stereotypes and prejudice about other people and minorities)	Students should agree on preferred travel companions on a night train.
Diversity, ableism, heteronormativity	• https://diversitaet.uni-graz.at/de/schon-gesehen/videos/videos-der-awarenesskampagne/ (four videos from a university's diversity awareness campaign) • https://diversitaet.uni-graz.at/de/schon-gesehen/videos/unialltag-auch-jenseits-von-binaritaet/ (a video about everyday, non-binary university life)	Students explore discriminatory practices and discuss potentially necessary localisation work in terms of linguistic and cultural adaptation for different contexts.
Politics, coming to terms with a controversial past	• https://www.youtube.com/watch?v=EiEzeyG0QRo (movie trailer in German) • https://www.youtube.com/watch?v=DhUOqY4t5rs (interview with film director Ruth Beckermann)	Students learn about Austrian history during and after the Nazi regime based on the movie "*Waldheims Walzer*" (2018) by linking it to other countries' problematic historical events.
Illness, disease, death	• http://vocal-medical.eu/user/module (language and culture-related activities for health care professionals) • https://www.medizinpopulaer.at/archiv/medizin-vorsorge/details/article/krisen-als-wendepunkt-leben-mit-hirntumor.html (magazine article about a student dealing with a brain tumour)	Students critically evaluate EU project materials on linguistics, cultural and religious aspects in healthcare and discuss a young person's way of dealing with a severe illness.

and time as key factors when discussing taboo topics. Not only is it essential for teachers and students to take time to get to know each other to create a meaningful working relationship and learning community between everyone in the classroom, "where wholeness is welcomed and students can be honest, even radically open, […] name their fears, voice their resistance" (hooks, 2010, p. 21). It also needs a power-sharing relationship, enacted through dialogue and reflection, within an ethic of reciprocity (Gibson & Cook-Sather, 2020, p. 23). On the one hand, teachers should "see students' experiences more clearly and learn from students' analyses of their experiences". On the other hand, students should experience "being seen and listened to as well as learn to see and listen to other students" (Gibson & Cook-Sather, 2020, p. 23). Another time-related factor is that addressing taboo topics cannot be accomplished in one or two lessons since they are complex, sensitive, and challenging.

To sum up, the classroom which was in focus in the discussion above can best be described as one where "students come together from a variety of linguistic, ethnic, and cultural backgrounds to learn an additional language [and which constitutes] a unique setting for exposing social and cultural underpinnings of identity categories" (Pavlenko, 2004, p. 65). In what follows, I will present a number of practical examples that turned out to be particularly suited for the TILLT foreign language classroom (see Table 21.1).

All the educational activities in Table 21.1 provide thematic contextualisation as well as a language and culture focus on a variety of audio-visual media content. The implications of the personal testimonials of my students and my teaching experience using the material on taboo topics for practice, research and professional development are discussed in the concluding section.

Conclusion

This contribution addressed language learning and teaching in translator education from the perspective of critical, engaged pedagogy. Such an approach embraces the willingness to be responsible, not pretending that teachers do not have the power to change the direction of their students' lives (hooks, 1994, p. 206). Prado and her colleagues (2021) understand this transformative effect as empowering individuals to engage with their immediate circles, the wider society, various institutions and the environment in order to bring about positive change.

The contribution discussed issues of identity and agency, two notions that Killick (2015) used in the context of higher education for describing the global student as one "whose *self-in-the-world* identity primarily and *act-in-the-world* agency secondarily constitute the capabilities which will enable him to make his way in the globalising world" (p. 180, original emphasis). The personal testimonials of undergraduate students discussed in this contribution highlight the importance of establishing a critical, anti-racist education at universities, which promotes anti-discriminatory practices as a transdisciplinary, cross-sectional responsibility (Aygün et al., 2020; Seidl, 2021). As for continuing professional development, higher education teachers, who have the opportunity to influence the student experience, also have a responsibility to continuously review and reshape their practice (Killick, 2015). Ultimately, our contemporary world needs teachers, students, and graduates who raise their voices against any kind of racism, homophobia or hostility towards minorities and vulnerable groups.

References

Allan, K. (2018). Taboo words and language: An overview. In K. Allan (Ed.), *The Oxford handbook of taboo words and language* (pp. 1–27). Oxford University Press.

Aygün, D., Freieck, L., Kasatschenko, T., & Zitzelsberger, O. (2020). Vielfalt bildet! Rassismuskritische Bildung an Hochschulen etablieren. *Zeitschrift für Hochschulentwicklung, 15*(3), 77–92.

Banegas, D. L., & Evripidou, D. (2021). Introduction: Comprehensive sexuality education in ELT. *ELT Journal, 75*(2), 127–132.

Ben Slamia, F. (2020). Translation strategies of taboo words in interlingual film subtitling. *International Journal of Linguistics, Literature and Translation, 3*(6), 82–98.

Blell, G., & Doff, S. (2014) It takes more than two for this tango: Moving beyond the self/other-binary in teaching about culture in the global EFL-classroom. *Zeitschrift für Interkulturellen Fremdsprachenunterricht, 19*(1), 77–96.

Brantmeier, E. J. (2013). Pedagogy of vulnerability: Definitions, assumptions, and applications. In J. Lin, R. Oxford, & E. J. Brantmeier (Eds.), *Re-envisioning higher education. Embodied pathways to wisdom and social transformation* (pp. 95–106). Information Age Publishing.

Cerezo Herrero, E., & Schmidhofer, A. (2021). 25 years of research on language training in TI programmes: Taking stock and ways forward. In A. Schmidhofer, & E. Cerezo Herrero (Eds.), *Foreign language training in translation and interpreting programmes* (pp. 17–44). Peter Lang.

Dewaele, J.-M. (2018). Linguistic taboos in a second or foreign language. In K. Allan (Ed.), *The Oxford handbook of taboo words and language* (pp. 218–232). Oxford University Press.

Dobutowitsch, F. (2020). *Lebensweltliche Mehrsprachigkeit an der Hochschule. Eine qualitative Studie über die sprachlichen Spielräume Studierender.* Waxmann.

Freire, P. (2018/2005). *Teachers as cultural workers. Letters to those who dare teach* (expanded edition). Routledge.

Gibson, S., & Cook-Sather, A. (2020). Politicised compassion and pedagogical partnership: A discourse and practice for social justice in the inclusive academy. *International Journal for Students as Partners, 4*(1), 16–33.

Grbić, N., & Wolf, M. (2021). *Translation und Migration: Dolmetschen als gesellschaftspolitische Aufgabe.* LIT Verlag.

Gregersen, T., & MacIntyre, P. (2021). The nonverbal channels of peacebuilding: What teachers, trainers and facilitators need to know. In R. Oxford, M. M. Olivero, M. Harrison, & T. Gregersen (Eds.), *Peacebuilding in language education. Innovations in theory and practice* (pp. 43–60). Multilingual Matters.

hooks, B. (1994). *Teaching to transgress. Education as the practice of freedom.* Routledge.

hooks, B. (2010). *Teaching critical thinking. Practical wisdom.* Routledge.

Kadrić, M., & Kaindl, K. (2016). Translation als zentrale Nebensache in einer globalisierten Welt – eine Einführung. In M. Kadrić, & K. Kaindl (Eds.), *Berufsziel Übersetzen und Dolmetschen. Grundlagen, Ausbildung, Arbeitsfelder* (pp. 1–15). Narr Francke Attempto.

Kadrić, M., Kaindl, K., & Reithofer, K. (2019). *Translatorische Methodik. 6., vollständig überarbeitete und erweiterte Auflage.* Facultas.

Killick, D. (2015). *Developing the global student. Higher education in an era of globalisation.* Routledge.

Massey, G., & Kiraly, D. (2019). The future of translator education: A dialogue. *Cultus: The Journal of Intercultural Mediation and Communication, 2019*(12), 15–34.

Nixon, J. (2008). *Towards the virtuous university. The moral basis of academic practice*. Routledge.

Pavlenko, A. (2004). Gender and sexuality in foreign and second language education: Critical and feminist approaches. In B. Norton, & K. Toohey (Eds.), *Critical pedagogies and language learning* (pp. 53–71). Cambridge University Press.

Prado, J., Uguralp-Cannon, G., Green, J. M., Harrison, M., & Frantz Smith, L. (2021). Seeking connection through difference: Finding the nexus of transformative learning, peacebuilding and language teaching. In R. Oxford, M. M. Olivero, M. Harrison, & T. Gregersen (Eds.), *Peacebuilding in language education. Innovations in theory and practice* (pp. 110–126). Multilingual Matters.

Schmidhofer, A., & Ahmann, H. (2015). Translationsrelevanter Fremdsprachenunterricht: Besonderheiten und Zielsetzungen. *Moderne Sprachen, 59*(1), 49–70.

Seidl, E. (2021). Sprach-, Kultur- und Diversitätskompetenz lehren und lernen. Ein Lehr-Lern-Szenario aus der translationsorientierten Sprachlehre. In M.-T. Gruber, K. Ogris, & B. Breser (Eds.), *Diversität im Kontext Hochschullehre: Best Practice* (pp. 181–197). Waxmann.

Siever, H. (2019). Metaphern für die Figur des Translators. In L. Heller, & T. Rozmysłowicz (Eds.), *Translation and intercultural communication* (pp. 65–88). Frank & Timme.

Sinclair, K. (2021). TranslatorInnen als SprachlehrerInnen: Eignung und Einsatz. Frank & Timme.

Stachl-Peier, U., & Schwarz, E. (Eds.). (2020). *Resources and tools for T&I education. Research studies, teaching concepts, best-practice results*. Frank & Timme.

Taibi, M., & El-Madkouri Maataoui, M. (2016). Interpreting taboo: The case of Arabic interpreters in Spanish public services. In M. Taibi (Ed.), *New insights into Arabic translation and interpreting* (pp. 69–90). Multilingual Matters.

Witte, A. (2021). The sentient body and intercultural situational attentiveness. In A. Witte, & T. Harden (Eds.), *Rethinking intercultural competence: Theoretical challenges and practical issues* (pp. 19–48). Peter Lang.

Conclusion

22 International Perspectives on Taboos in Foreign Language Education

Tyson Seburn

Introduction

To suggest that the English language learning classroom is a microcosm representation of the society in which it operates or for which it prepares learners also suggests that the teacher and the learner explore topics and language that reflect the outside world and the people within it. It is in the classroom then that learners are able to freely make mistakes without judgement and experiment with expressing their ideas before doing so in a foreign language with foreign language speakers who are less interested in this language learning experience and more so in interaction towards a particular goal. The forgiving safety net of the language learning classroom needs to be tried out and bounced on as much as possible while we have access to it. Thus, it is essential that the language learning environment creates space for a variety of simple and more complex communicative situations. These situations can include seemingly benign topic areas such as banking, hobbies, and entertainment, but even within these, learners bring with them their own identities, experiences, and values. To return to the suggestion that our classrooms are microcosms of wider society with differing identities, differing lived experiences, and differing perspectives, it is through our curricula, our pedagogy, our teaching materials that we as an education profession are obligated to combine representation of identity and what this volume describes as "tabooed" topics. By referring to ideas presented, explained, and supported throughout this volume, I would like to succinctly summarise the contributors' collective argument: that we as foreign language educators have the power and obligation to promulgate three ideals of the language learning space through a critical pedagogy: (1) that language can create meaningful connections across groups of people, (2) that the materials provide opportunity to practice language relevant to today's world and learners' lives within it, and (3) that ultimately they belong as users of the target language alongside everyone else.

In their introduction, Ludwig and Summer (this volume) provide a framework for what foreign language educators and course designers should consider in order to achieve these outcomes: the social positionalities in which our teaching is situated, key characteristics of taboo topics, how critical pedagogy aligns with taboo topic use in the classroom, and the role of teacher education in equipping

DOI: 10.4324/9781003220701-27

us with the tools required to operationalise critical pedagogy through course design, teaching materials, and pedagogy. Throughout the three sections of this volume (I – Theoretical Overviews, II – Empirical Inquiries, III – Specific Taboos and Practical Examples), the authors elaborate on each aspect from their identities, expertises, and experiences. In this concluding chapter, I wish to highlight how the author contributions work together to support the three ideals of the foreign language learning space by first drawing together examples they give of the social positionalities tabooed topics are determined by. Then, we will move on to how critical pedagogy lends itself to bring these tabooed topics into the curriculum in order to demonstrate these three ideals by reviewing several exemplars from this volume. To participate in this effort, I will contribute areas of my own work in inclusive practices, which primarily focuses on the English language teaching (ELT) context as a program director, teacher, and materials writer within it, and complement the authors' arguments with treatment from a Canadian context, too, as perhaps a North American perspective is not evident elsewhere in this volume. For the purposes of this chapter and to equally value its participants, I refer to foreign language education, foreign language teaching, and foreign language learning interchangeably to describe the spaces in which we occupy as a profession, unless the agent is specifically the teacher or the student.

Social Positionalities of Tabooed Topics (Practical and Theoretical)

The way in which we situate our classrooms and thus the lesson's topic areas, identities represented within materials, and useful language outcomes to a large extent depend on the context where language learning occurs, but also where our learners will use that language in their futures. Within any context, we must also acknowledge that one or more groups of people hold the power to determine who is included and who is not in many decision-making activities and what identities are considered valid to value. As educators, when we acknowledge these existing power structures impact our learners, we can also recognise the role we have played in perpetuating power structures that may have excluded our learners. As people reading this volume, as educators, curriculum designers, materials writers, program directors, or some combination of each, we must acknowledge that we too yield at least some power to impact the way our learners see themselves, communicate with others, and either continue to uphold or endeavour to improve the social positionality taboo topics hold for others. As a result, we must also acknowledge "the responsibility we have held in excluding up to now. When we can identify that there is a problem and accept that we have contributed to it, we can embrace the power we have to correct it" (Seburn, 2021, p. 16). We can determine how these power structures may impact our learners' views of themselves as English language users. In this regard, Ludwig and Summer (this volume) suggest that although "there are still boundaries that should not be crossed, today's society seems to be increasingly open and accepting towards things that used to be frowned upon" and thus opportunity to include an examination of these power structures may be afforded in our classrooms.

More globally, however, which boundaries still exist and which attitudes have become more accepting is context dependent and should be part of a context-specific consideration on how to approach including taboos within a foreign language curriculum. What appears to be socially acceptable at times is not reflected in education. For example, while "legislation recognizing and protecting sexual and gender minorities across much of the world from the late twentieth century onwards" has been implemented, a 2016 UNESCO report concluded that

> the education sector as a whole appeared to be reluctant to accord recognition to LGBTQ+ students. The report pointed out that materials remained firmly heteronormative in character, stereotypical in terms of gender roles and blind to varieties of gender and sexual diversity.
>
> (Gray, this volume)

This finding is supported by a variety of research into ELT coursebooks that uncovered invisibility, underrepresentation, and diminutive portrayal of minority groups (Gray, 2013; Hawthorne, 2020; Nelson, 2019; Yuen, 2011) and was impetus for moving theory to practice in *How to Write Inclusive Materials* (Seburn, 2021), a self-study training course for materials writers and teachers who develop their own materials. As a concrete example of this phenomenon of acceptance versus practicality, Borgwaldt and Amarasinghe (this volume) explain that in Sri Lankan society, there are definite incongruences between theory and practice when it comes to sex and sexuality. For example, "while menstruation is significant turning point [for people who can], talking about it is not" and "where practical life and attitude towards LGBTQ issues has progressed, on paper at least there can still be criminal convictions for non-heterosexual acts" (Borgwaldt & Amarasinghe, this volume). They note that while the first can lead to very awkward reactions if spoken about publicly, the latter can lead to workplace discrimination or unemployment, domestic violence, bullying, and lack of mental health support for victims experiencing these things.

With regard to mental health, some societies have begun to shift from traditionally thinking of it as a sign of weakness to a normalised aspect of life, even to the point of corporate involvement in promoting this public consciousness. For example, one of the largest media companies in Canada, Bell openly supports an annual campaign ("Let's Talk", https://letstalk.bell.ca/en/) on television and social media, which publicly purports to aim for breaking down barriers and stigma to discussing mental health. On the surface, this visibility has opened lines of communication across the country and raised funds for mental health programs. Yet still, in practice, even companies like Bell that seem to lead the charge continue to have employment policies and working conditions that allegedly lead to some mental health issues. Other societies, on the other hand, continue to perpetuate a stigmatised view of mental health altogether by keeping it among a list of things to keep to oneself. Ludwig and Martinez (this volume) note that this belief "makes it harder or even impossible for affected individuals to open up about their mental health problems and seek help" and that members of minoritised groups, such as LGBTQ+, are more vulnerable to mental health issues given how society ignores their specific life experiences, treats their existence, or debates the importance of including them in educational curricula at all.

Even in contexts where LGBTQ+ rights seem to have progressed and mental health awareness campaigns aim to normalise talking about it as equal to any type of health concern, racism of all sorts evades meaningful discourse, by manifesting itself as defensiveness even at the thought of its existence. Unless you experience it directly yourself, because racism is so normalised and ordinary in our societies, people can require dramatic events, such as the death of George Floyd, to even acknowledge it exists. Still then, the popularity of support wains over time. In many cases where advocates draw attention to anti-racist action, talking about it can bring about intense cognitive dissonance and a vehement pushback on claims meant to cause change or "backfire effect" (Lewandowski et al., 2012), especially for white people. Braselmann (this volume) discusses how "this defensive reaction is a product of an informed and increasingly liberal society in which most people would claim that they are not racist" so any suggestion that a self-identifying liberal individual participates in racist social undertones, uphold racist policies, or contribute to racist attitudes through unconscious (or conscious) language choices can be extremely unwelcomed as an affront to their very core nature. Compounding this, what kind of racism depends on which society we choose to look at, what recent events have recently made the prevailing news, and what the leaders of these places exemplify: anti-Black racism, anti-Asian racism, and anti-Indigenous racism. In places like Canada, where multiculturalism is regarded both outside and within as one of its primary strengths, daily examples of micro- and macro-aggressions from all three types of racism form part of the tapestry that accompanies any positives we may gain from this diversity, though this may be disputed by the aforementioned self-identifying liberal individuals. These same individuals also comprise many of the teachers in our profession simply due to the nature of working across cultures and demographics, so "while studies have shown that young adults experience racism in schools much more frequently and openly than they do outside of the educational setting, e.g., in their free time and after school activities" (Moffit & Juang, 2019 as cited in Braselmann, this volume), collectively acknowledging the racism that exists within our education systems is a difficult goal to reach. Thus, including discussions of racism—as an attitude that currently exists not outside somewhere to other people, but within our societies, within our schools, to our learners and teachers—as an essential part of the foreign language education curriculum is met with equal discomfort.

As a result, how can we claim to be including our learners and their experiences in our classroom spaces, when there are many topics about which cultural perspective plays a role in what we talk about and what we don't? This discomfort, this denial, this desperate reaction from adults is all the more support for the essential role educational spaces play, especially those like language teaching and learning, whose primary concentration is communication between people, in countering these attitudes before they can manifest so wholeheartedly. Living in this space and using it to guide our curriculum is the basis of critical pedagogy, which we'll focus on now.

Critical Pedagogy and Its Practical Application to Foreign Language Education

As Ludwig and Summer begin this volume purporting: a critical pedagogy not only creates a language learning space that engages learners with practising language that is relevant to their lives and experiences but also exposes them to viewpoints that differ from their own, which can act as insightful reflection on why these differences exist and how to avoid communication breakdown as a result. The first method towards this is to understand what and how critical pedagogy operates in education, then apply this to the foreign language education environment. Within this volume, we have seen both in a myriad of examples which fall within the eight categories to taboo topics they suggest: cultural taboos; gender, sex, and sexuality; relationships; drugs and addictions, consumerism, and human rights; (mental) health and illnesses; and violence.

First, through critical pedagogy, direct learner involvement in the curriculum creates investment in the learning and better engagement with the material, by selecting the topic area, providing materials from their own lives, and generally helping inform the curricula through issues that are important to them. It gives reason to practise. Ignoring this diminishes the learner role as investor in the learning, as critical thinkers, and as sources of diverse perspectives. There are notable examples throughout this volume that we can review here.

Gray (this volume) gives the example of textbooks that assume who its learners are and what experiences they must have. In one study of working-class learners, the textbooks in use showed little representation of the student body and

> where limited representation of working class characters did occur (in textbooks from the 1970s), students were not invited to identify with them and there was generally no serious engagement with issues relating to working conditions, union activity and disputes – although these were mentioned in passing.
>
> (Gray, this volume)

This, according to Gray, was "an active withholding of lexis related to working-class life and struggles" which not only prevented learners from practising ways to express themselves and their experiences in English but also exemplified to learners that their lives and struggles were something to be avoided, not discussed, and not valued as much as the people's lives in the textbooks. Additionally, by not involving learner experiences in this language learning process, the opportunity to learn how to talk about their situation in a new society as an immigrant and therefore express themselves in a way that accurately details their experiences also severely reduces their ability to use target language to understand access supports that might help improve their lives. For example, if in Canada, we avoided talking about the immigrant experience with immigrants and merely used materials that show affluent citizens taking holidays at their summer cottages, we would not only be devaluing immigrant experiences as lesser than the affluent citizens but also denying them the opportunity to express any problem areas they are encountering in their lives or knowing what supports exist that can help them improve life.

In another example, Ludwig and Martinez (this volume) discuss how including mental health units connect with the reality of teen lives today insofar as it is "real-life related and student-oriented and could elicit genuine responses from students". The foreign language learning classroom can provide space to share concerns and learn ways to cope with stressors like bullying, problems with family and friends, and negative feelings about themselves, as well as common indicators of mental health concerns, like social withdrawal, eating habits, and even anger. Space for this language learning context enables teens to identify with the material as they are issues they personally deal with or know others who do. It demystifies the stigma while also creating connections with others. Leaving topics like mental health out of the curriculum first assumes it is being discussed elsewhere in their lives and, second, disconnects language teaching spaces from what learners really want to talk about. Connecting to this idea of a negotiated syllabus between teachers and learners (via Ludwig & Summer, this volume), in a study by Summer and Steinbock (this volume), they found that most teen learners showed interest in topics they encountered even passively in peer conversations and media, things like illness, racism, and sexuality. In fact, a high percentage (70%–81%) of teens agreed that these types of "taboo" topics were actually important and exciting to cover in class and did not feel that they would be embarrassed to discuss them with others. Even when we question the relevance of, the interest level of, or the reactions to some taboo topics, it may simply be our prejudices or discomfort that is the driving force for perpetuating the status quo, not theirs.

Critical pedagogy also engages learners with the language used in the topic areas and through this discussion and exposure to similar and differing experiences, it then supports

> the development of active, engaged citizens who will [...] critically inquire into why the lives of so many human beings, perhaps including their own, are materially, psychologically, socially, and spiritually inadequate—citizens who will be prepared to seek out solutions to the problems they define and encounter, and take action accordingly.
> (Crookes, 2013, p. 8, as cited in Ludwig & Summer, this volume)

By helping connect students with views, ideas, and opinions different from their own, it can motivate them to not only critically think about the source of these differences but also their own views critically to understand how they shape beliefs and reactions to others. On a practical level, materials writers or teachers working with materials can incorporate a "disruptive approach" as part of critical pedagogy through a five-step framework, which aims to bring together empathy for the experiences of individuals within tabooed topics even among those who don't directly share these experiences so everyone can create solutions (Seburn, 2021, pp. 130–133). First, teachers identify a social norm that is unfair to and/or marginalises at least one group of people. Second, they situate this social norm for learners through visuals, texts, and critical questions. Third, marginalised experiences of the social norm provide insight into how it affects them negatively. Fourth, learners work together to build personal connections to problems caused by this social norm, like it has for the marginalised individuals. Finally, they work together to improve the situation through language practice activities. Examples of implementing part or all of this framework for inclusive materials design are included throughout this volume.

In a Sri Lankan class using films as input, Amarasinghe and Borgwaldt (this volume) examine smoking among women in Western cultures to counter a bias towards smoking that exists in Sri Lankan culture: a prejudice that labels women who smoke as immoral or less cultured. Through the use of film, students learn about the "facts, functions, and the historical development of smoking in Western societies and Western films" (Amarasinghe & Borgwaldt, this volume) which can help students understand why women smoke rather than simply from non-Western stereotypes when encountering smokers in reality or fiction. This type of examination of behaviour in another culture can "be used as a catapult to examining a common Sri Lankan behaviour and how people from other countries may feel a similar bias towards eating with hands rather than utensils" (Amarasinghe & Borgwaldt, this volume), for instance. Drawing parallels between these two can help students rethink future examples of judgements formed by a cultural norm and potentially improve communication between cultures before this judgement impacts perspective. In another example, Stadler-Heer (this volume) discusses how race impacts storytelling through folktales in the South African context. When using this type of literature in class, white scholars and learners can critically examine where the stories originate from, whose perspectives are driving the plots (spoiler: white people!), and how these storytellers' identities impact what happens in the story, to whom, and what the moral is. This exercise can lead to learners recognising how their language choices are impacted by their socio-economic, racial, and gender identities, for example, and thus how their choices can become more conscious. The first step towards change is acknowledging reality after all. But also, Stadler-Heer shows that this also benefits the teacher, in particular their "need to revisit their understanding of knowledge production and the role they play in developing knowledge in the first place, particularly as they are the ones selecting and telling stories" (this volume). In another chapter of this volume, Braselmann argues that even in educational spaces that appear homogeneous where topics like racism can seem less relevant on a personal level (e.g., a language learning class in Germany with white students and a white teacher), critically examining whiteness and privilege together in class can focus on the structural rather than the individual level of racism: using critical thinking here "strives to enable learners to question and actively and intellectually challenge any societal structure, belief or narrative that is related to the power of one group over another". This awareness of power structures and dynamics also affords learners the ability to critique whose language and whose beliefs are valued in their materials and then beyond in their societies so that they can decide for themselves whether that power structure is benefitting or hurting their (language learning) education—a Freirean problem-posing approach to education, i.e., an aspect of critical pedagogy. Ludwig and Summer (this volume) note it best in their introduction that

> by developing lesson plans and activities that are student-centred, possibly even student-generated, [we] guide learners towards tracing the roots of taboos by widening their horizons and learning more about the origins of social injustices, discovering power relations and cultural conventions, exploring consequences of tabooing certain topics, and finding possible solutions.

On a very practical lesson-based level, by sourcing material from texts that students bring in or encounter in their lives, language practice lessons can use them to identify multiple perspectives, identify problems and voice concerns, and offer solutions to participate (Kalantzis & Cope, 2012, as cited in Ludwig & Summer, this volume). Rather than from nothing, which can be a very intimidating stance to take as a lesson planner, these texts can provide the teacher with a starting point for building a critical pedagogy language learning lesson. For example, Becker (this volume) discusses how texts make up a culture's representation of a taboo topic. This means that a culture's representation, stigmatisation, and beliefs about a topic like mental health are the result of every single text in learners' lives, such as news reports, young adult literature, and YouTube videos. In practice, Becker argues, teachers should source a variety of different text types (even from learners themselves) based on the different perspectives they offer (e.g., texts portraying depression as an illness vs. texts portraying depression as dangerous and unwanted). Doing so allows learners to not only potentially see their attitudes reflected in some but not all texts, expose them to multiple perspectives they may not have connected with before, and discuss how these all contribute to their society's landscape on the topic. As an educational activity, it enables learners to focus on two primary linguistic functions: (a) practice language for different functions (e.g., agreeing/disagreeing appropriately, a range of grammatical structures, topically related vocabulary that's acceptable for use) and (b) re-examine how their own beliefs impact their language choices. Using another modern (and underused?) text type, poetry slams, Ludwig and Martinez (this volume) provide a sample lesson on mental health, where first, the key characteristics of the text type are introduced, then students use the content to analyse the main symptoms of a mental health issue like bipolar disorder. Following this, they work together to brainstorm strategies to communicate and help people with bipolar disorder, given the content they heard in the poetry slam.

In all practical lesson-based examples, including those in other chapters throughout this volume, a social norm that marginalises or certainly is under-discussed and thus causes stigmatisation is chosen as the taboo topic. Voices of those impacted are amplified to be equal to those in society that always dominate the discourse. Opportunity for learners from within and outside these voices is directed to use the content to build connections to their own lives. Finally, using language that emerges from the topic areas, ways to improve society's approach or support for the benefit of everyone is made possible through discussion with each other. The last consideration and perhaps one of the most important then is how to enable teachers to recognise critical pedagogy's importance and empower them to feel able to work with it in their own classes: through teacher education.

The Role of Teacher Education in Critical Pedagogy

Having critical discussions through a language learning process is fine when a teacher understands what critical pedagogy is and is not, what its benefits are, and how it operates in a lesson plan. Getting to this very practical stage, however, itself presents a number of challenges. The primary agent in any education environment is the teacher themselves and their attitudes towards including the taboo topics that are essential for critical pedagogy need to be addressed before anything meaningful can happen in the classroom. As mentioned in their opening chapter, Ludwig and Summer (this volume) refer to the Kelly's four attitudes that teachers adopt in this regard (1986): exclusive neutrality, exclusive partiality, neutral impartiality, and committed impartiality, each of which (though particularly the first two) may prevent a critical pedagogy approach to language learning because the teacher's own attitude regards these taboo topics as not belonging in the classroom or contributes to their fear that learners could express views different from their own. In their chapter, Gerlach and Lüke (this volume) reinforce the Freirean notion that classrooms are not neutral: "In order to unearth existing inequalities, teachers need to address existing discriminations and power relations in teaching and in the classroom itself" before being able to move past this notion of neutrality. This perceived neutrality may reflect "rather traditional views of language and education within society or the neoliberal turn in English language teaching" (Gerlach & Lüke, this volume) that values language as a vehicle for economic growth over any other rationale for communication. These issues move towards the essential role that teacher education as well as in-service teacher training play in "promoting both critical foreign language pedagogy and taboo literacy. Therefore, teacher education programmes, in which critical literacy plays a marginal role, as has been observed by Gray (2019), are bound to fail" (Ludwig & Summer, this volume).

Referring to English language teacher education specifically but certainly regardless of the target language, Gerlach and Lüke (this volume) suggest that to prepare teachers to build and engage learners in a critical pedagogy curriculum, teacher education needs to prioritise opportunity for teachers to question their mission for teaching English so that they can develop a critical consciousness about educational practices and look at how their identity contributes to these as normal. Secondly, they argue for teacher education to help teachers to build a broad theoretical knowledge base about language, language teaching, and the school system. Focusing on these as part of their training enables new (especially) and practising teachers to think about the power dynamics involved in ELT, how they may prioritise one group of people over another, how hiring is done, which version of English is valued and which is devalued, and other such critical examinations of the industry and profession. Additionally, this work offers teachers an opportunity to reflect on how they are positioned to participate in these existing practices or change them. Finally, it gives teachers the opportunity to interrogate the materials they are asked to work with in differing institutional settings. If teacher education focused more on training teachers to

> collaboratively plan, research and theorize (critical) teaching, they might be more empowered to emancipate themselves from the dominant methods, such as the ones presented in textbooks; initiate reflective phases to explore their own identities [...] they might have been the subject of discriminatory practices themselves or they might have greater awareness of discriminatory practices occurring in their immediate environment.
>
> (Gerlach & Lüke, this volume)

Stadler-Heer (this volume) too concludes that more content- and skill-specific continuous professional development are necessary to give teachers the confidence to teach using topics outside their comfort zone and apply inclusive practices appropriately to the language they use for instruction, demonstration, or interaction with students as these can both perpetuate power dynamics and hierarchies. Without this language awareness and practice at materials design, even the most willing teacher's efforts at critical pedagogy may fail or at worst, contribute to how a learner feels about language learning and themselves as learners. With specific regard to anti-racist teaching practice, Braselmann (this volume) believes that teacher education plays a vital role in preparing teachers to handle racism in language itself and teaching materials by making space for teachers to learn "strategies for identifying and addressing racism in different learner groups". Ludwig and Summer (this volume) themselves agree and suggest that

> the integration of critical pedagogy into [Teaching English as a Foreign Language] programmes [...] and an interdisciplinary approach with psychology with a focus on handling taboos and the conflicts that come with them could potentially help teachers develop strategies for dealing with... unexpected conflicts.

Concluding Thoughts

As illustrate, there are numerous intersections between the field of critical foreign language pedagogy and the teaching and learning of foreign languages that become apparent not only at the methodological level but also at the level of content.

These characteristics and implementations of a critical pedagogy approach to the language teaching and learning classroom that are theorised, situated within context, and operationalised on actual lessons accomplish solidly provide evidence for how we began this chapter: that we as language educators have the power and obligation to promulgate three ideals of the foreign language learning space through a critical pedagogy: (1) that language can create meaningful connections across groups of people, (2) that the materials provide opportunity to practice language relevant to today's world and learners' lives within it, and (3) that ultimately they belong as users of the target language alongside everyone else.

Moving forward, to continue equipping those in our profession, including our learners, to tackle injustice and build connections through communicative critical pedagogy, it is imperative that teacher training and education programmes (e.g., CELTA, DipTESOL for ELT) and localised teaching associations not only include but focus on inclusive practices and materials design as essential components to any teachers' professional development.

References

Gray, J. (2013). LGBT invisibility and heteronormativity in ELT materials. In J. Gray (Ed.), *Critical perspectives on language teaching materials* (pp. 40–63). Palgrave Macmillan.

Gray, J. (2019). Critical language teacher education? In S. Walsh, & S. Mann (Eds.), *The Routledge Handbook of English Language Teacher Education* (pp. 68–81). Routledge.

Hawthorne, A. (2020). *Black in the British: Analysing the visual representation of Black people in British Council teaching materials* [Master's thesis, Lancaster University]. British Council: Teaching English.

Kalantzis, M., & Cope, B. (2012). *Literacies*. Cambridge University Press.

Kelly, T. E. (1986). Discussing controversial issues: Four perspectives on the teacher's role. *Theory and Research in Social Education, 14*(2), 113–138.

Lewandowsky, S., Ecker, U. K. H., Seifert, C. M., Schwarz, N., & Cook, J. (2012). Misinformation and its correction: Continued influence and successful debiasing. *Psychological Science in the Public Interest, 13*(3), 106–131.

Moffit, U., & Juang L. P. (2019). 'We don't do that in Germany!' A critical race theory examination of Turkish heritage young adult's school experiences. *Ethnicities, 19*(5), 830–857.

Nelson, J. (2019). *"I thought Canadians were white!" An intersectional gendered visual analysis of race, nation, gender, and LGBT+ representation in ESL/ELL textbooks* [Master's thesis, The University of British Columbia]. UBC Open Collections. https://open.library.ubc.ca/soa/cIRcle/collections/ubctheses/24/items/1.0378577

Seburn, T. (2021). *How to write inclusive materials*. ELTTeacher2Writer.

Yuen, K. M. (2011). The representation of foreign cultures in English textbooks. *ELT Journal, 65*(4), 458–466.

Appendix

Questionnaire: Topics in School Education

Note: This appendix includes the English translation of the German questionnaire "Themen im Unterricht" (topics in school education) developed for 13–19-year-olds in Germany.

Introductory text

Hello and welcome to our survey! Are you between 13- and 19-year-old and do you currently go to or have you been to school? If so, we'd like to ask you about your experiences in your school days and spare time in terms of possible teaching topics. We are two researchers working in the field of English language teaching.

With this survey, we would like to find out what topics from your everyday life you would like to deal with in class. The focus is on topics that may not have been addressed much or not at all in the classroom. Such topics could be, for example, illnesses, experiences of violence or drug abuse. If a topic concerns you personally, we suggest you get help.

Please answer honestly; the survey is anonymous. This means no one can see who gave which answers.

We will use the results to develop lesson sequences that are thematically related to students' interests and needs.

Thank you for your support!

1. Let's begin with your spare time: Which topics are you interested in in your spare time?
   [18 topics (see Table 7.1) + 5-point Likert scale (*very much – not at all*)]
2. a) Which topics do you encounter without necessarily wanting to through other people (e.g., friends or strangers)?
   [Six topics: drugs, racism, violence, bullying, sex and dangers, sex and love]
   b) How do you encounter these topics?
   [pictures/photos, memes, videos, links, chat comments, others]

3 Now we'd like to ask you about your experience during school lessons: Which topics have you dealt with and how frequently?
[18 topics (see Table 7.1) – 5-point Likert scale (*very often–not at all*)]
4 The topics you read about can also be called taboos or taboo topics. They could also be dealt with at school. Please rate the following statements:
- I consider dealing with taboos in school … [interesting, embarrassing, exciting, motivating, frightening, important] [5-point Likert scale (*strongly agree–strongly disagree*)]
5 Please think about your English lessons in particular: Regardless of your current or previous English teachers, how much would you like to deal with the following topics in English lessons?
[18 topics (see Table 7.1) + 5-point Likert scale (*very much–not at all*)]
6 Image, you would deal with one of these topics in an English lesson. You would watch a short film and analyse a song about a topic such as drugs or racism. Then you would discuss the topic. Would you like to participate in such a lesson?
[5-point Likert scale (*very much–not at all*)]
7 With which format would you like to work with in English lessons when dealing with taboo topics? You can click multiple items.
[feature films, short films (e.g., YouTube), songs, social media (internet), invite experts, invited affected people, role-plays, literary texts (e.g., novels, poems), comics and graphic novels, picturebooks]
8 Imagine you are personally affected by a topic (e.g., bullying, violence in the family). Would you want to deal with such a topic in English lessons?
[yes, probably, maybe, unlikely, no]

Socio-demographics:
[age, rural/urban area, federal state in Germany, religion, multilingual background, gender]

Finally, if you feel like it: What is your general opinion on whether taboo topics should be dealt with in English lessons? [open answers]

Thank you very much for participating in this survey!

And as we've said: If an issue affects you personally, you can always get external help. Surely there is someone at your school (counsellor, psychologist, etc.) to whom you can confide in and who can find solutions. Help hotlines for are also available here: https://www.nummergegenkummer.de/kinder-und-jugendtelefon.html

Index

Note: **Bold** page numbers refer to tables and *italic* page numbers refer to figures.

Abel, J. 156
Abolitionista! (comic book series) 159
Action Comics #1 (DC Comics) 158
addictions/addictive behaviour **75**, 87, 219, 242, 253
aggravated sexting behaviour 143–144, *144*
Akbari, R. 41
American Psychiatric Association 129
American Psychological Association (APA) 61–62
Anglophone English language teachers 23
animals: aid 190; education for 181–184; and environmental sustainability 182; global strategy for 187; improvements in 182; rebellion 6; welfare 182
animation films: and fictional stories 116; short 113–123
anti-racism 171–172; language teaching 169–170, 172
Asher, J.: *13 Reasons Why* 95
Audrey: A Story of Child Sex Trafficking (H.E.A.T. Watch) 159

Bachtin, M. 32, 34
Bad Romance 162
Baker, W. 209
Banegas, D. L. 41
Barthes, R. 32
Basic Instinct 210
Beautiful Thing 29
Bend it like Beckham 213
Berman, J. 198
Best, J. 152
Bhabha, H. 209
Black Lives Matter movement 6, 83, 168
Bland, J. 89

Block, D. 26
Bogart, H. 211
Bogle, K. A. 152
Bonnet, A. 86, 98
borderline personality disorder (BPD): affect dysregulation as core component of 133; classroom example 132–137; in ELT 132–137; interpersonal problems of people with 133–134; lifetime prevalence of 133; overview 132–134; sample lesson sequence on **136–137**
Breakfast at Tiffany's 210
Bredella, L. 37
Breidbach, S. 42
Brosnan, M. 141
bullying 74, 81, 94–97, **119**, 121, 131, 143, 163, 208, 251, 254; cyberbullying 9, 14, 131, 147
Burnett, F. H.: *The Secret Garden* 198
Byram, M. 183, 209

Charter on Education for Democratic Citizenship and Human Rights Education (Council of Europe) 113
children: protective factors 59; resilience, defined 58; risk factors/stressors 58–59; vulnerability factors 58–59
circumvention strategies 34
Clarke, D. F. 15
class 9, 174; social 25–26; working 24–27, 29
comics: Comics Code of 1954 156; human trafficking in 158–161
Common European Framework of References (CEFR) 13, 106, 210
communicative language teaching (CLT) 6, 23

Index

competence development 63, 81
conspiracy theories 74, 85
controversial issues/topics 49, 50, 52, 55, 71, 73, 79, 81, 93, 98, 99, 156, 174, 214, 220, 226, 235; in foreign language education 3–18; taboos and 7–11
Cook, J. 4
Cotterall, S. 6
COVID-19 pandemic 25, 58, 61, 83, 127, 196, 241
critical animal pedagogy 184–189
critical foreign language education/ pedagogy 5–7
critical issues 9, 17, 222
criticality: in language teacher education 41–43; in language teaching 41–43
critical language teacher education: principles for **44**; principles of 43–45; workshop on **46**
critical literacy 11–12, 41–42
critical pedagogy 5–7, 181–184, 223–224, 254; Crookes' definition of 6; and foreign language education 253–257; and language teacher education 40–41; practical application to 253–257; teacher education in 257–258
critical race theory (CRT) 168–170
Crookes, G. 5–6, 11
cultural hybridity 209
cultural injustice 25
cultural learning 32, 33; in EFL classroom 32–33
cultural taboos: domains, in Sri Lanka *207*, 207–208; in foreign language feature films 210–213; in Sri Lanka 206–210
"culture as text" approach 33
Cyrus, M. 127

Dahlgren, R. L. 17
Dean, J. 210
death 51, 53, **75**, 98, 157, 182, 187, 195–204, **243**
Der blaue Engel 210
Dewaele, J.-M. 53
Dietrich, M. 210
differentiation 6, 81, 163
digital competence 147, 162, 165
Digital Competence Framework 2.1 (DigComp) 147; copyright and licencing 152; and sexting **148**
digital media 9, 11, 72, 152
disability: as sensitive and challenging topic 114–115; and short animation films 113–123

Disability Awareness Education (DAE): in ELT 113–123; in film-based ELT 116; importance of 115, 122; objectives of 117; overcoming bias 114
discourses 34–37; classroom 53; defined 34; environmental 186; supremacist 229; transformative 3
discrimination: collaboratively created mind map for *176*; teaching sequence on **174**; text ensemble for **177**
discursivity of taboos 33–35
disenfranchised grief 197–198
diversity, defined 113
Doka, K. 197
Donaldson, S. 188; *Zoopolis* 188–189
Dörnyei, Z. 82
drugs 59, 74, **75**, 83, 86, 87, 156, 165, 211, 219, 221, 226, 253, 261, 262

eco-criticism/ecocritical 183, 186, 187, 192
Edes, I. 71, 78
education: for animal welfare 181–184; guidelines for dealing with taboos **15**; research 94; for sustainable development 181–184
Education for Sustainable Development (ESD) 181–184
Élite: controversial topics in *220*; key scenes of first season 222, **223**; lesson on HIV 223–226; overview of topics 222, **223**; practical example 222–226; relevance for foreign language classroom 220–222; selected key scenes and themes of **223**; taboo topics in 219–220
English as a foreign language (EFL) classroom: cultural learning in 32–33; global education in 181–192; pre-service teachers' opinion on taboos in **87**; taboos in 35–37; using *Ian* in advanced 118–122
English language teaching (ELT): Disability Awareness Education in 115–118; human trafficking in 161–165; learner perceptions of taboo topics in 71–79; mental health in 130–132; pedagogical alliance in 93–99; and pre-service teachers 89; pre-service teachers' attitudes towards taboos for 86–89; racism in 169–172; sexting in 149–152; and short animation film 115–118
Enriquez, G. 11
entrepreneurialism 25
eruption 14

ethical and practical questions 51–54
European Commission 147
European Union 147, 187
Everything I have is Blue: Short Fiction by Working Class Men about More-or-less Gay Life 28
experimental sexting 143–144, *144*
Extinction Rebellion 6
extinctions, learning to die in age of 196–197

Facebook 72, 158
Fake Chat App 225
fake news 74, **75**
Fasching-Varner, K. 43
Fight the New Drug 157–158
fluid identities 209
Francione, G. 188
Frankfurt school 41
Fraser, N. 24, 25, 29
Freire, P. 5, 16, 41, 44, 79, 221, 238
Freud, S. 4
Fridays for Future movement 184
fuck in rap lyrics 108–109
#FundaMentalSDG 127

Gal, S. 24
Gavin, J. 141
Geddes, P. 184
gender: diversity 28; dysphoria 129; and foreign language classroom 231–232; identification 29, 208; minorities 25, 27; reassignment 74–77, 85; stereotypes 41, 146
gender norms 230–231; practical example 233–235
Gerlach, D. 6, 11, 43; *Kritische Fremdsprachendidaktik (Critical Foreign Language Education)* 6
gig economy 25
Girl on the Line 36
Giroux, H. A. 42, 73, 170, 171
global capitalism 25
global education 181–192
globalisation: and advocacy for animals 187; and human trafficking 157
Global North 25
Global Report on Trafficking in Persons 2020 (United Nations) 157
Gopalkrishnan, N. 131
graphic novels, human trafficking in 158–161
Gray, J. 16, 71, 253, 257
Gunda 191

Hallet, W. 36; cultural meaning-making 33; intertextual approach 32–37; poststructuralist notion of intertextuality 32
Halpert, M. 126
Hawkins, M. 40
Heads Together campaign 127
H.E.A.T. *Watch Series:* excerpt from *161*; panel sequence from *160*; representation of human trafficking in 159–160
Heise, U. 196
Helsper, W. 93–94
Hepburn, A. 210
Hericks, U. 86, 98
Hess, D. E. 10
HIV/AIDS 222, 223–226, **224**; sources for internet research on **225**
homosexuality 74, 75, **75**, 81, 82, 85, 208, 218, 219
human animals 181
human trafficking 157–158; in comics 158–161; control wheel to explore comic and graphic novel renderings of *164*, 164–165; in ELT 161–165; in graphic novels 158–161; lesson sequence on 162–165; polaris power and comic and graphic novel renderings of *164*, 164–165; representation, in H.E.A.T. *Watch Series* 159–160

Ian 117–119, 122; dissolve and disintegration effect in *120*; personal responses to 121; students' individual receptions of 121; teaching sequence on **119**; using in advanced EFL classroom 118–122
illnesses 3, 32, 34, 36, 59, 74, **75**, 76, 83, 85, 126–132, 134, 136, 138, 198, 219, 242, **243**, 253, 254, 256, 261
inclusive pedagogy 6
individualism 25
Inggs, J. 230
inquiry-based learning 6
Instagram 9, 72
interdisciplinary teaching ideas 189–192
international perspectives on taboos 249–259
internet memes 151–152
Irvine, J. 24

Janks, H. 14, 41
Jay, T. 103
Jones, N. 134–136, *135*
Jones, O. 196

Kaltenbrunner, G. K. 4
Kaye, P. 3
Kazazoğlu, S. 71
Kelly, T. E. 17
Kernberg, O. 132
Killick, D. 239, 244
The King's Speech 115
Klein, C. 156
König, L. 53
Kossakovsky, V. 191
Kramsch, C. 55, 209, 221
Kristeva, J. 32
Kumaravadivelu, B. 6
Kutcher, S. 127
Kymlicka, W. 188; *Zoopolis* 188–189

Ladwig, B. 185, 188
Lady Gaga 162
language teacher education: critical approaches and 40–41; criticality in 41–43; taboos in 81–91
language teaching, criticality in 41–43
language use 230–231; and foreign language classroom 231–232; practical example 233–235
Las Encinas (fictional elite school) 219
"learner-centredness" (re-)consideration of 13, 16, 98, 136
learner perceptions of taboo topics in ELT 71–79
lesson sequence on human trafficking 162–165
LGBTQ+: identities 24, 25; language learners 27; people 25; recognition 28; rights 252; students 27–28
lifestyles 3, 7, 9, 219, 220, 221; environmentally destructive lifestyles **75**, 76, 77
literacy: critical 11–12; taboo 11–12
literary texts, and films 37
López-Gopar, M. E. 78

The Maltese Falcon 211
market fundamentalism 25
Matthews, S. 228, 230, 233; "Decolonizing while white?" 228
Meddings, L. 7
Meme Generator site 151
Mendez, P. 28
mental disorders 127–130
mental health 127–130; addressing in ELT 130–132; literacy, components of 128–130, *129*

#mentalhealthmatters 127
Merse, T. 84, 175
migration 26, 59, **75**, 86, 90, 155–157, 161, 241
Miller, W. 127
"monosemination" 33
#moveformentalhealth 127
"multilingual turn" 23
multimediality 36
multimodal text ensembles 173; addressing racism with 172–177; cooperatively designed 172–177
music videos 13, 16, 162, **177**
mutilation: genital mutilation 50; self-mutilation 74, 75, **75**, 82, 83, 85–87, 132, 133

Naezer, M. 146
Nakano, S. 53
Nation, I. S. P. 63
neoliberalism 25, 26
Ness, P.: *Release* 36
Nettles, B.: *A Free Me: How Taylor Escaped Becoming a Victim of Human Trafficking* 162
Nieweler, A. 221
nigga in rap lyrics 108–109
Niven, J.: *All the Bright Places* 36
Nixon, R. 196
Noah, T. 127
non-human animals 181
Norton, B. 40, 42

O'Connor, S. 127
Oevermann, U. 94
online chat 74, 84, 147, 209
Oosterhout, L. van 146
oppressive institutions 44
Outcault, R. F.: *The Yellow Kid* 156
Oxford Dictionary of English 4

Palacio, R. J.: *Wonder* 115
PARSNIP: in ELT 73; model 7, 14, 241; policy 7; topics *8*, **200**, 206
pedagogical alliance in ELT 93–99; implications for teaching practice 98; interview analysis 95–98; introduction to 94–95; overview 93–94; research methodology 94–95; teacher-learner relationship in structural theory 94; theoretical background 94
pedagogic framework for taboos *12*, 12–17

Pennycook, A. 23
personal resources/resilience factors **59**, 60
physical health literacy 128
picturebooks 11, 32, 42, 77, 78, 88, 115, 162, 262
Pip 117
Pizziconi, B. 106
poetry slams, and borderline personality disorder in English language teaching 134–137
Polaris 164
political economy of taboos 23–29
pop culture 10, 78, 89, 107, 110, 162
poverty 40, **75**, 219
The Present 117
pre-service teachers 81; attitudes towards potential of taboos for ELT 86–89; experience with taboos 83–86; opinion on taboos in English classroom **87**; perceptions of challenges related to taboos 89; and taboo topics *84*
Pride 29
primary sexting 144
privacy 51, 53, 54
privilege 174; collaboratively created mind map for **175**; teaching sequence on **174**; text ensemble for **177**
Purcell, K.: *Trafficked* 162

Quammen, D.: *The Song of the Dodo* 202
questionnaire 72, 73, 78, 79, 82, 261

race/racism 169–172; addressing 171–172; challenges and principles 171–172; and cooperatively designed multimodal text ensembles 172–177; countering in educational contexts 169; teaching sequence on **174**; terms, concepts, and principles 169–171
radicalism 74, **75**, 76, 77, 82, 83
rap lyrics: *nigga* and *fuck* in **108**, 108–109; STWs in 105–106
Rebel without a Cause 210
refuge 75, 86, 90, 155
Regan, T. 188
religious conflicts 75, 82, 85
resilience 25; defined 58; personal resources/resilience factors **59**, 60; promoting, in classroom 61–65; promoting, in foreign language classroom 63–65; recommendations for school subjects 61–63; social resources/

resilience factors 60, **60**; theoretical approach 58–61
Rich, A. 29
Ricketts, W. 28
Rigby, K. 196
Rosenfeld, E. 126
Rucka, G.: *Wonder Woman: The Hiketeia* 158

Sarıçoban, A. 71
Satrapi, M.: *Persepolis* 156
Schweitzer, A. 186
Scranton, R. 197
secondary sexting 144
Seiler, W. 59
sex 7, 31, 74, **75**, 82, 85, 142, 143, 145, 146, 155, 207, 219, 220, 238, 239; and love 74, **75**, 86; trafficking 163
sexting: aggravated 143–144, *144*; components of DigComp 2.1 to **148**; and DigComp 2.1 **148**; in ELT 149–152; example of sexting situation *150*; experimental 143–144, *144*; and foreign language classroom 146–147; German law on 145; laws on 145; overview 141–142; primary 144; and religious groups 146; secondary 144; and teenage generation 142–145
short animation films: addressing disability through 113–123; in ELT 115–118
Silvera, A. 200; *They Both Die at the End* 200–201
Slamia, B. 240
slam performances 134–136
"slow violence" 196
social media 54, 162–163, 165, 251; channels 83; platforms 9, 127; posts 32
social positionalities of tabooed topics 250–253
social resources/resilience factors 60, **60**
socioeconomic injustice 25
Soscisurvey platform 72
South Africa: addressing language use and gender norms 230–231; addressing whiteness 229–230; debating tricky topics **233**; suggested activities for task cycle **234**
Spaemann, R. 188
Spiegelman, A.: *Maus: A Survivor's Tale* 156, 158
Sri Lanka: Buddha statues in 209; cultural taboo of eating with hand **212**; cultural taboo of smoking among females **212**;

cultural taboos in 206–210; domains of cultural taboos in *207*, 207–208; homosexuality in 208; sexual minorities (LGBTQ+) in 208
The State of the World's Children 2021 report (UNICEF) 127
Steinberg, S. W. 5, 6, 145
Stern, A. 132
Stone, E. 127
Stone, S. 210
structural theory 94
swearing 103
swear/taboo words (STWs): categories *104*; corpus-based views 105–106; defining and categorizing *104*, 104–105; foreign-language 106; multiple functions of *105*, 105–106; negligence of 107; *nigga* and *fuck* in rap lyrics 108–109; offensiveness of 106; overview 103–104; practical example 108–109; in rap lyrics 105–106; as recognizable lexical items 104; relevance for foreign language education 106–107; theoretical background 104–106
Swift, G.: *Waterland* 35

taboo literacy 4, 11–12, 13, 16, 18, 50, 78, 81, 88, 89, 91, 109, 189, 206–214, 223–224, 238, 239, 241, 242, 257; definition of 4–5
taboos 195; average rating of interest in English lessons 77; and controversial topics 7–11; dealt with at school **75, 76**; different perspectives on 36–37; discursivity and textuality of 33–35; educational guidelines for dealing with **15**; in the EFL classroom 35–37; in *Élite* 219–220; in ELT 82; in foreign language education 3–18; integrating literary texts and films 37; international perspectives on 249–259; in language teacher education 81–91; multimediality 36; neglected at schools **86**; past and present 4–5; pedagogic framework for *12*, 12–17; political economy of 23–29; potential challenges with *88*; pre-service teachers' experience with 83–86, *84*; selecting 73–74; social positionalities of 250–253; teaching guidelines 14–15, **15**, 203; textual networks 35–36; in translator and interpreter training 237–244
Taguchi, T. 82
Tan, S.: *The Rabbits* 198, 201

tasks: "Eating Animals" 191–192; "Farm Animal Husbandry" 191; "Take Political Action" 192
teacher education 89–90; and critical pedagogy 257–258
teacher-learner relationship in structural theory 94
teenage generation, and sexting 142–145
TEFL (Teaching English as a Foreign Language) 81, 83, 90
terminology and concept 49–51
text ensembles: cooperative design of 173; defined 173; discrimination **177**; multimodal 173; privilege **177**; for racism **177**
texts 10, 32, 33–37, 41, 42, 77, 78, 84, 89, 90, 94, 115, 134, 151, 152, 169, 172, 173, 175, 176, 201, 202, 203, 221, 222, 224–226, 230, 235, 237, 238, 256, 261
textuality of taboos 33–35
textual networks 35–36
Their Future in Your Hands 190
Theravada Buddhism 207; religious teachings of 208
Thornbury, S. 7
TikTok 9, 137
"Topics in school education" ("Themen im Unterricht"): in class 75–76; descriptive survey results 74–77; English lessons 76–77; research methodology 72–74; selecting taboos and challenging topics 73–74; spare time 74–75; survey design 72–73; survey questionnaire **73**
translation: foreign language classroom 239–241; LX classroom **243**; TILLT 237, 239, 242
translator and interpreter training: practical examples 241–244; student voices 241–244; taboo topics in 237–244; theoretical background 238–239; translation-oriented foreign language classroom 239–241
Trumm, T. 34

unemployment 75, 208, 251
UNESCO 27, 196, 251
UNICEF: *The State of the World's Children 2021* report 127
United Nations (UN): 2020 *Global Report on Trafficking in Persons* 157; Convention on the Rights of Persons with Disabilities 113

"verbal violence" 103
violence 14, 28, 74, **75**, 82, 83, 85, 105, 126, 128, 146, 158, 159, 160, 161, 181, 187, 196, 198, 208, 209, 219, 251, 253, 261, 262; *see also individual entries*
Villacanas de Castro, L. S. 41
Vizzini, N.: *It's Kind of a Funny Story* 37
Vonnegut, K.: *Galápagos* 198, 201

Wei, Y. 127
West, G. B. 14
Wharton, S. 84

whiteness 229–230; and foreign language classroom 231–232; practical example 233–235
Williams, L. 196
Wilson, R. 52
World Health Organization (WHO) 126, 132, 196; International Classification of Diseases (ICD-11) by 129; *Mental Health Day* 127
World War II 58

young adult novels 16, 62, 95, 162, 200
You're not for sale (Council of Europe) 159